The Ultimate CASPER COMICS COLLECTION!

The Ultimate CASPER® COMICS COLLECTION!

ibooks
graphic
novels
new york
www.ibooks.net

Distributed by Publishers Group West

An ibooks, inc. Book
24 West 25th street, New York, NY 10010

All rights reserved, including the right to reproduce this book or portions
thereof in any form whatsoever.
All media is digitally recolored from the
original black and white master files.

Distributed by Publishers Group West
1700 Fourth Street, Berkeley, CA 94710
www.pgw.com

Editor: Sid Jacobson

Design: Mat Postawa
Cover Art: Ernie Colon
Special Thanks to:
Shannon Denton
Eric Spikes
Fabio

First published by ibooks, inc. October 2005

ISBN 1-59687-823-1

Printed in the USA

INTRODUCTION

SID JACOBSON

I was there at the birth of Casper. Well, at least, at the birth of Casper at Harvey Comics in 1952 when the company took over publication of the Paramount animation character. It had been published prior to that, in 1949 and 1950, by St. John Publishing with little if any success. That company had also published Little Audrey for 24 issues, from 1948 to 1952, with a great deal more popularity.

Certainly when Harvey took over the publishing of Casper— as well as Little Audrey and several other Paramount prop- erties—it was Audrey that was deemed the important one. Even Herman and Katnip—a more violent pair of Tom and Jerry actalikes—was considered more important than the little spook.

I firmly and unashamedly believe that it was what we did to change the Casper character and background that caused it to become what it ultimately did. Before Warren Kremer, as art editor and artist, and myself, as editor, took over the reins, Casper was little more than a ghost who dwelled mainly in a cemetery and of whom one creature after anoth- er was frightened. Finally, in this setup, one usually young character found him friendly and in some small way helpful. And Casper had made a friend.

We changed that formula. Immensely. That new Casper (we're talking "new" in 1959) is what is presented on these pages. We moved him into a haunted house. We created three uncles (whose first names varied but were collectively known as the Ghostly Trio). We created a "tuff" little friend named Spooky. A ghost horse named Nightmare. And per- haps, most importantly, a good little witch girl named Wendy and her three aunts, the Witch Sisters.

With that we created a whole new world around Casper that we called the Enchanted Forest. This place was filled with fairy tale like settings and creatures, such as elves and fairies and gnomes and others that we and our superb writers created.

Casper was no longer a dead kid who had become a ghost. In our scheme, Casper was one of the magical creatures in the Enchanted Forest who was born a ghost, just as a fairy is born a fairy and an ogre an ogre. The stories now no longer involved simply making a friend. Casper had become, more or less, a superhero. He had his own special powers, such as flying and becoming invisible and going through walls, and he could defeat some evil being or turn a terrible wrong into a right.

He also had some very special friends, who had their own prominence and, very soon, their own magazines.

Soon Casper became one of the most popular characters in all of comics and, by following the scenario we had made, in all of film and TV animation.

We should make it clear that we did not originate Casper the Friendly Ghost. A creative and charming man named Seymour Reit did. He created the idea, and wrote the original story, and an artist—and very dear friend of both Warren and myself—Joe Oriolo, created the original look and sold the first story to Famous Studios, the animation arm of Paramount Pictures.
That happened back in the early 1940s, so if you have enough fingers on your hands, you can figure Casper as being over sixty years old. Once again, it proves the basic premise of the character: Don't judge a book by the cover. A ghost can be very, very friendly. And someone looking like a kid can be sixty plus years old.

All the Casper stories in this collection, as well as the covers, were drawn by Warren Kremer, who got better and better as he became more accustomed to his new role as an animator. Warren was originally an illustrator and one of the best illustrators in the field of comics. But he did even better as an animator. In my estimation—and that of a host of artists and critics—he was the best ever in his field.

It is a shame that his name has been hidden for years. Much as it had been fought, company policy refused to allow creators to put their name on their work. And so the names of Warren Kremer, Ernie Colon, Howie Post, Marty Taras, Jim Miele, Lee Donahue——and I can go on and on- sit nowhere near their prized output.

And though his name isn't there, all the Spooky stories here were drawn by Howie Post, one of the zaniest pencillers ever allowed near a drawing board. Several of the other pages were drawn by a very young Ernie Colon, who in later years became one of the two prime artists for Casper and Richie Rich.

The writers include Ralph Newman, Jim Miele, Charlie Strauss and Carl Wessler. The inkers were Lee Donahue, Helen Cason, Ruth Leon and Jacqueline Roettcher.

Before I allow you to enjoy these delightful and exciting sto- ries from the early Casper days, I'd like to point out some- thing quite fascinating in the very first story in this collection, "Real Gone." The artist character in the story is a self cari- cature of Warren Kremer, and the Harvey in the story is a depiction of Alfred Harvey.

Now, go—enjoy!

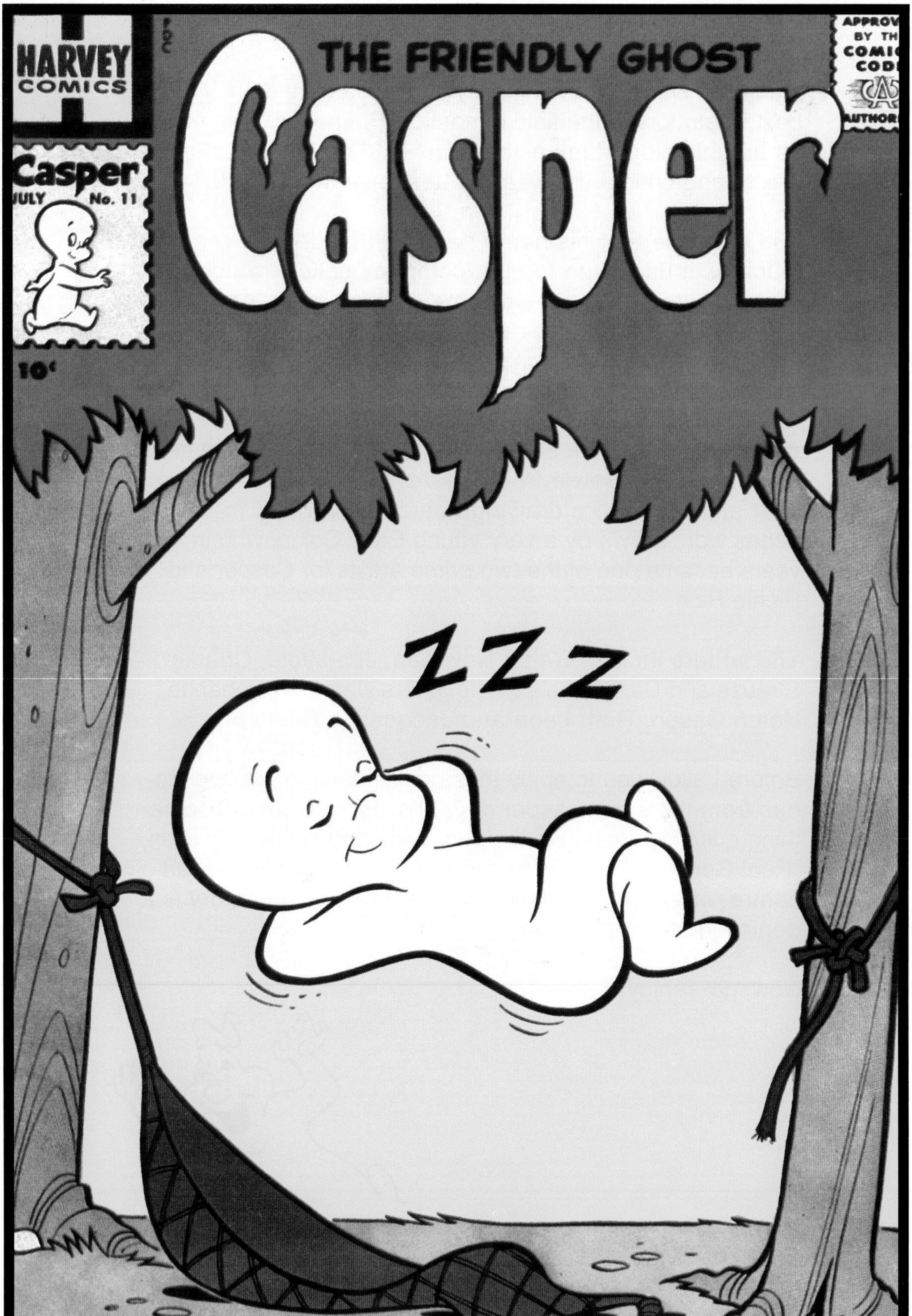
HARVEY COMICS
THE FRIENDLY GHOST
Casper
Casper
JULY No. 11
10¢
ZZZ

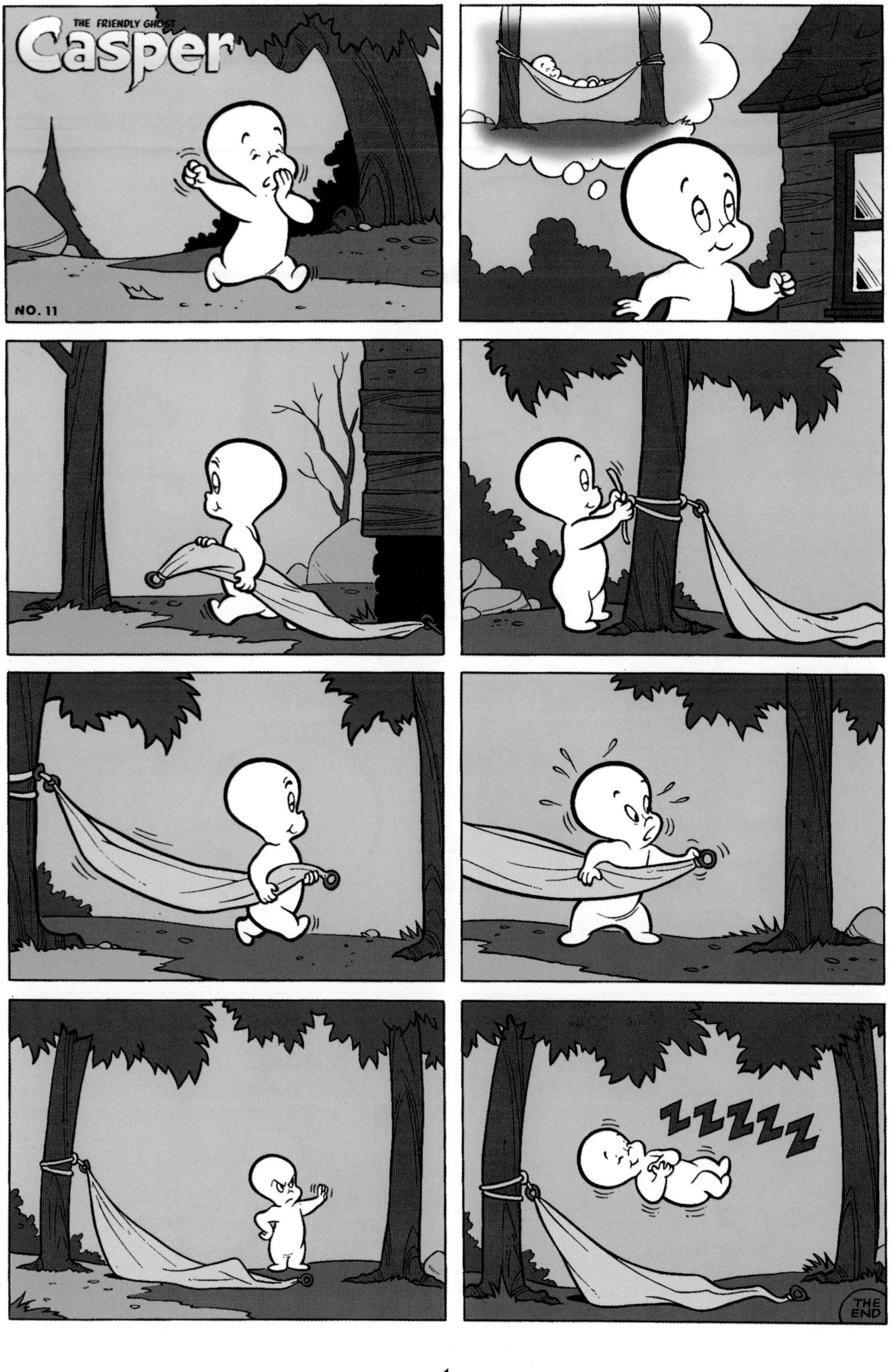
THE FRIENDLY GHOST
Casper
NO. 11
ZZZZZ
THE END

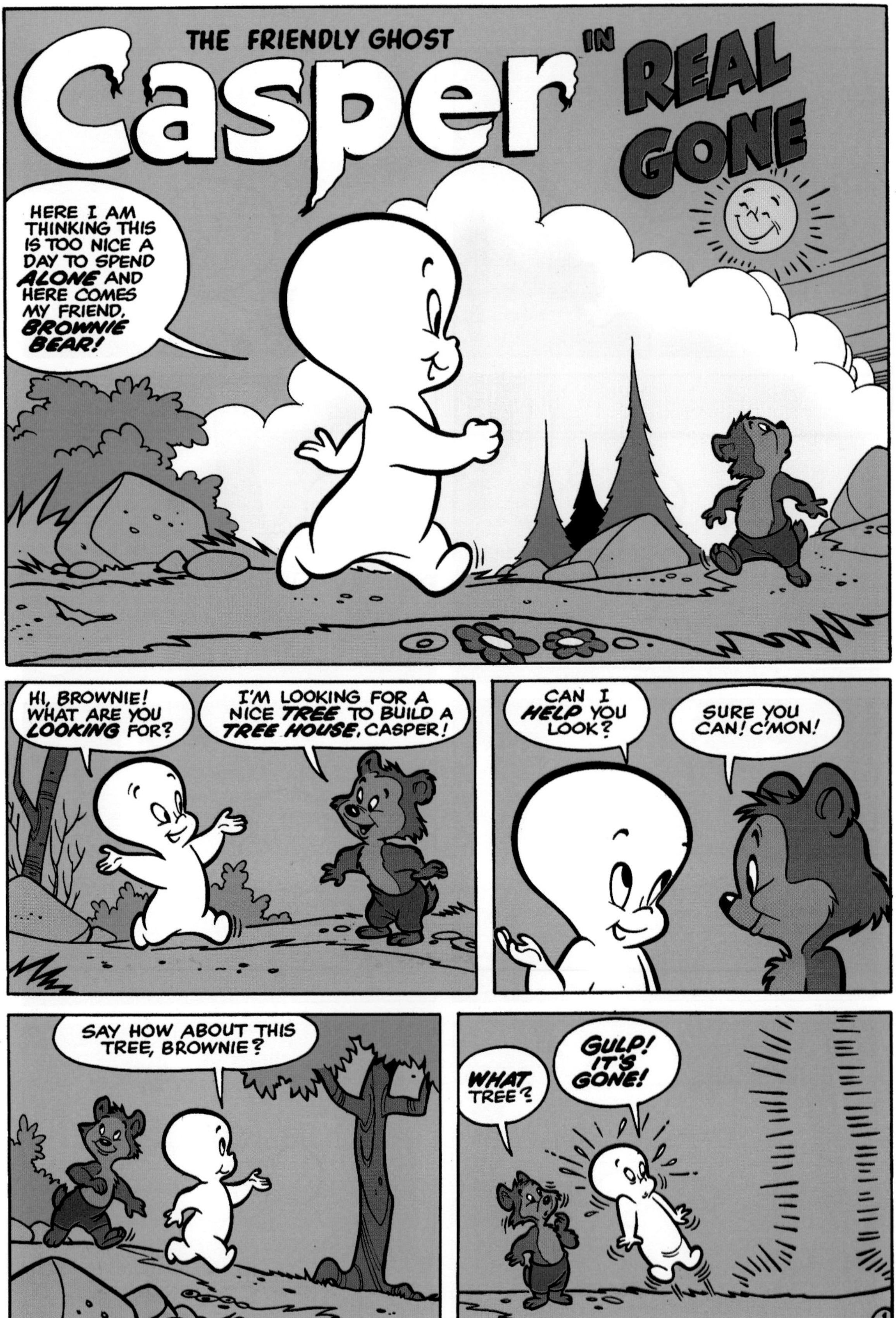
THE FRIENDLY GHOST
Casper
IN
REAL GONE
HERE I AM THINKING THIS IS TOO NICE A DAY TO SPEND ALONE AND HERE COMES MY FRIEND, BROWNIE BEAR!
HI, BROWNIE! WHAT ARE YOU LOOKING FOR?
I'M LOOKING FOR A NICE TREE TO BUILD A TREE HOUSE, CASPER!
CAN I HELP YOU LOOK?
SURE YOU CAN! C'MON!
SAY HOW ABOUT THIS TREE, BROWNIE?
WHAT TREE?
GULP! IT'S GONE!
1

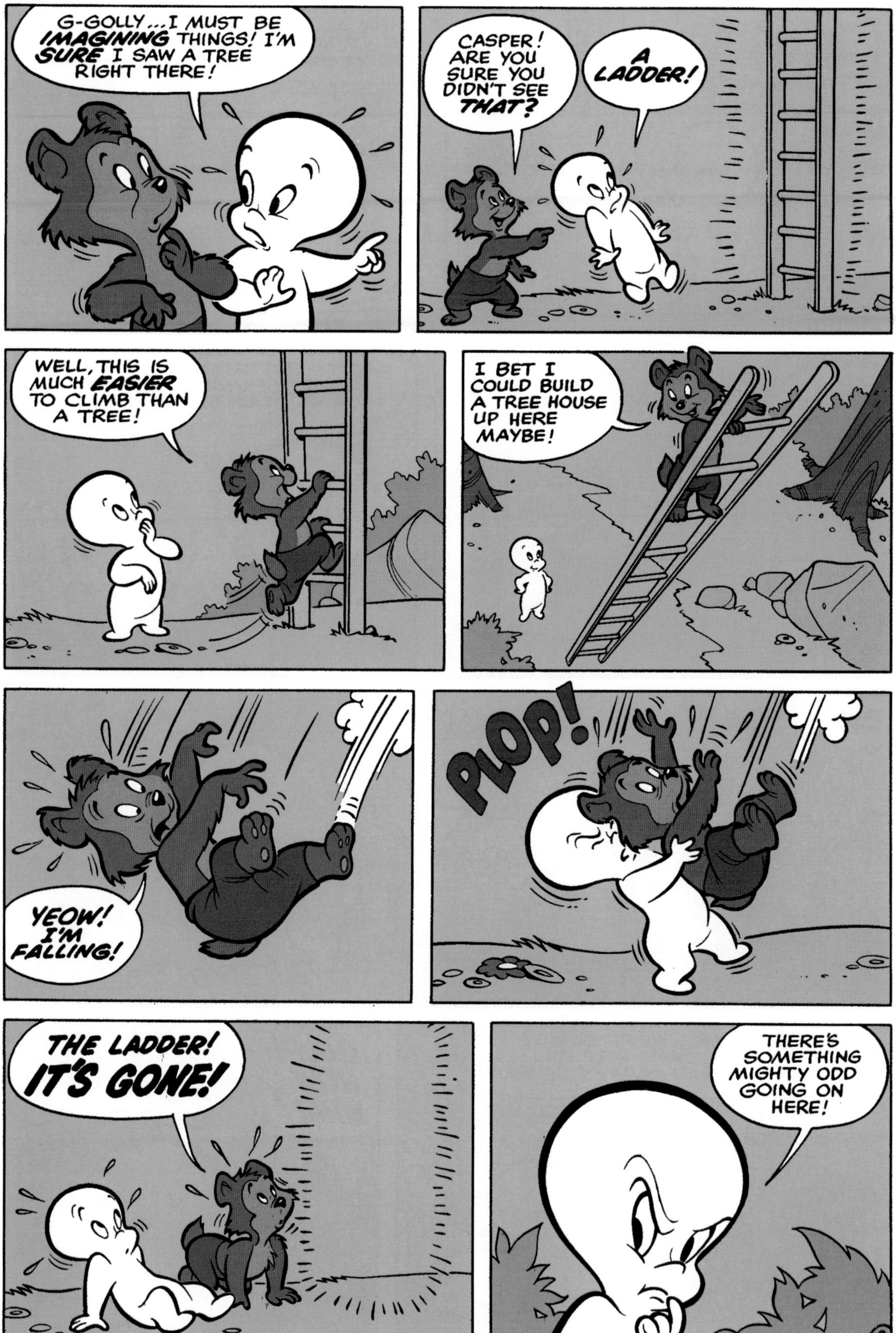
G-GOLLY...I MUST BE IMAGINING THINGS! I'M SURE I SAW A TREE RIGHT THERE!
CASPER! ARE YOU SURE YOU DIDN'T SEE THAT?
A LADDER!
WELL, THIS IS MUCH EASIER TO CLIMB THAN A TREE!
I BET I COULD BUILD A TREE HOUSE UP HERE MAYBE!
YEOW! I'M FALLING!
PLOP!
THE LADDER! IT'S GONE!
THERE'S SOMETHING MIGHTY ODD GOING ON HERE!
2

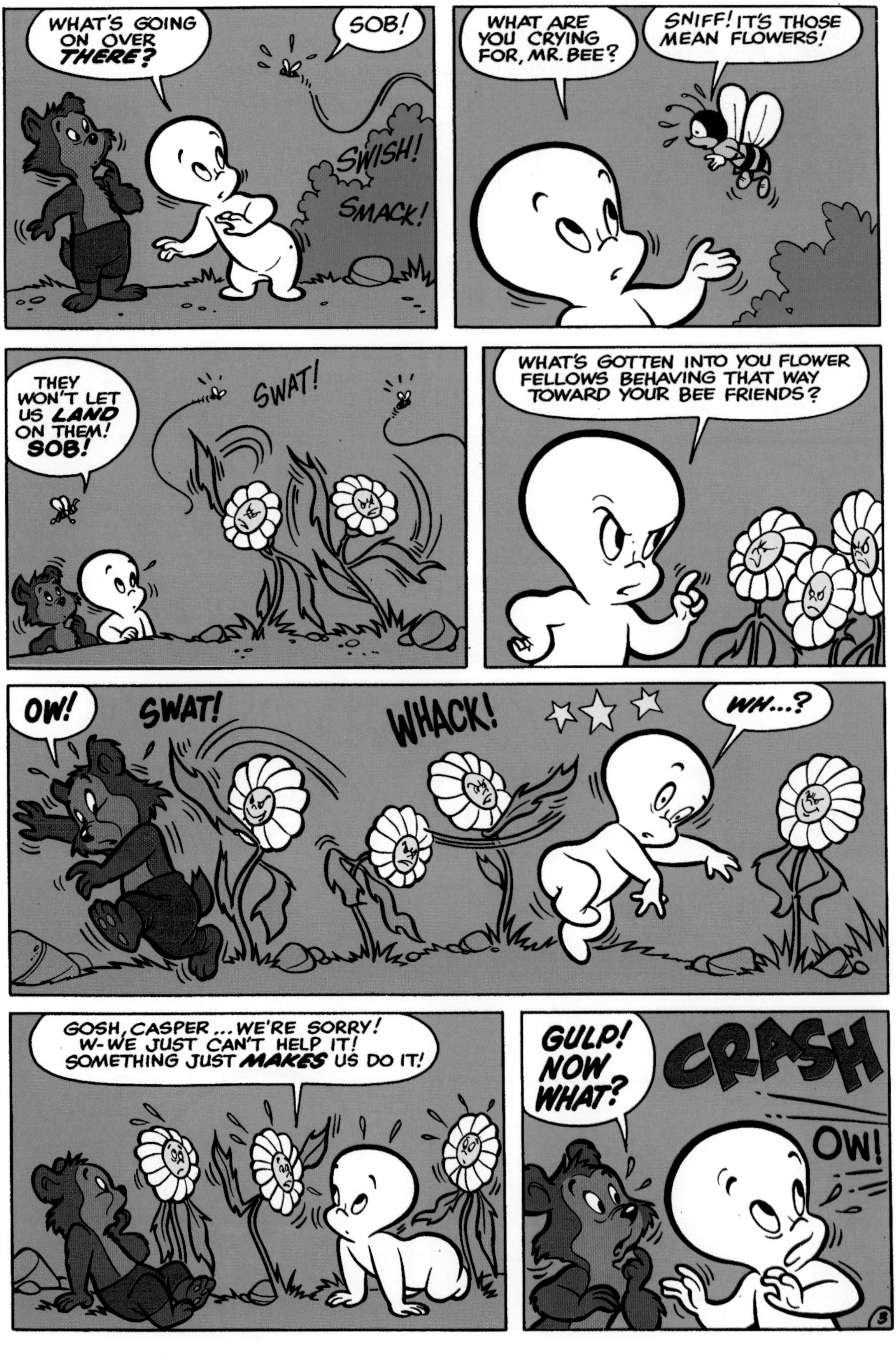
WHAT'S GOING ON OVER THERE?
SOB!
SWISH!
SMACK!
WHAT ARE YOU CRYING FOR, MR. BEE?
SNIFF! IT'S THOSE MEAN FLOWERS!
THEY WON'T LET US LAND ON THEM! SOB!
SWAT!
WHAT'S GOTTEN INTO YOU FLOWER FELLOWS BEHAVING THAT WAY TOWARD YOUR BEE FRIENDS?
OW!
SWAT!
WHACK!
WH...?
GOSH, CASPER ... WE'RE SORRY! W-WE JUST CAN'T HELP IT! SOMETHING JUST MAKES US DO IT!
GULP! NOW WHAT?
CRASH
OW!
3

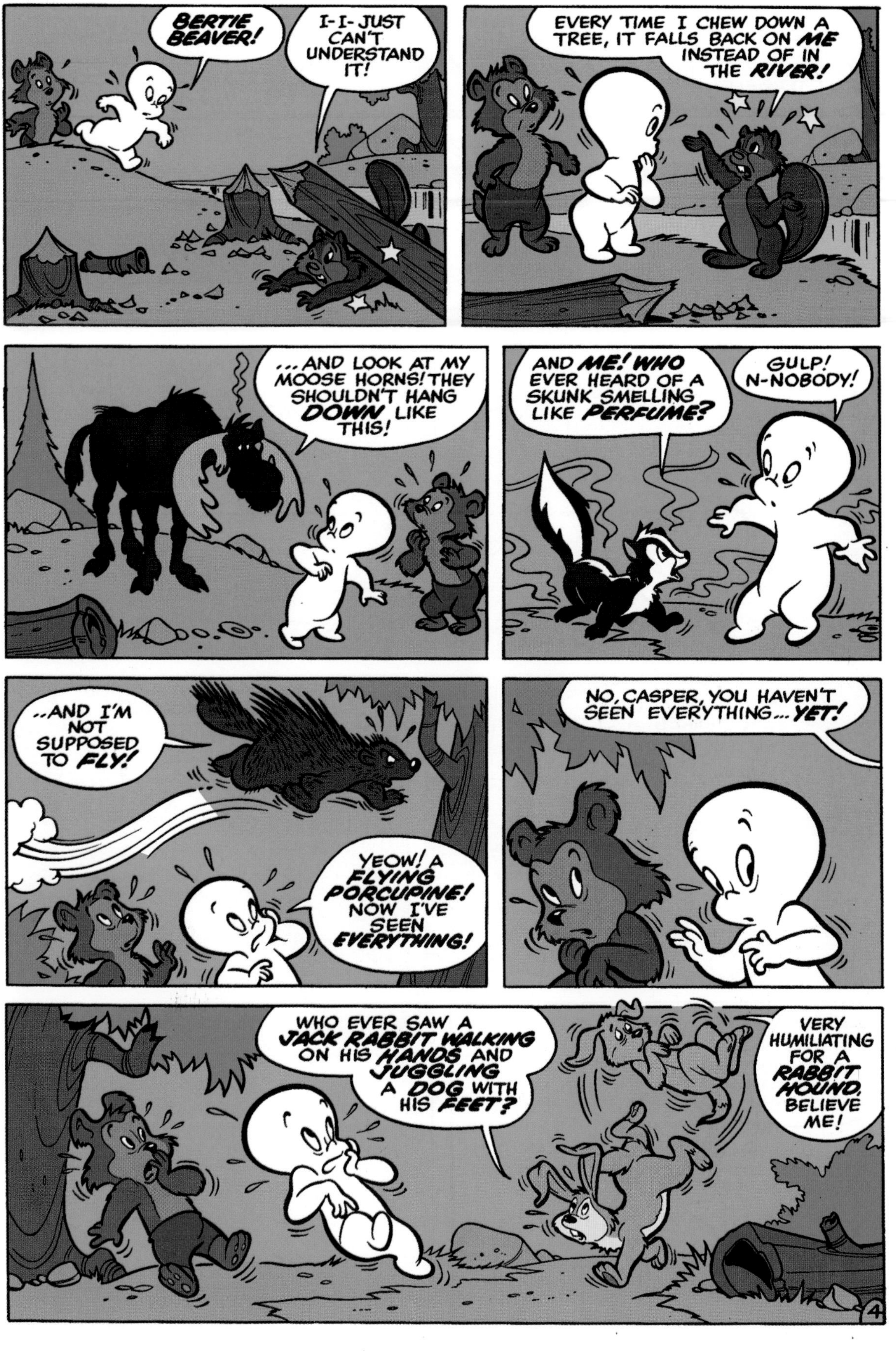

BERTIE BEAVER!
I-I- JUST CAN'T UNDERSTAND IT!
EVERY TIME I CHEW DOWN A TREE, IT FALLS BACK ON ME INSTEAD OF IN THE RIVER!
...AND LOOK AT MY MOOSE HORNS! THEY SHOULDN'T HANG DOWN LIKE THIS!
AND ME! WHO EVER HEARD OF A SKUNK SMELLING LIKE PERFUME?
GULP! N-NOBODY!
..AND I'M NOT SUPPOSED TO FLY!
YEOW! A FLYING PORCUPINE! NOW I'VE SEEN EVERYTHING!
NO, CASPER, YOU HAVEN'T SEEN EVERYTHING... YET!
WHO EVER SAW A JACK RABBIT WALKING ON HIS HANDS AND JUGGLING A DOG WITH HIS FEET?
VERY HUMILIATING FOR A RABBIT HOUND, BELIEVE ME!
4

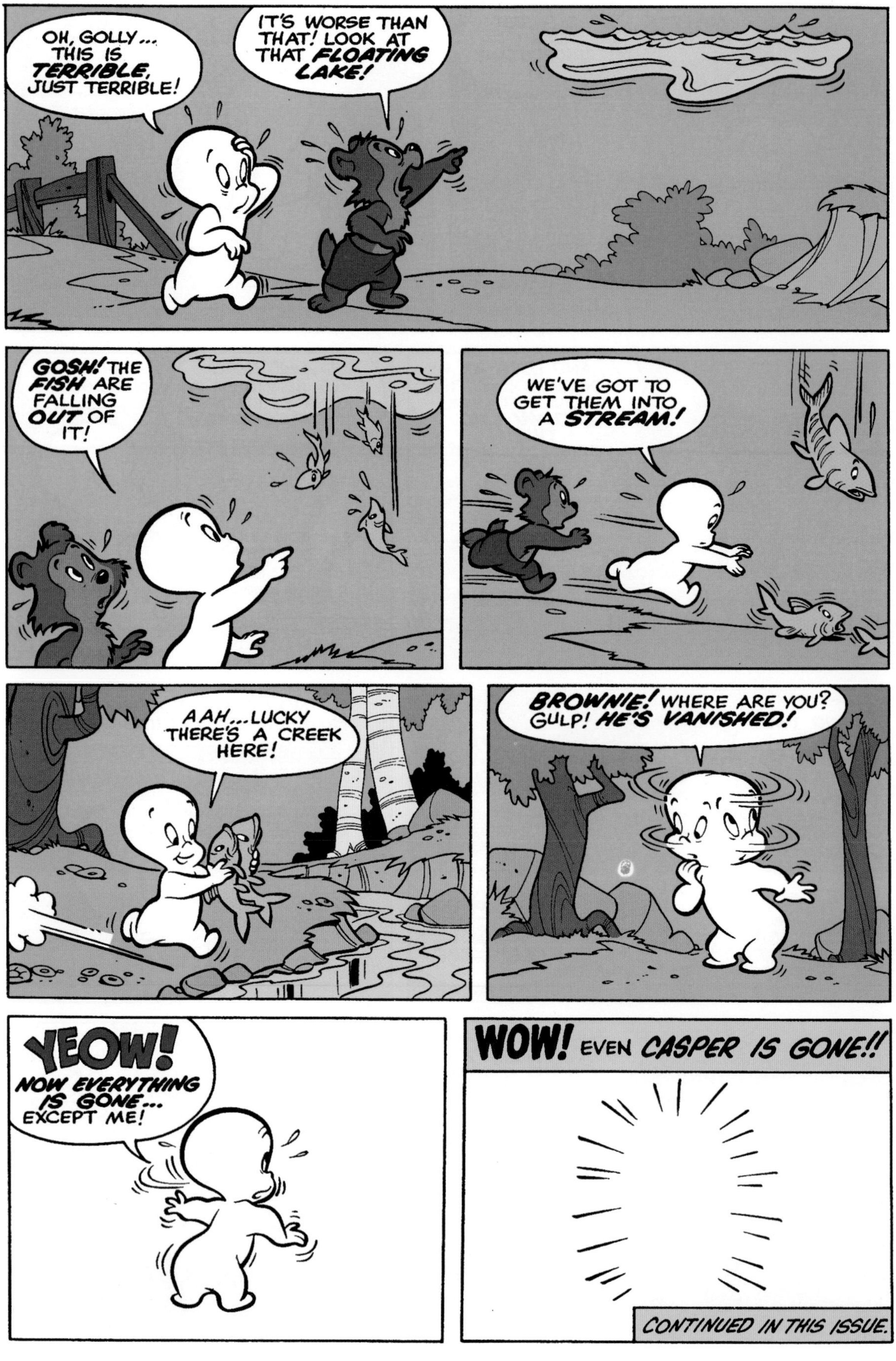

OH, GOLLY... THIS IS TERRIBLE, JUST TERRIBLE!
IT'S WORSE THAN THAT! LOOK AT THAT FLOATING LAKE!
GOSH! THE FISH ARE FALLING OUT OF IT!
WE'VE GOT TO GET THEM INTO A STREAM!
AAH... LUCKY THERE'S A CREEK HERE!
BROWNIE! WHERE ARE YOU? GULP! HE'S VANISHED!
YEOW! NOW EVERYTHING IS GONE... EXCEPT ME!
WOW! EVEN CASPER IS GONE!!
CONTINUED IN THIS ISSUE.

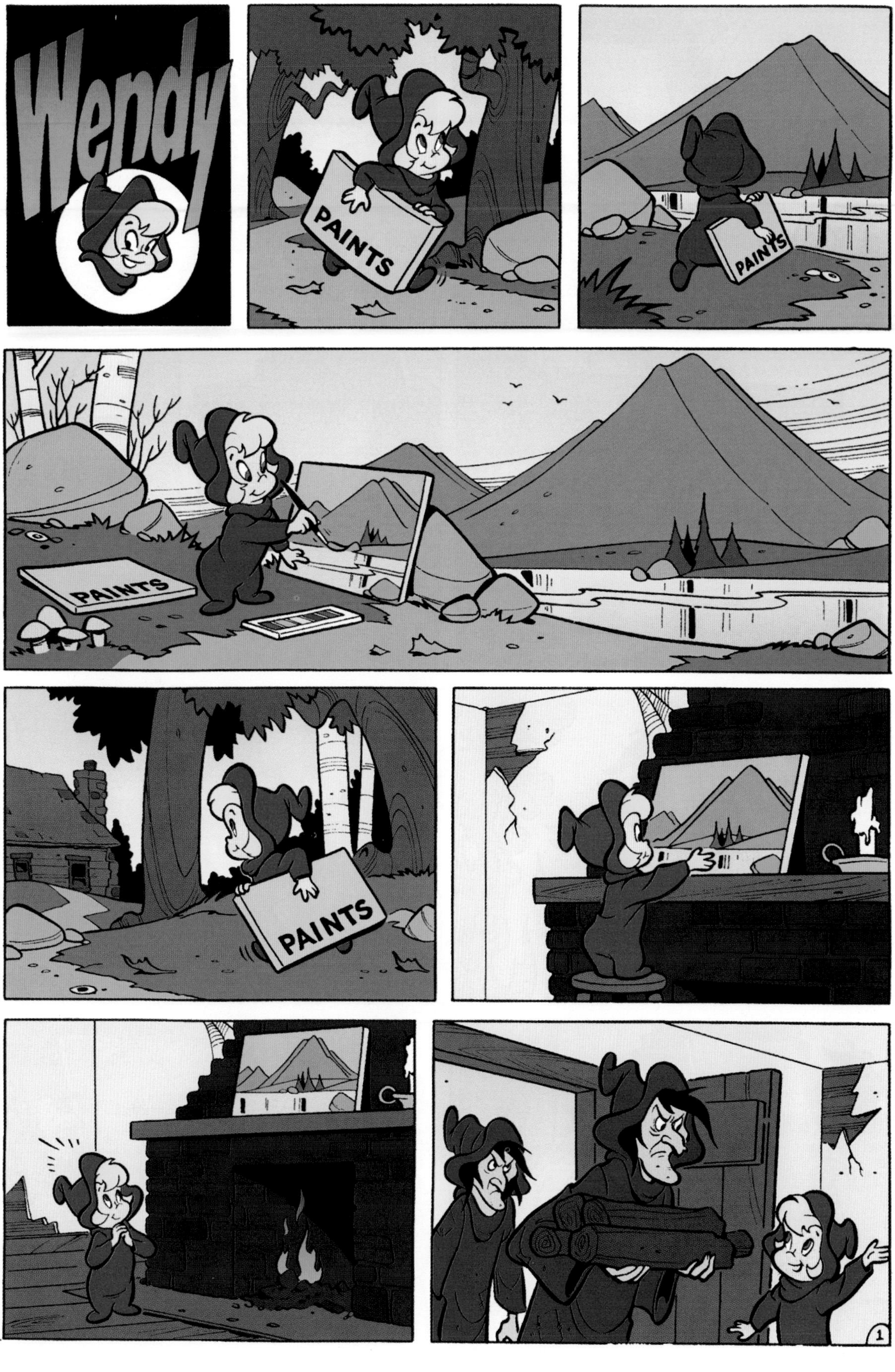
Wendy
PAINTS
PAINTS
PAINTS
PAINTS
1

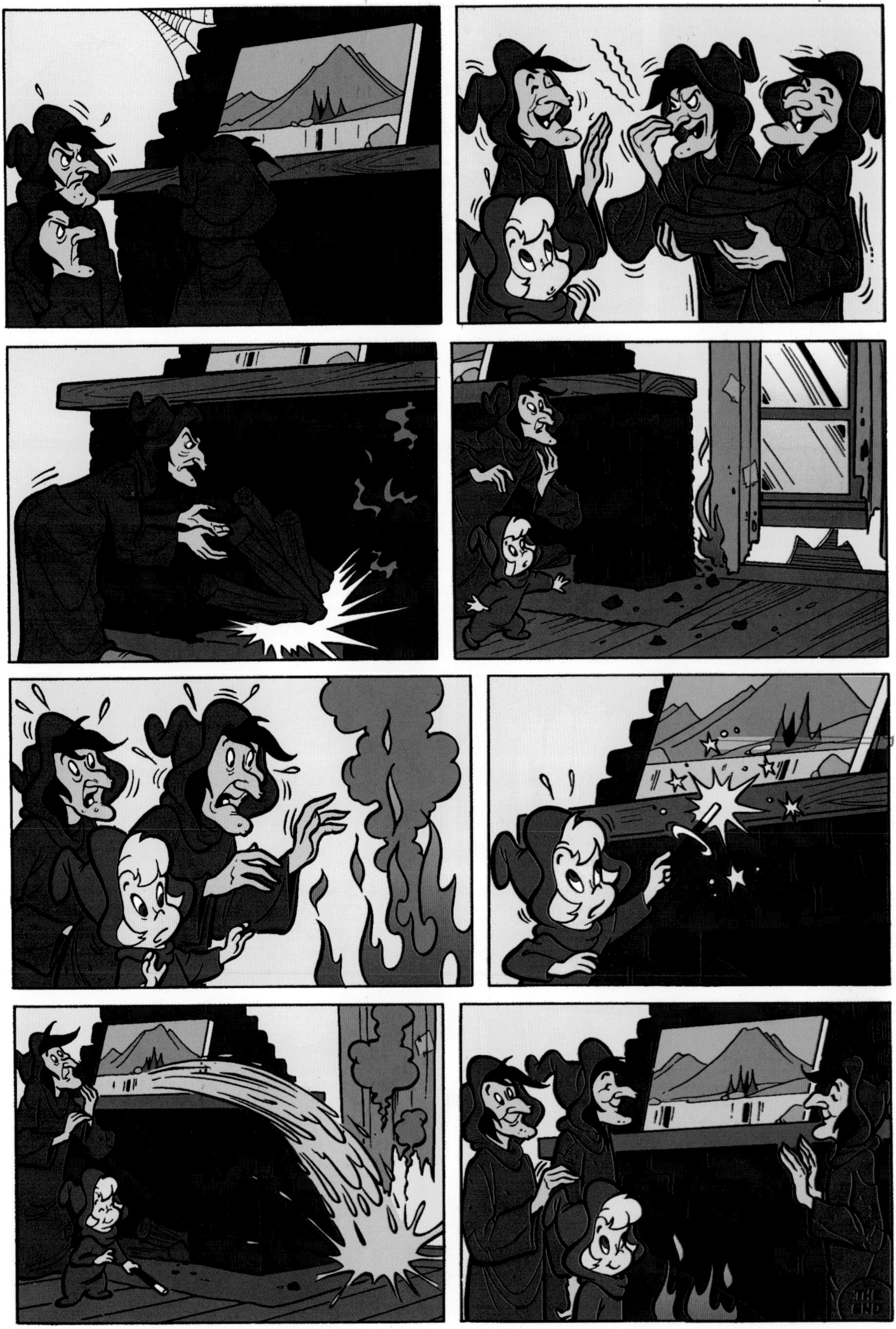
THE END

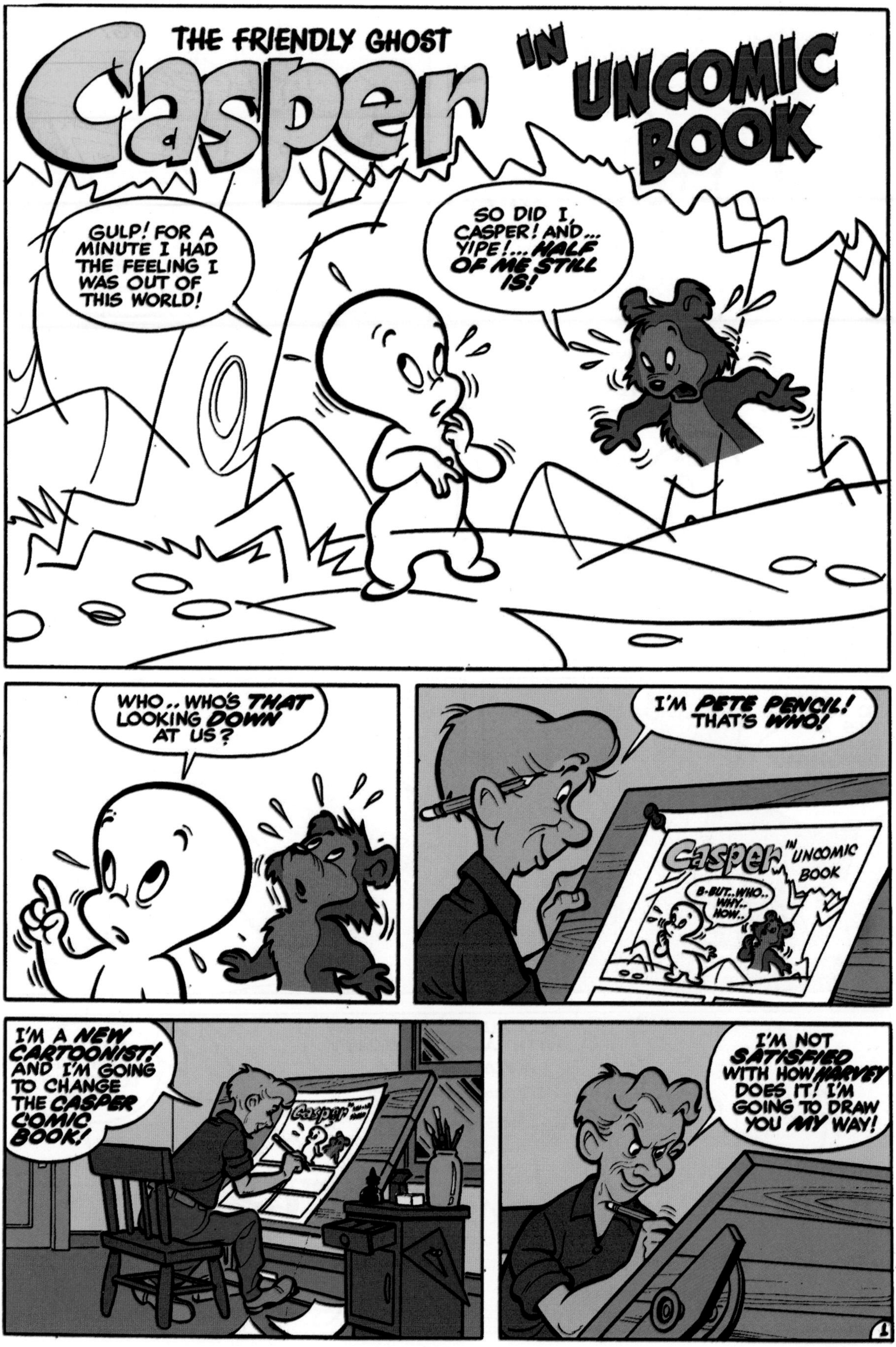
THE FRIENDLY GHOST
Casper
IN
UNCOMIC BOOK
GULP! FOR A MINUTE I HAD THE FEELING I WAS OUT OF THIS WORLD!
SO DID I, CASPER! AND... YIPE!... HALF OF ME STILL IS!
WHO.. WHO'S THAT LOOKING DOWN AT US?
I'M PETE PENCIL! THAT'S WHO!
Casper IN UNCOMIC BOOK
B-BUT.. WHO.. WHY.. HOW..
I'M A NEW CARTOONIST! AND I'M GOING TO CHANGE THE CASPER COMIC BOOK!
I'M NOT SATISFIED WITH HOW HARVEY DOES IT! I'M GOING TO DRAW YOU MY WAY!
1

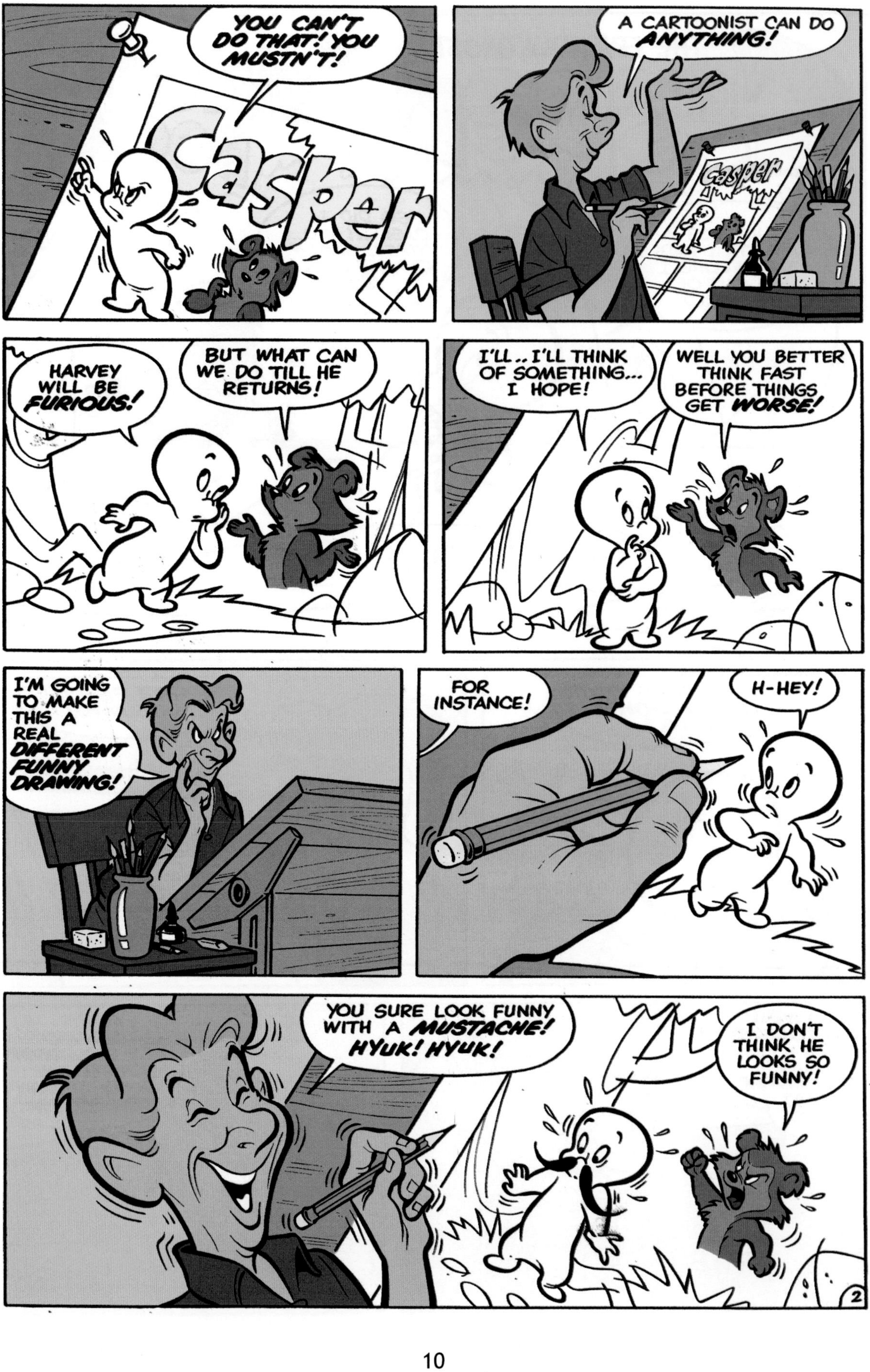
YOU CAN'T DO THAT! YOU MUSTN'T!
Casper
A CARTOONIST CAN DO ANYTHING!
HARVEY WILL BE FURIOUS!
BUT WHAT CAN WE DO TILL HE RETURNS!
I'LL.. I'LL THINK OF SOMETHING... I HOPE!
WELL YOU BETTER THINK FAST BEFORE THINGS GET WORSE!
I'M GOING TO MAKE THIS A REAL DIFFERENT FUNNY DRAWING!
FOR INSTANCE!
H-HEY!
YOU SURE LOOK FUNNY WITH A MUSTACHE! HYUK! HYUK!
I DON'T THINK HE LOOKS SO FUNNY!
2

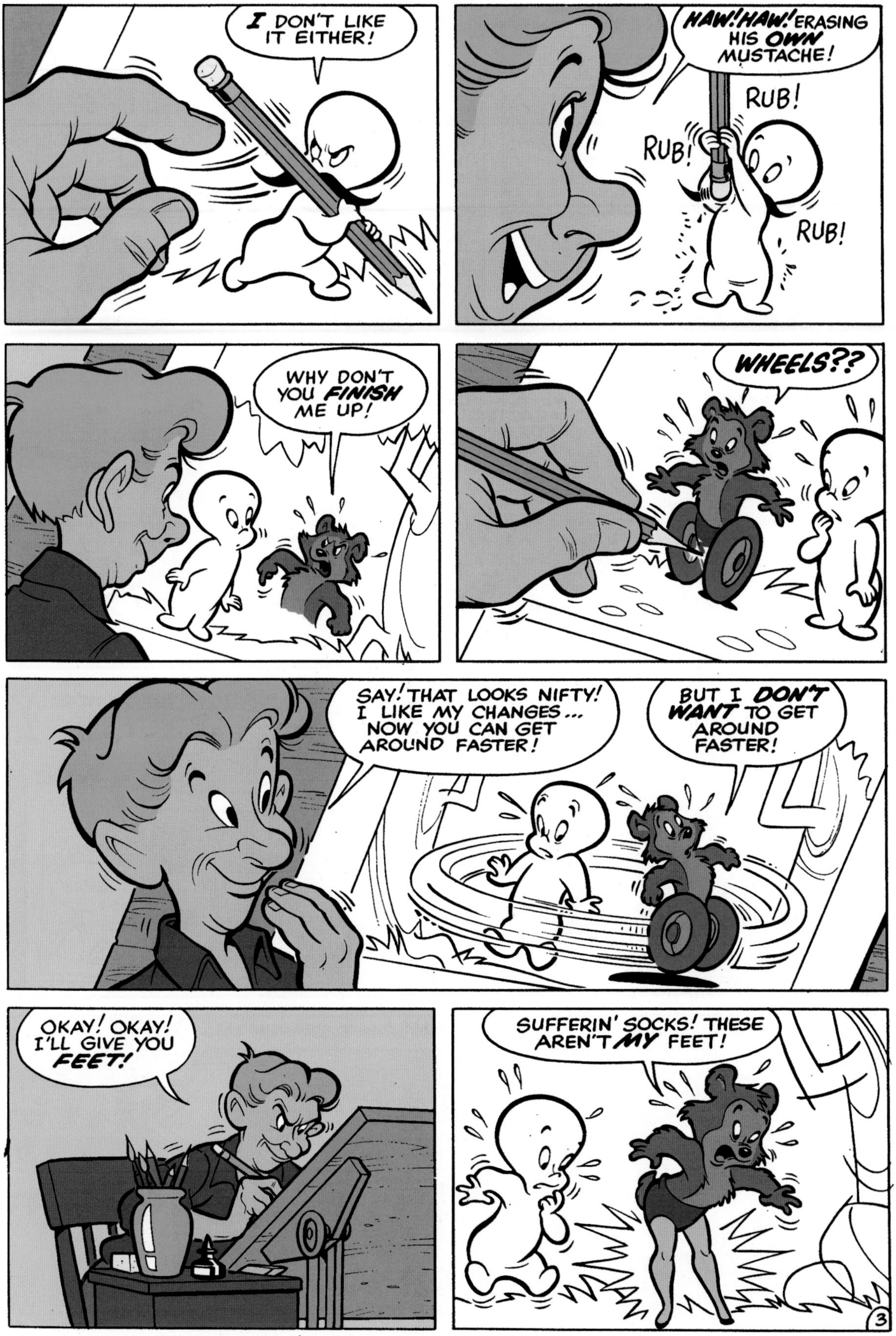
I DON'T LIKE IT EITHER!
HAW! HAW! ERASING HIS OWN MUSTACHE!
RUB!
RUB!
RUB!
WHY DON'T YOU FINISH ME UP!
WHEELS??
SAY! THAT LOOKS NIFTY! I LIKE MY CHANGES... NOW YOU CAN GET AROUND FASTER!
BUT I DON'T WANT TO GET AROUND FASTER!
OKAY! OKAY! I'LL GIVE YOU FEET!
SUFFERIN' SOCKS! THESE AREN'T MY FEET!
3

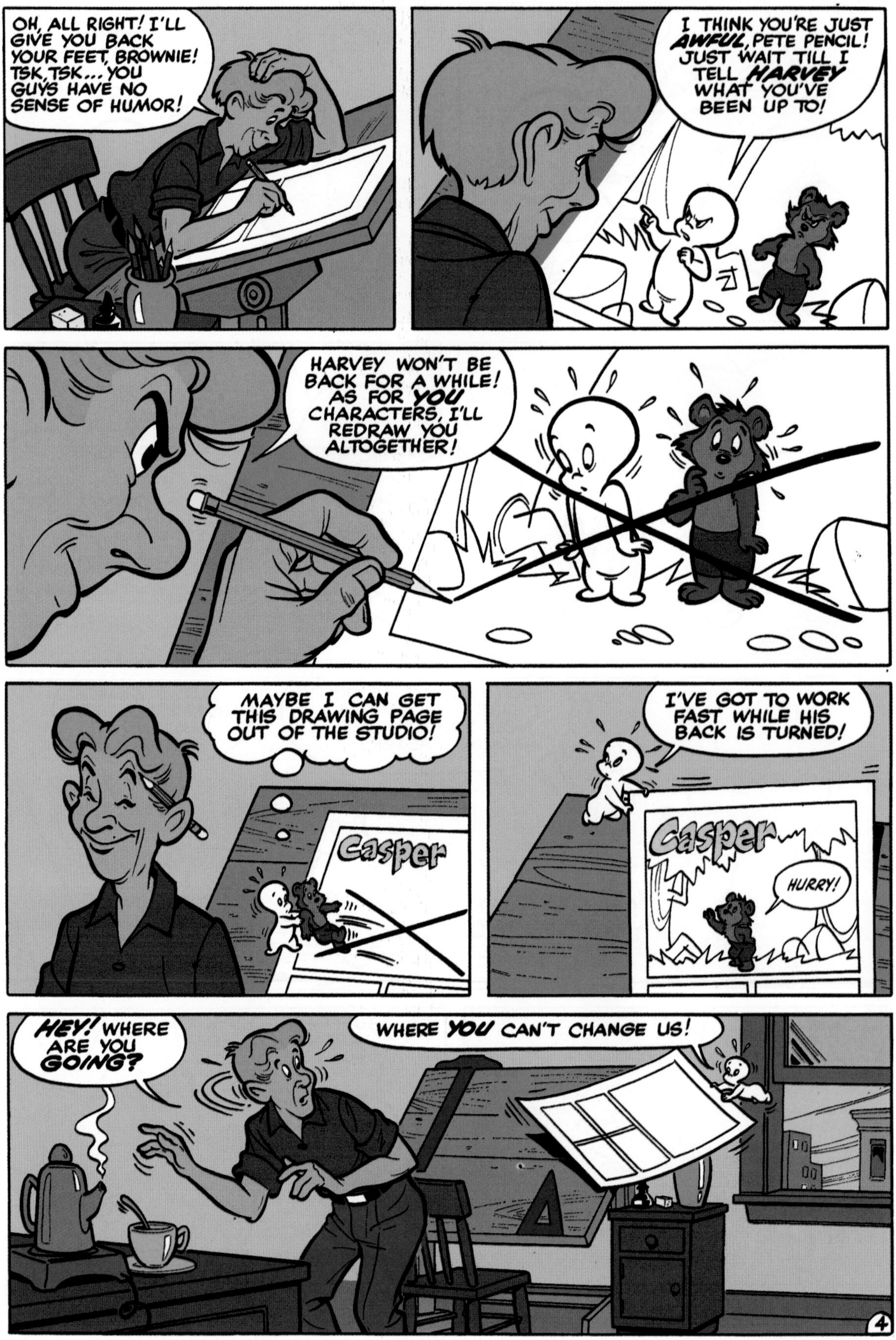
OH, ALL RIGHT! I'LL GIVE YOU BACK YOUR FEET, BROWNIE! TSK,TSK... YOU GUYS HAVE NO SENSE OF HUMOR!
I THINK YOU'RE JUST AWFUL, PETE PENCIL! JUST WAIT TILL I TELL HARVEY WHAT YOU'VE BEEN UP TO!
HARVEY WON'T BE BACK FOR A WHILE! AS FOR YOU CHARACTERS, I'LL REDRAW YOU ALTOGETHER!
MAYBE I CAN GET THIS DRAWING PAGE OUT OF THE STUDIO!
Casper
I'VE GOT TO WORK FAST WHILE HIS BACK IS TURNED!
Casper
HURRY!
HEY! WHERE ARE YOU GOING?
WHERE YOU CAN'T CHANGE US!
4

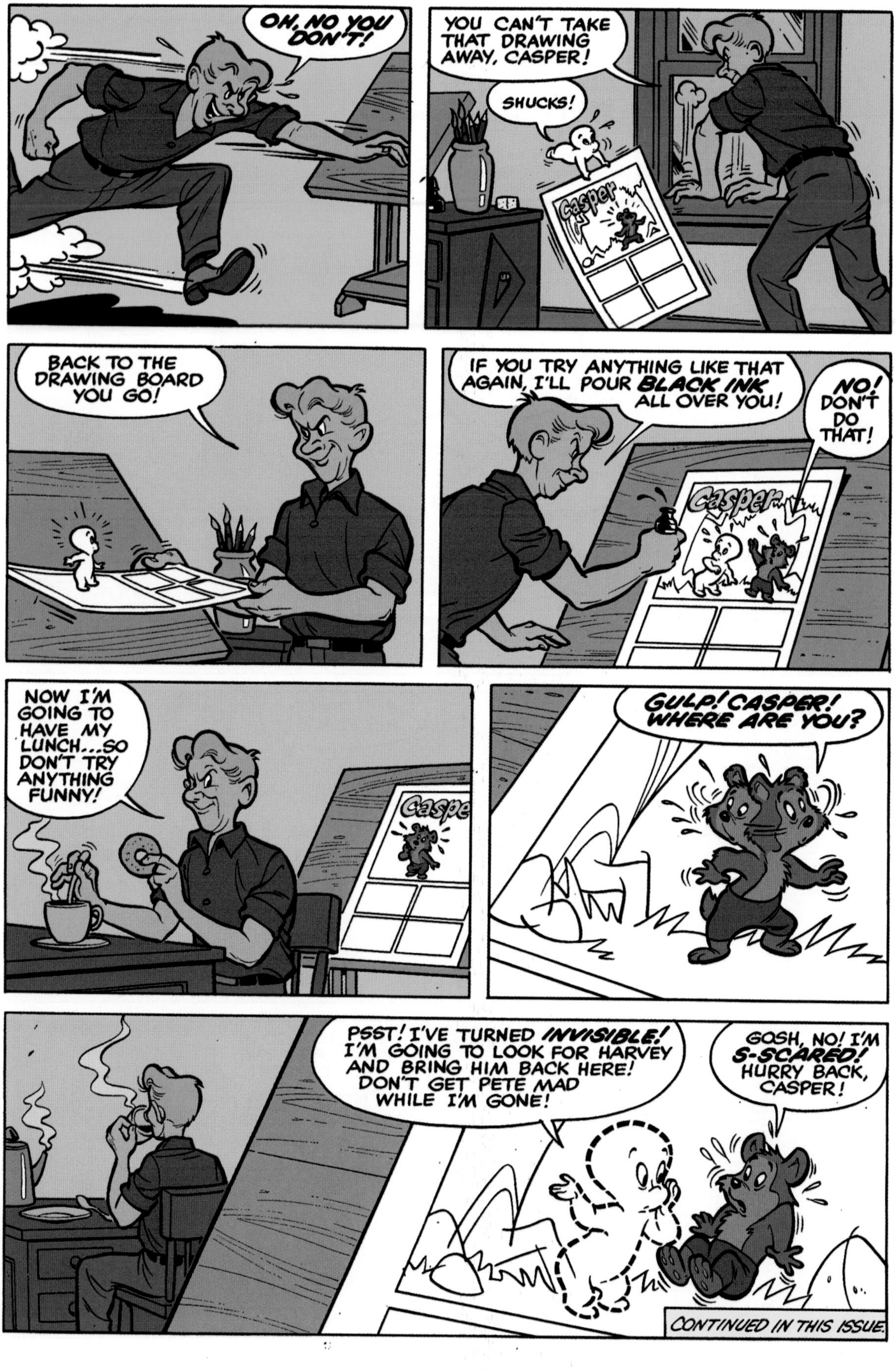

OH, NO YOU DON'T!
YOU CAN'T TAKE THAT DRAWING AWAY, CASPER!
SHUCKS!
Casper
BACK TO THE DRAWING BOARD YOU GO!
IF YOU TRY ANYTHING LIKE THAT AGAIN, I'LL POUR BLACK INK ALL OVER YOU!
NO! DON'T DO THAT!
Casper
NOW I'M GOING TO HAVE MY LUNCH...SO DON'T TRY ANYTHING FUNNY!
Caspe
GULP! CASPER! WHERE ARE YOU?
PSST! I'VE TURNED INVISIBLE! I'M GOING TO LOOK FOR HARVEY AND BRING HIM BACK HERE! DON'T GET PETE MAD WHILE I'M GONE!
GOSH, NO! I'M S-SCARED! HURRY BACK, CASPER!
CONTINUED IN THIS ISSUE.

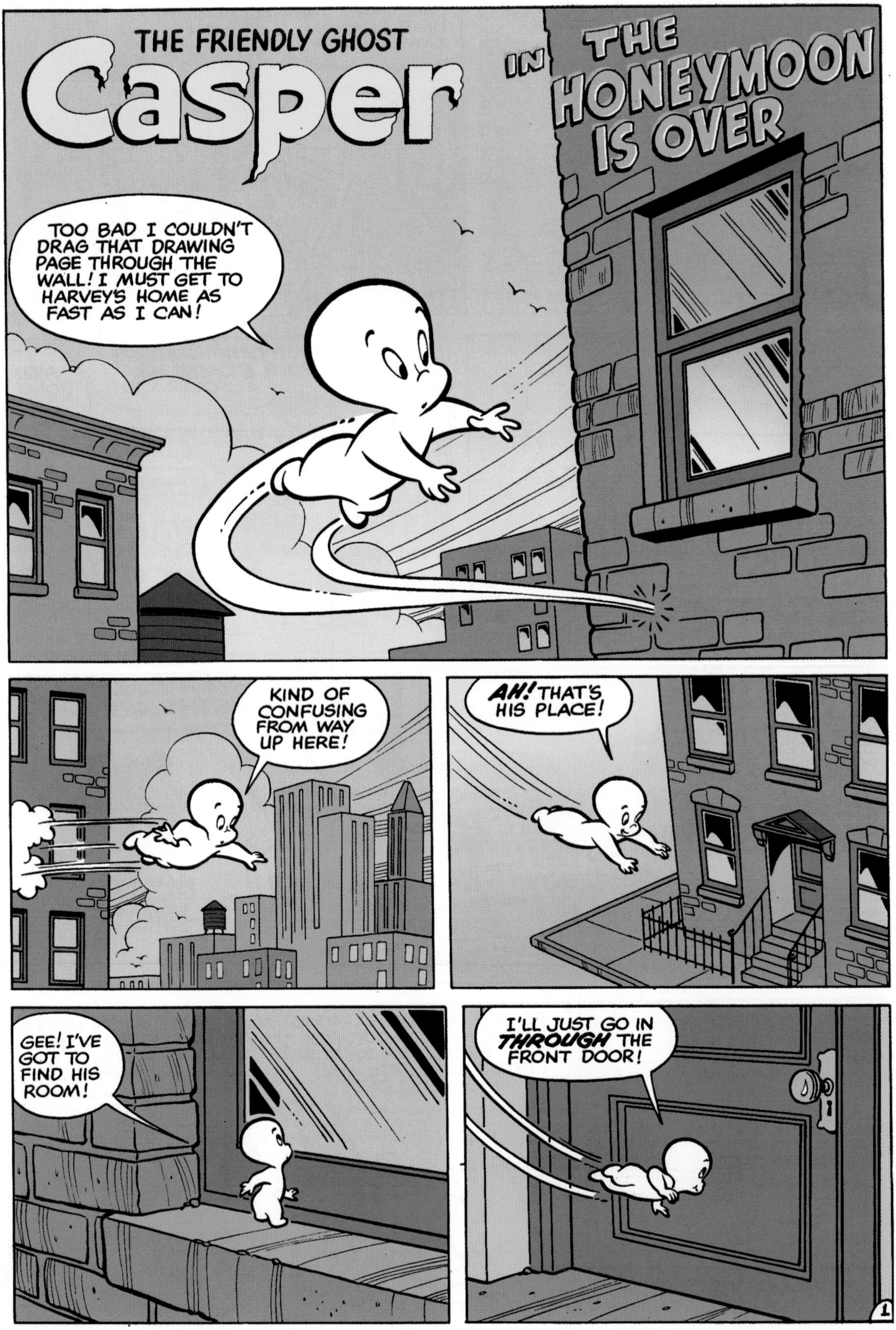
THE FRIENDLY GHOST
Casper
IN
THE HONEYMOON IS OVER
TOO BAD I COULDN'T DRAG THAT DRAWING PAGE THROUGH THE WALL! I MUST GET TO HARVEY'S HOME AS FAST AS I CAN!
KIND OF CONFUSING FROM WAY UP HERE!
AH! THAT'S HIS PLACE!
GEE! I'VE GOT TO FIND HIS ROOM!
I'LL JUST GO IN THROUGH THE FRONT DOOR!
1

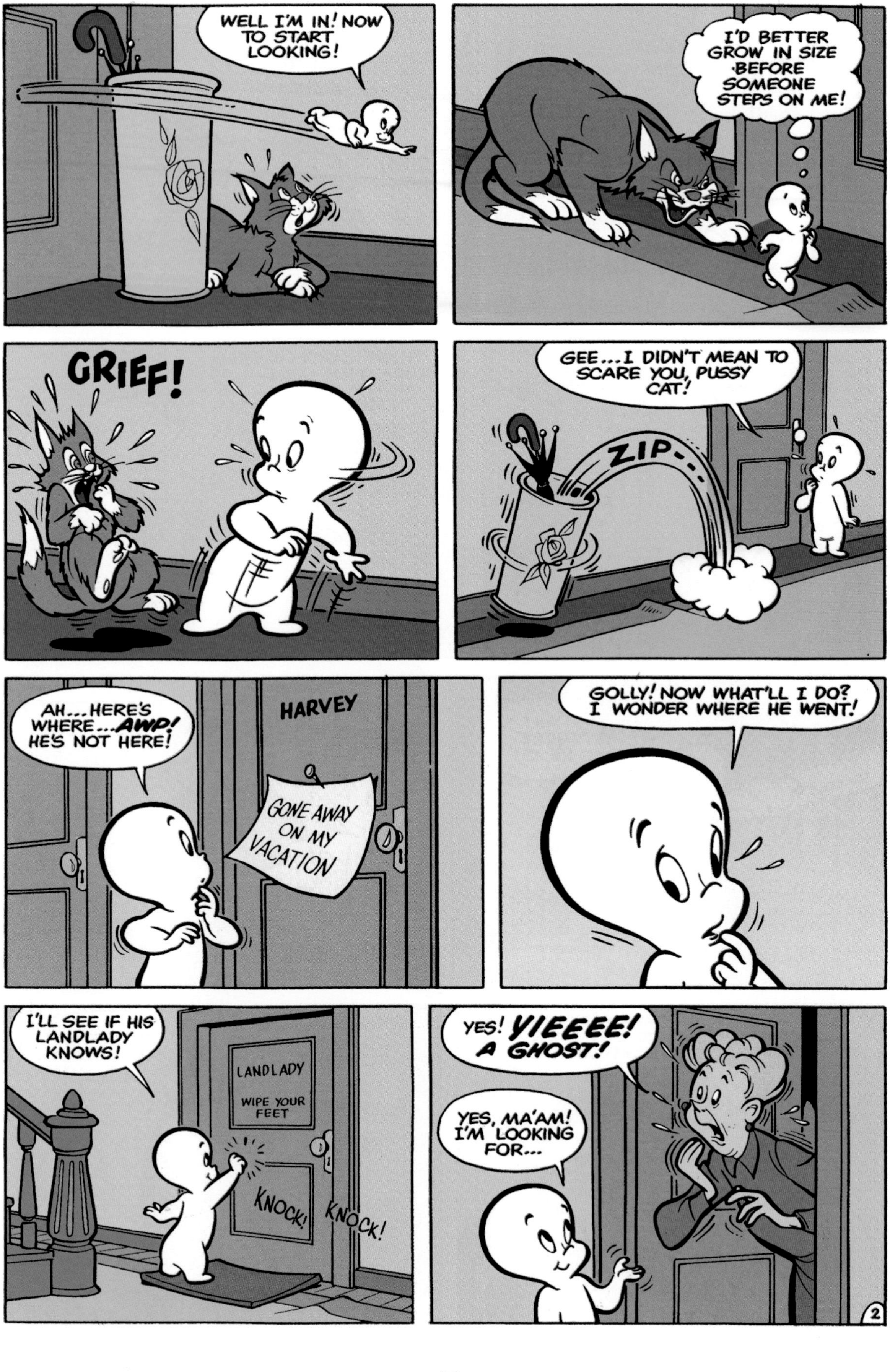
WELL I'M IN! NOW TO START LOOKING!
I'D BETTER GROW IN SIZE BEFORE SOMEONE STEPS ON ME!
GRIEF!
GEE...I DIDN'T MEAN TO SCARE YOU, PUSSY CAT!
ZIP...
AH...HERE'S WHERE...AWP! HE'S NOT HERE!
HARVEY
GONE AWAY ON MY VACATION
GOLLY! NOW WHAT'LL I DO? I WONDER WHERE HE WENT!
I'LL SEE IF HIS LANDLADY KNOWS!
LANDLADY
WIPE YOUR FEET
KNOCK! KNOCK!
YES, MA'AM! I'M LOOKING FOR...
YES! YIEEEE! A GHOST!
2

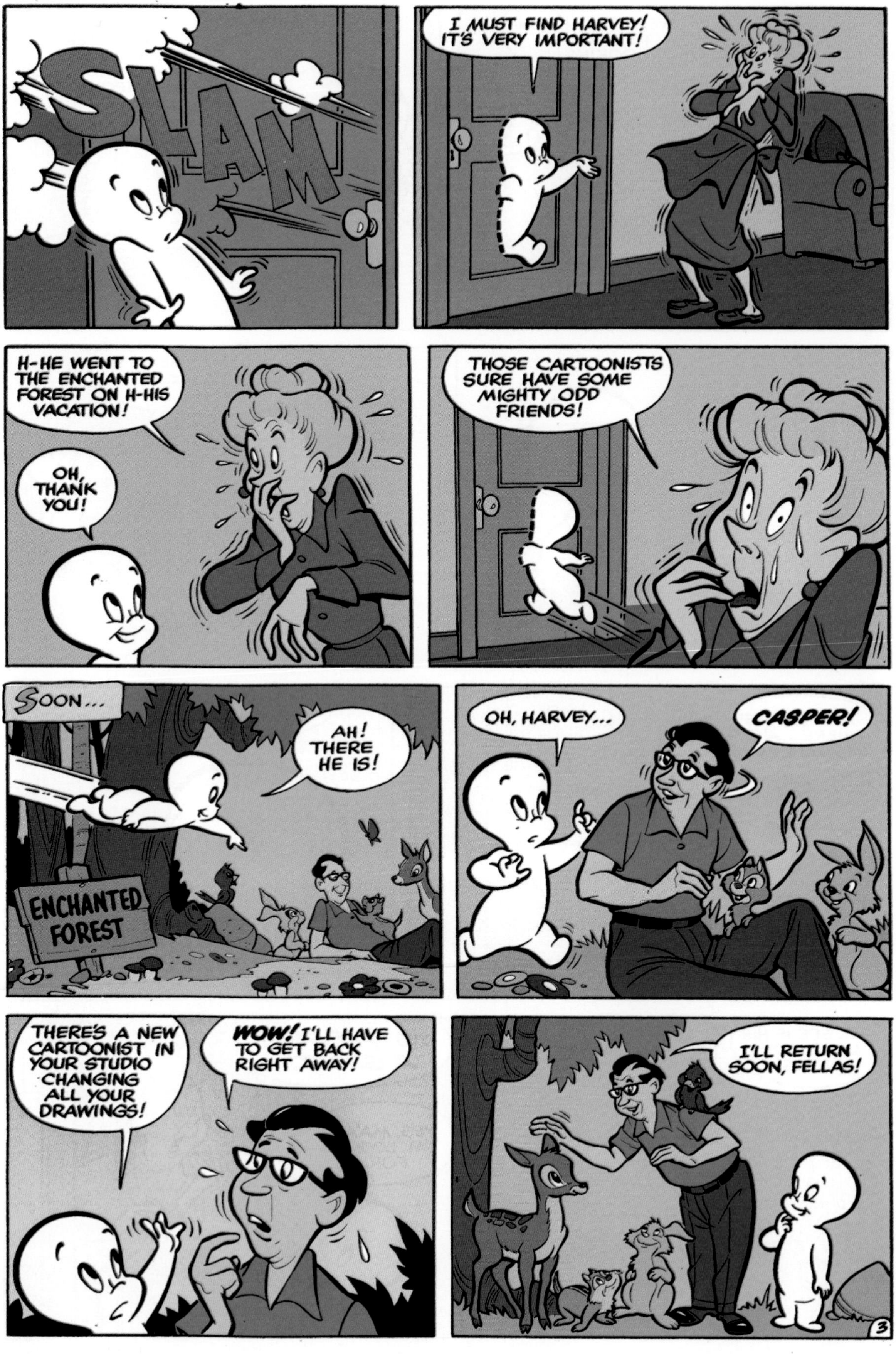
SLAM
I MUST FIND HARVEY! IT'S VERY IMPORTANT!
H-HE WENT TO THE ENCHANTED FOREST ON H-HIS VACATION!
OH, THANK YOU!
THOSE CARTOONISTS SURE HAVE SOME MIGHTY ODD FRIENDS!
SOON...
AH! THERE HE IS!
ENCHANTED FOREST
OH, HARVEY...
CASPER!
THERE'S A NEW CARTOONIST IN YOUR STUDIO CHANGING ALL YOUR DRAWINGS!
WOW! I'LL HAVE TO GET BACK RIGHT AWAY!
I'LL RETURN SOON, FELLAS!
3

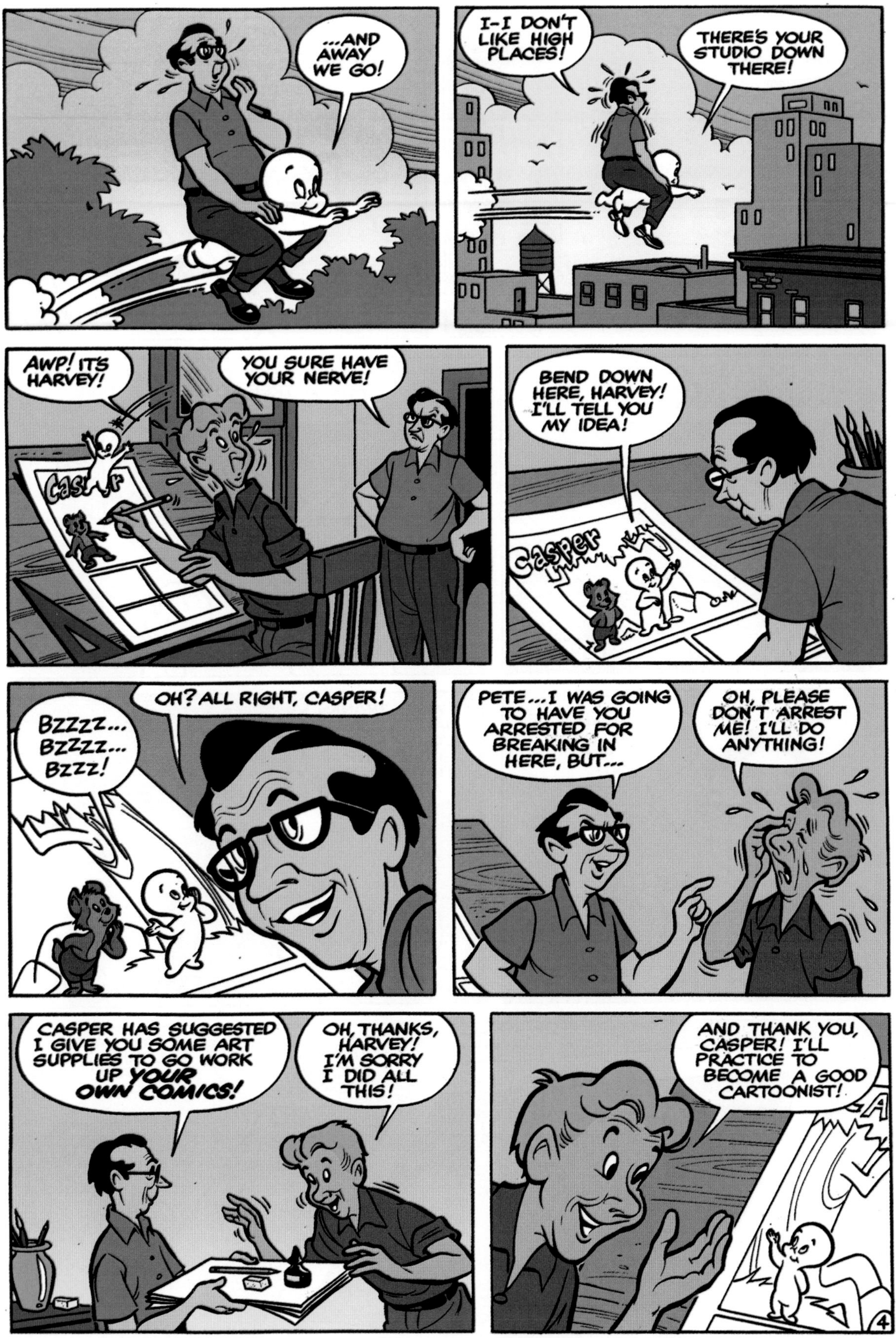
...AND AWAY WE GO!
I-I DON'T LIKE HIGH PLACES!
THERE'S YOUR STUDIO DOWN THERE!
AWP! IT'S HARVEY!
YOU SURE HAVE YOUR NERVE!
BEND DOWN HERE, HARVEY! I'LL TELL YOU MY IDEA!
BZZZZ... BZZZZ... BZZZ!
OH? ALL RIGHT, CASPER!
PETE...I WAS GOING TO HAVE YOU ARRESTED FOR BREAKING IN HERE, BUT...
OH, PLEASE DON'T ARREST ME! I'LL DO ANYTHING!
CASPER HAS SUGGESTED I GIVE YOU SOME ART SUPPLIES TO GO WORK UP YOUR OWN COMICS!
OH, THANKS, HARVEY! I'M SORRY I DID ALL THIS!
AND THANK YOU, CASPER! I'LL PRACTICE TO BECOME A GOOD CARTOONIST!
4

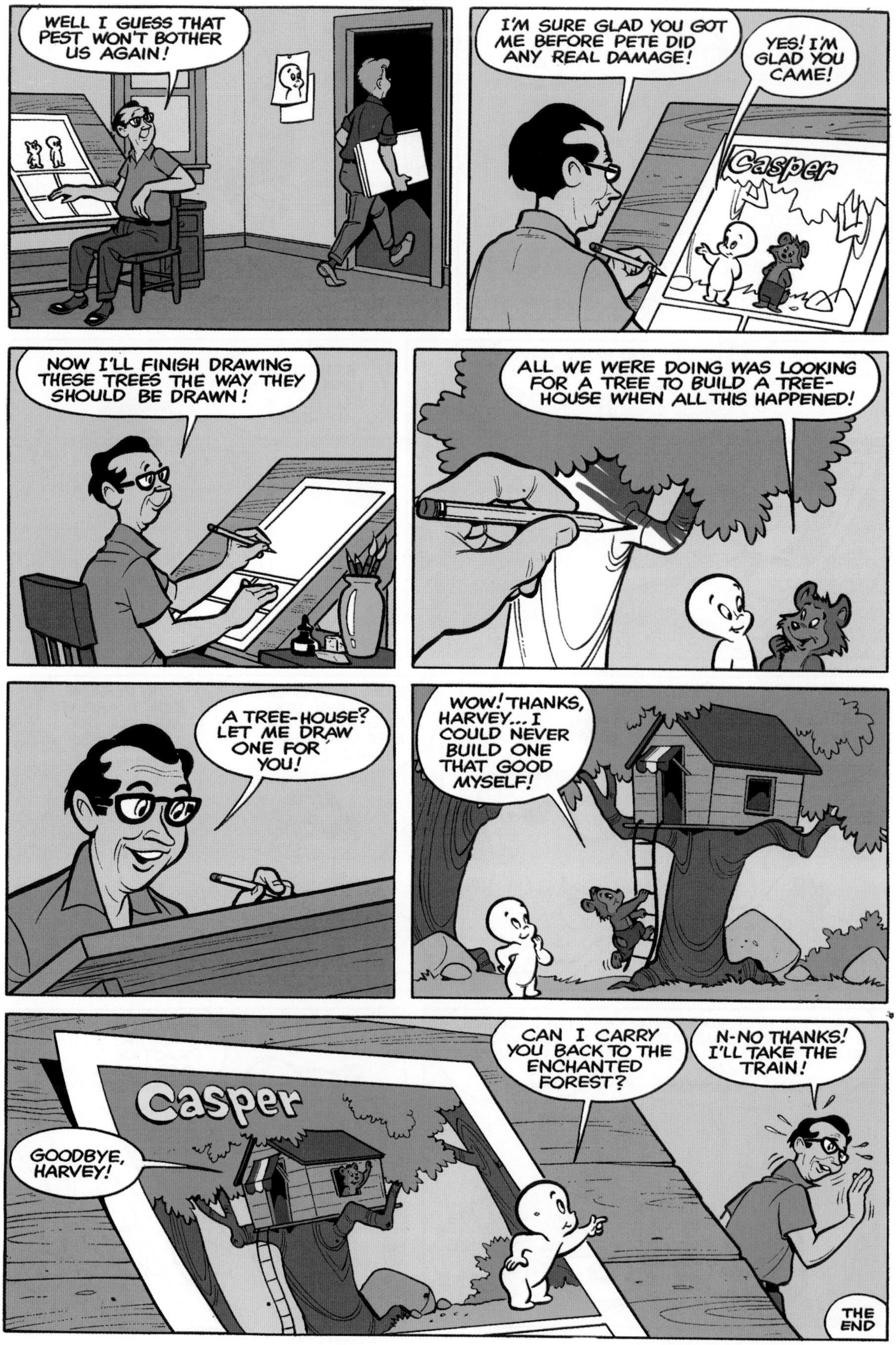

WELL I GUESS THAT PEST WON'T BOTHER US AGAIN!
I'M SURE GLAD YOU GOT ME BEFORE PETE DID ANY REAL DAMAGE!
YES! I'M GLAD YOU CAME!
Casper
NOW I'LL FINISH DRAWING THESE TREES THE WAY THEY SHOULD BE DRAWN!
ALL WE WERE DOING WAS LOOKING FOR A TREE TO BUILD A TREE-HOUSE WHEN ALL THIS HAPPENED!
A TREE-HOUSE? LET ME DRAW ONE FOR YOU!
WOW! THANKS, HARVEY... I COULD NEVER BUILD ONE THAT GOOD MYSELF!
Casper
GOODBYE, HARVEY!
CAN I CARRY YOU BACK TO THE ENCHANTED FOREST?
N-NO THANKS! I'LL TAKE THE TRAIN!
THE END

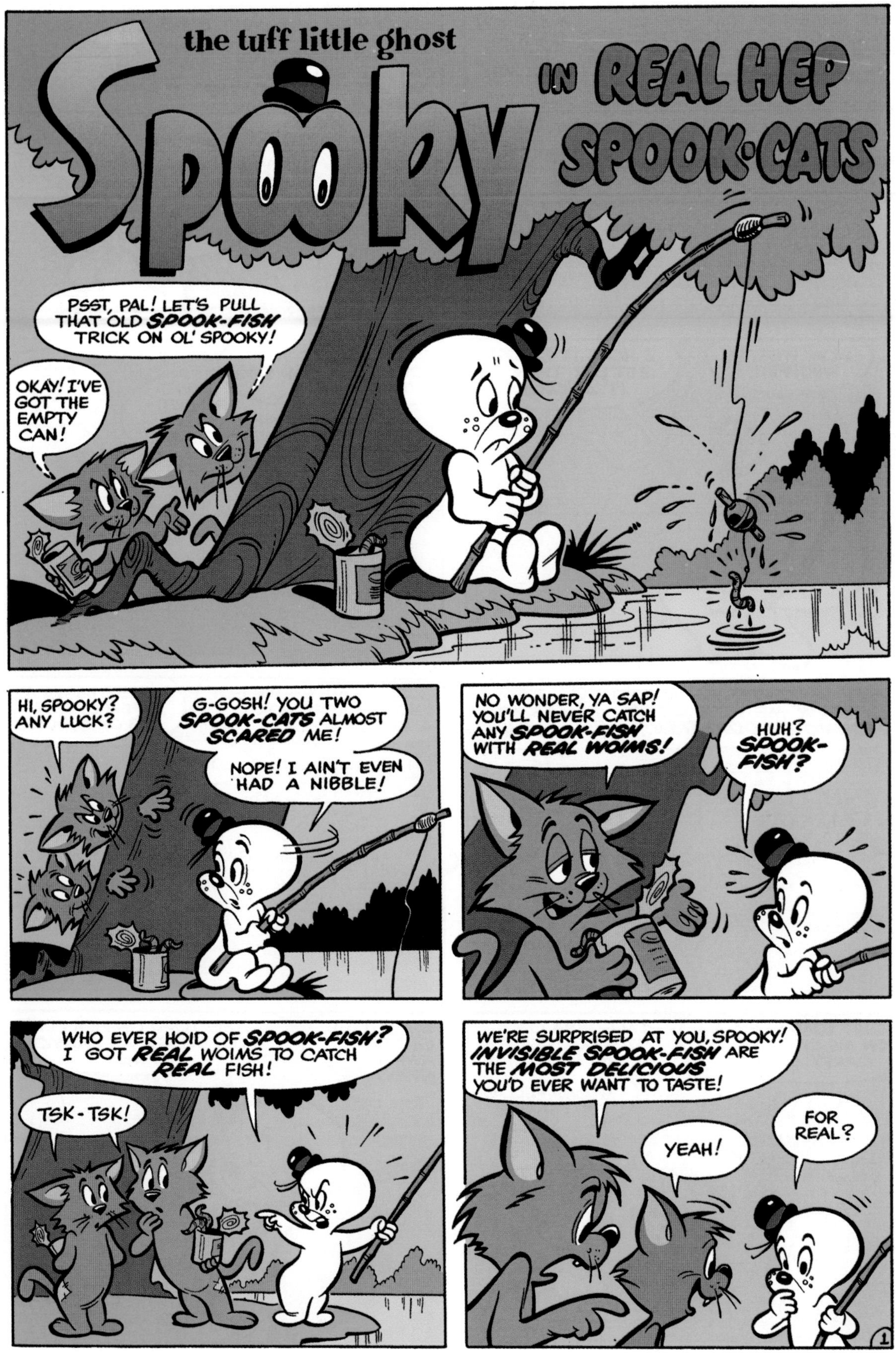
the tuff little ghost
Spooky
IN REAL HEP SPOOK-CATS
PSST, PAL! LET'S PULL THAT OLD SPOOK-FISH TRICK ON OL' SPOOKY!
OKAY! I'VE GOT THE EMPTY CAN!
HI, SPOOKY? ANY LUCK?
G-GOSH! YOU TWO SPOOK-CATS ALMOST SCARED ME!
NOPE! I AIN'T EVEN HAD A NIBBLE!
NO WONDER, YA SAP! YOU'LL NEVER CATCH ANY SPOOK-FISH WITH REAL WOIMS!
HUH? SPOOK-FISH?
WHO EVER HOID OF SPOOK-FISH? I GOT REAL WOIMS TO CATCH REAL FISH!
TSK-TSK!
WE'RE SURPRISED AT YOU, SPOOKY! INVISIBLE SPOOK-FISH ARE THE MOST DELICIOUS YOU'D EVER WANT TO TASTE!
YEAH!
FOR REAL?
1

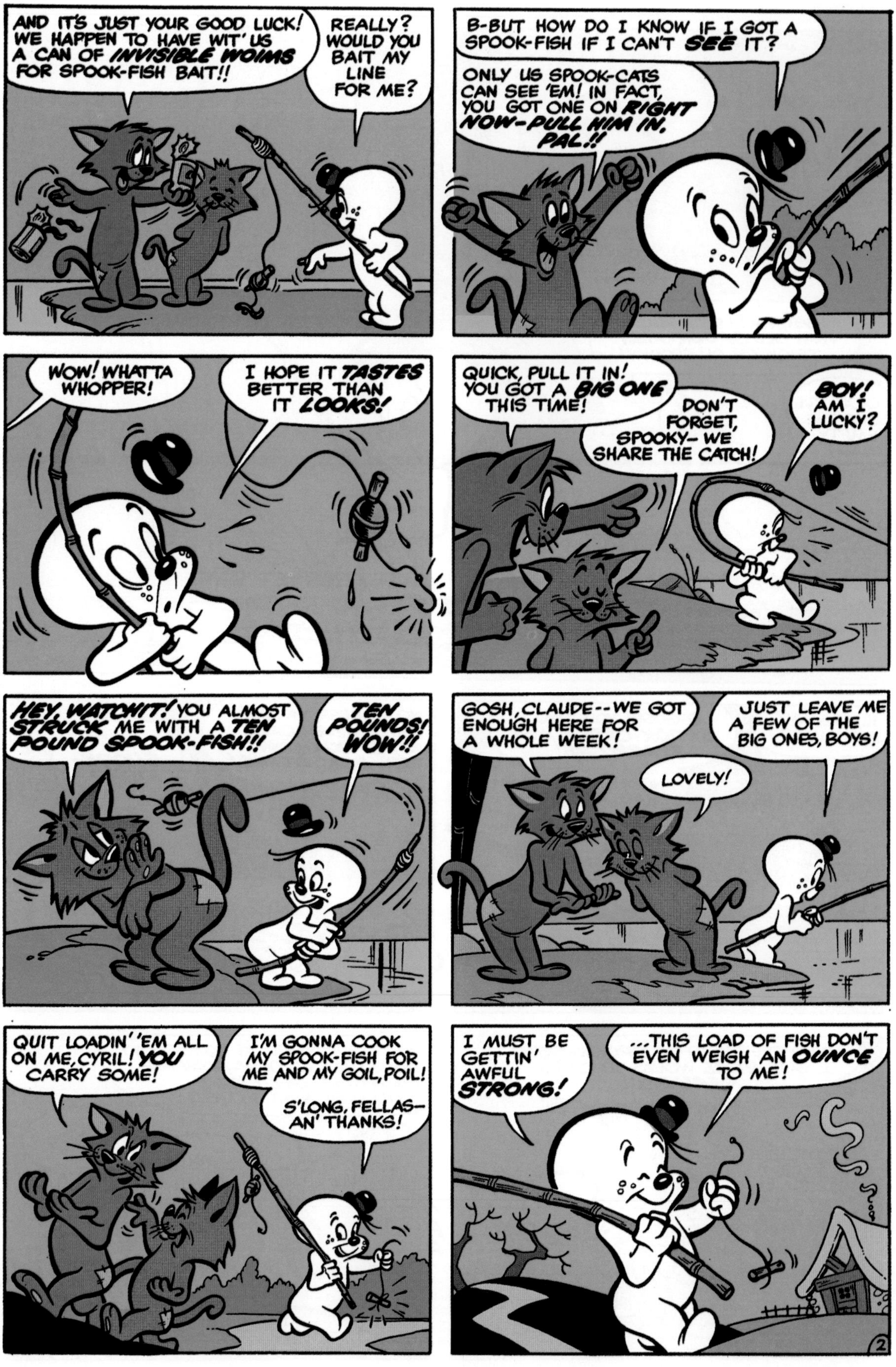
AND IT'S JUST YOUR GOOD LUCK! WE HAPPEN TO HAVE WIT' US A CAN OF INVISIBLE WOIMS FOR SPOOK-FISH BAIT!!
REALLY? WOULD YOU BAIT MY LINE FOR ME?
B-BUT HOW DO I KNOW IF I GOT A SPOOK-FISH IF I CAN'T SEE IT?
ONLY US SPOOK-CATS CAN SEE 'EM! IN FACT, YOU GOT ONE ON RIGHT NOW-PULL HIM IN, PAL!!
WOW! WHATTA WHOPPER!
I HOPE IT TASTES BETTER THAN IT LOOKS!
QUICK, PULL IT IN! YOU GOT A BIG ONE THIS TIME!
DON'T FORGET, SPOOKY- WE SHARE THE CATCH!
BOY! AM I LUCKY?
HEY, WATCHIT! YOU ALMOST STRUCK ME WITH A TEN POUND SPOOK-FISH!!
TEN POUNDS! WOW!!
GOSH, CLAUDE--WE GOT ENOUGH HERE FOR A WHOLE WEEK!
LOVELY!
JUST LEAVE ME A FEW OF THE BIG ONES, BOYS!
QUIT LOADIN' 'EM ALL ON ME, CYRIL! YOU CARRY SOME!
I'M GONNA COOK MY SPOOK-FISH FOR ME AND MY GOIL, POIL!
S'LONG, FELLAS- AN' THANKS!
I MUST BE GETTIN' AWFUL STRONG!
...THIS LOAD OF FISH DON'T EVEN WEIGH AN OUNCE TO ME!
2

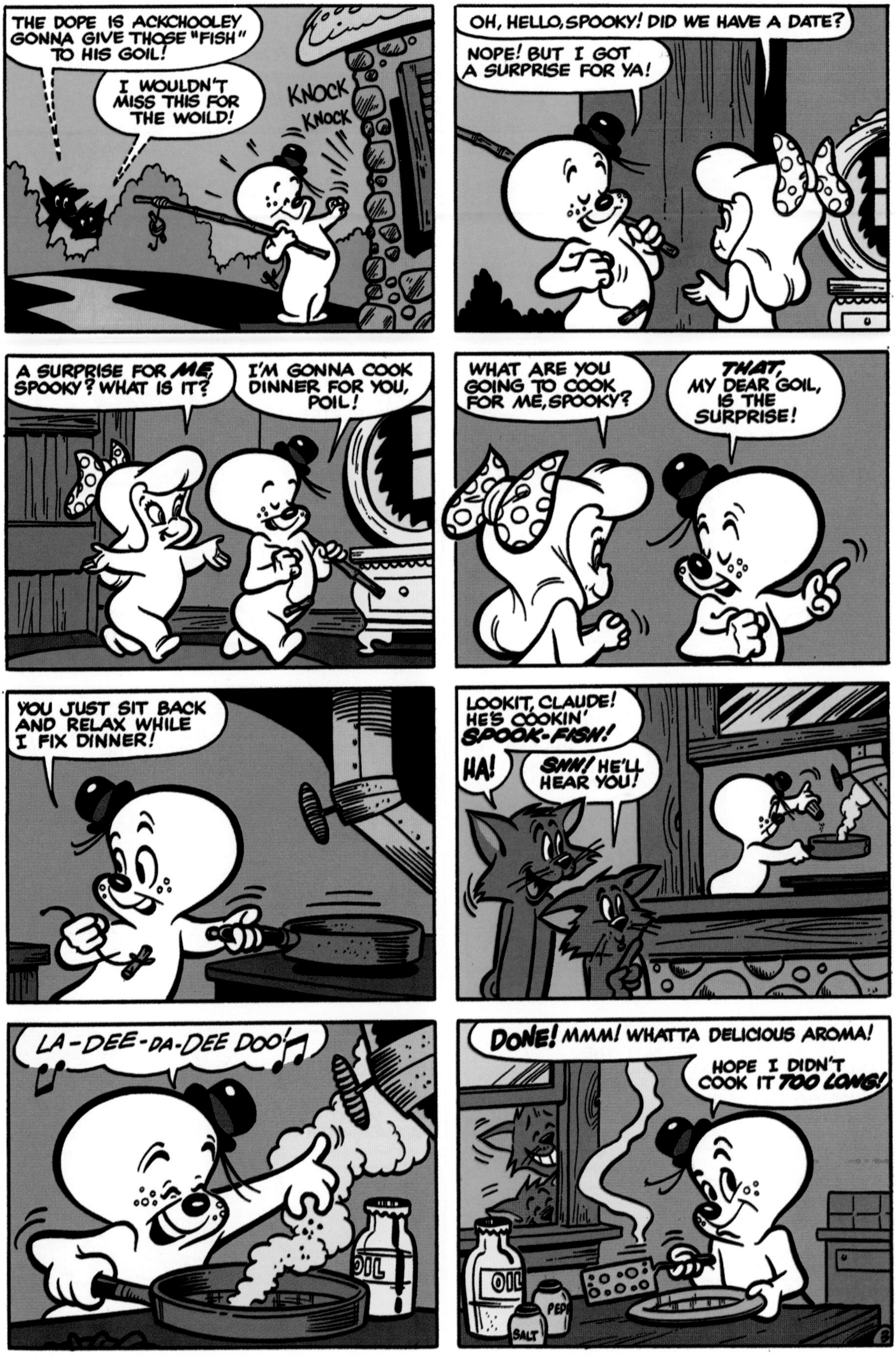
THE DOPE IS ACKCHOOLEY GONNA GIVE THOSE "FISH" TO HIS GOIL!
I WOULDN'T MISS THIS FOR THE WOILD!
KNOCK KNOCK
OH, HELLO, SPOOKY! DID WE HAVE A DATE?
NOPE! BUT I GOT A SURPRISE FOR YA!
A SURPRISE FOR ME, SPOOKY? WHAT IS IT?
I'M GONNA COOK DINNER FOR YOU, POIL!
WHAT ARE YOU GOING TO COOK FOR ME, SPOOKY?
THAT, MY DEAR GOIL, IS THE SURPRISE!
YOU JUST SIT BACK AND RELAX WHILE I FIX DINNER!
LOOKIT, CLAUDE! HE'S COOKIN' SPOOK-FISH!
HA!
SHH! HE'LL HEAR YOU!
LA-DEE-DA-DEE DOO!
OIL
DONE! MMM! WHATTA DELICIOUS AROMA!
HOPE I DIDN'T COOK IT TOO LONG!
OIL
SALT
PEP

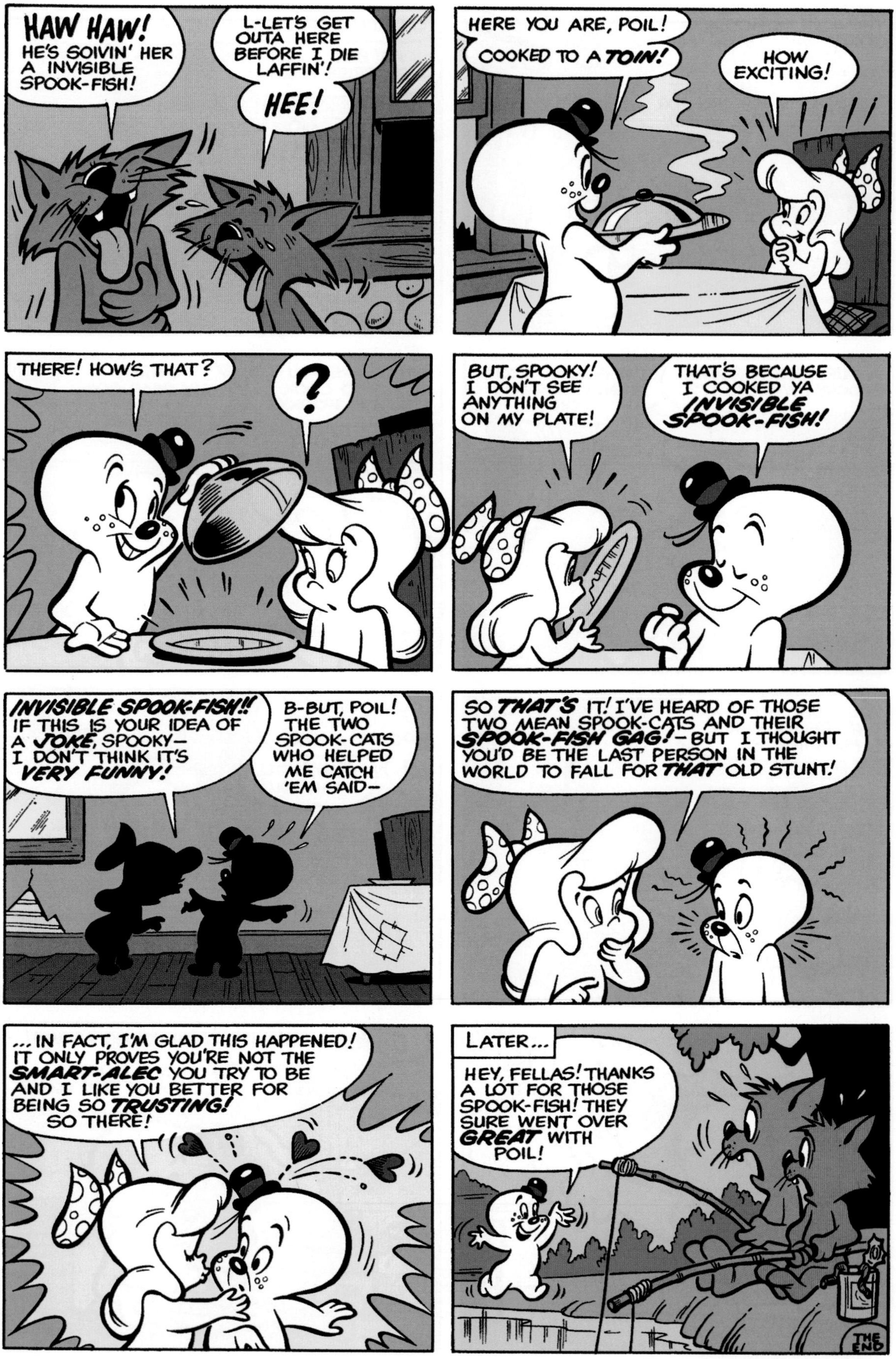
HAW HAW! HE'S SOIVIN' HER A INVISIBLE SPOOK-FISH!
L-LET'S GET OUTA HERE BEFORE I DIE LAFFIN'!
HEE!
HERE YOU ARE, POIL!
COOKED TO A TOIN!
HOW EXCITING!
THERE! HOW'S THAT?
?
BUT, SPOOKY! I DON'T SEE ANYTHING ON MY PLATE!
THAT'S BECAUSE I COOKED YA INVISIBLE SPOOK-FISH!
INVISIBLE SPOOK-FISH!! IF THIS IS YOUR IDEA OF A JOKE, SPOOKY— I DON'T THINK IT'S VERY FUNNY!
B-BUT, POIL! THE TWO SPOOK-CATS WHO HELPED ME CATCH 'EM SAID—
SO THAT'S IT! I'VE HEARD OF THOSE TWO MEAN SPOOK-CATS AND THEIR SPOOK-FISH GAG! —BUT I THOUGHT YOU'D BE THE LAST PERSON IN THE WORLD TO FALL FOR THAT OLD STUNT!
...IN FACT, I'M GLAD THIS HAPPENED! IT ONLY PROVES YOU'RE NOT THE SMART-ALEC YOU TRY TO BE AND I LIKE YOU BETTER FOR BEING SO TRUSTING! SO THERE!
LATER...
HEY, FELLAS! THANKS A LOT FOR THOSE SPOOK-FISH! THEY SURE WENT OVER GREAT WITH POIL!
THE END

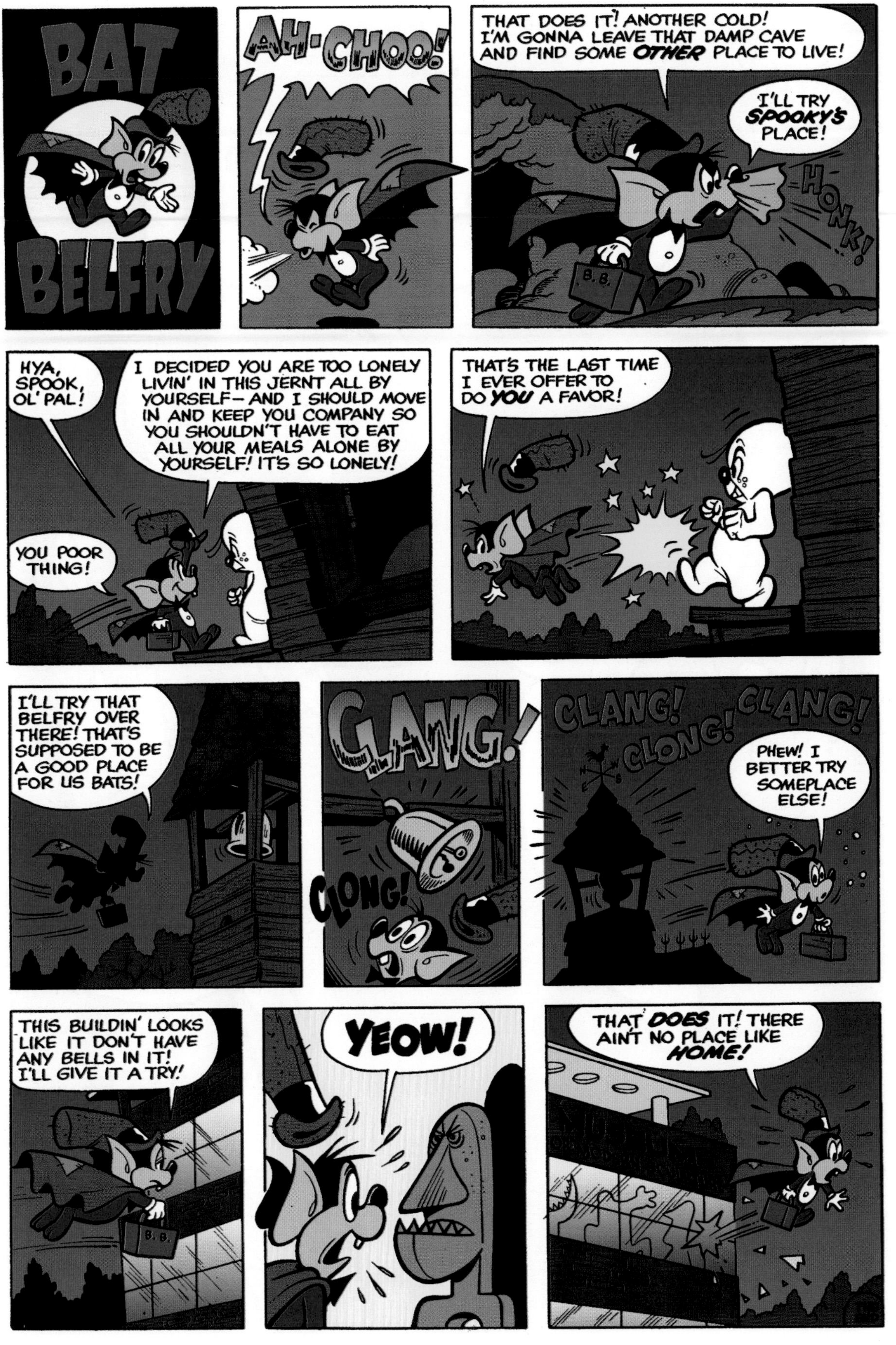
BAT BELFRY
AH-CHOO!
THAT DOES IT! ANOTHER COLD! I'M GONNA LEAVE THAT DAMP CAVE AND FIND SOME OTHER PLACE TO LIVE!
I'LL TRY SPOOKY'S PLACE!
HONK!
HYA, SPOOK, OL' PAL!
I DECIDED YOU ARE TOO LONELY LIVIN' IN THIS JERNT ALL BY YOURSELF— AND I SHOULD MOVE IN AND KEEP YOU COMPANY SO YOU SHOULDN'T HAVE TO EAT ALL YOUR MEALS ALONE BY YOURSELF! IT'S SO LONELY!
YOU POOR THING!
THAT'S THE LAST TIME I EVER OFFER TO DO YOU A FAVOR!
I'LL TRY THAT BELFRY OVER THERE! THAT'S SUPPOSED TO BE A GOOD PLACE FOR US BATS!
CLANG!
CLONG!
CLANG! CLONG! CLANG!
PHEW! I BETTER TRY SOMEPLACE ELSE!
THIS BUILDIN' LOOKS LIKE IT DON'T HAVE ANY BELLS IN IT! I'LL GIVE IT A TRY!
YEOW!
THAT DOES IT! THERE AIN'T NO PLACE LIKE HOME!

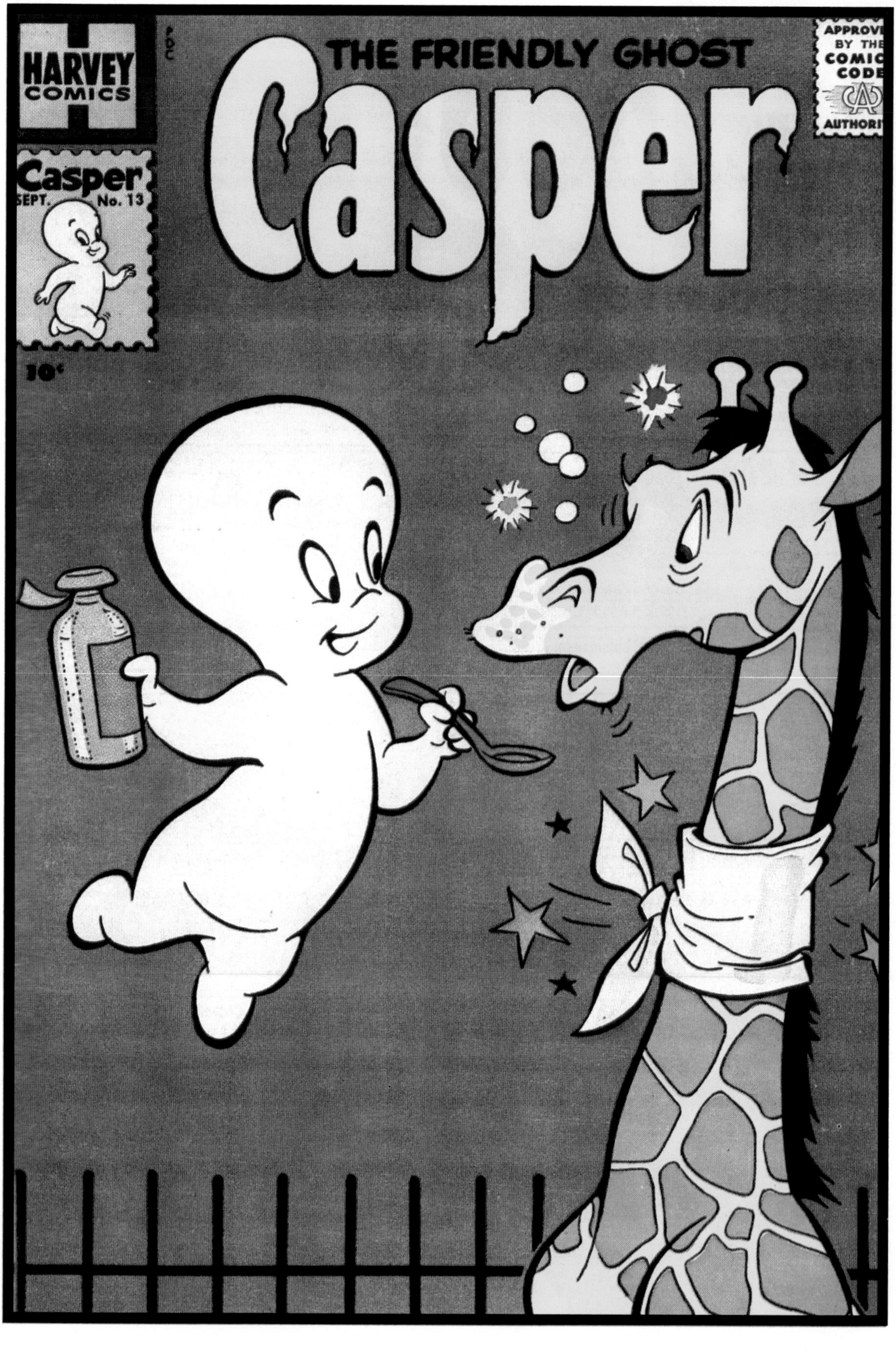
HARVEY COMICS
THE FRIENDLY GHOST
Casper
Casper SEPT. No. 13
10¢
APPROV BY THE COMIC CODE AUTHORIT

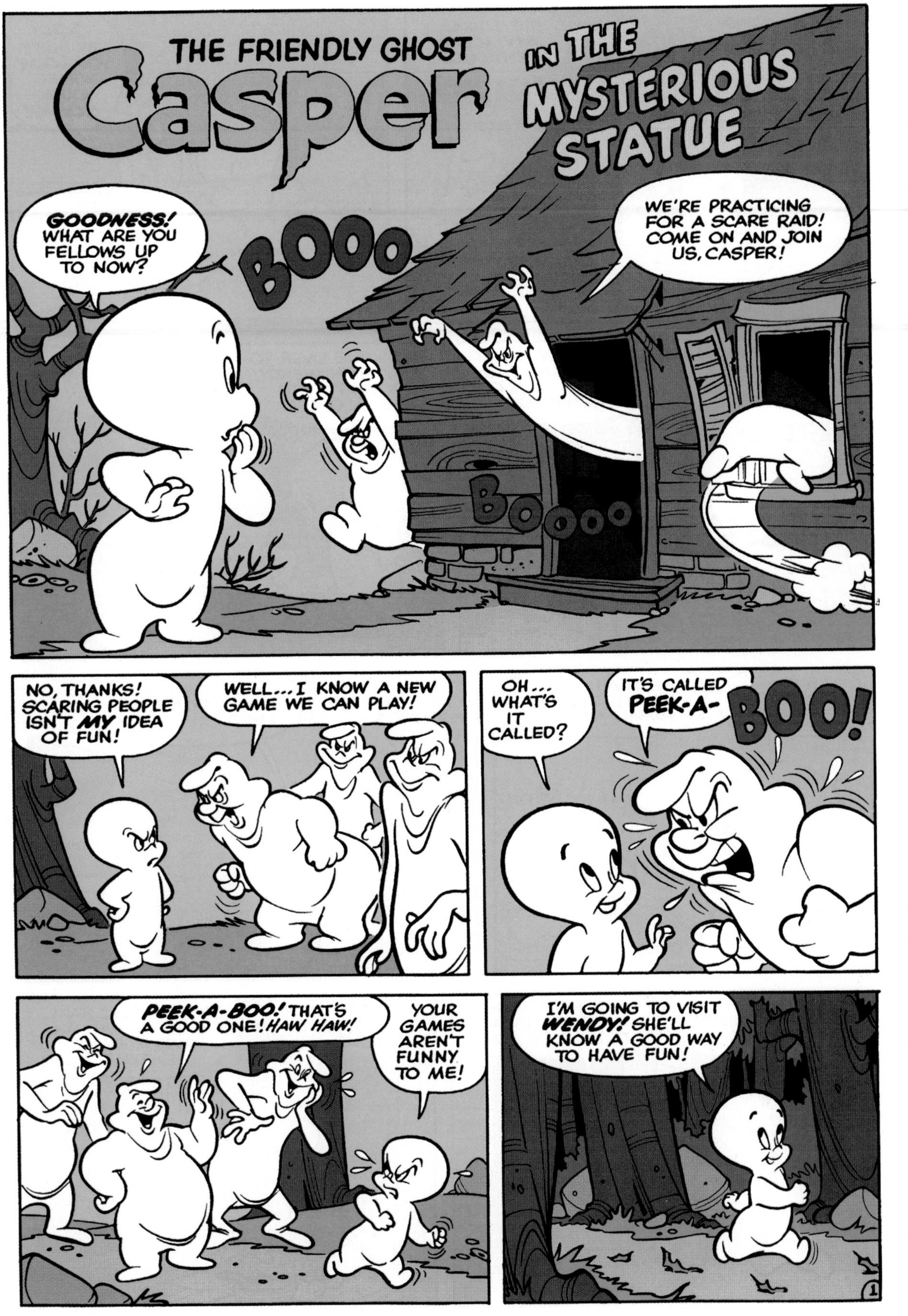

THE FRIENDLY GHOST
Casper
IN THE MYSTERIOUS STATUE
GOODNESS! WHAT ARE YOU FELLOWS UP TO NOW?
BOOO
WE'RE PRACTICING FOR A SCARE RAID! COME ON AND JOIN US, CASPER!
BOOOO
NO, THANKS! SCARING PEOPLE ISN'T MY IDEA OF FUN!
WELL... I KNOW A NEW GAME WE CAN PLAY!
OH... WHAT'S IT CALLED?
IT'S CALLED PEEK-A-BOO!
PEEK-A-BOO! THAT'S A GOOD ONE! HAW HAW!
YOUR GAMES AREN'T FUNNY TO ME!
I'M GOING TO VISIT WENDY! SHE'LL KNOW A GOOD WAY TO HAVE FUN!
1

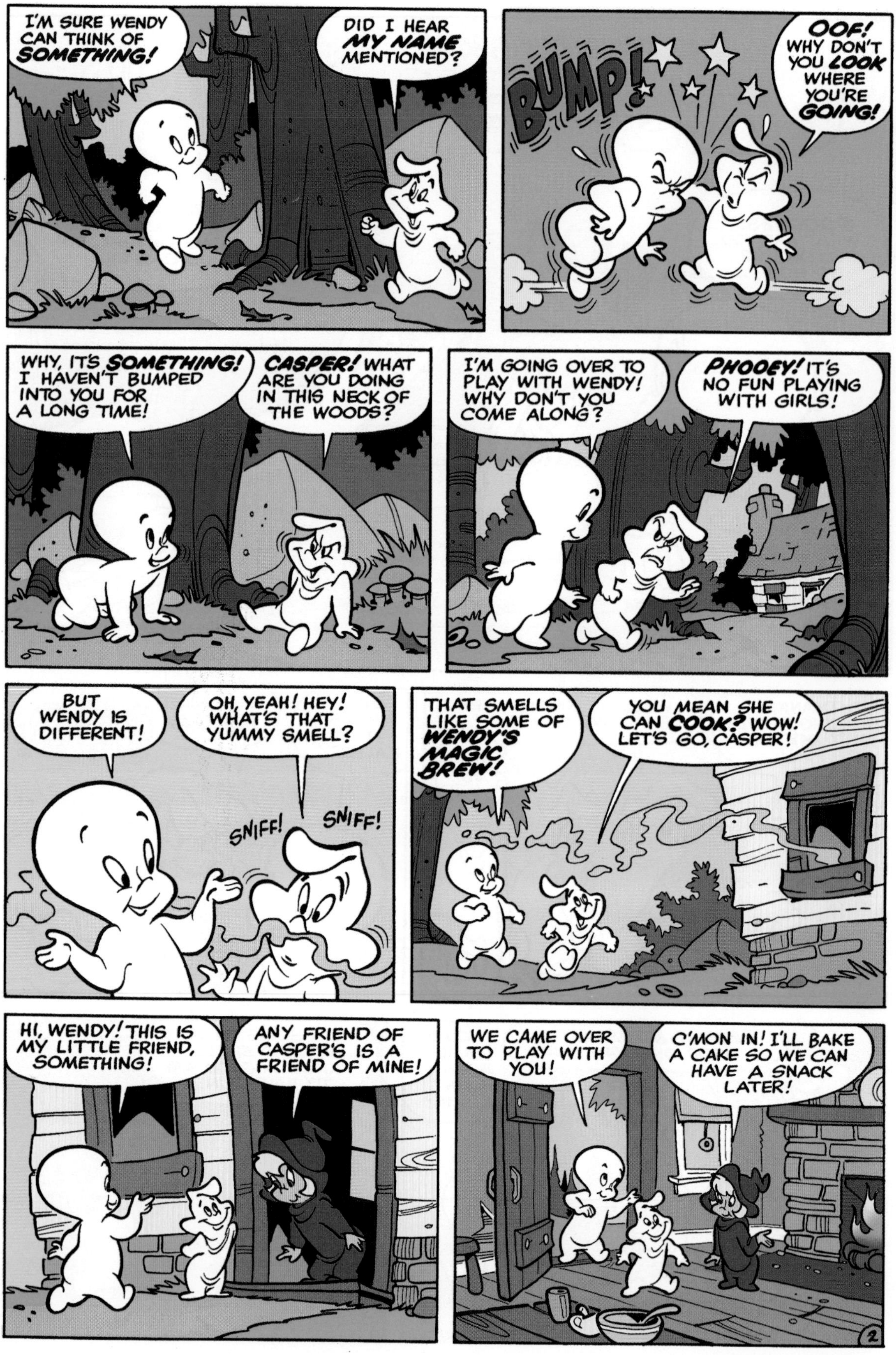

I'M SURE WENDY CAN THINK OF SOMETHING!
DID I HEAR MY NAME MENTIONED?
BUMP!
OOF! WHY DON'T YOU LOOK WHERE YOU'RE GOING!
WHY, IT'S SOMETHING! I HAVEN'T BUMPED INTO YOU FOR A LONG TIME!
CASPER! WHAT ARE YOU DOING IN THIS NECK OF THE WOODS?
I'M GOING OVER TO PLAY WITH WENDY! WHY DON'T YOU COME ALONG?
PHOOEY! IT'S NO FUN PLAYING WITH GIRLS!
BUT WENDY IS DIFFERENT!
OH, YEAH! HEY! WHAT'S THAT YUMMY SMELL?
SNIFF!
SNIFF!
THAT SMELLS LIKE SOME OF WENDY'S MAGIC BREW!
YOU MEAN SHE CAN COOK? WOW! LET'S GO, CASPER!
HI, WENDY! THIS IS MY LITTLE FRIEND, SOMETHING!
ANY FRIEND OF CASPER'S IS A FRIEND OF MINE!
WE CAME OVER TO PLAY WITH YOU!
C'MON IN! I'LL BAKE A CAKE SO WE CAN HAVE A SNACK LATER!
2

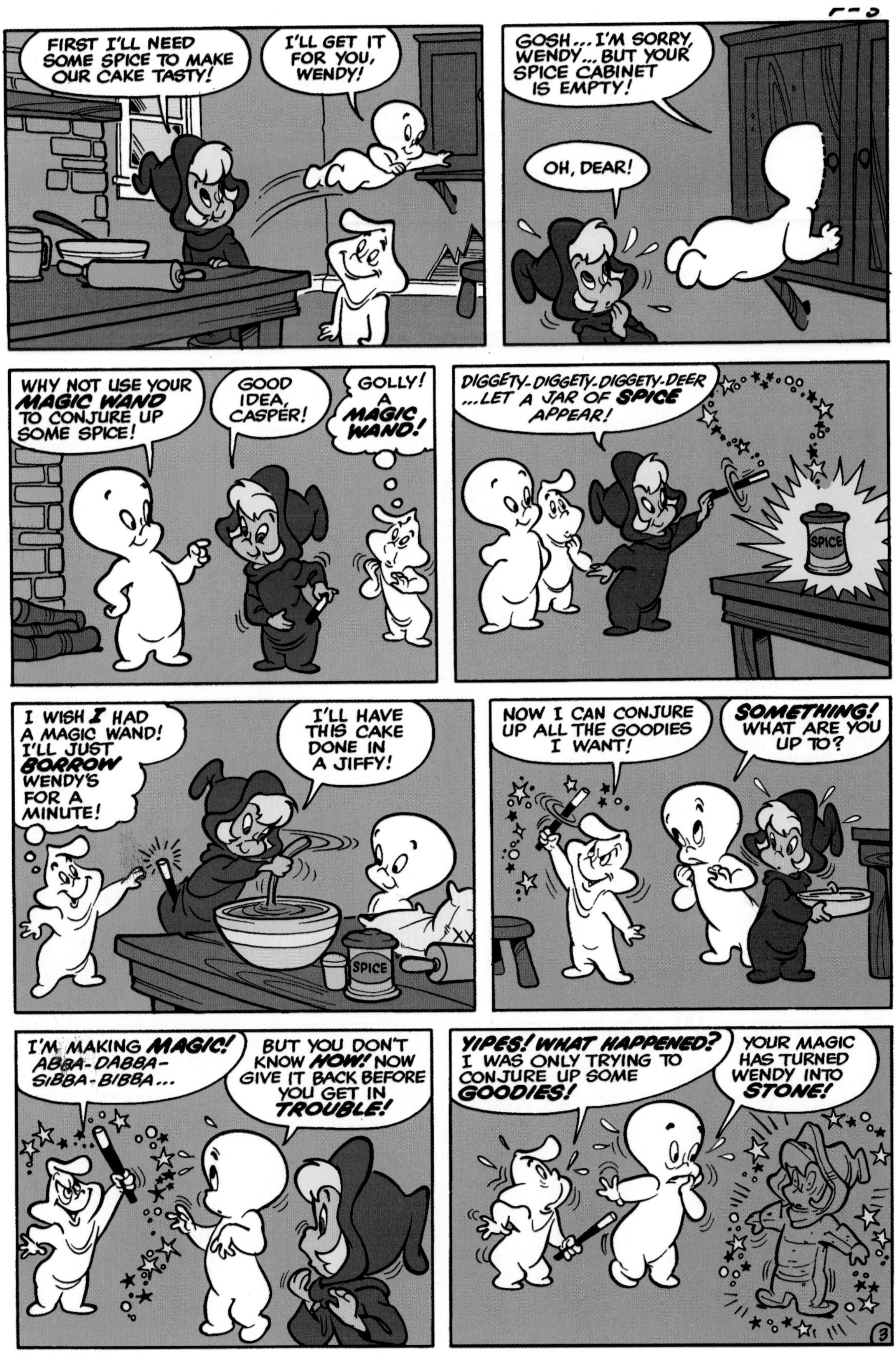
F-3
FIRST I'LL NEED SOME SPICE TO MAKE OUR CAKE TASTY!
I'LL GET IT FOR YOU, WENDY!
GOSH... I'M SORRY, WENDY... BUT YOUR SPICE CABINET IS EMPTY!
OH, DEAR!
WHY NOT USE YOUR MAGIC WAND TO CONJURE UP SOME SPICE!
GOOD IDEA, CASPER!
GOLLY! A MAGIC WAND!
DIGGETY-DIGGETY-DIGGETY-DEER ...LET A JAR OF SPICE APPEAR!
SPICE
I WISH I HAD A MAGIC WAND! I'LL JUST BORROW WENDY'S FOR A MINUTE!
I'LL HAVE THIS CAKE DONE IN A JIFFY!
SPICE
NOW I CAN CONJURE UP ALL THE GOODIES I WANT!
SOMETHING! WHAT ARE YOU UP TO?
I'M MAKING MAGIC! ABBA-DABBA-SIBBA-BIBBA...
BUT YOU DON'T KNOW HOW! NOW GIVE IT BACK BEFORE YOU GET IN TROUBLE!
YIPES! WHAT HAPPENED? I WAS ONLY TRYING TO CONJURE UP SOME GOODIES!
YOUR MAGIC HAS TURNED WENDY INTO STONE!
3

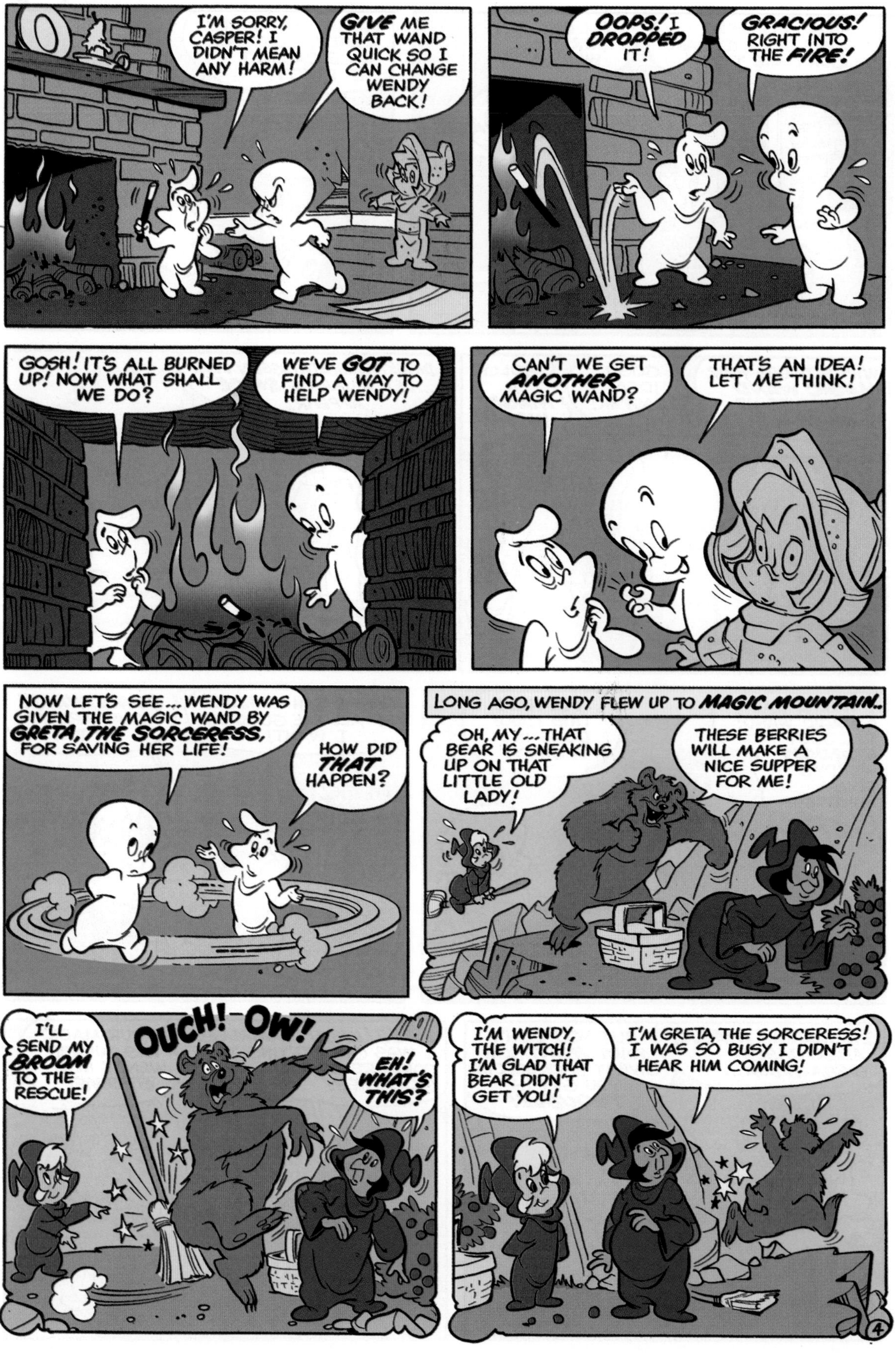
I'M SORRY, CASPER! I DIDN'T MEAN ANY HARM!
GIVE ME THAT WAND QUICK SO I CAN CHANGE WENDY BACK!
OOPS! I DROPPED IT!
GRACIOUS! RIGHT INTO THE FIRE!
GOSH! IT'S ALL BURNED UP! NOW WHAT SHALL WE DO?
WE'VE GOT TO FIND A WAY TO HELP WENDY!
CAN'T WE GET ANOTHER MAGIC WAND?
THAT'S AN IDEA! LET ME THINK!
NOW LET'S SEE... WENDY WAS GIVEN THE MAGIC WAND BY GRETA, THE SORCERESS, FOR SAVING HER LIFE!
HOW DID THAT HAPPEN?
LONG AGO, WENDY FLEW UP TO MAGIC MOUNTAIN..
OH, MY... THAT BEAR IS SNEAKING UP ON THAT LITTLE OLD LADY!
THESE BERRIES WILL MAKE A NICE SUPPER FOR ME!
I'LL SEND MY BROOM TO THE RESCUE!
OUCH! - OW!
EH! WHAT'S THIS?
I'M WENDY, THE WITCH! I'M GLAD THAT BEAR DIDN'T GET YOU!
I'M GRETA, THE SORCERESS! I WAS SO BUSY I DIDN'T HEAR HIM COMING!
4

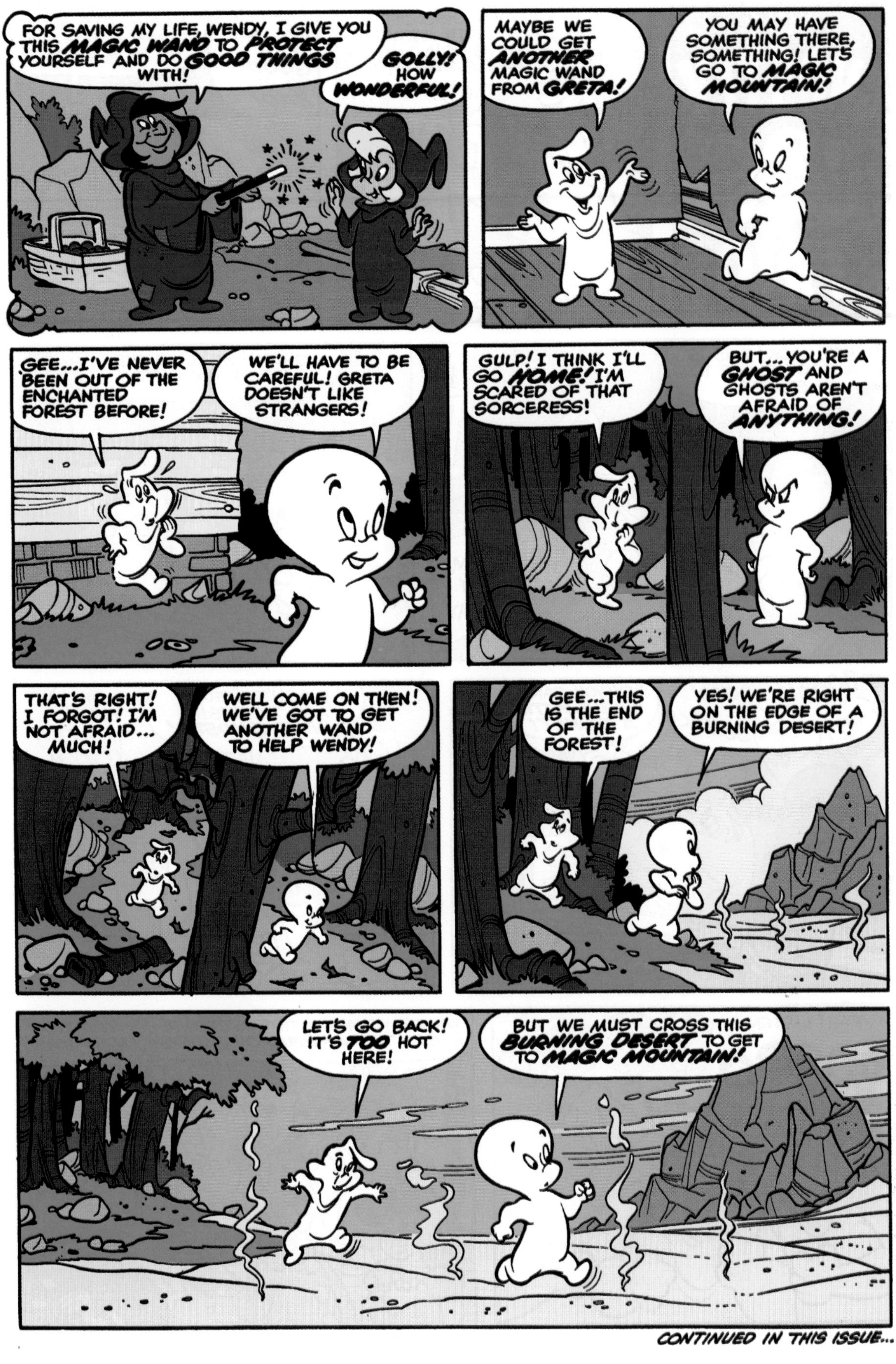
FOR SAVING MY LIFE, WENDY, I GIVE YOU THIS MAGIC WAND TO PROTECT YOURSELF AND DO GOOD THINGS WITH!
GOLLY! HOW WONDERFUL!
MAYBE WE COULD GET ANOTHER MAGIC WAND FROM GRETA!
YOU MAY HAVE SOMETHING THERE, SOMETHING! LET'S GO TO MAGIC MOUNTAIN!
GEE...I'VE NEVER BEEN OUT OF THE ENCHANTED FOREST BEFORE!
WE'LL HAVE TO BE CAREFUL! GRETA DOESN'T LIKE STRANGERS!
GULP! I THINK I'LL GO HOME! I'M SCARED OF THAT SORCERESS!
BUT...YOU'RE A GHOST AND GHOSTS AREN'T AFRAID OF ANYTHING!
THAT'S RIGHT! I FORGOT! I'M NOT AFRAID... MUCH!
WELL COME ON THEN! WE'VE GOT TO GET ANOTHER WAND TO HELP WENDY!
GEE...THIS IS THE END OF THE FOREST!
YES! WE'RE RIGHT ON THE EDGE OF A BURNING DESERT!
LET'S GO BACK! IT'S TOO HOT HERE!
BUT WE MUST CROSS THIS BURNING DESERT TO GET TO MAGIC MOUNTAIN!

CONTINUED IN THIS ISSUE...

THE GHOSTLY TRIO

THAT CASPER!

YEAH! GOING OFF TO PLAY WITH *WENDY* WHEN HE COULD GO ON *SCARE RAIDS* WITH US!

LET HIM GO! HE'S *TOO GOOD* TO BE *BAD!*

YEAH! LET'S GO TO TOWN AND SCARE US UP SOME FUN!

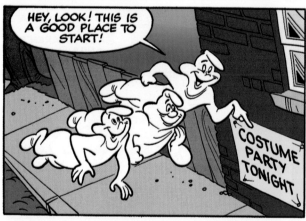

HEY, LOOK! THIS IS A GOOD PLACE TO START!

COSTUME PARTY TONIGHT

C'MON! WE'LL BE THE LIFE OF THE PARTY!

BOOO! BOOO! SCREECH!

HEY! YOU CAN'T CRASH IN HERE *WITHOUT A TICKET!*

WE DON'T NEED ANY TICKETS! WE'RE *GHOSTS!*

OH YEAH!

YEAH! LISTEN...

BOOOO BOOO OOO

WHAT'S WRONG WITH THIS CROWD! AREN'T THEY *AFRAID* OF GHOSTS?

AFRAID? HAW HAW!

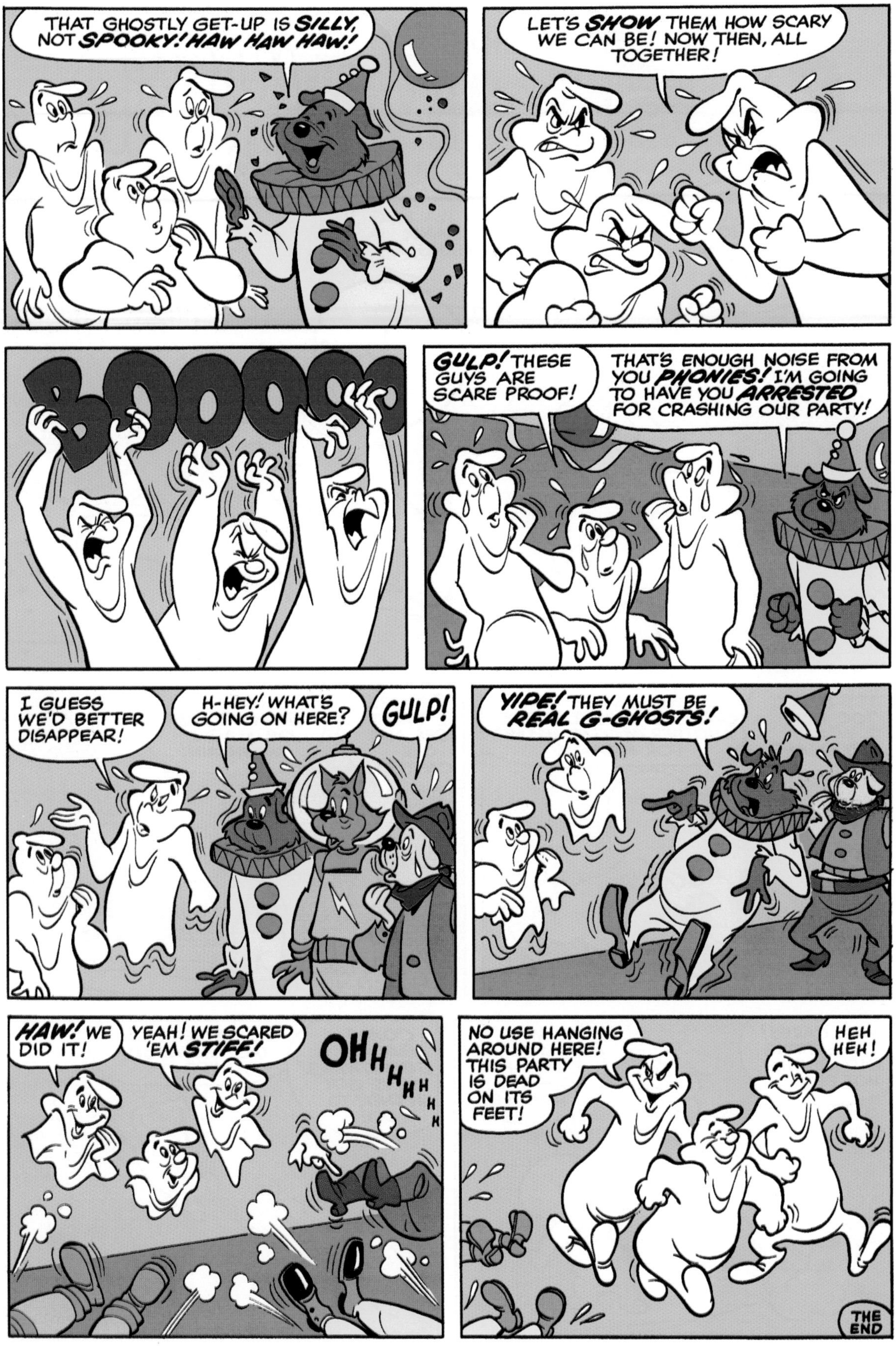
THAT GHOSTLY GET-UP IS SILLY, NOT SPOOKY! HAW HAW HAW!
LET'S SHOW THEM HOW SCARY WE CAN BE! NOW THEN, ALL TOGETHER!
BOOOOO
GULP! THESE GUYS ARE SCARE PROOF!
THAT'S ENOUGH NOISE FROM YOU PHONIES! I'M GOING TO HAVE YOU ARRESTED FOR CRASHING OUR PARTY!
I GUESS WE'D BETTER DISAPPEAR!
H-HEY! WHAT'S GOING ON HERE?
GULP!
YIPE! THEY MUST BE REAL G-GHOSTS!
HAW! WE DID IT!
YEAH! WE SCARED 'EM STIFF!
OHHHHHHH
NO USE HANGING AROUND HERE! THIS PARTY IS DEAD ON ITS FEET!
HEH HEH!
THE END

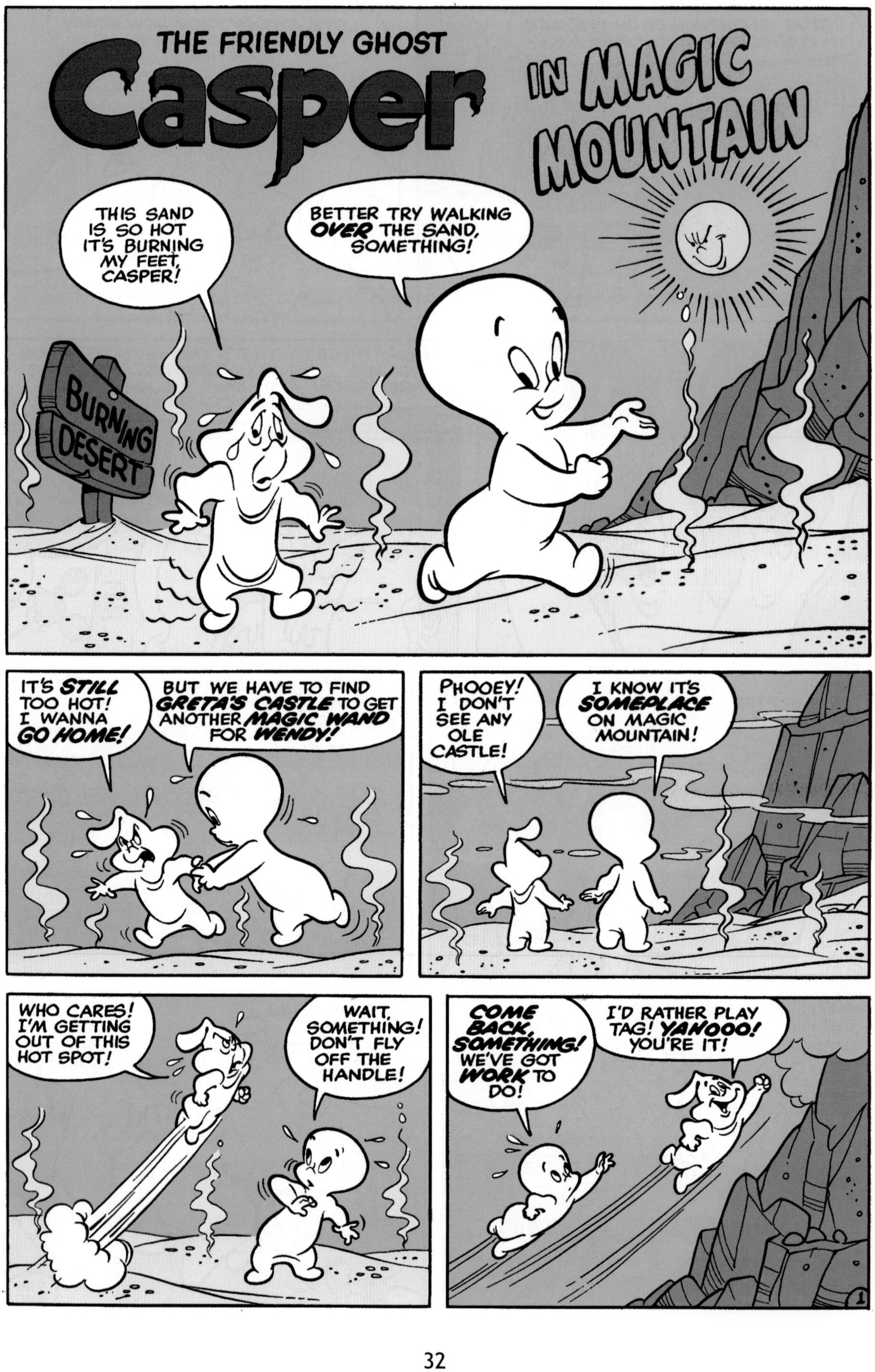
THE FRIENDLY GHOST
Casper
IN MAGIC MOUNTAIN
THIS SAND IS SO HOT IT'S BURNING MY FEET, CASPER!
BETTER TRY WALKING OVER THE SAND, SOMETHING!
BURNING DESERT
IT'S STILL TOO HOT! I WANNA GO HOME!
BUT WE HAVE TO FIND GRETA'S CASTLE TO GET ANOTHER MAGIC WAND FOR WENDY!
PHOOEY! I DON'T SEE ANY OLE CASTLE!
I KNOW IT'S SOMEPLACE ON MAGIC MOUNTAIN!
WHO CARES! I'M GETTING OUT OF THIS HOT SPOT!
WAIT, SOMETHING! DON'T FLY OFF THE HANDLE!
COME BACK, SOMETHING! WE'VE GOT WORK TO DO!
I'D RATHER PLAY TAG! YAHOOO! YOU'RE IT!

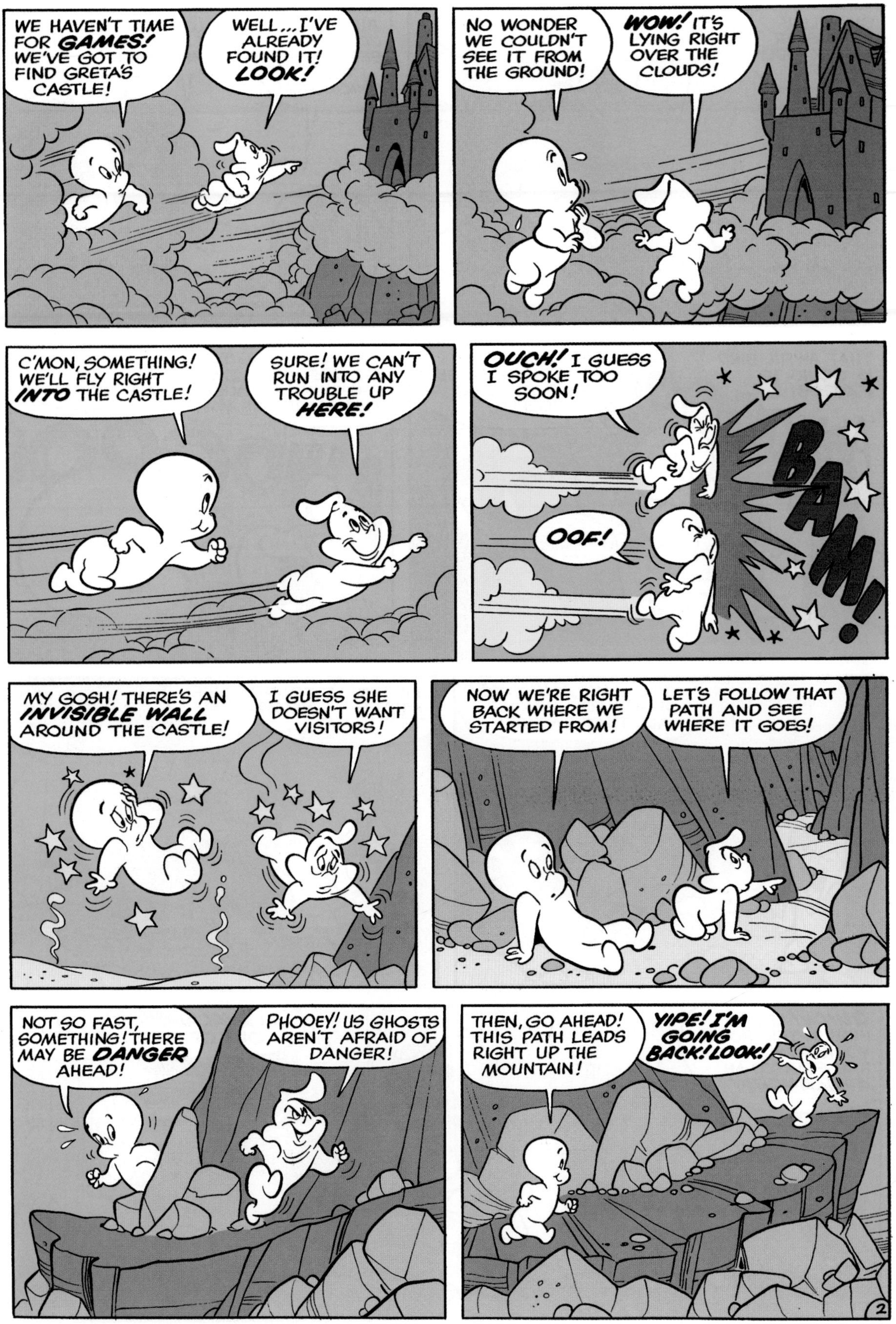
WE HAVEN'T TIME FOR GAMES! WE'VE GOT TO FIND GRETA'S CASTLE!
WELL... I'VE ALREADY FOUND IT! LOOK!
NO WONDER WE COULDN'T SEE IT FROM THE GROUND!
WOW! IT'S LYING RIGHT OVER THE CLOUDS!
C'MON, SOMETHING! WE'LL FLY RIGHT INTO THE CASTLE!
SURE! WE CAN'T RUN INTO ANY TROUBLE UP HERE!
OUCH! I GUESS I SPOKE TOO SOON!
OOF!
BAM!
MY GOSH! THERE'S AN INVISIBLE WALL AROUND THE CASTLE!
I GUESS SHE DOESN'T WANT VISITORS!
NOW WE'RE RIGHT BACK WHERE WE STARTED FROM!
LET'S FOLLOW THAT PATH AND SEE WHERE IT GOES!
NOT SO FAST, SOMETHING! THERE MAY BE DANGER AHEAD!
PHOOEY! US GHOSTS AREN'T AFRAID OF DANGER!
THEN, GO AHEAD! THIS PATH LEADS RIGHT UP THE MOUNTAIN!
YIPE! I'M GOING BACK! LOOK!
2

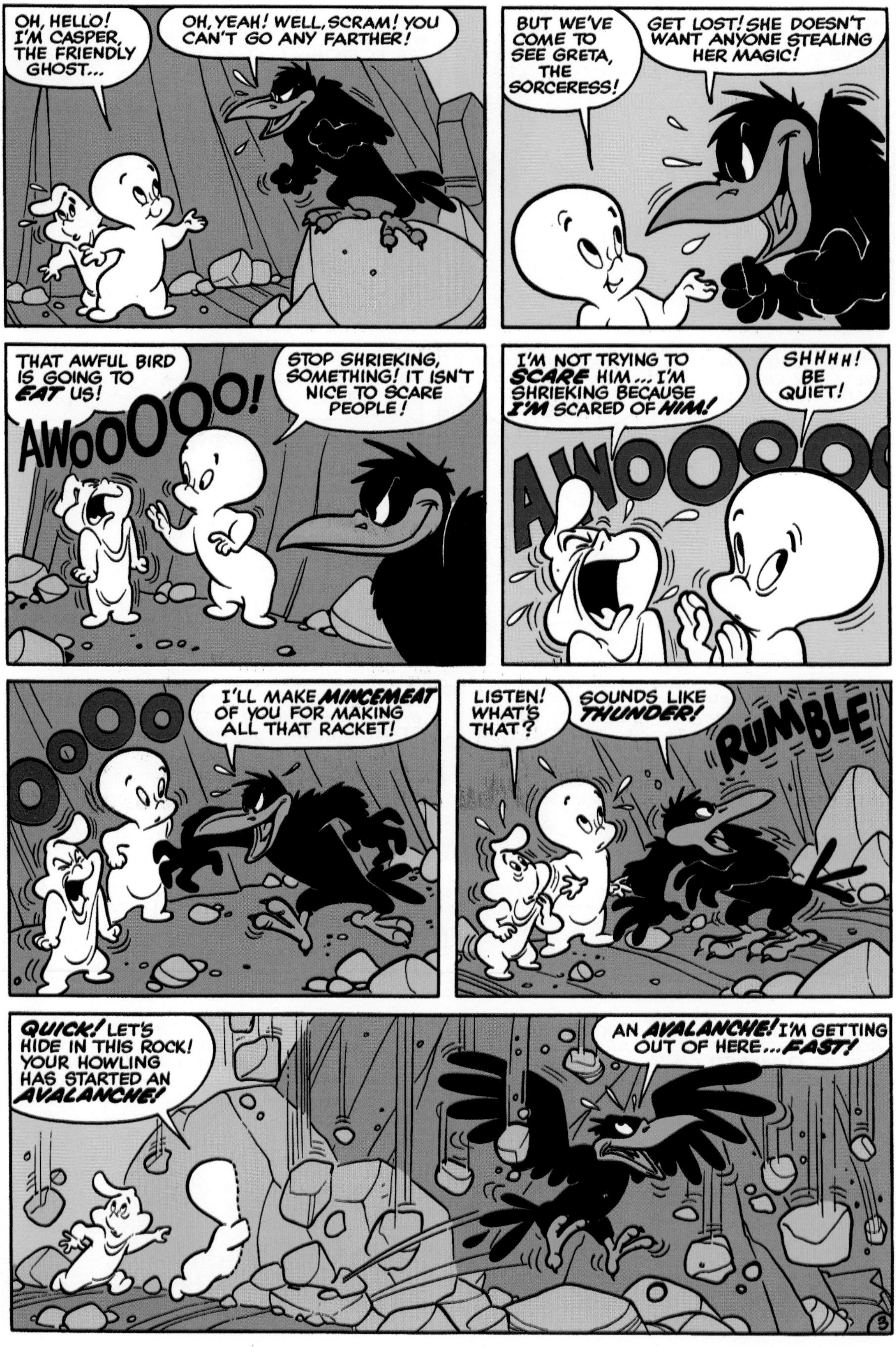
OH, HELLO! I'M CASPER, THE FRIENDLY GHOST...
OH, YEAH! WELL, SCRAM! YOU CAN'T GO ANY FARTHER!
BUT WE'VE COME TO SEE GRETA, THE SORCERESS!
GET LOST! SHE DOESN'T WANT ANYONE STEALING HER MAGIC!
THAT AWFUL BIRD IS GOING TO EAT US!
AWOOOOO!
STOP SHRIEKING, SOMETHING! IT ISN'T NICE TO SCARE PEOPLE!
I'M NOT TRYING TO SCARE HIM... I'M SHRIEKING BECAUSE I'M SCARED OF HIM!
SHHHH! BE QUIET!
AWOOOOO
OOOOO
I'LL MAKE MINCEMEAT OF YOU FOR MAKING ALL THAT RACKET!
LISTEN! WHAT'S THAT?
SOUNDS LIKE THUNDER!
RUMBLE
QUICK! LET'S HIDE IN THIS ROCK! YOUR HOWLING HAS STARTED AN AVALANCHE!
AN AVALANCHE! I'M GETTING OUT OF HERE... FAST!
3

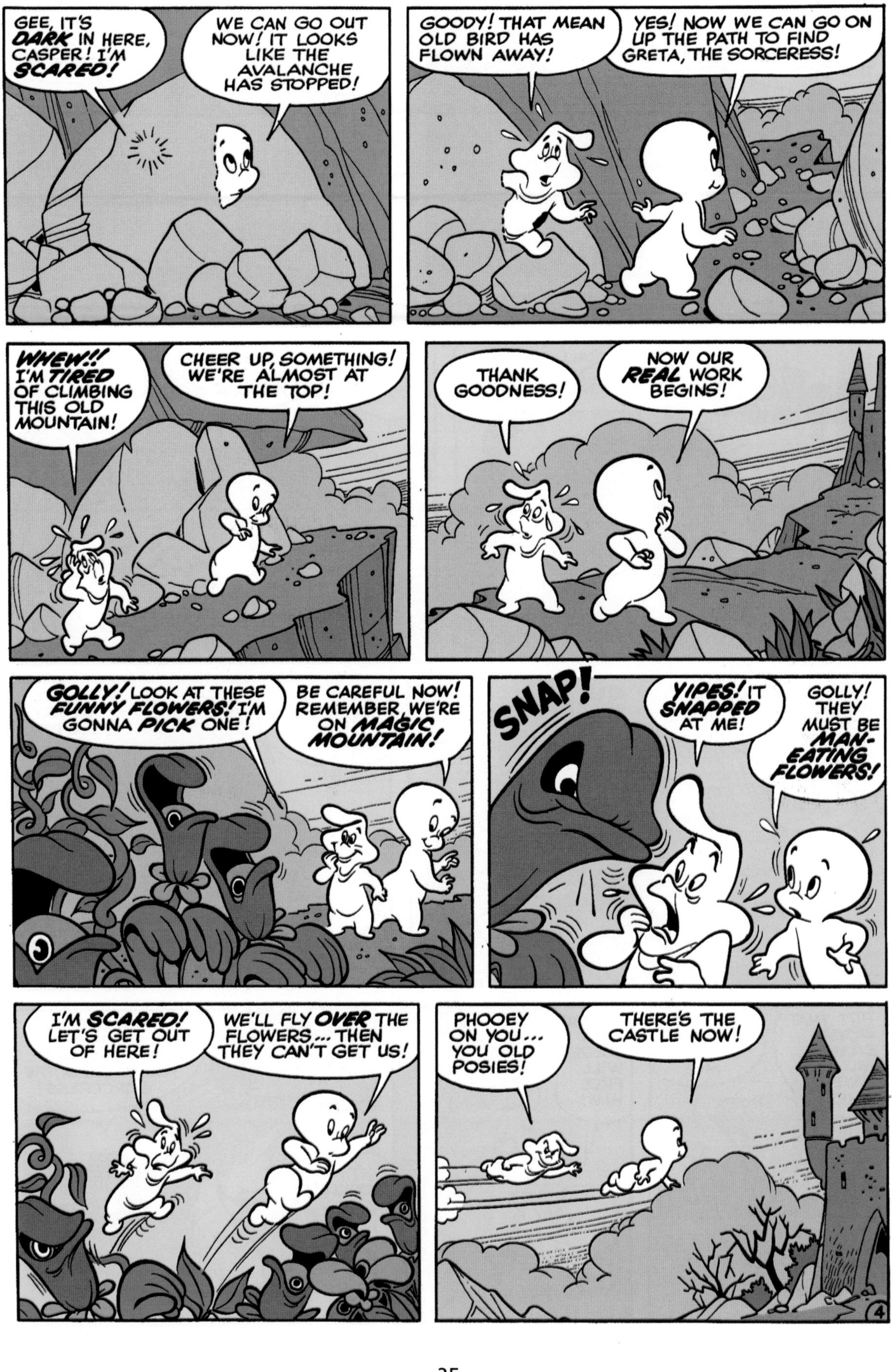
GEE, IT'S DARK IN HERE, CASPER! I'M SCARED!
WE CAN GO OUT NOW! IT LOOKS LIKE THE AVALANCHE HAS STOPPED!
GOODY! THAT MEAN OLD BIRD HAS FLOWN AWAY!
YES! NOW WE CAN GO ON UP THE PATH TO FIND GRETA, THE SORCERESS!
WHEW!! I'M TIRED OF CLIMBING THIS OLD MOUNTAIN!
CHEER UP, SOMETHING! WE'RE ALMOST AT THE TOP!
THANK GOODNESS!
NOW OUR REAL WORK BEGINS!
GOLLY! LOOK AT THESE FUNNY FLOWERS! I'M GONNA PICK ONE!
BE CAREFUL NOW! REMEMBER, WE'RE ON MAGIC MOUNTAIN!
SNAP!
YIPES! IT SNAPPED AT ME!
GOLLY! THEY MUST BE MAN-EATING FLOWERS!
I'M SCARED! LET'S GET OUT OF HERE!
WE'LL FLY OVER THE FLOWERS... THEN THEY CAN'T GET US!
PHOOEY ON YOU... YOU OLD POSIES!
THERE'S THE CASTLE NOW!
4

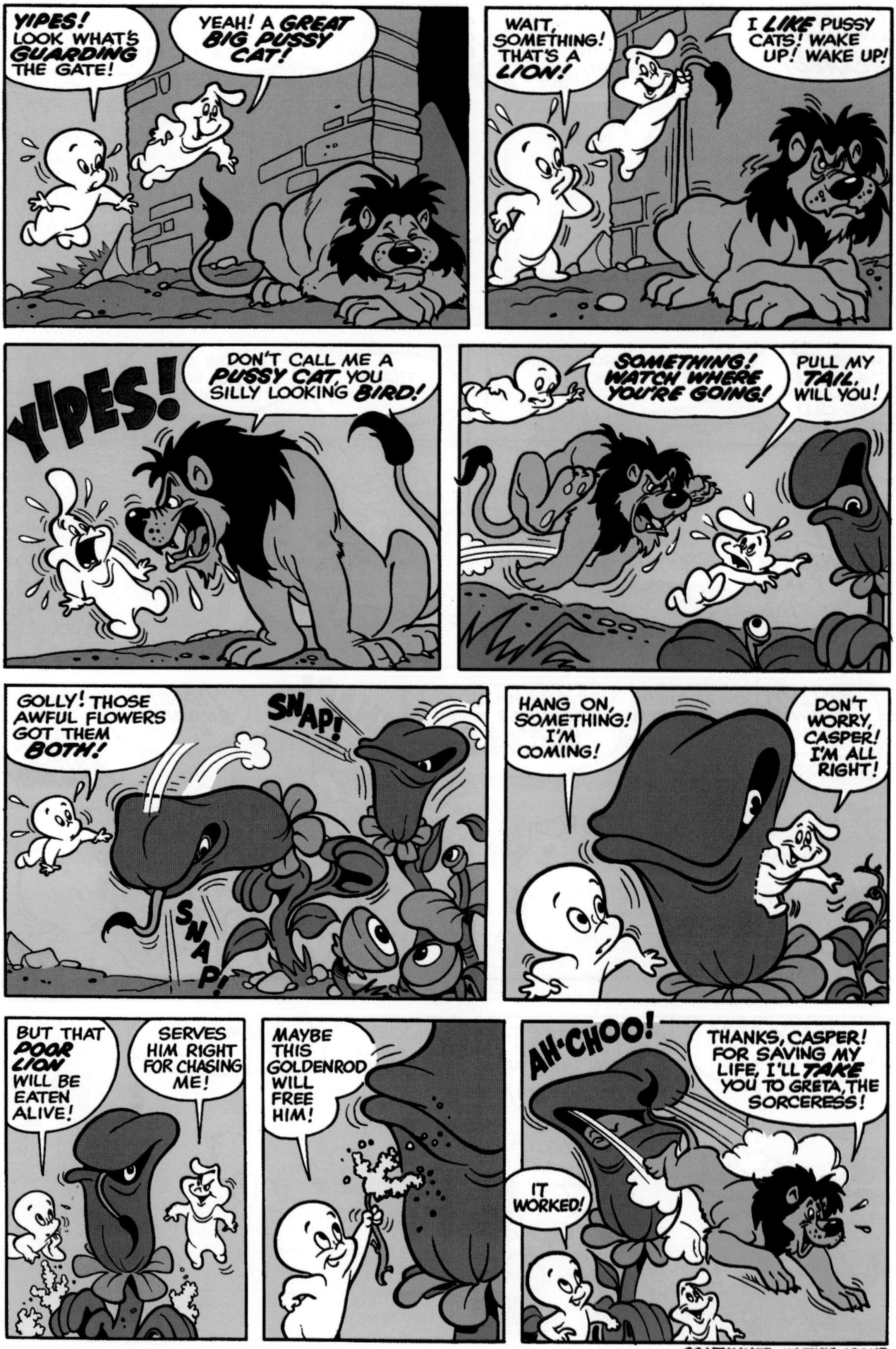
YIPES! LOOK WHAT'S GUARDING THE GATE!
YEAH! A GREAT BIG PUSSY CAT!
WAIT, SOMETHING! THAT'S A LION!
I LIKE PUSSY CATS! WAKE UP! WAKE UP!
YIPES!
DON'T CALL ME A PUSSY CAT, YOU SILLY LOOKING BIRD!
SOMETHING! WATCH WHERE YOU'RE GOING!
PULL MY TAIL, WILL YOU!
GOLLY! THOSE AWFUL FLOWERS GOT THEM BOTH!
SNAP!
SNAP!
HANG ON, SOMETHING! I'M COMING!
DON'T WORRY, CASPER! I'M ALL RIGHT!
BUT THAT POOR LION WILL BE EATEN ALIVE!
SERVES HIM RIGHT FOR CHASING ME!
MAYBE THIS GOLDENROD WILL FREE HIM!
AH-CHOO!
THANKS, CASPER! FOR SAVING MY LIFE, I'LL TAKE YOU TO GRETA, THE SORCERESS!
IT WORKED!

CONTINUED IN THIS ISSUE.

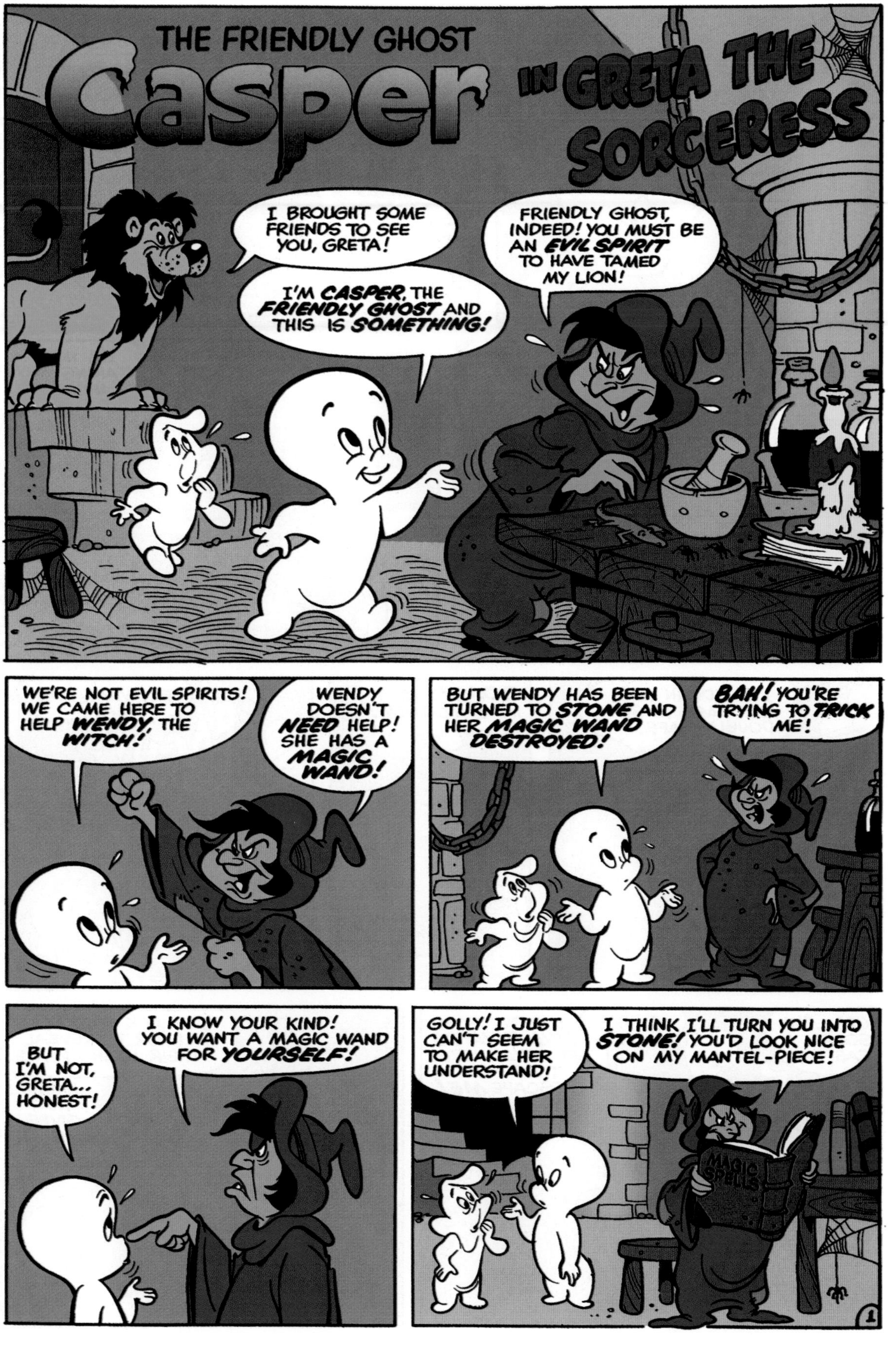
THE FRIENDLY GHOST
Casper
IN GRETA THE SORCERESS
I BROUGHT SOME FRIENDS TO SEE YOU, GRETA!
I'M CASPER, THE FRIENDLY GHOST AND THIS IS SOMETHING!
FRIENDLY GHOST, INDEED! YOU MUST BE AN EVIL SPIRIT TO HAVE TAMED MY LION!
WE'RE NOT EVIL SPIRITS! WE CAME HERE TO HELP WENDY, THE WITCH!
WENDY DOESN'T NEED HELP! SHE HAS A MAGIC WAND!
BUT WENDY HAS BEEN TURNED TO STONE AND HER MAGIC WAND DESTROYED!
BAH! YOU'RE TRYING TO TRICK ME!
I KNOW YOUR KIND! YOU WANT A MAGIC WAND FOR YOURSELF!
BUT I'M NOT, GRETA... HONEST!
GOLLY! I JUST CAN'T SEEM TO MAKE HER UNDERSTAND!
I THINK I'LL TURN YOU INTO STONE! YOU'D LOOK NICE ON MY MANTEL-PIECE!
MAGIC SPELLS
1

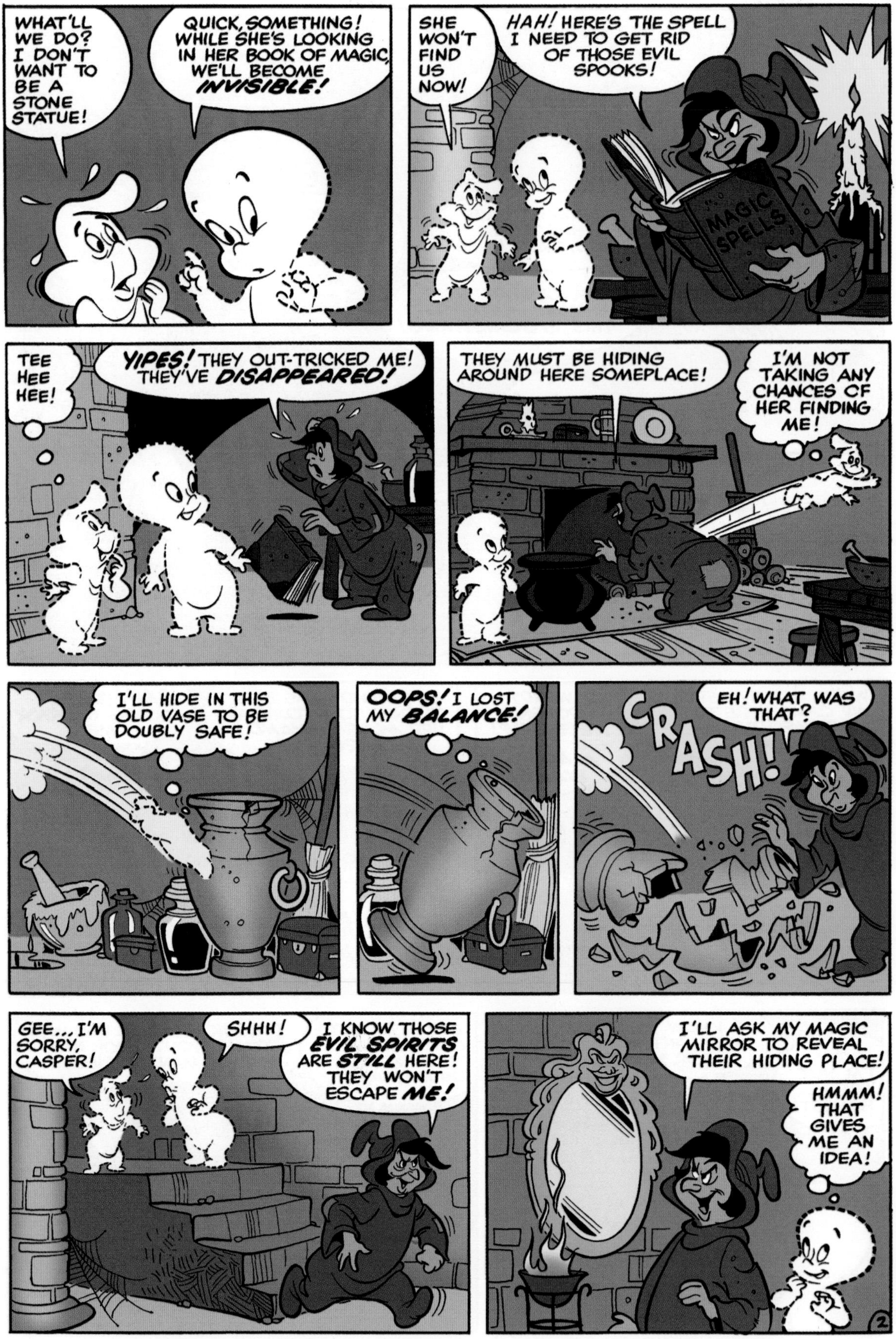
WHAT'LL WE DO? I DON'T WANT TO BE A STONE STATUE!
QUICK, SOMETHING! WHILE SHE'S LOOKING IN HER BOOK OF MAGIC, WE'LL BECOME INVISIBLE!
SHE WON'T FIND US NOW!
HAH! HERE'S THE SPELL I NEED TO GET RID OF THOSE EVIL SPOOKS!
MAGIC SPELLS
TEE HEE HEE!
YIPES! THEY OUT-TRICKED ME! THEY'VE DISAPPEARED!
THEY MUST BE HIDING AROUND HERE SOMEPLACE!
I'M NOT TAKING ANY CHANCES OF HER FINDING ME!
I'LL HIDE IN THIS OLD VASE TO BE DOUBLY SAFE!
OOPS! I LOST MY BALANCE!
CRASH!
EH! WHAT WAS THAT?
GEE... I'M SORRY, CASPER!
SHHH!
I KNOW THOSE EVIL SPIRITS ARE STILL HERE! THEY WON'T ESCAPE ME!
I'LL ASK MY MAGIC MIRROR TO REVEAL THEIR HIDING PLACE!
HMMM! THAT GIVES ME AN IDEA!
2

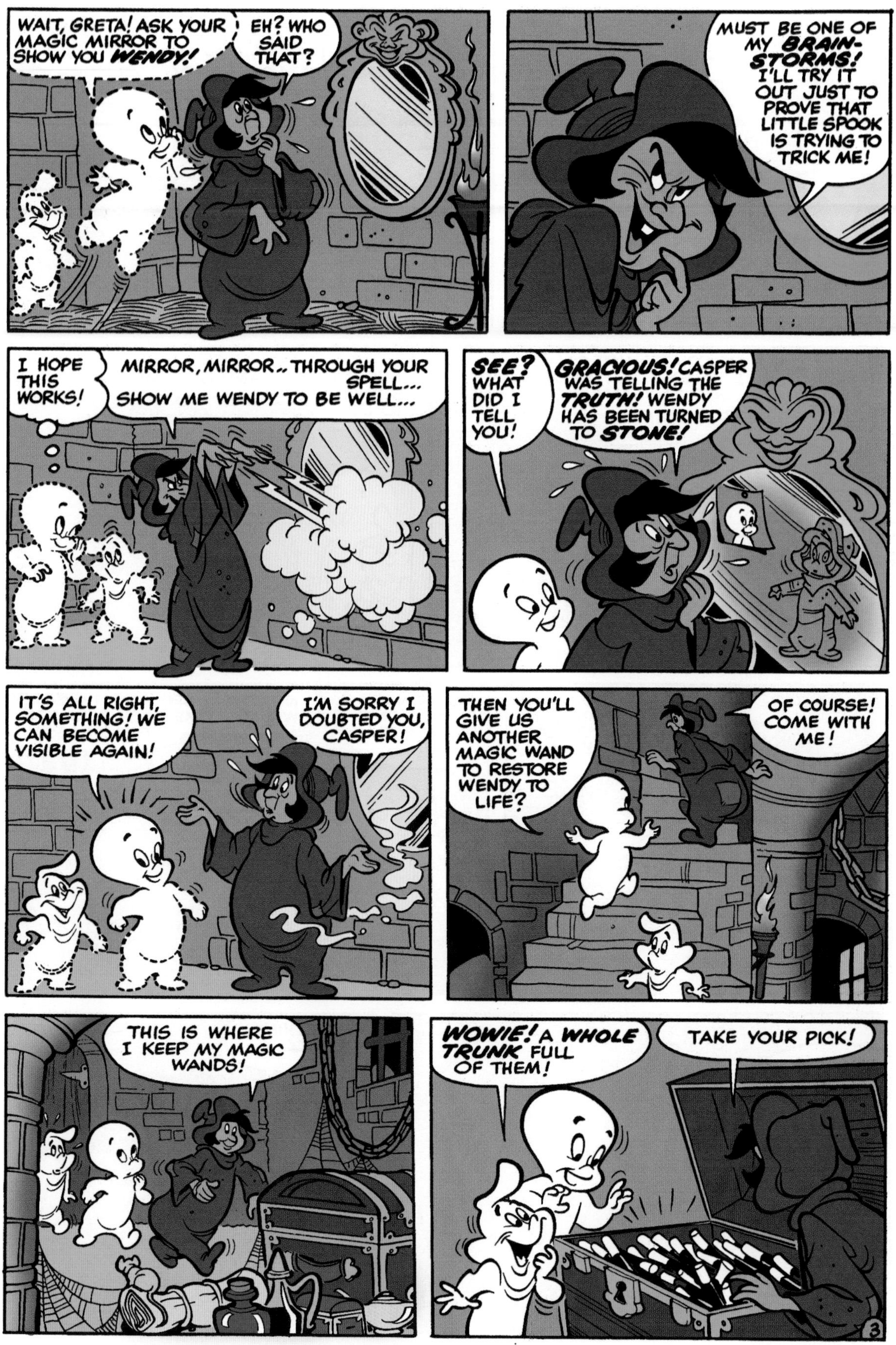
WAIT, GRETA! ASK YOUR MAGIC MIRROR TO SHOW YOU WENDY!
EH? WHO SAID THAT?
MUST BE ONE OF MY BRAIN-STORMS! I'LL TRY IT OUT JUST TO PROVE THAT LITTLE SPOOK IS TRYING TO TRICK ME!
I HOPE THIS WORKS!
MIRROR, MIRROR.. THROUGH YOUR SPELL... SHOW ME WENDY TO BE WELL...
SEE? WHAT DID I TELL YOU!
GRACIOUS! CASPER WAS TELLING THE TRUTH! WENDY HAS BEEN TURNED TO STONE!
IT'S ALL RIGHT, SOMETHING! WE CAN BECOME VISIBLE AGAIN!
I'M SORRY I DOUBTED YOU, CASPER!
THEN YOU'LL GIVE US ANOTHER MAGIC WAND TO RESTORE WENDY TO LIFE?
OF COURSE! COME WITH ME!
THIS IS WHERE I KEEP MY MAGIC WANDS!
WOWIE! A WHOLE TRUNK FULL OF THEM!
TAKE YOUR PICK!
3

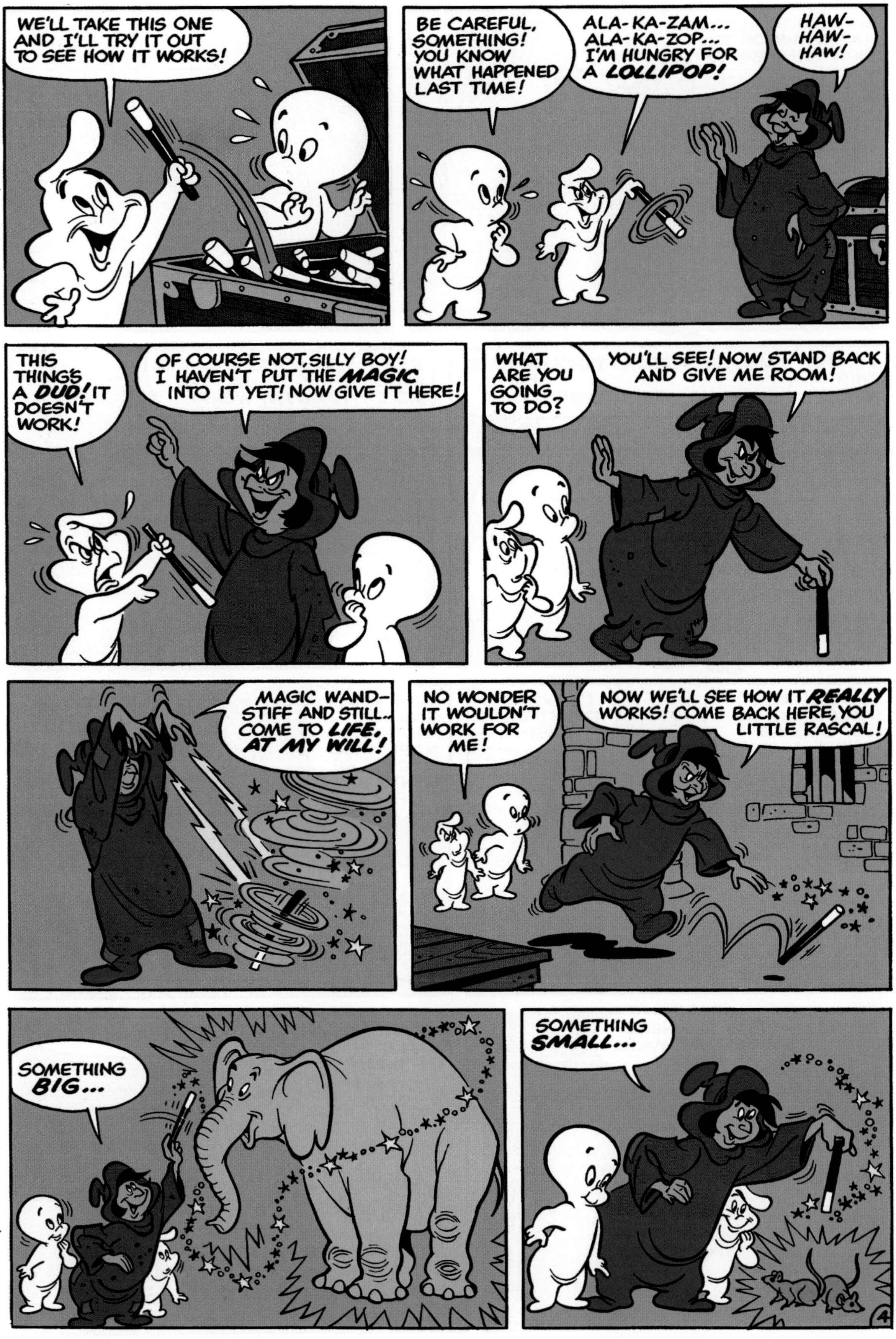
WE'LL TAKE THIS ONE AND I'LL TRY IT OUT TO SEE HOW IT WORKS!
BE CAREFUL, SOMETHING! YOU KNOW WHAT HAPPENED LAST TIME!
ALA-KA-ZAM... ALA-KA-ZOP... I'M HUNGRY FOR A LOLLIPOP!
HAW-HAW-HAW!
THIS THING'S A DUD! IT DOESN'T WORK!
OF COURSE NOT, SILLY BOY! I HAVEN'T PUT THE MAGIC INTO IT YET! NOW GIVE IT HERE!
WHAT ARE YOU GOING TO DO?
YOU'LL SEE! NOW STAND BACK AND GIVE ME ROOM!
MAGIC WAND-STIFF AND STILL.. COME TO LIFE, AT MY WILL!
NO WONDER IT WOULDN'T WORK FOR ME!
NOW WE'LL SEE HOW IT REALLY WORKS! COME BACK HERE, YOU LITTLE RASCAL!
SOMETHING BIG...
SOMETHING SMALL...
4

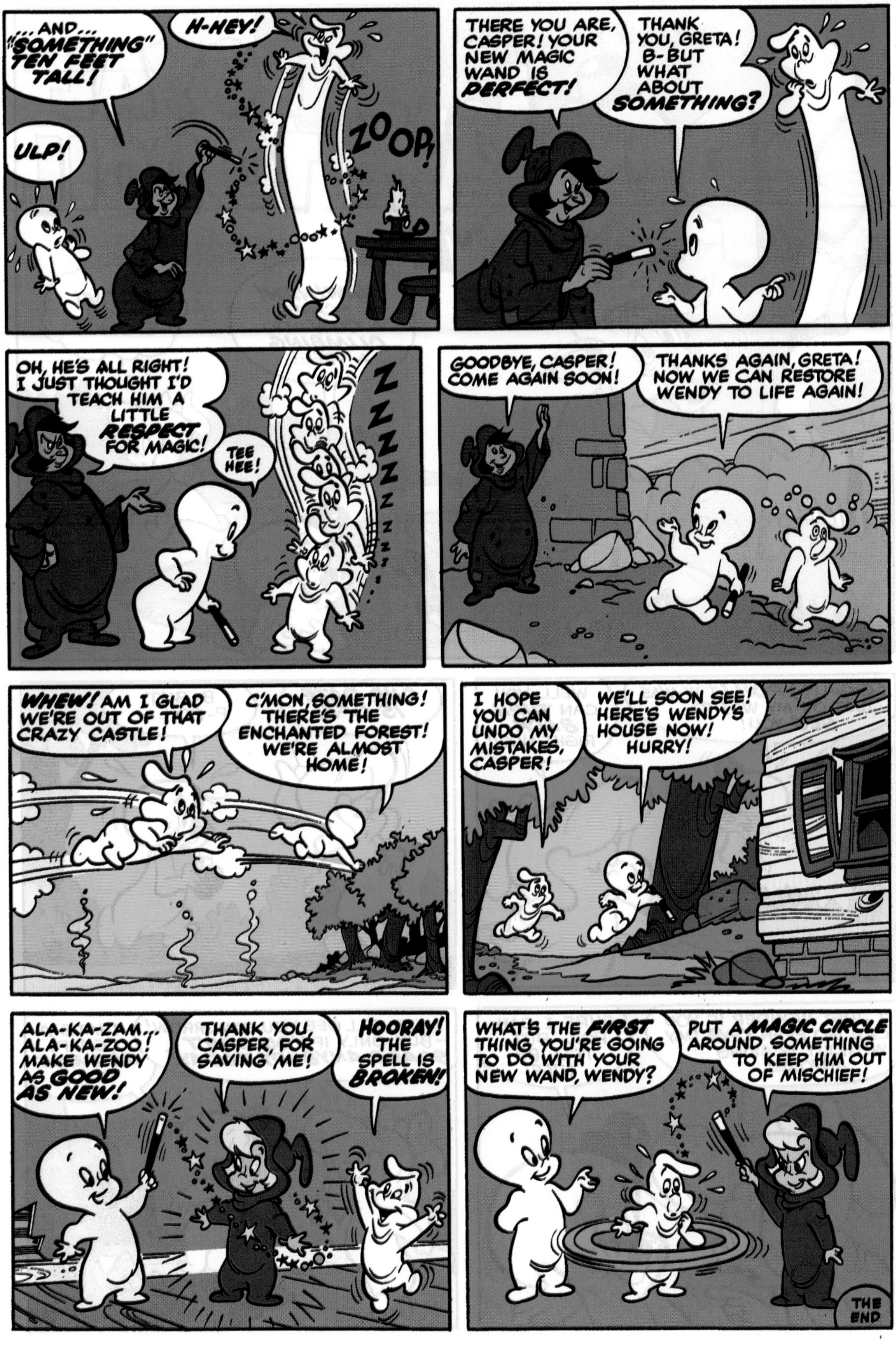
...AND... "SOMETHING" TEN FEET TALL!
H-HEY!
ULP!
ZOOP!
THERE YOU ARE, CASPER! YOUR NEW MAGIC WAND IS PERFECT!
THANK YOU, GRETA! B-BUT WHAT ABOUT SOMETHING?
OH, HE'S ALL RIGHT! I JUST THOUGHT I'D TEACH HIM A LITTLE RESPECT FOR MAGIC!
TEE HEE!
GOODBYE, CASPER! COME AGAIN SOON!
THANKS AGAIN, GRETA! NOW WE CAN RESTORE WENDY TO LIFE AGAIN!
WHEW! AM I GLAD WE'RE OUT OF THAT CRAZY CASTLE!
C'MON, SOMETHING! THERE'S THE ENCHANTED FOREST! WE'RE ALMOST HOME!
I HOPE YOU CAN UNDO MY MISTAKES, CASPER!
WE'LL SOON SEE! HERE'S WENDY'S HOUSE NOW! HURRY!
ALA-KA-ZAM... ALA-KA-ZOO! MAKE WENDY AS GOOD AS NEW!
THANK YOU, CASPER, FOR SAVING ME!
HOORAY! THE SPELL IS BROKEN!
WHAT'S THE FIRST THING YOU'RE GOING TO DO WITH YOUR NEW WAND, WENDY?
PUT A MAGIC CIRCLE AROUND SOMETHING TO KEEP HIM OUT OF MISCHIEF!
THE END

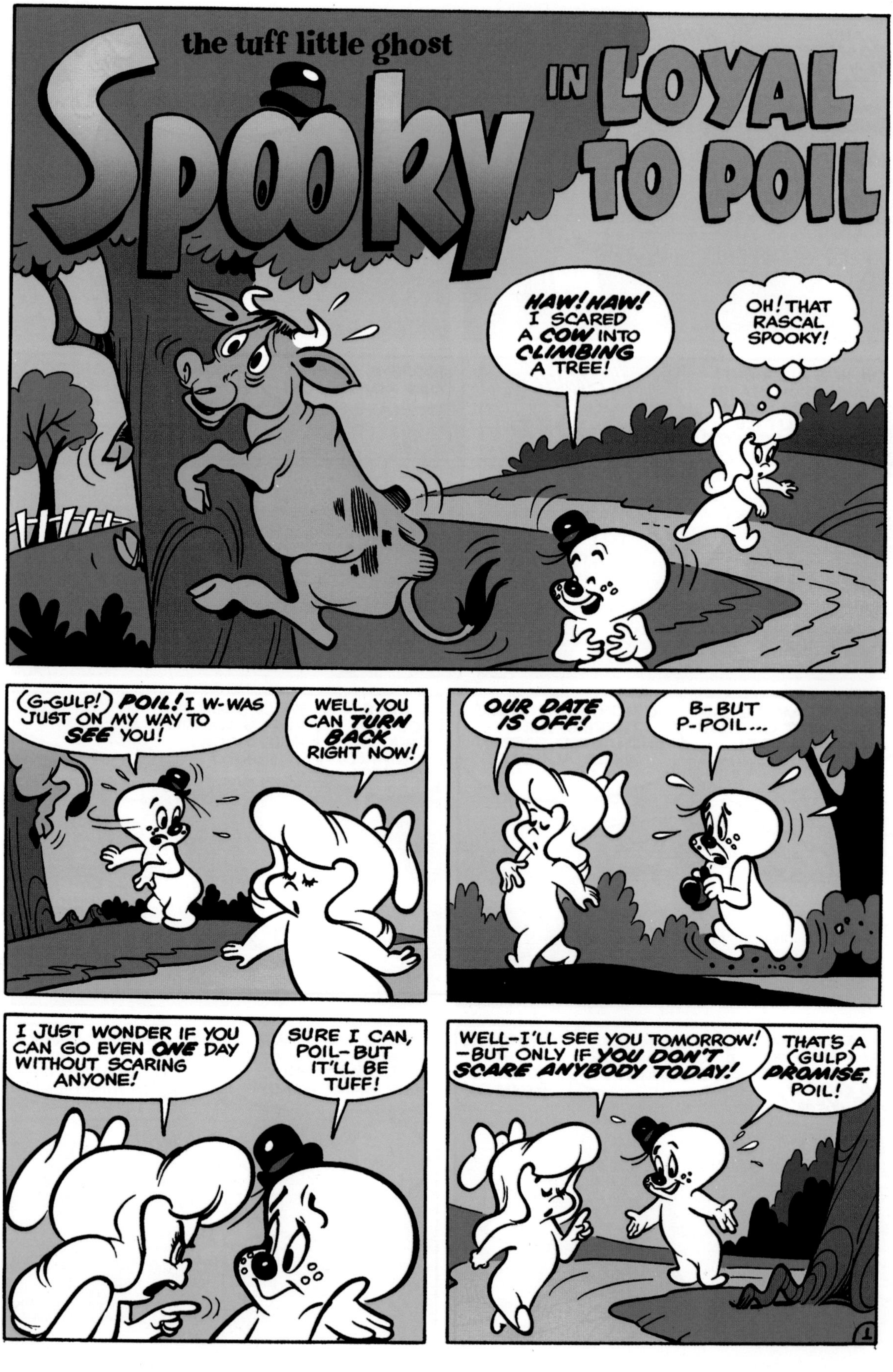
the tuff little ghost
Spooky
IN LOYAL TO POIL
HAW! HAW! I SCARED A COW INTO CLIMBING A TREE!
OH! THAT RASCAL SPOOKY!
(G-GULP!) POIL! I W-WAS JUST ON MY WAY TO SEE YOU!
WELL, YOU CAN TURN BACK RIGHT NOW!
OUR DATE IS OFF!
B-BUT P-POIL...
I JUST WONDER IF YOU CAN GO EVEN ONE DAY WITHOUT SCARING ANYONE!
SURE I CAN, POIL-BUT IT'LL BE TUFF!
WELL-I'LL SEE YOU TOMORROW! -BUT ONLY IF YOU DON'T SCARE ANYBODY TODAY!
THAT'S A (GULP) PROMISE, POIL!
1

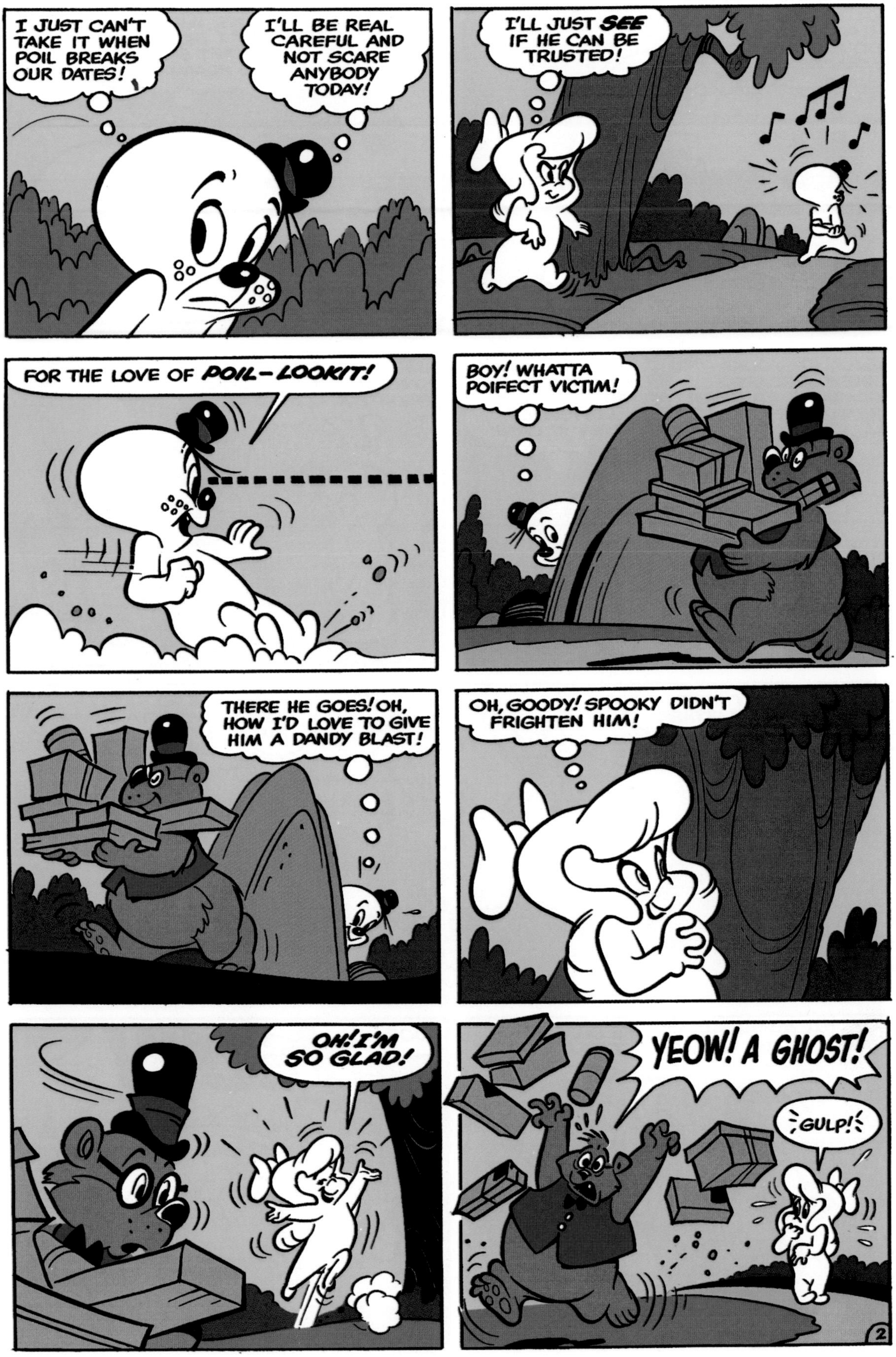
I JUST CAN'T TAKE IT WHEN POIL BREAKS OUR DATES!
I'LL BE REAL CAREFUL AND NOT SCARE ANYBODY TODAY!
I'LL JUST SEE IF HE CAN BE TRUSTED!
FOR THE LOVE OF POIL-LOOKIT!
BOY! WHATTA POIFECT VICTIM!
THERE HE GOES! OH, HOW I'D LOVE TO GIVE HIM A DANDY BLAST!
OH, GOODY! SPOOKY DIDN'T FRIGHTEN HIM!
OH! I'M SO GLAD!
YEOW! A GHOST!
GULP!
2

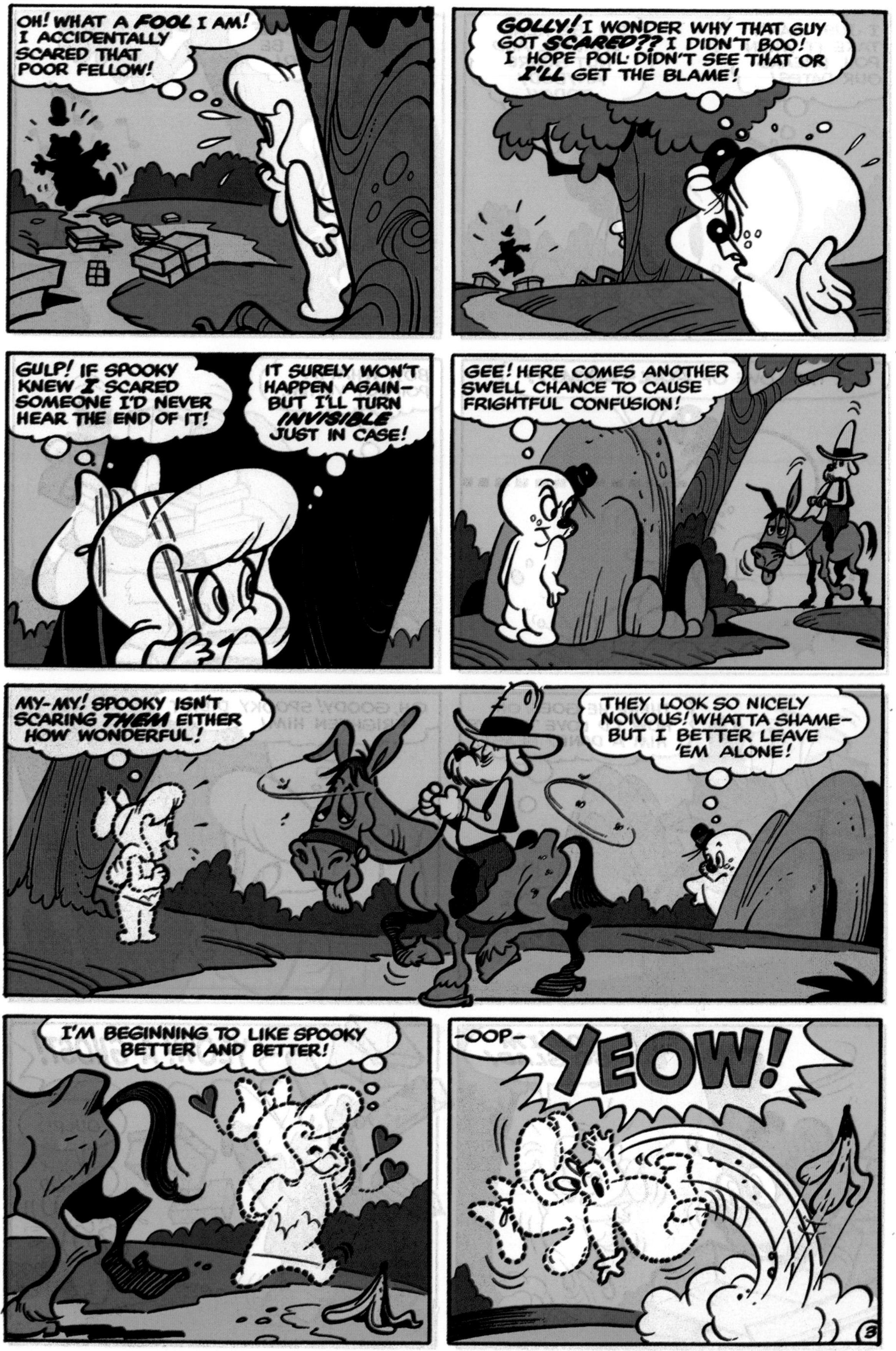
OH! WHAT A FOOL I AM! I ACCIDENTALLY SCARED THAT POOR FELLOW!
GOLLY! I WONDER WHY THAT GUY GOT SCARED?? I DIDN'T BOO! I HOPE POIL DIDN'T SEE THAT OR I'LL GET THE BLAME!
GULP! IF SPOOKY KNEW I SCARED SOMEONE I'D NEVER HEAR THE END OF IT!
IT SURELY WON'T HAPPEN AGAIN- BUT I'LL TURN INVISIBLE JUST IN CASE!
GEE! HERE COMES ANOTHER SWELL CHANCE TO CAUSE FRIGHTFUL CONFUSION!
MY-MY! SPOOKY ISN'T SCARING THEM EITHER HOW WONDERFUL!
THEY LOOK SO NICELY NOIVOUS! WHATTA SHAME- BUT I BETTER LEAVE 'EM ALONE!
I'M BEGINNING TO LIKE SPOOKY BETTER AND BETTER!
-OOP-
YEOW!
3

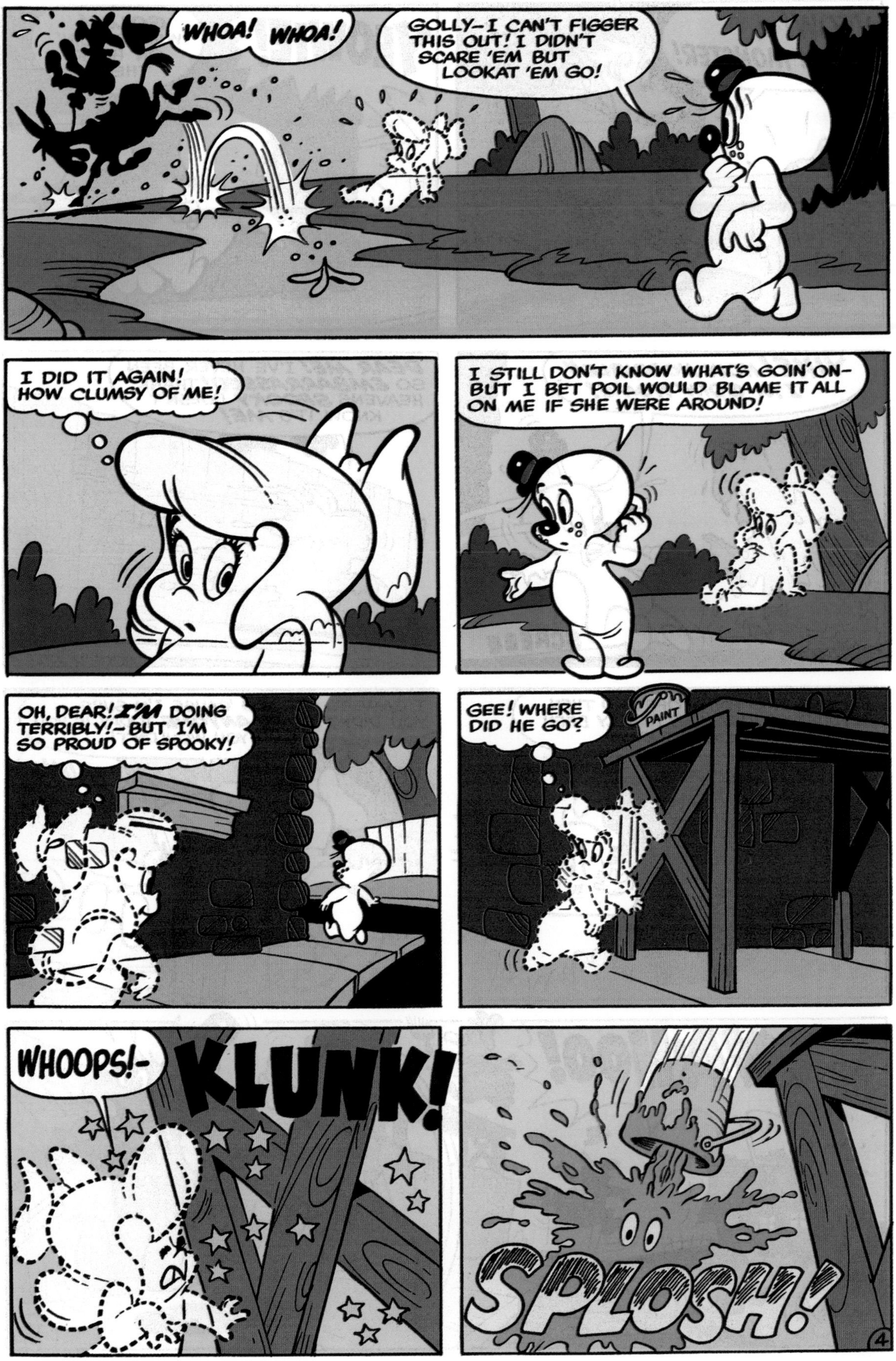
WHOA! WHOA!
GOLLY—I CAN'T FIGGER THIS OUT! I DIDN'T SCARE 'EM BUT LOOKAT 'EM GO!
I DID IT AGAIN! HOW CLUMSY OF ME!
I STILL DON'T KNOW WHAT'S GOIN' ON- BUT I BET POIL WOULD BLAME IT ALL ON ME IF SHE WERE AROUND!
OH, DEAR! I'M DOING TERRIBLY!—BUT I'M SO PROUD OF SPOOKY!
GEE! WHERE DID HE GO?
PAINT
WHOOPS!-
KLUNK!
SPLOSH!
4

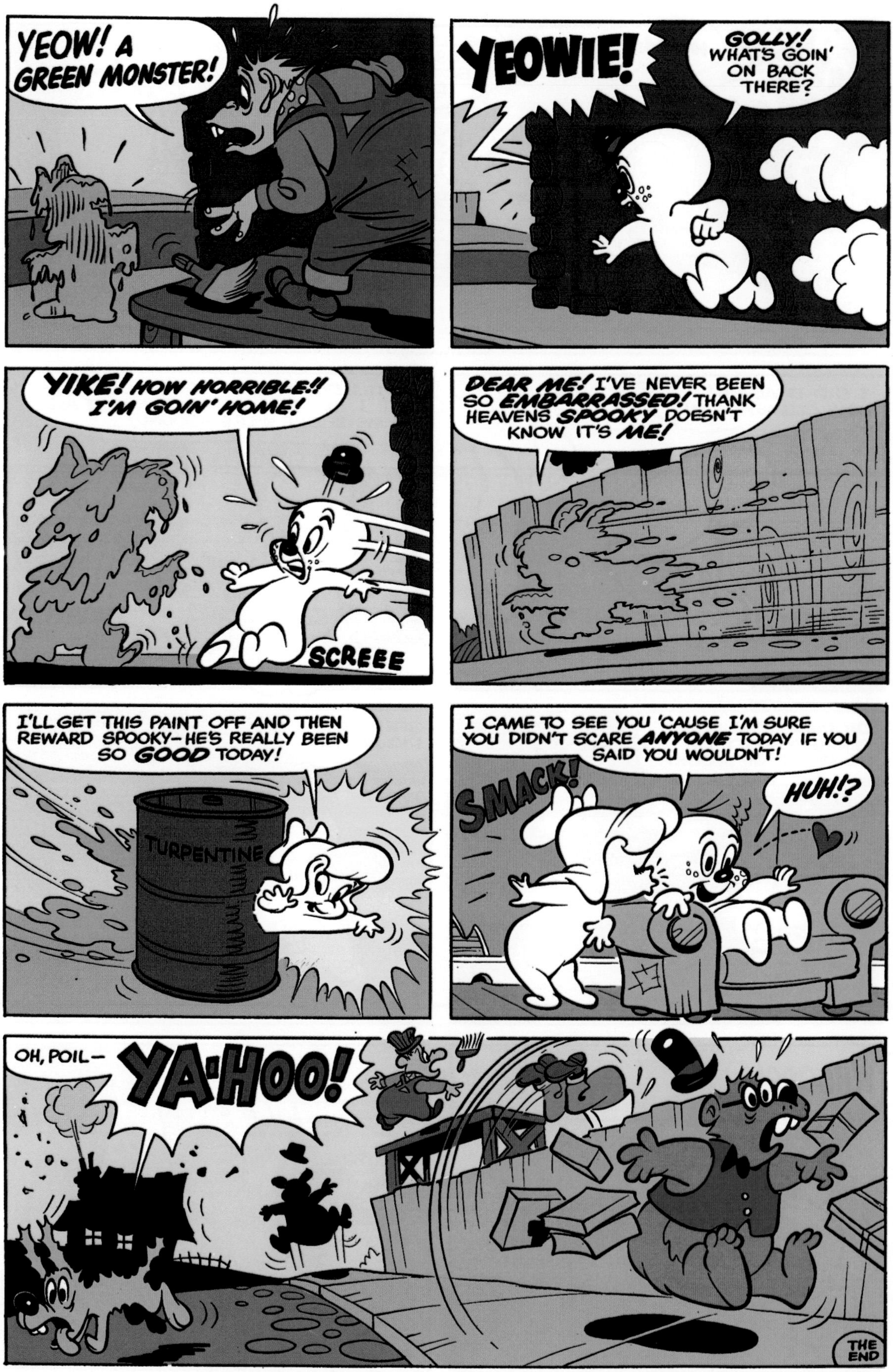
YEOW! A GREEN MONSTER!
YEOWIE!
GOLLY! WHAT'S GOIN' ON BACK THERE?
YIKE! HOW HORRIBLE!! I'M GOIN' HOME!
SCREEE
DEAR ME! I'VE NEVER BEEN SO EMBARRASSED! THANK HEAVENS SPOOKY DOESN'T KNOW IT'S ME!
I'LL GET THIS PAINT OFF AND THEN REWARD SPOOKY- HE'S REALLY BEEN SO GOOD TODAY!
TURPENTINE
I CAME TO SEE YOU 'CAUSE I'M SURE YOU DIDN'T SCARE ANYONE TODAY IF YOU SAID YOU WOULDN'T!
SMACK!
HUH!?
OH, POIL-
YA-HOO!
THE END

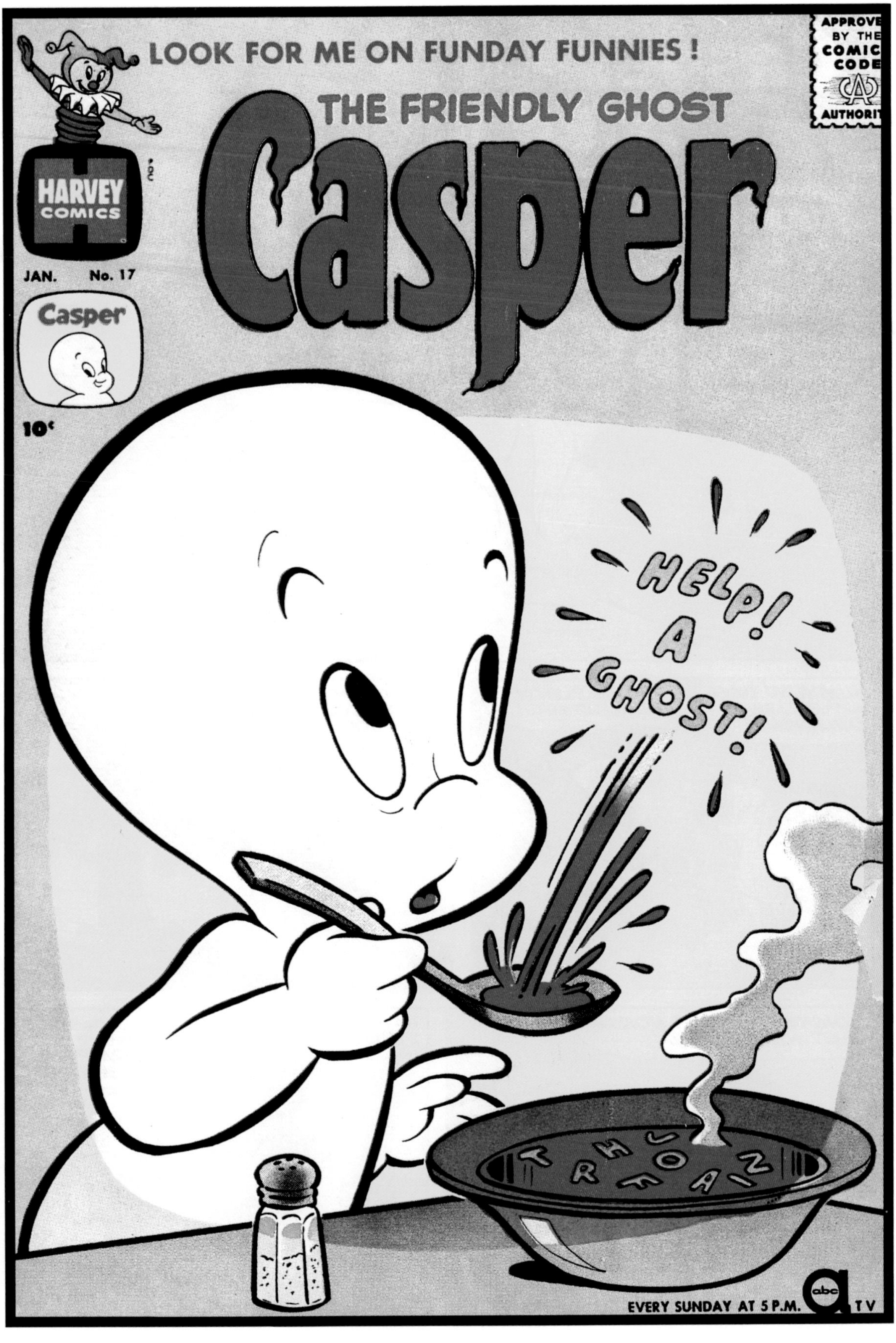

LOOK FOR ME ON FUNDAY FUNNIES !
APPROVE
BY THE
COMIC
CODE
AUTHORIT
HARVEY
COMICS
THE FRIENDLY GHOST
Casper
JAN.
No. 17
Casper
10¢
HELP! A GHOST!
EVERY SUNDAY AT 5 P.M.
abc
TV

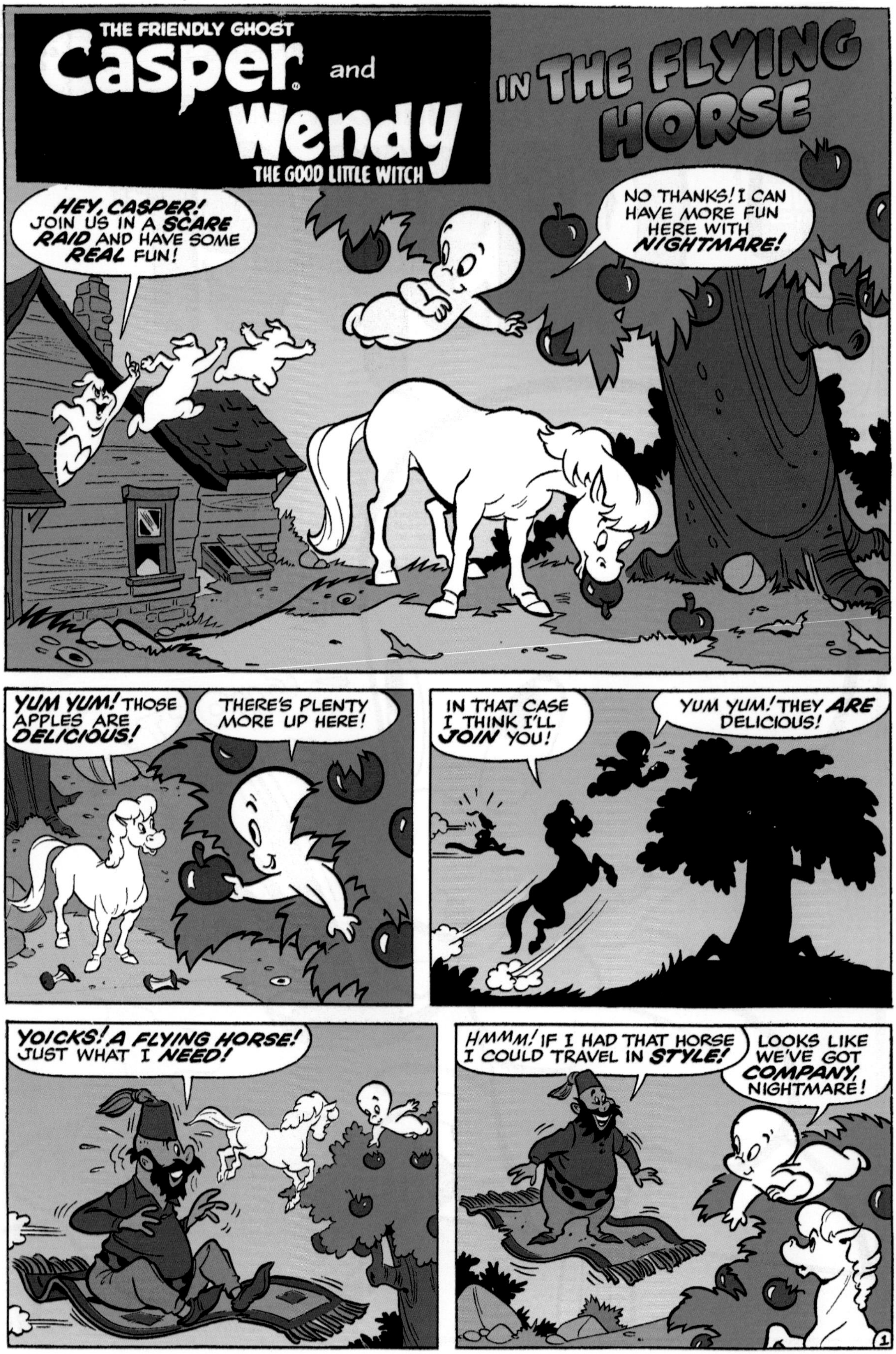
THE FRIENDLY GHOST
Casper and
Wendy
THE GOOD LITTLE WITCH
IN THE FLYING HORSE
HEY, CASPER! JOIN US IN A SCARE RAID AND HAVE SOME REAL FUN!
NO THANKS! I CAN HAVE MORE FUN HERE WITH NIGHTMARE!
YUM YUM! THOSE APPLES ARE DELICIOUS!
THERE'S PLENTY MORE UP HERE!
IN THAT CASE I THINK I'LL JOIN YOU!
YUM YUM! THEY ARE DELICIOUS!
YOICKS! A FLYING HORSE! JUST WHAT I NEED!
HMMM! IF I HAD THAT HORSE I COULD TRAVEL IN STYLE!
LOOKS LIKE WE'VE GOT COMPANY, NIGHTMARE!
1

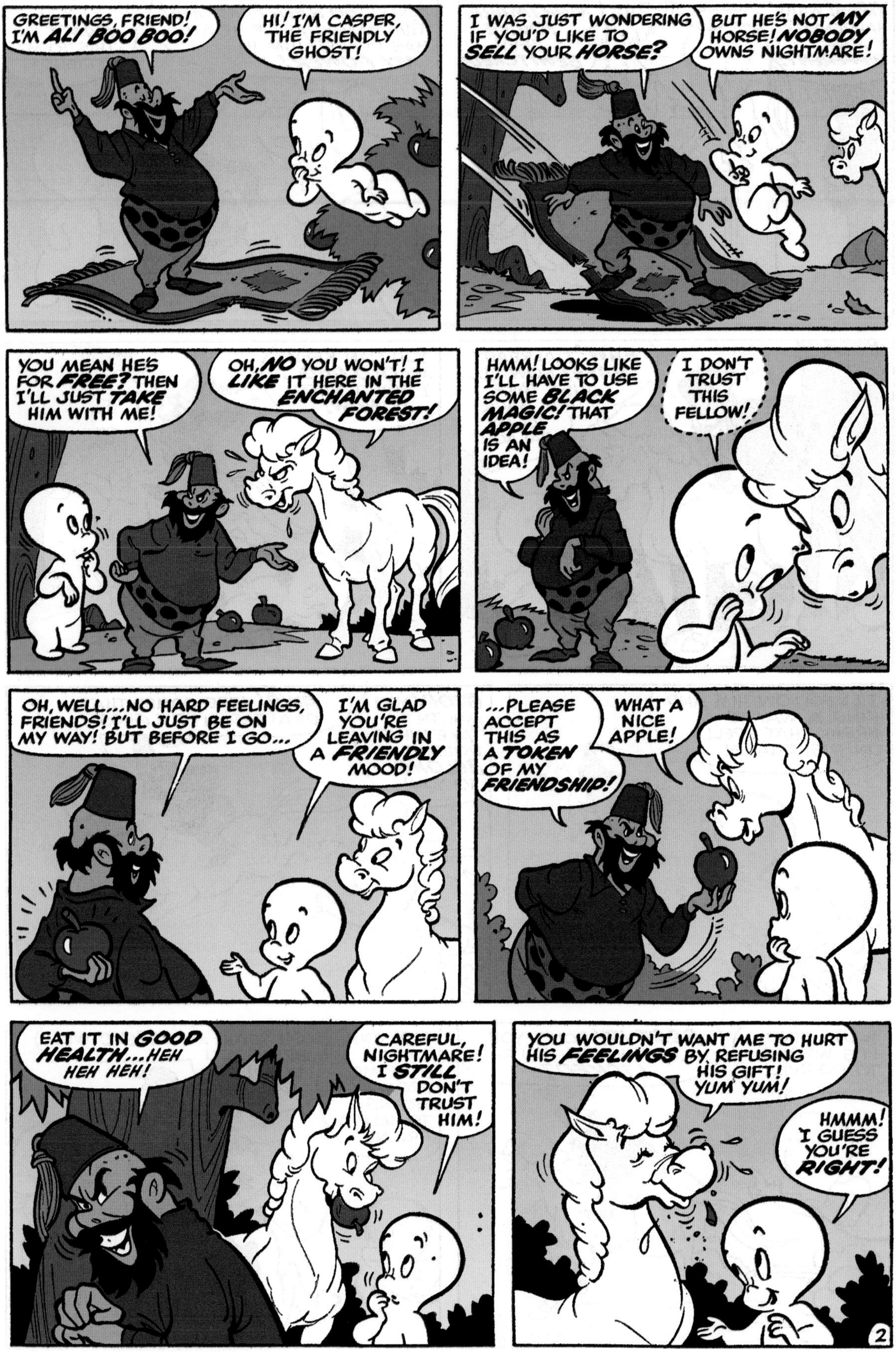
GREETINGS, FRIEND! I'M ALI BOO BOO!
HI! I'M CASPER, THE FRIENDLY GHOST!
I WAS JUST WONDERING IF YOU'D LIKE TO SELL YOUR HORSE?
BUT HE'S NOT MY HORSE! NOBODY OWNS NIGHTMARE!
YOU MEAN HE'S FOR FREE? THEN I'LL JUST TAKE HIM WITH ME!
OH, NO YOU WON'T! I LIKE IT HERE IN THE ENCHANTED FOREST!
HMM! LOOKS LIKE I'LL HAVE TO USE SOME BLACK MAGIC! THAT APPLE IS AN IDEA!
I DON'T TRUST THIS FELLOW!
OH, WELL... NO HARD FEELINGS, FRIENDS! I'LL JUST BE ON MY WAY! BUT BEFORE I GO...
I'M GLAD YOU'RE LEAVING IN A FRIENDLY MOOD!
...PLEASE ACCEPT THIS AS A TOKEN OF MY FRIENDSHIP!
WHAT A NICE APPLE!
EAT IT IN GOOD HEALTH... HEH HEH HEH!
CAREFUL, NIGHTMARE! I STILL DON'T TRUST HIM!
YOU WOULDN'T WANT ME TO HURT HIS FEELINGS BY REFUSING HIS GIFT! YUM YUM!
HMMM! I GUESS YOU'RE RIGHT!
2

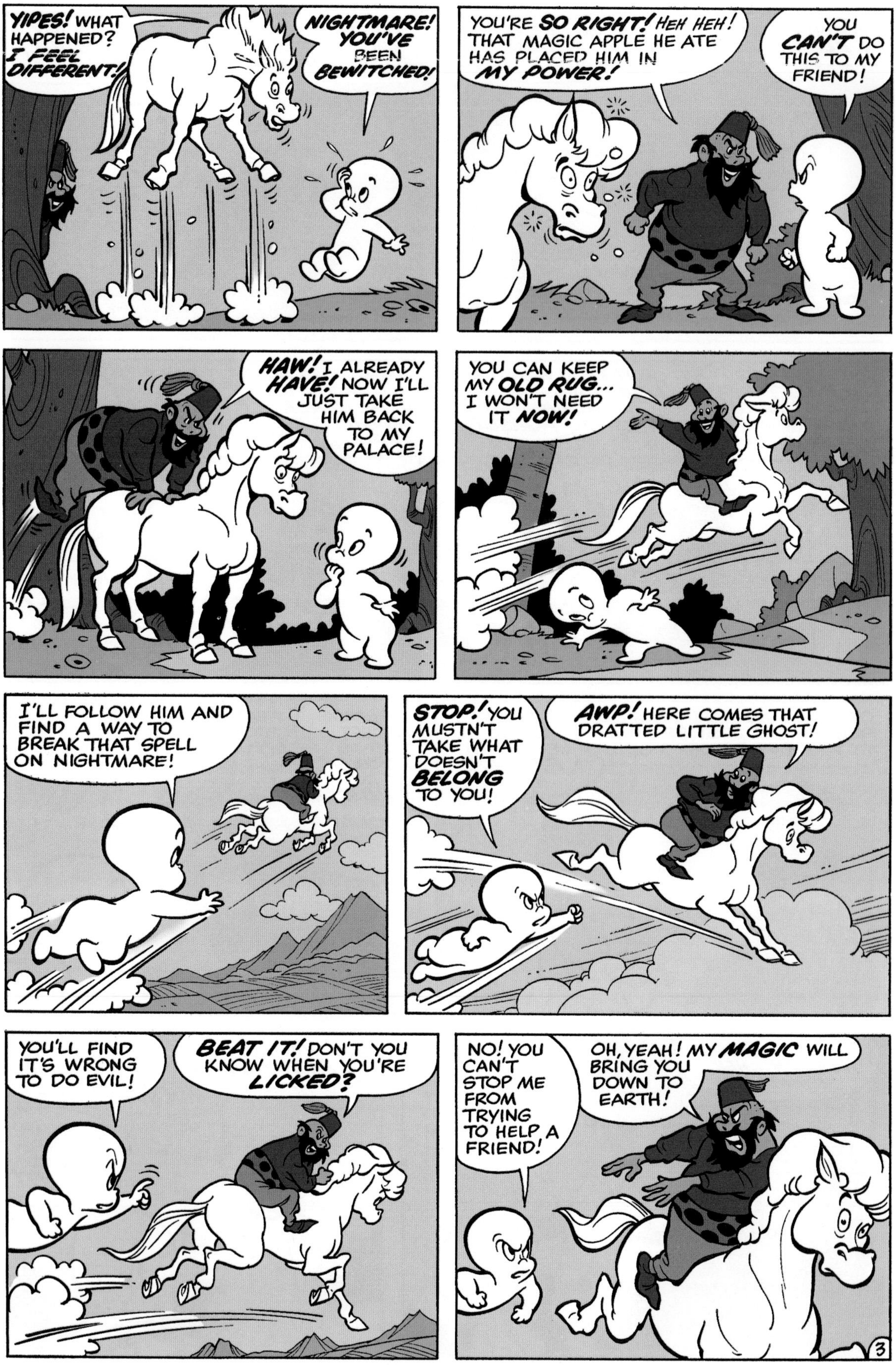
YIPES! WHAT HAPPENED? I FEEL DIFFERENT!
NIGHTMARE! YOU'VE BEEN BEWITCHED!
YOU'RE SO RIGHT! HEH HEH! THAT MAGIC APPLE HE ATE HAS PLACED HIM IN MY POWER!
YOU CAN'T DO THIS TO MY FRIEND!
HAW! I ALREADY HAVE! NOW I'LL JUST TAKE HIM BACK TO MY PALACE!
YOU CAN KEEP MY OLD RUG... I WON'T NEED IT NOW!
I'LL FOLLOW HIM AND FIND A WAY TO BREAK THAT SPELL ON NIGHTMARE!
STOP! YOU MUSTN'T TAKE WHAT DOESN'T BELONG TO YOU!
AWP! HERE COMES THAT DRATTED LITTLE GHOST!
YOU'LL FIND IT'S WRONG TO DO EVIL!
BEAT IT! DON'T YOU KNOW WHEN YOU'RE LICKED?
NO! YOU CAN'T STOP ME FROM TRYING TO HELP A FRIEND!
OH, YEAH! MY MAGIC WILL BRING YOU DOWN TO EARTH!
3

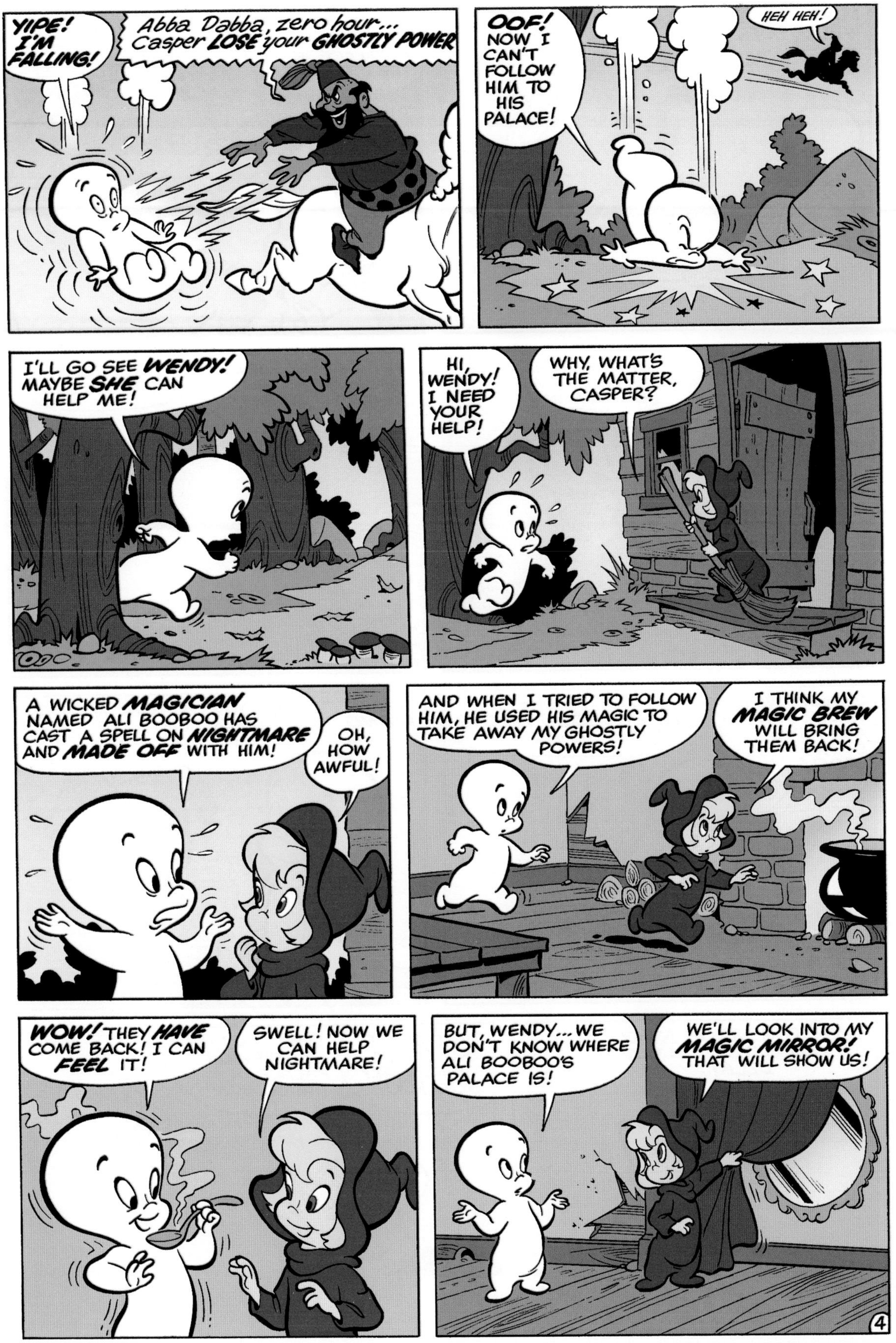
YIPE! I'M FALLING!
Abba Dabba, zero hour... Casper LOSE your GHOSTLY POWER
OOF! NOW I CAN'T FOLLOW HIM TO HIS PALACE!
HEH HEH!
I'LL GO SEE WENDY! MAYBE SHE CAN HELP ME!
HI, WENDY! I NEED YOUR HELP!
WHY, WHAT'S THE MATTER, CASPER?
A WICKED MAGICIAN NAMED ALI BOOBOO HAS CAST A SPELL ON NIGHTMARE AND MADE OFF WITH HIM!
OH, HOW AWFUL!
AND WHEN I TRIED TO FOLLOW HIM, HE USED HIS MAGIC TO TAKE AWAY MY GHOSTLY POWERS!
I THINK MY MAGIC BREW WILL BRING THEM BACK!
WOW! THEY HAVE COME BACK! I CAN FEEL IT!
SWELL! NOW WE CAN HELP NIGHTMARE!
BUT, WENDY... WE DON'T KNOW WHERE ALI BOOBOO'S PALACE IS!
WE'LL LOOK INTO MY MAGIC MIRROR! THAT WILL SHOW US!
4

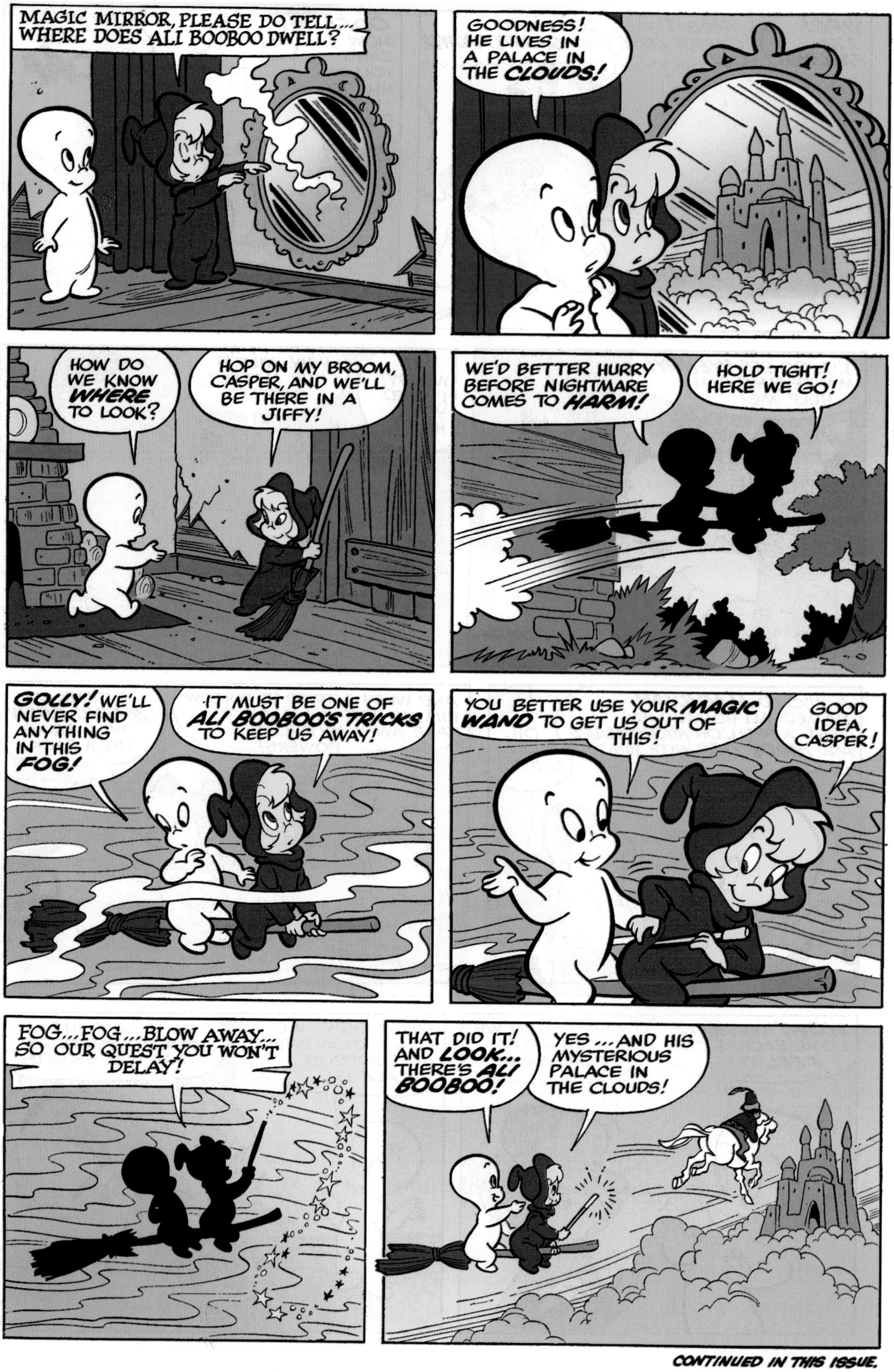
MAGIC MIRROR, PLEASE DO TELL... WHERE DOES ALI BOOBOO DWELL?
GOODNESS! HE LIVES IN A PALACE IN THE CLOUDS!
HOW DO WE KNOW WHERE TO LOOK?
HOP ON MY BROOM, CASPER, AND WE'LL BE THERE IN A JIFFY!
WE'D BETTER HURRY BEFORE NIGHTMARE COMES TO HARM!
HOLD TIGHT! HERE WE GO!
GOLLY! WE'LL NEVER FIND ANYTHING IN THIS FOG!
IT MUST BE ONE OF ALI BOOBOO'S TRICKS TO KEEP US AWAY!
YOU BETTER USE YOUR MAGIC WAND TO GET US OUT OF THIS!
GOOD IDEA, CASPER!
FOG...FOG...BLOW AWAY... SO OUR QUEST YOU WON'T DELAY!
THAT DID IT! AND LOOK... THERE'S ALI BOOBOO!
YES ...AND HIS MYSTERIOUS PALACE IN THE CLOUDS!

CONTINUED IN THIS ISSUE.

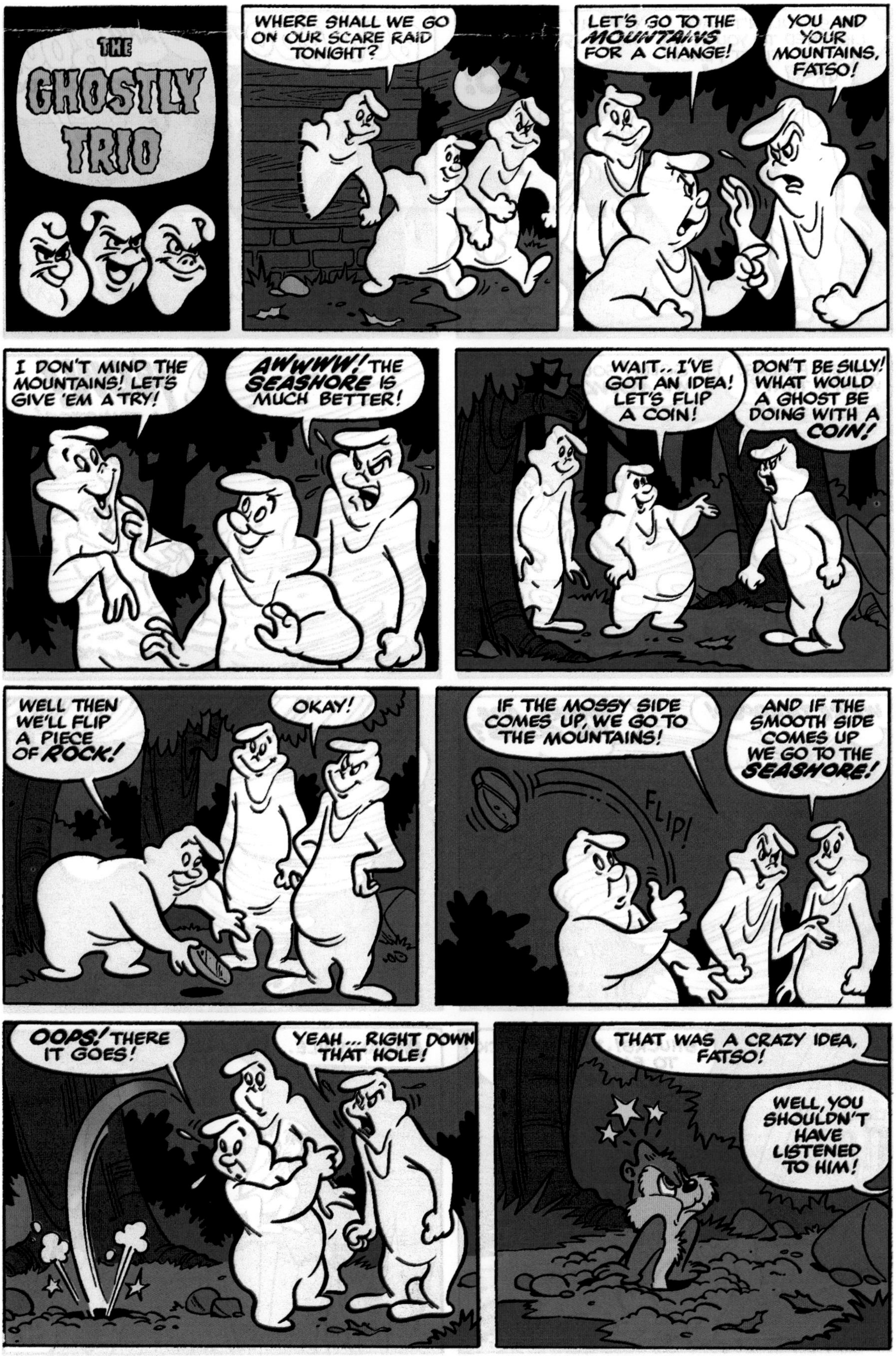
THE GHOSTLY TRIO
WHERE SHALL WE GO ON OUR SCARE RAID TONIGHT?
LET'S GO TO THE MOUNTAINS FOR A CHANGE!
YOU AND YOUR MOUNTAINS, FATSO!
I DON'T MIND THE MOUNTAINS! LET'S GIVE 'EM A TRY!
AWWWW! THE SEASHORE IS MUCH BETTER!
WAIT.. I'VE GOT AN IDEA! LET'S FLIP A COIN!
DON'T BE SILLY! WHAT WOULD A GHOST BE DOING WITH A COIN!
WELL THEN WE'LL FLIP A PIECE OF ROCK!
OKAY!
IF THE MOSSY SIDE COMES UP, WE GO TO THE MOUNTAINS!
AND IF THE SMOOTH SIDE COMES UP WE GO TO THE SEASHORE!
FLIP!
OOPS! THERE IT GOES!
YEAH... RIGHT DOWN THAT HOLE!
THAT WAS A CRAZY IDEA, FATSO!
WELL, YOU SHOULDN'T HAVE LISTENED TO HIM!

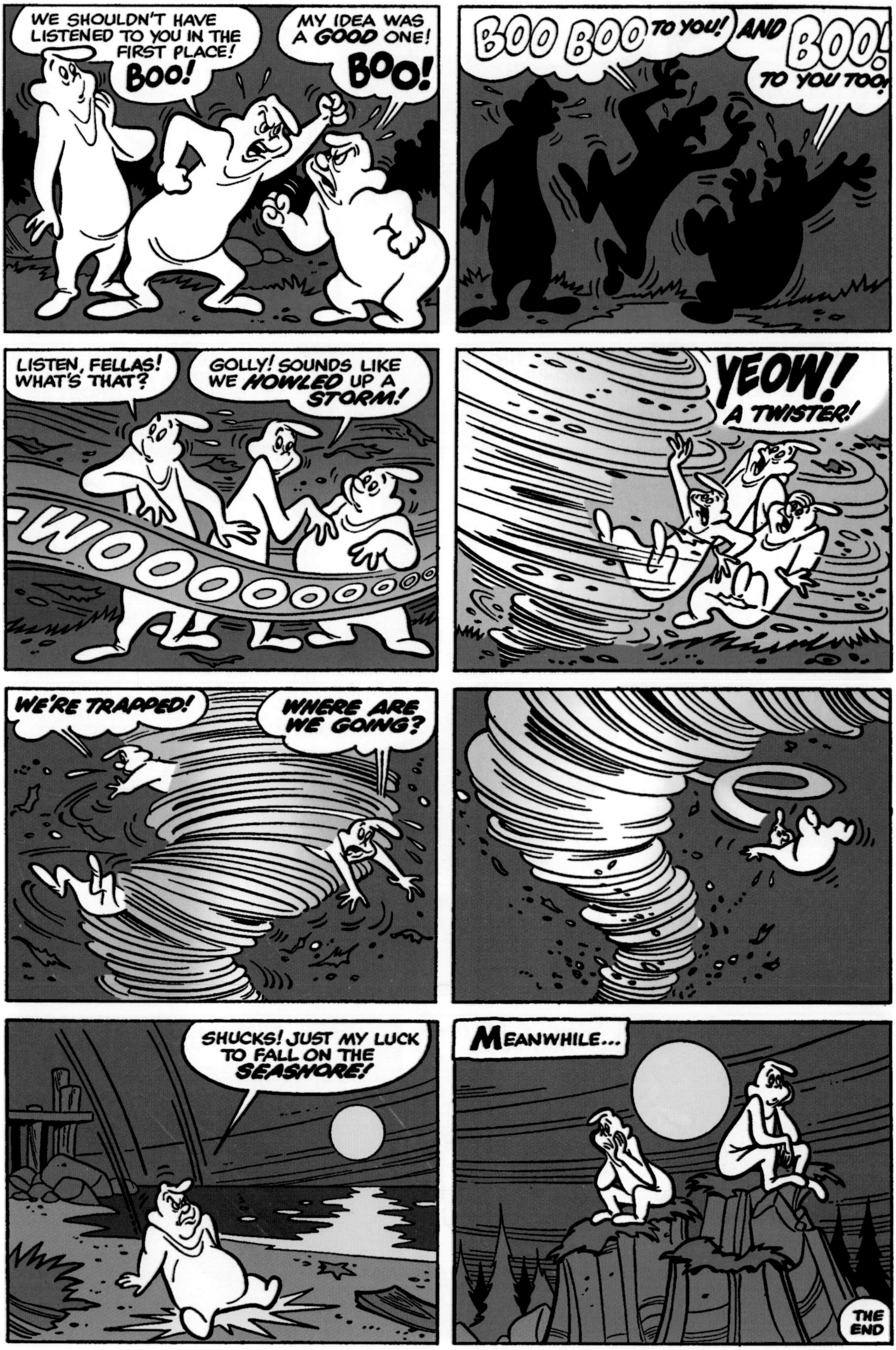
WE SHOULDN'T HAVE LISTENED TO YOU IN THE FIRST PLACE! BOO!
MY IDEA WAS A GOOD ONE! BOO!
BOO BOO TO YOU!
AND BOO! TO YOU TOO!
LISTEN, FELLAS! WHAT'S THAT?
GOLLY! SOUNDS LIKE WE HOWLED UP A STORM!
WOOOOOOOOOO
YEOW! A TWISTER!
WE'RE TRAPPED!
WHERE ARE WE GOING?
SHUCKS! JUST MY LUCK TO FALL ON THE SEASHORE!
MEANWHILE...
THE END

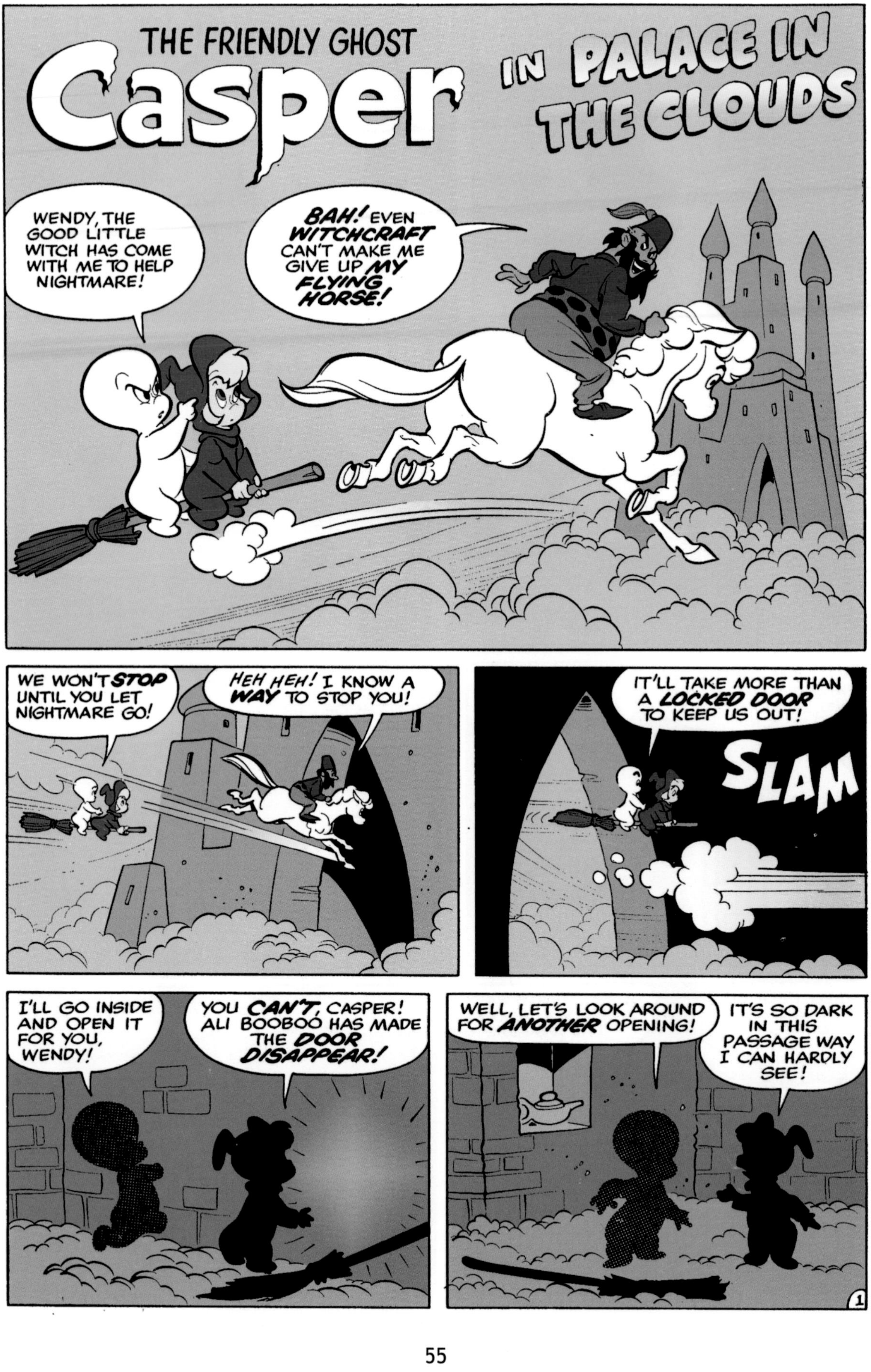

THE FRIENDLY GHOST
Casper
IN PALACE IN THE CLOUDS
WENDY, THE GOOD LITTLE WITCH HAS COME WITH ME TO HELP NIGHTMARE!
BAH! EVEN WITCHCRAFT CAN'T MAKE ME GIVE UP MY FLYING HORSE!
WE WON'T STOP UNTIL YOU LET NIGHTMARE GO!
HEH HEH! I KNOW A WAY TO STOP YOU!
IT'LL TAKE MORE THAN A LOCKED DOOR TO KEEP US OUT!
SLAM
I'LL GO INSIDE AND OPEN IT FOR YOU, WENDY!
YOU CAN'T, CASPER! ALI BOOBOO HAS MADE THE DOOR DISAPPEAR!
WELL, LET'S LOOK AROUND FOR ANOTHER OPENING!
IT'S SO DARK IN THIS PASSAGE WAY I CAN HARDLY SEE!
1

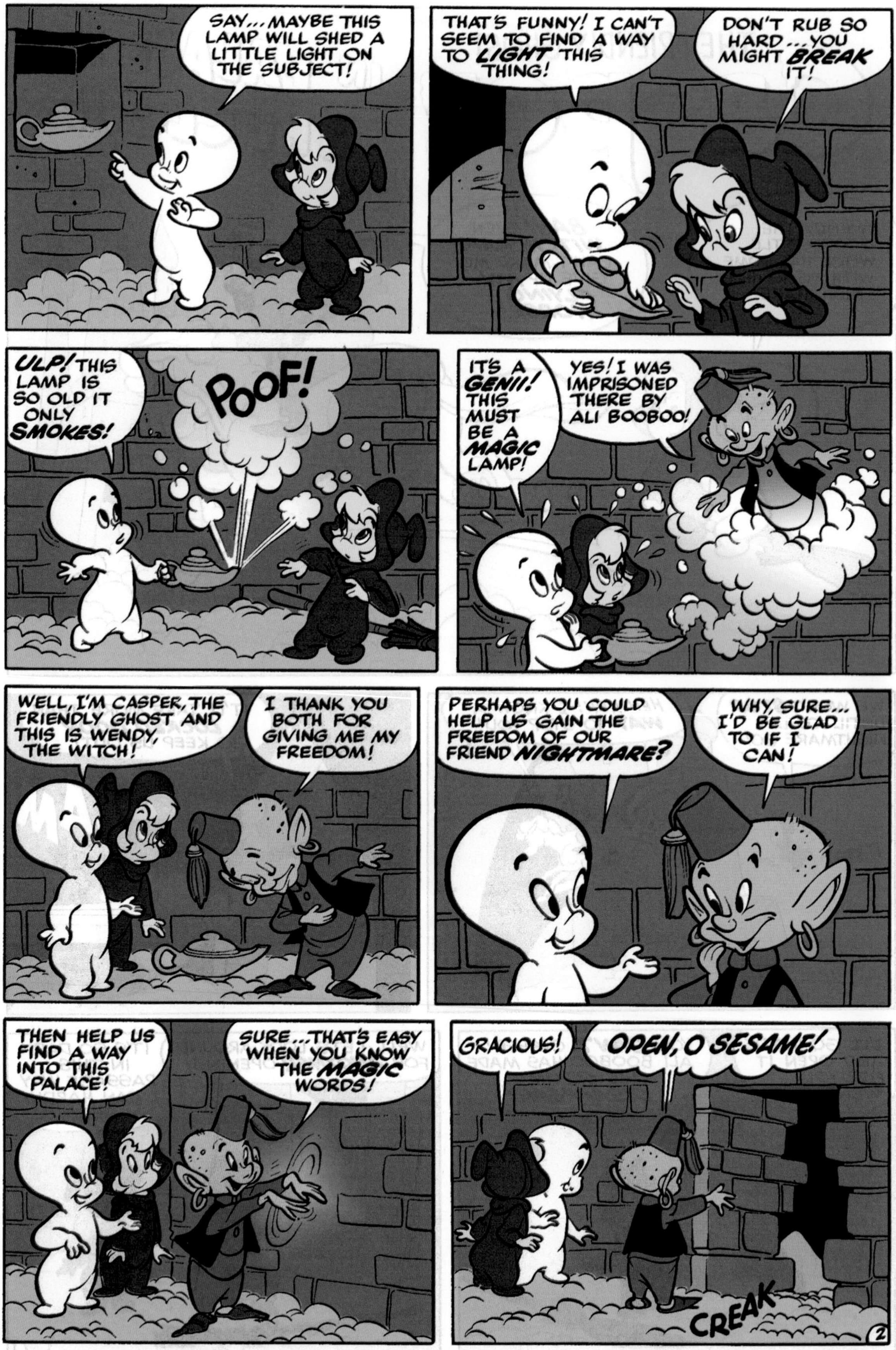
SAY... MAYBE THIS LAMP WILL SHED A LITTLE LIGHT ON THE SUBJECT!
THAT'S FUNNY! I CAN'T SEEM TO FIND A WAY TO LIGHT THIS THING!
DON'T RUB SO HARD... YOU MIGHT BREAK IT!
ULP! THIS LAMP IS SO OLD IT ONLY SMOKES!
POOF!
IT'S A GENII! THIS MUST BE A MAGIC LAMP!
YES! I WAS IMPRISONED THERE BY ALI BOOBOO!
WELL, I'M CASPER, THE FRIENDLY GHOST AND THIS IS WENDY, THE WITCH!
I THANK YOU BOTH FOR GIVING ME MY FREEDOM!
PERHAPS YOU COULD HELP US GAIN THE FREEDOM OF OUR FRIEND NIGHTMARE?
WHY, SURE... I'D BE GLAD TO IF I CAN!
THEN HELP US FIND A WAY INTO THIS PALACE!
SURE... THAT'S EASY WHEN YOU KNOW THE MAGIC WORDS!
GRACIOUS!
OPEN, O SESAME!
CREAK
2

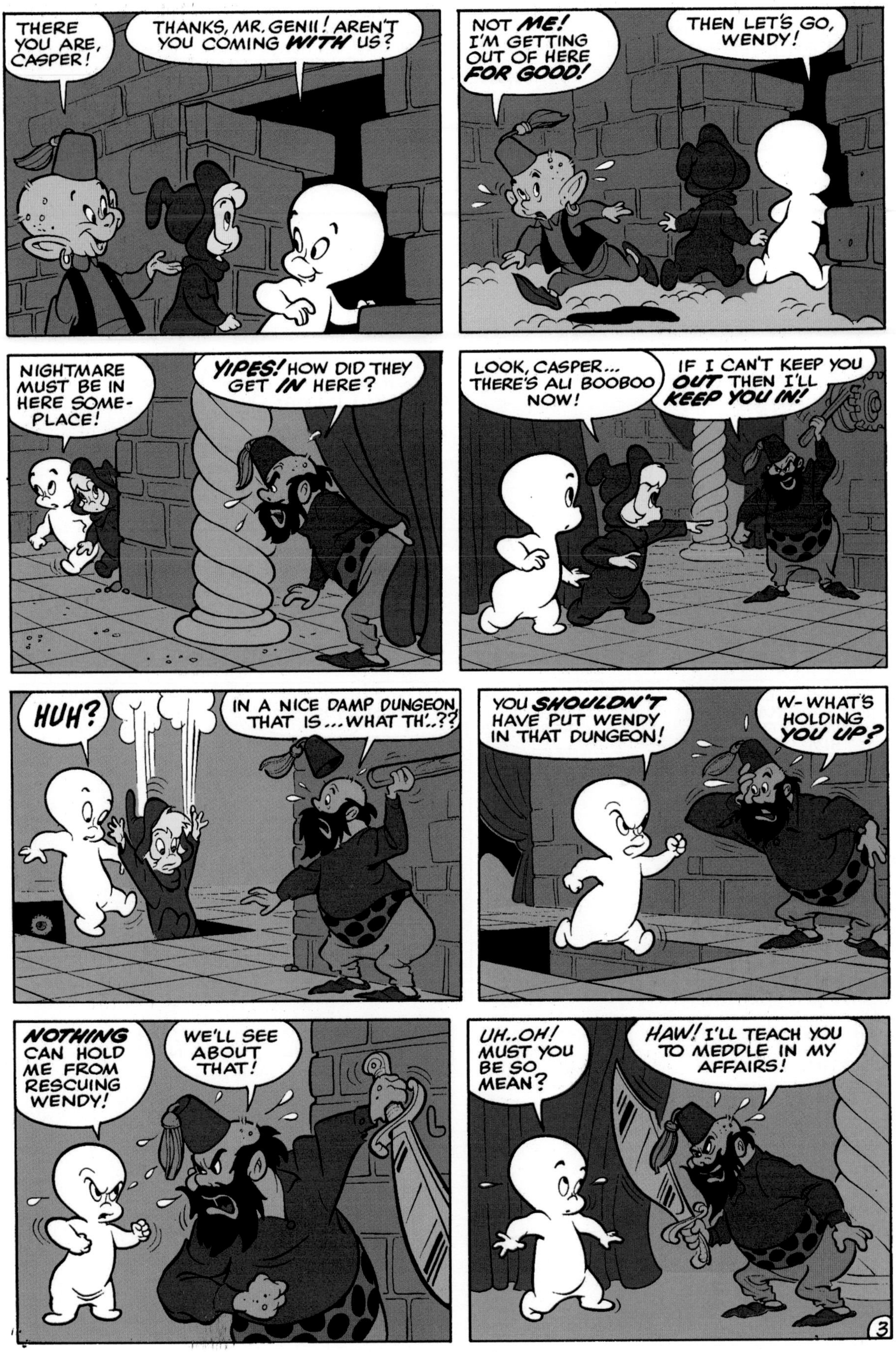
THERE YOU ARE, CASPER!
THANKS, MR. GENII! AREN'T YOU COMING WITH US?
NOT ME! I'M GETTING OUT OF HERE FOR GOOD!
THEN LET'S GO, WENDY!
NIGHTMARE MUST BE IN HERE SOME-PLACE!
YIPES! HOW DID THEY GET IN HERE?
LOOK, CASPER... THERE'S ALI BOOBOO NOW!
IF I CAN'T KEEP YOU OUT THEN I'LL KEEP YOU IN!
HUH?
IN A NICE DAMP DUNGEON, THAT IS... WHAT TH'..??
YOU SHOULDN'T HAVE PUT WENDY IN THAT DUNGEON!
W-WHAT'S HOLDING YOU UP?
NOTHING CAN HOLD ME FROM RESCUING WENDY!
WE'LL SEE ABOUT THAT!
UH..OH! MUST YOU BE SO MEAN?
HAW! I'LL TEACH YOU TO MEDDLE IN MY AFFAIRS!
3

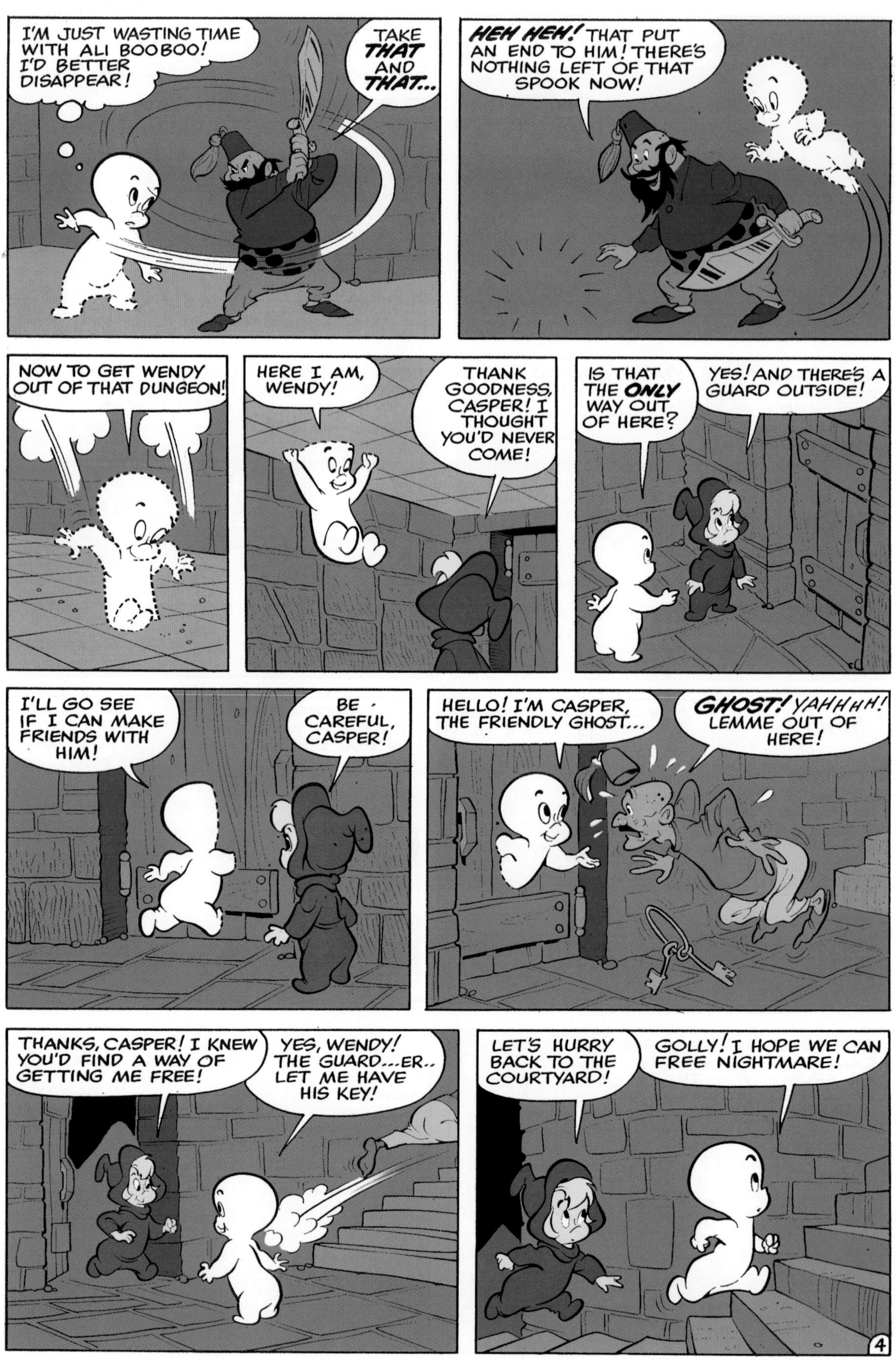
I'M JUST WASTING TIME WITH ALI BOOBOO! I'D BETTER DISAPPEAR!
TAKE THAT AND THAT...
HEH HEH! THAT PUT AN END TO HIM! THERE'S NOTHING LEFT OF THAT SPOOK NOW!
NOW TO GET WENDY OUT OF THAT DUNGEON!
HERE I AM, WENDY!
THANK GOODNESS, CASPER! I THOUGHT YOU'D NEVER COME!
IS THAT THE ONLY WAY OUT OF HERE?
YES! AND THERE'S A GUARD OUTSIDE!
I'LL GO SEE IF I CAN MAKE FRIENDS WITH HIM!
BE CAREFUL, CASPER!
HELLO! I'M CASPER, THE FRIENDLY GHOST...
GHOST! YAHHHH! LEMME OUT OF HERE!
THANKS, CASPER! I KNEW YOU'D FIND A WAY OF GETTING ME FREE!
YES, WENDY! THE GUARD...ER.. LET ME HAVE HIS KEY!
LET'S HURRY BACK TO THE COURTYARD!
GOLLY! I HOPE WE CAN FREE NIGHTMARE!
4

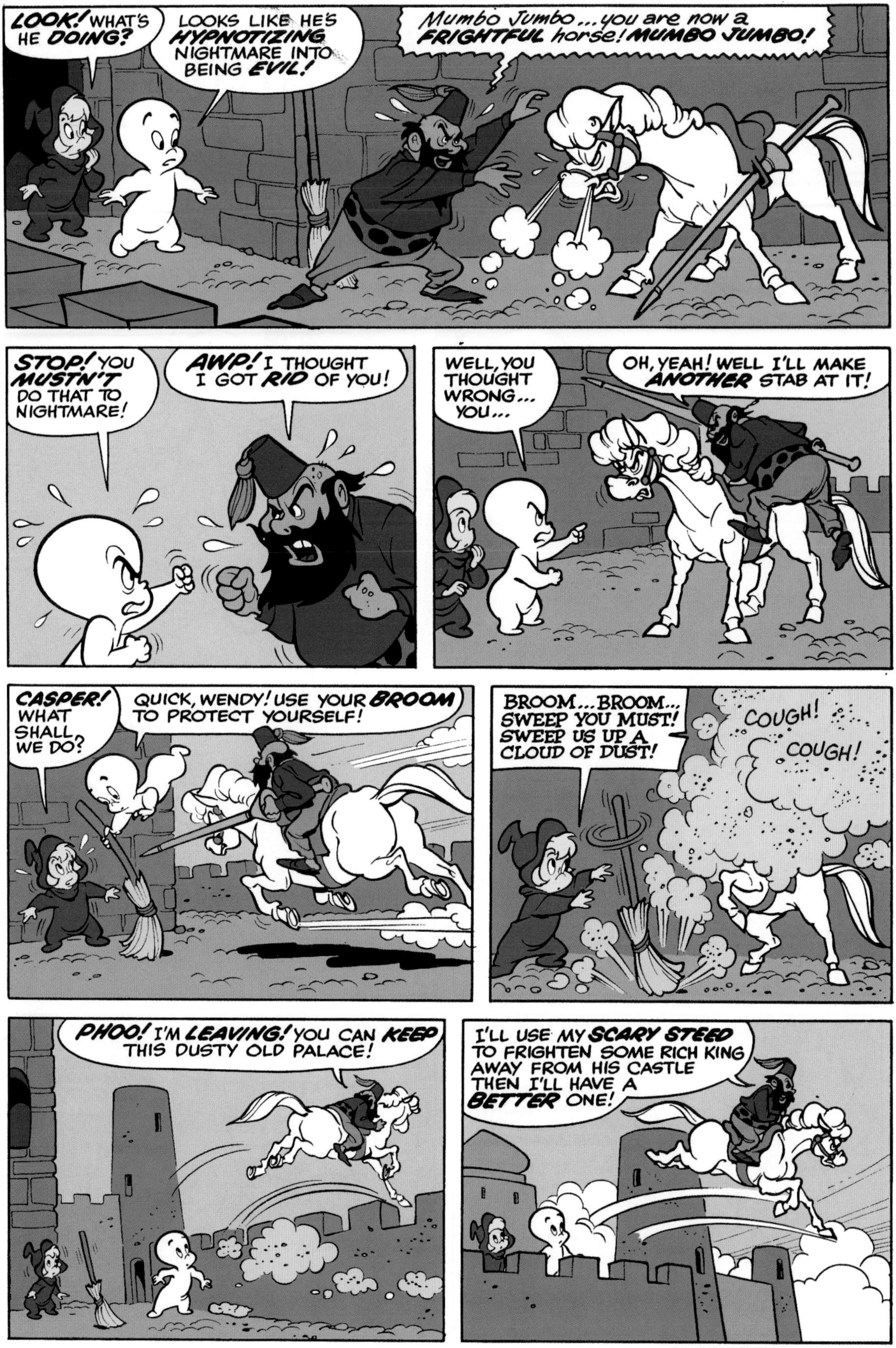
LOOK! WHAT'S HE DOING?
LOOKS LIKE HE'S HYPNOTIZING NIGHTMARE INTO BEING EVIL!
Mumbo Jumbo ...you are now a FRIGHTFUL horse! MUMBO JUMBO!
STOP! YOU MUSTN'T DO THAT TO NIGHTMARE!
AWP! I THOUGHT I GOT RID OF YOU!
WELL, YOU THOUGHT WRONG... YOU...
OH, YEAH! WELL I'LL MAKE ANOTHER STAB AT IT!
CASPER! WHAT SHALL WE DO?
QUICK, WENDY! USE YOUR BROOM TO PROTECT YOURSELF!
BROOM...BROOM... SWEEP YOU MUST! SWEEP US UP A CLOUD OF DUST!
COUGH! COUGH!
PHOO! I'M LEAVING! YOU CAN KEEP THIS DUSTY OLD PALACE!
I'LL USE MY SCARY STEED TO FRIGHTEN SOME RICH KING AWAY FROM HIS CASTLE THEN I'LL HAVE A BETTER ONE!

CONTINUED IN THIS ISSUE.

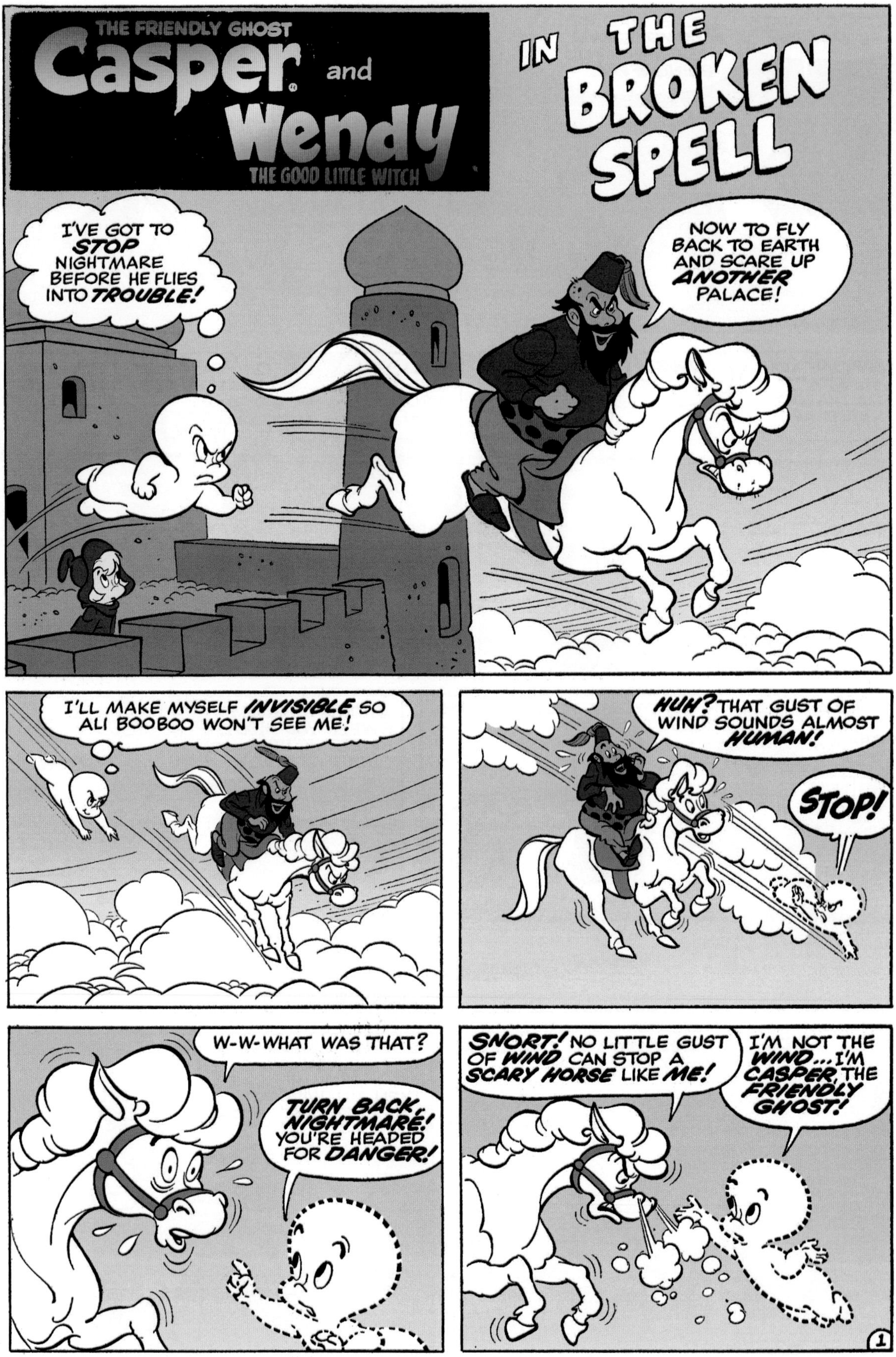
THE FRIENDLY GHOST
Casper and Wendy
THE GOOD LITTLE WITCH
IN THE BROKEN SPELL
I'VE GOT TO STOP NIGHTMARE BEFORE HE FLIES INTO TROUBLE!
NOW TO FLY BACK TO EARTH AND SCARE UP ANOTHER PALACE!
I'LL MAKE MYSELF INVISIBLE SO ALI BOOBOO WON'T SEE ME!
HUH? THAT GUST OF WIND SOUNDS ALMOST HUMAN!
STOP!
W-W-WHAT WAS THAT?
TURN BACK, NIGHTMARE! YOU'RE HEADED FOR DANGER!
SNORT! NO LITTLE GUST OF WIND CAN STOP A SCARY HORSE LIKE ME!
I'M NOT THE WIND...I'M CASPER, THE FRIENDLY GHOST!
1

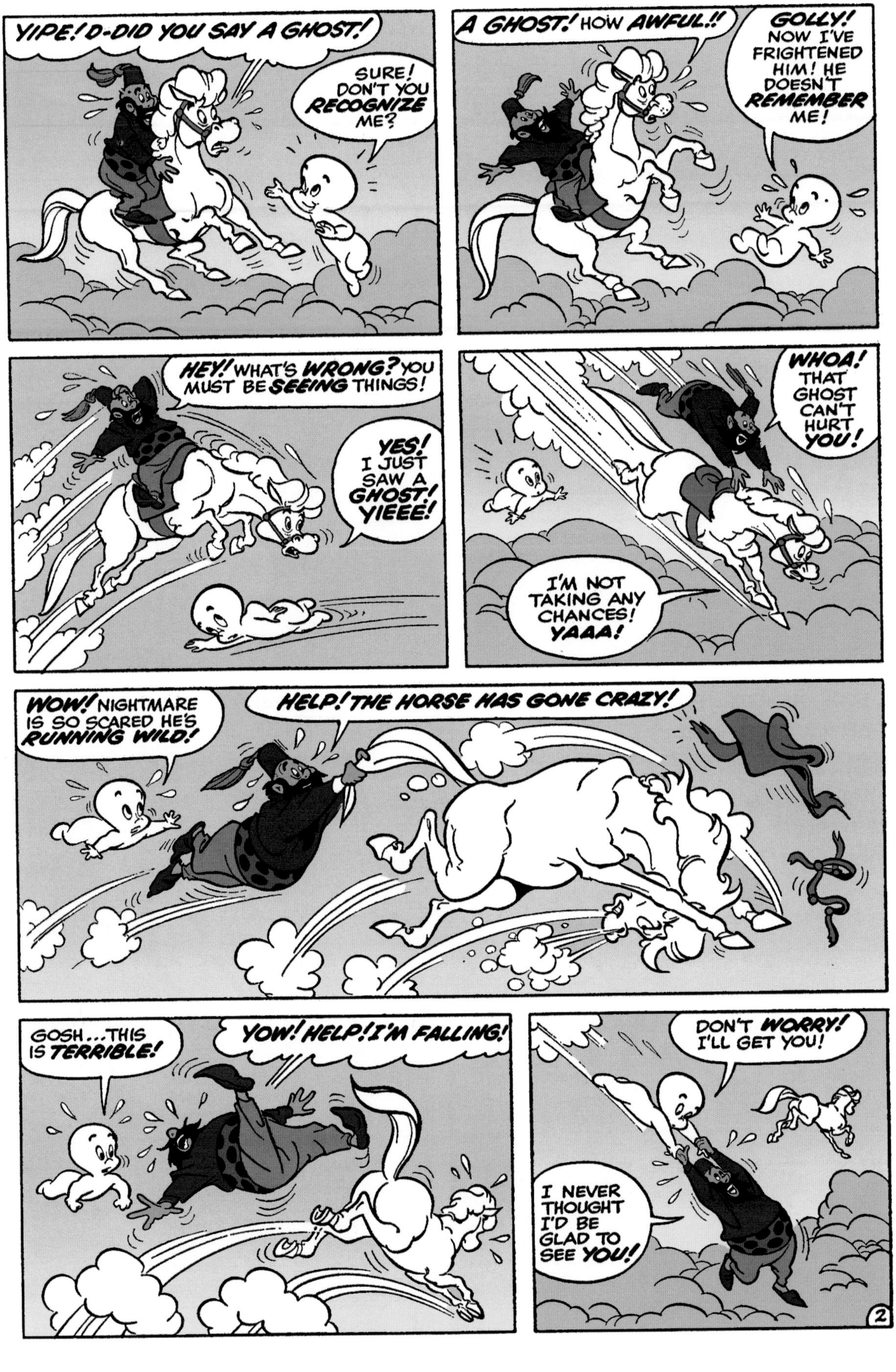
YIPE! D-DID YOU SAY A GHOST?
SURE! DON'T YOU RECOGNIZE ME?
A GHOST! HOW AWFUL!!
GOLLY! NOW I'VE FRIGHTENED HIM! HE DOESN'T REMEMBER ME!
HEY! WHAT'S WRONG? YOU MUST BE SEEING THINGS!
YES! I JUST SAW A GHOST! YIEEE!
WHOA! THAT GHOST CAN'T HURT YOU!
I'M NOT TAKING ANY CHANCES! YAAA!
WOW! NIGHTMARE IS SO SCARED HE'S RUNNING WILD!
HELP! THE HORSE HAS GONE CRAZY!
GOSH... THIS IS TERRIBLE!
YOW! HELP! I'M FALLING!
DON'T WORRY! I'LL GET YOU!
I NEVER THOUGHT I'D BE GLAD TO SEE YOU!
2

THERE YOU ARE! *SAFE* AND *SOUND*!

YOU *SAVED* MY LIFE, CASPER! HOW CAN I *EVER* REPAY YOU?

WELL...YOU CAN *UNDO* YOUR MAGIC SPELL AND MAKE NIGHTMARE HIS *OLD SELF* AGAIN!

I'VE HAD *ENOUGH* OF FLYING HORSES! BUT I *CAN'T BREAK* THE SPELL!

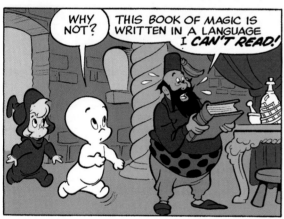

WHY NOT?

THIS BOOK OF MAGIC IS WRITTEN IN A LANGUAGE I *CAN'T READ!*

MAYBE *YOU* CAN HELP US OUT, WENDY!

WELL, I'LL *TRY*, CASPER!

BOOK, OH, BOOK...PLEASE CHANGE INTO A LANGUAGE I CAN READ!

I PLEAD...

ABBA DABA
BABBLE BOOO
GAZICK GAZA
MICKEY MOO
ZIPPY ZICH
BALY BOOO

HOORAY! THAT DID IT!

YEAH! IT SAYS TO MAKE A MAGIC BREW!

FIRST... MAKE A MAGIC BREW-- THEN—

WENDY CAN MIX UP THE MAGIC BREW IF YOU HAVE THE THINGS TO MAKE IT!

ER., LET'S SEE NOW, WHERE DID I PUT ALL THAT STUFF!

IT'S NOT HERE....OR HERE... OR IN HERE!

I'LL HELP YOU LOOK FOR IT!

3

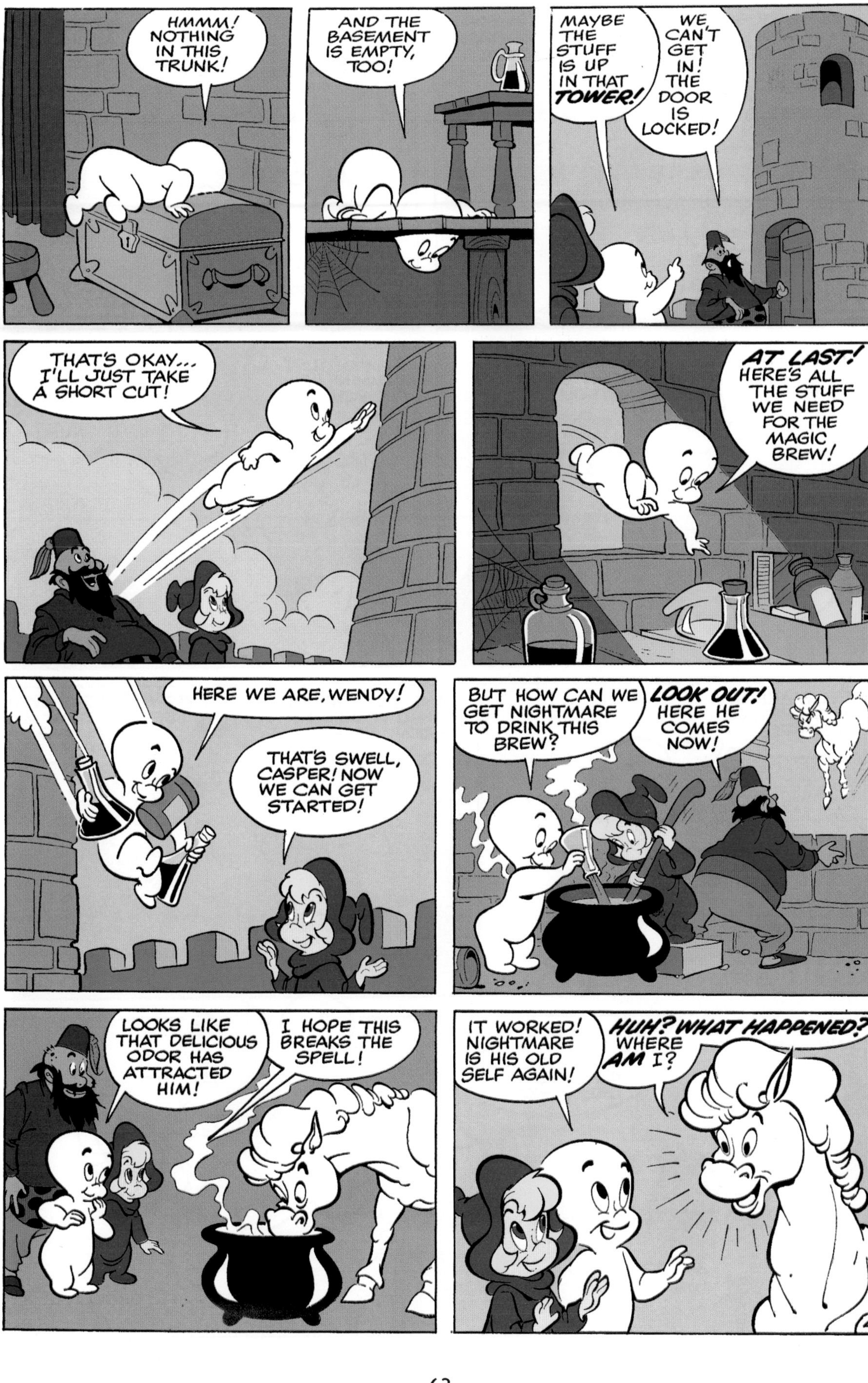
HMMM! NOTHING IN THIS TRUNK!
AND THE BASEMENT IS EMPTY, TOO!
MAYBE THE STUFF IS UP IN THAT TOWER!
WE CAN'T GET IN! THE DOOR IS LOCKED!
THAT'S OKAY... I'LL JUST TAKE A SHORT CUT!
AT LAST! HERE'S ALL THE STUFF WE NEED FOR THE MAGIC BREW!
HERE WE ARE, WENDY!
THAT'S SWELL, CASPER! NOW WE CAN GET STARTED!
BUT HOW CAN WE GET NIGHTMARE TO DRINK THIS BREW?
LOOK OUT! HERE HE COMES NOW!
LOOKS LIKE THAT DELICIOUS ODOR HAS ATTRACTED HIM!
I HOPE THIS BREAKS THE SPELL!
IT WORKED! NIGHTMARE IS HIS OLD SELF AGAIN!
HUH? WHAT HAPPENED? WHERE AM I?
4

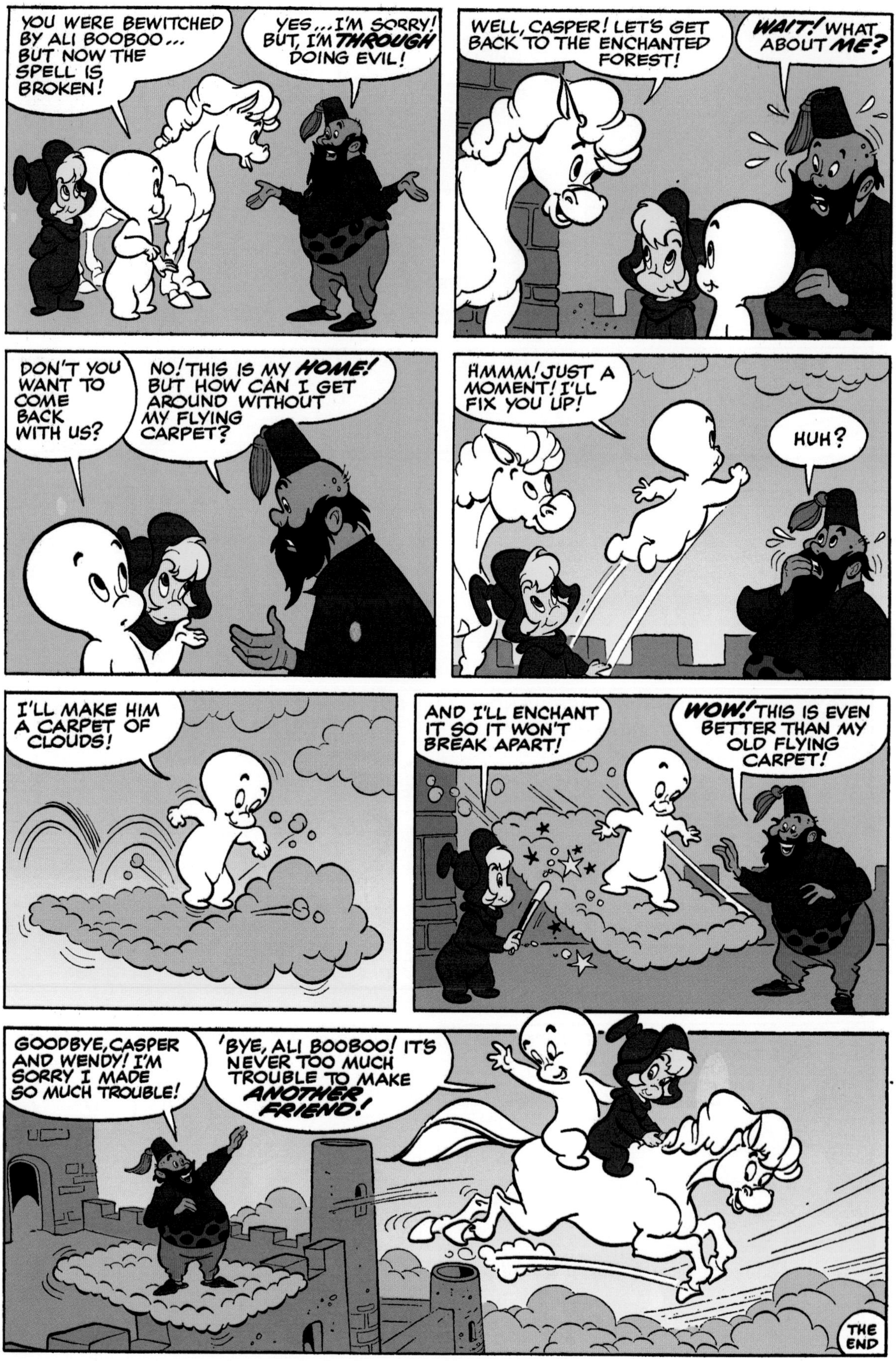
YOU WERE BEWITCHED BY ALI BOOBOO... BUT NOW THE SPELL IS BROKEN!
YES... I'M SORRY! BUT, I'M THROUGH DOING EVIL!
WELL, CASPER! LET'S GET BACK TO THE ENCHANTED FOREST!
WAIT! WHAT ABOUT ME?
DON'T YOU WANT TO COME BACK WITH US?
NO! THIS IS MY HOME! BUT HOW CAN I GET AROUND WITHOUT MY FLYING CARPET?
HMMM! JUST A MOMENT! I'LL FIX YOU UP!
HUH?
I'LL MAKE HIM A CARPET OF CLOUDS!
AND I'LL ENCHANT IT SO IT WON'T BREAK APART!
WOW! THIS IS EVEN BETTER THAN MY OLD FLYING CARPET!
GOODBYE, CASPER AND WENDY! I'M SORRY I MADE SO MUCH TROUBLE!
'BYE, ALI BOOBOO! IT'S NEVER TOO MUCH TROUBLE TO MAKE ANOTHER FRIEND!
THE END

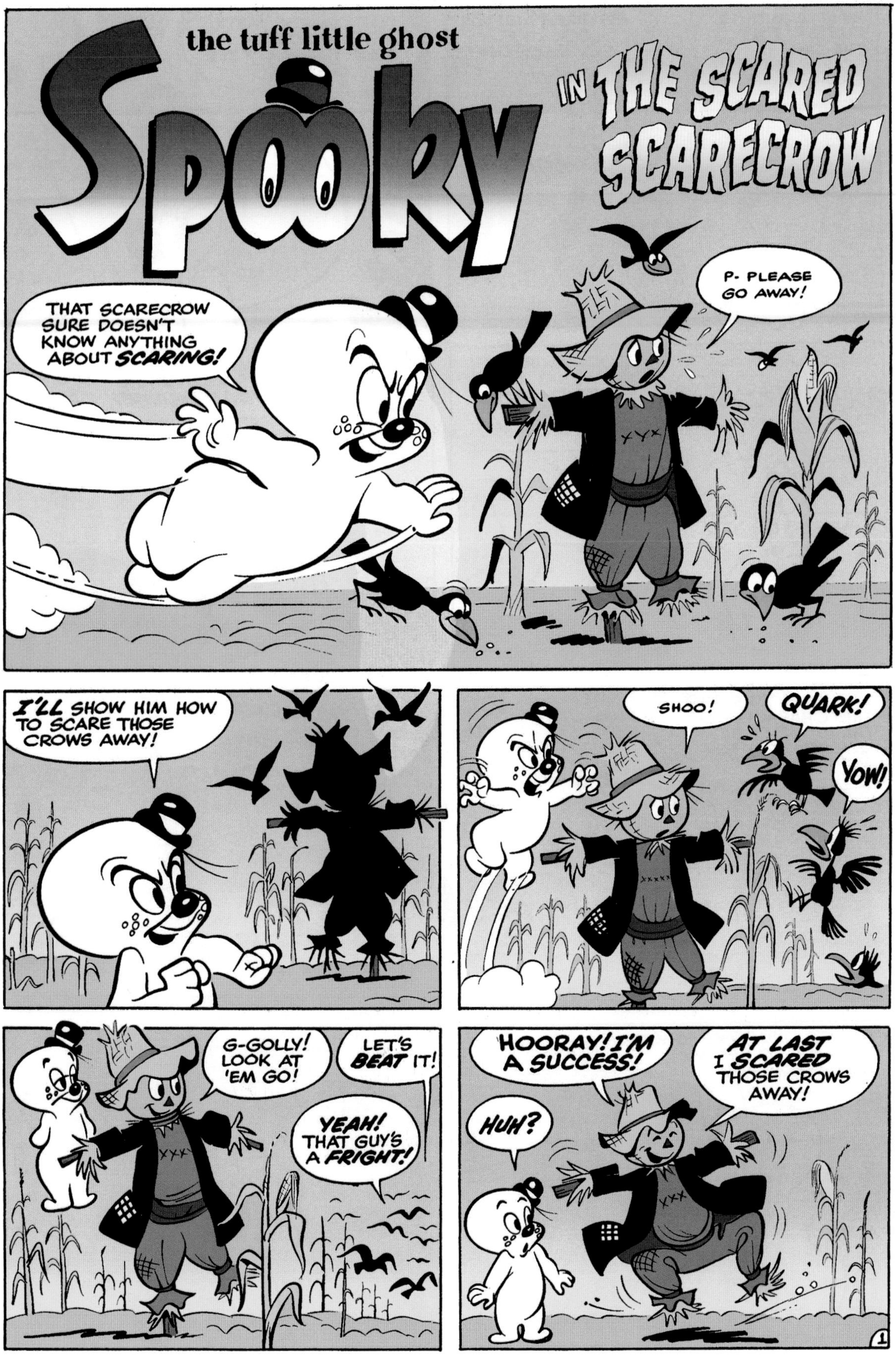
the tuff little ghost
Spooky
IN THE SCARED SCARECROW
THAT SCARECROW SURE DOESN'T KNOW ANYTHING ABOUT SCARING!
P- PLEASE GO AWAY!
I'LL SHOW HIM HOW TO SCARE THOSE CROWS AWAY!
SHOO!
QUARK!
YOW!
G-GOLLY! LOOK AT 'EM GO!
LET'S BEAT IT!
YEAH! THAT GUY'S A FRIGHT!
HOORAY! I'M A SUCCESS!
AT LAST I SCARED THOSE CROWS AWAY!
HUH?
1

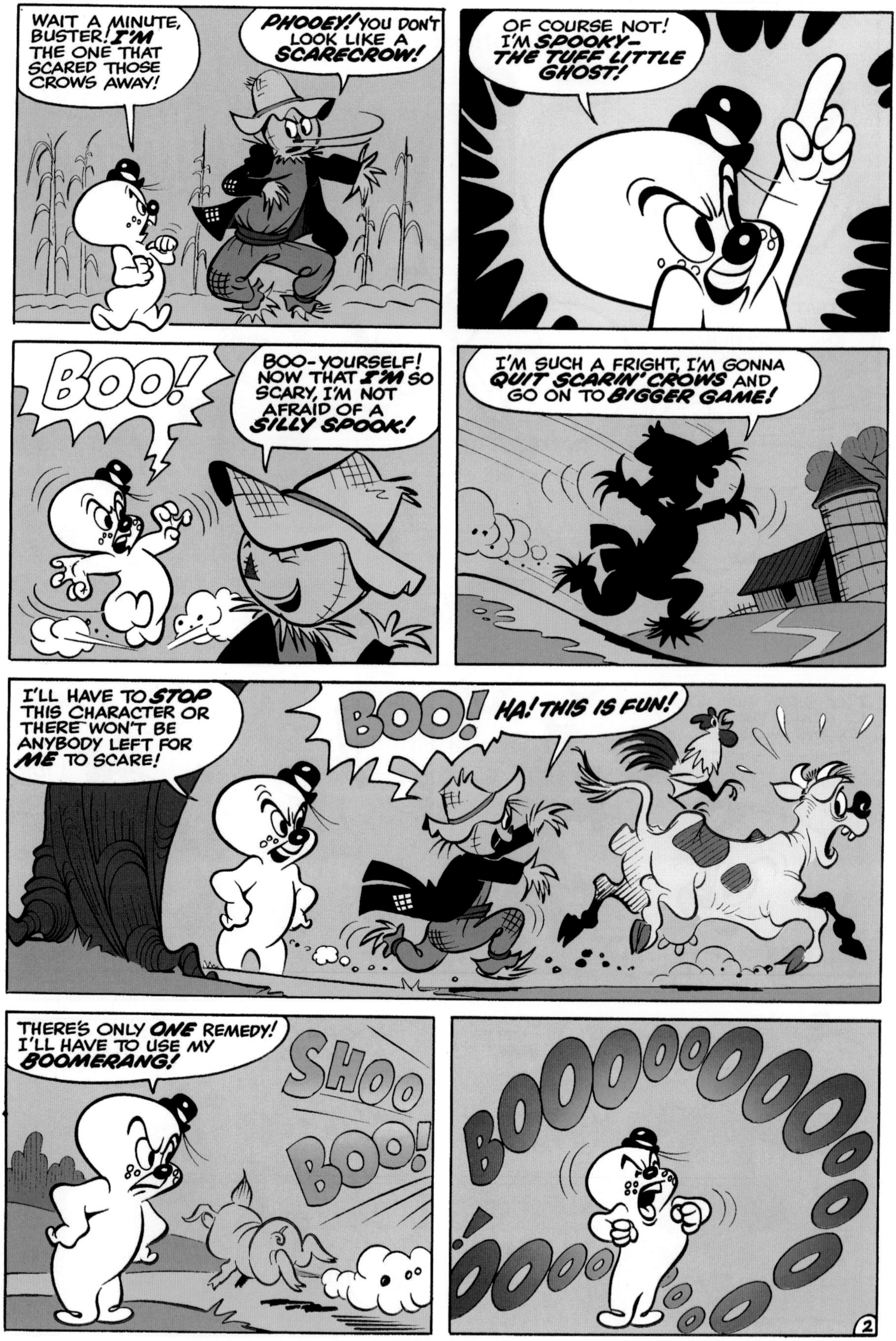
WAIT A MINUTE, BUSTER! I'M THE ONE THAT SCARED THOSE CROWS AWAY!
PHOOEY! YOU DON'T LOOK LIKE A SCARECROW!
OF COURSE NOT! I'M SPOOKY-THE TUFF LITTLE GHOST!
BOO!
BOO-YOURSELF! NOW THAT I'M SO SCARY, I'M NOT AFRAID OF A SILLY SPOOK!
I'M SUCH A FRIGHT, I'M GONNA QUIT SCARIN' CROWS AND GO ON TO BIGGER GAME!
I'LL HAVE TO STOP THIS CHARACTER OR THERE WON'T BE ANYBODY LEFT FOR ME TO SCARE!
BOO!
HA! THIS IS FUN!
THERE'S ONLY ONE REMEDY! I'LL HAVE TO USE MY BOOMERANG!
SHOO
BOO!
BOOOOOOOOOOOOOOOOOOOOOOO!
2

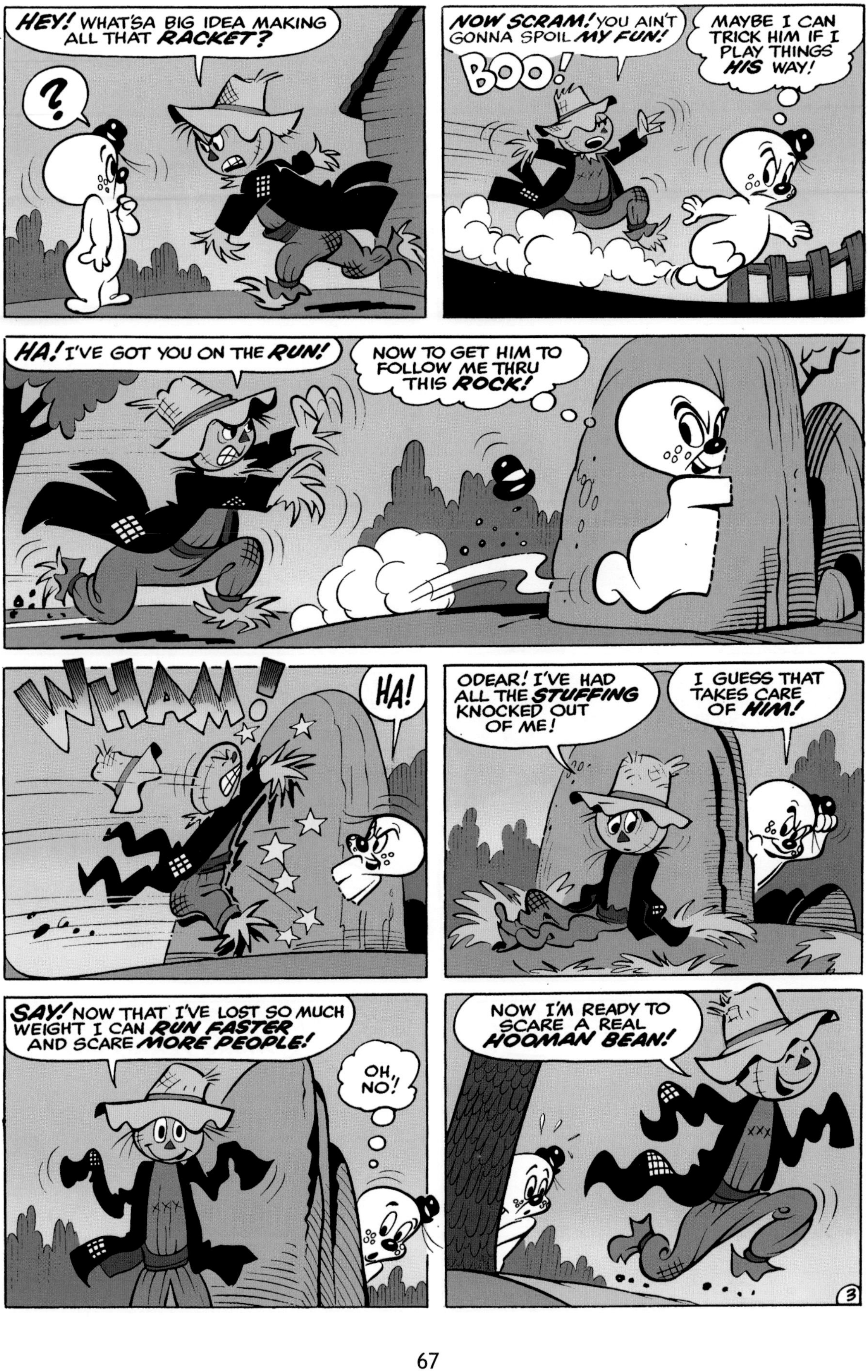
HEY! WHAT'SA BIG IDEA MAKING ALL THAT RACKET?
?
NOW SCRAM! YOU AIN'T GONNA SPOIL MY FUN!
BOO!
MAYBE I CAN TRICK HIM IF I PLAY THINGS HIS WAY!
HA! I'VE GOT YOU ON THE RUN!
NOW TO GET HIM TO FOLLOW ME THRU THIS ROCK!
WHAM!
HA!
ODEAR! I'VE HAD ALL THE STUFFING KNOCKED OUT OF ME!
I GUESS THAT TAKES CARE OF HIM!
SAY! NOW THAT I'VE LOST SO MUCH WEIGHT I CAN RUN FASTER AND SCARE MORE PEOPLE!
OH, NO!
NOW I'M READY TO SCARE A REAL HOOMAN BEAN!
3

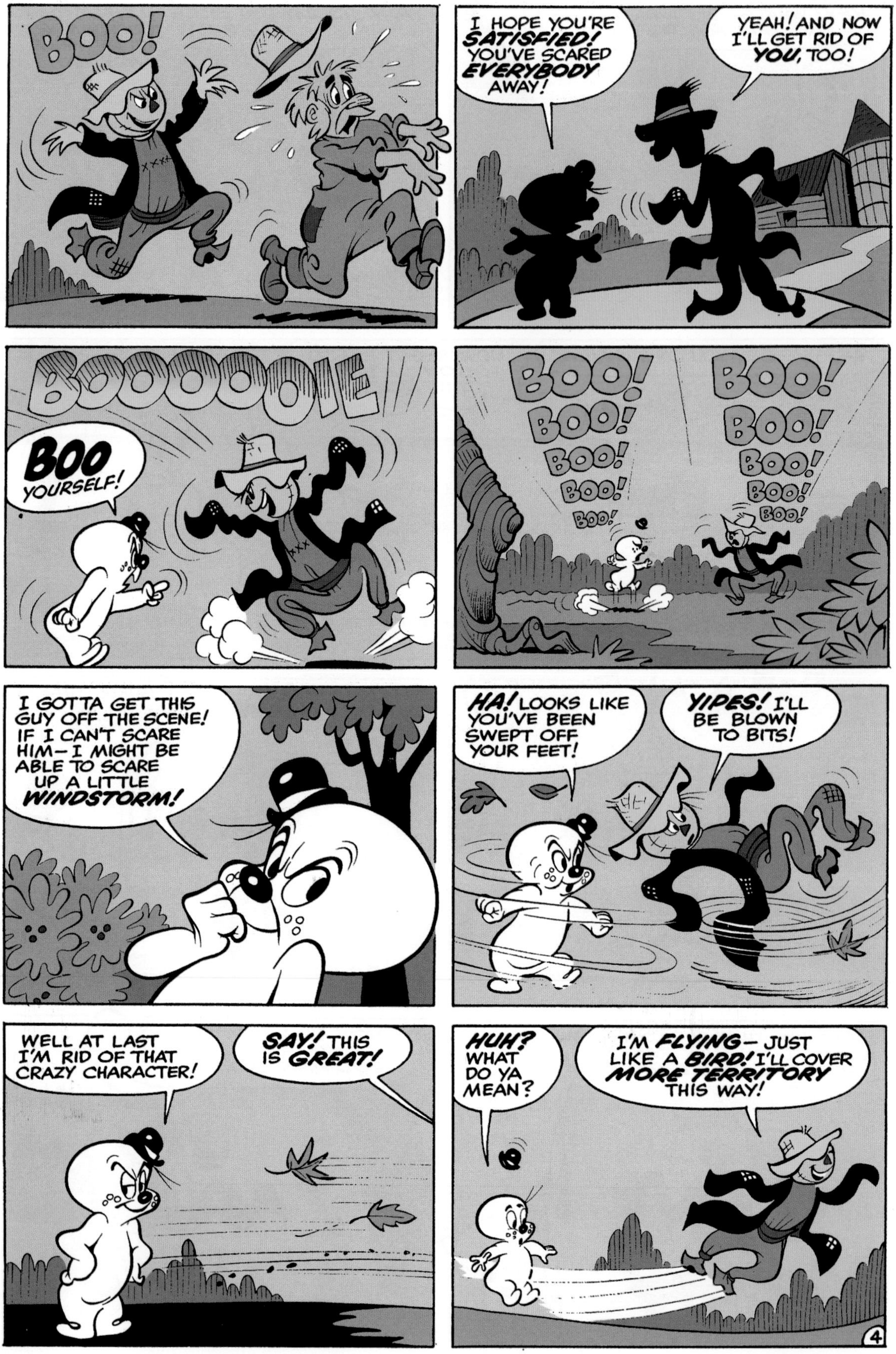
BOO!
I HOPE YOU'RE SATISFIED! YOU'VE SCARED EVERYBODY AWAY!
YEAH! AND NOW I'LL GET RID OF YOU, TOO!
BOOOOOIE
BOO YOURSELF!
BOO! BOO! BOO! BOO! BOO!
BOO! BOO! BOO! BOO! BOO!
I GOTTA GET THIS GUY OFF THE SCENE! IF I CAN'T SCARE HIM—I MIGHT BE ABLE TO SCARE UP A LITTLE WINDSTORM!
HA! LOOKS LIKE YOU'VE BEEN SWEPT OFF YOUR FEET!
YIPES! I'LL BE BLOWN TO BITS!
WELL AT LAST I'M RID OF THAT CRAZY CHARACTER!
SAY! THIS IS GREAT!
HUH? WHAT DO YA MEAN?
I'M FLYING— JUST LIKE A BIRD! I'LL COVER MORE TERRITORY THIS WAY!
4

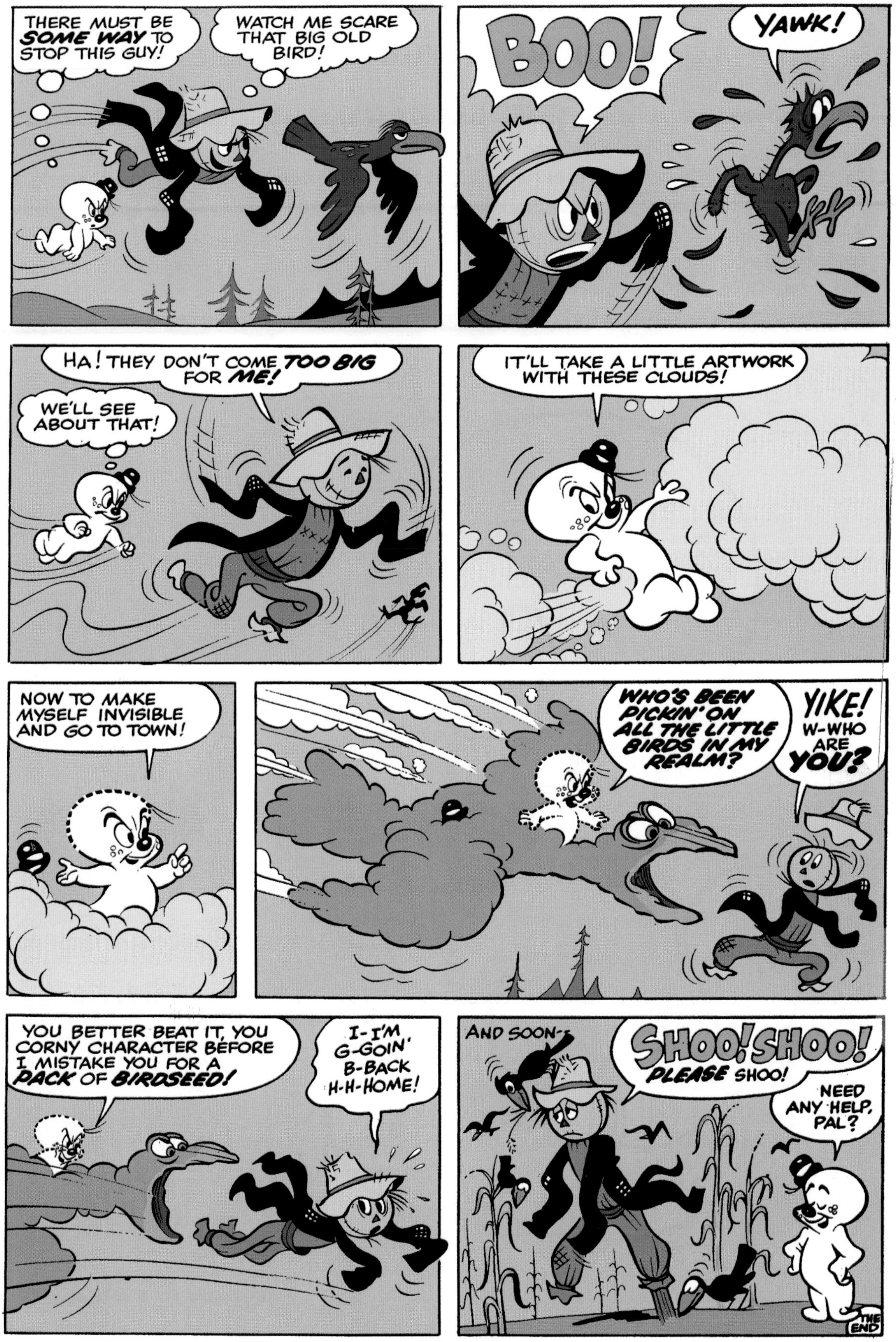
THERE MUST BE SOME WAY TO STOP THIS GUY!
WATCH ME SCARE THAT BIG OLD BIRD!
BOO!
YAWK!
HA! THEY DON'T COME TOO BIG FOR ME!
WE'LL SEE ABOUT THAT!
IT'LL TAKE A LITTLE ARTWORK WITH THESE CLOUDS!
NOW TO MAKE MYSELF INVISIBLE AND GO TO TOWN!
WHO'S BEEN PICKIN' ON ALL THE LITTLE BIRDS IN MY REALM?
YIKE! W-WHO ARE YOU?
YOU BETTER BEAT IT, YOU CORNY CHARACTER BEFORE I MISTAKE YOU FOR A PACK OF BIRDSEED!
I-I'M G-GOIN' B-BACK H-H-HOME!
AND SOON--
SHOO! SHOO! PLEASE SHOO!
NEED ANY HELP, PAL?
THE END

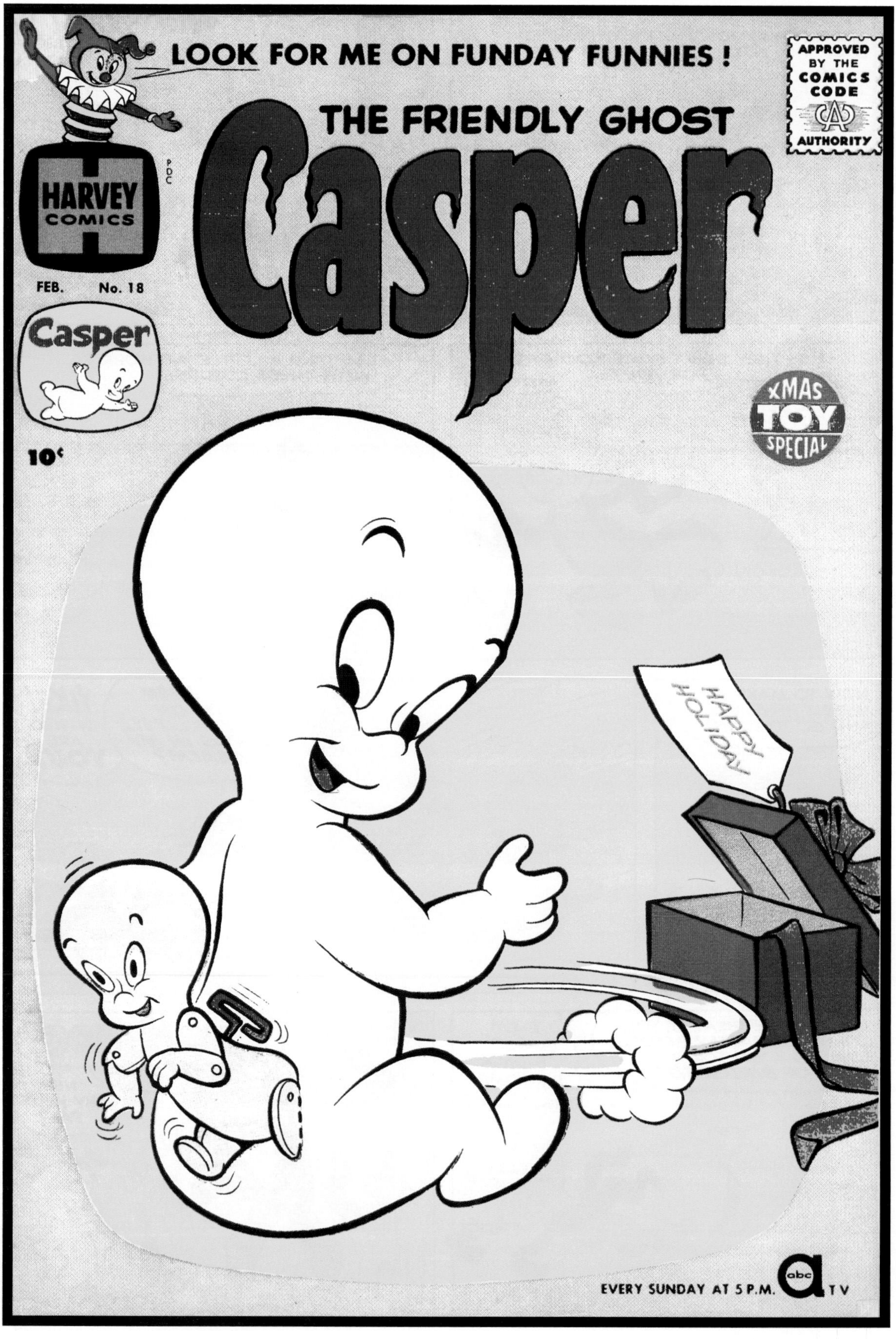
LOOK FOR ME ON FUNDAY FUNNIES !
THE FRIENDLY GHOST
Casper
HARVEY COMICS
APPROVED BY THE COMICS CODE AUTHORITY
FEB.
No. 18
Casper
10¢
XMAS TOY SPECIAL
HAPPY HOLIDAY
EVERY SUNDAY AT 5 P.M.
abc TV

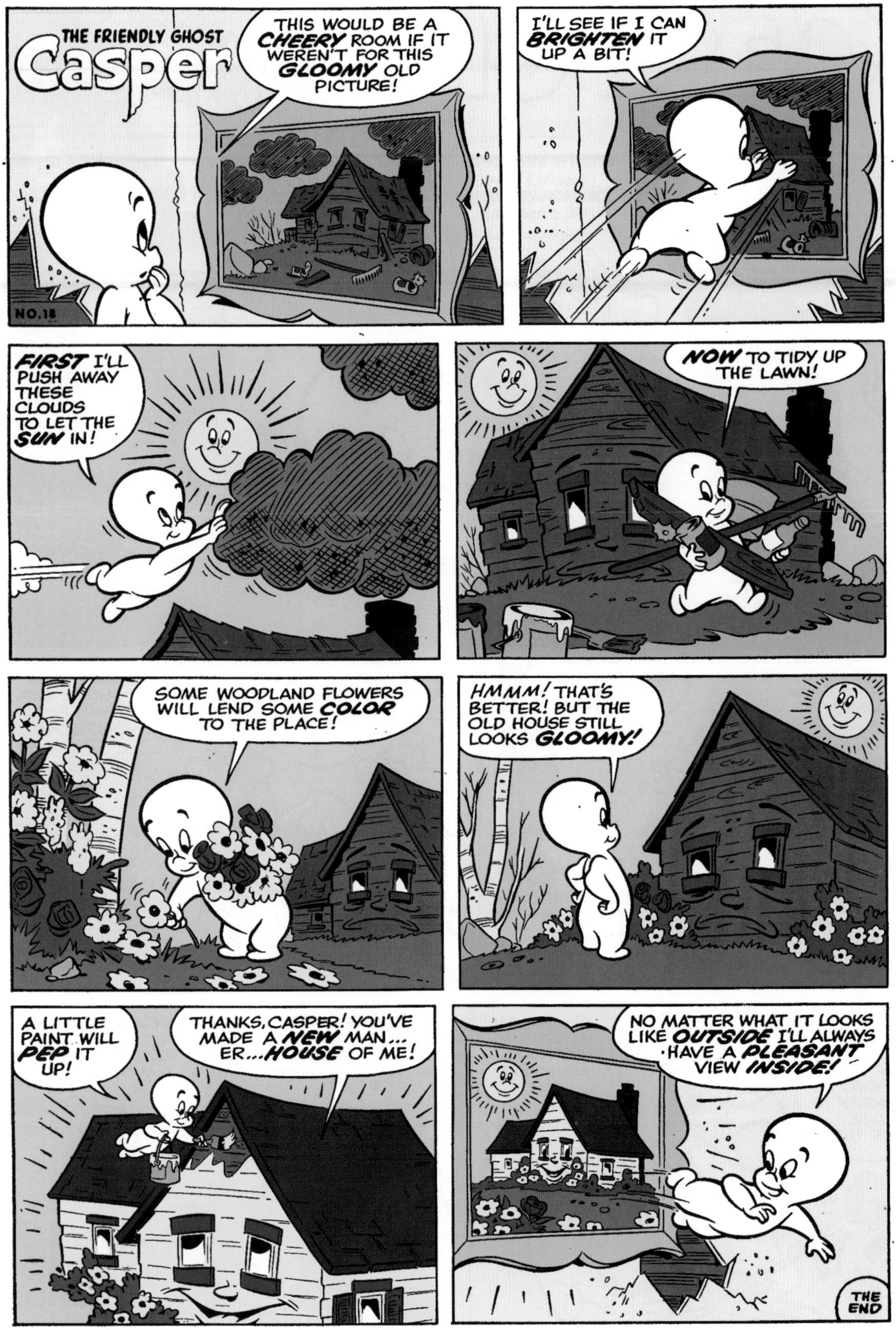
THE FRIENDLY GHOST
Casper
THIS WOULD BE A CHEERY ROOM IF IT WEREN'T FOR THIS GLOOMY OLD PICTURE!
NO.18
I'LL SEE IF I CAN BRIGHTEN IT UP A BIT!
FIRST I'LL PUSH AWAY THESE CLOUDS TO LET THE SUN IN!
NOW TO TIDY UP THE LAWN!
SOME WOODLAND FLOWERS WILL LEND SOME COLOR TO THE PLACE!
HMMM! THAT'S BETTER! BUT THE OLD HOUSE STILL LOOKS GLOOMY!
A LITTLE PAINT WILL PEP IT UP!
THANKS, CASPER! YOU'VE MADE A NEW MAN... ER...HOUSE OF ME!
NO MATTER WHAT IT LOOKS LIKE OUTSIDE I'LL ALWAYS HAVE A PLEASANT VIEW INSIDE!
THE END

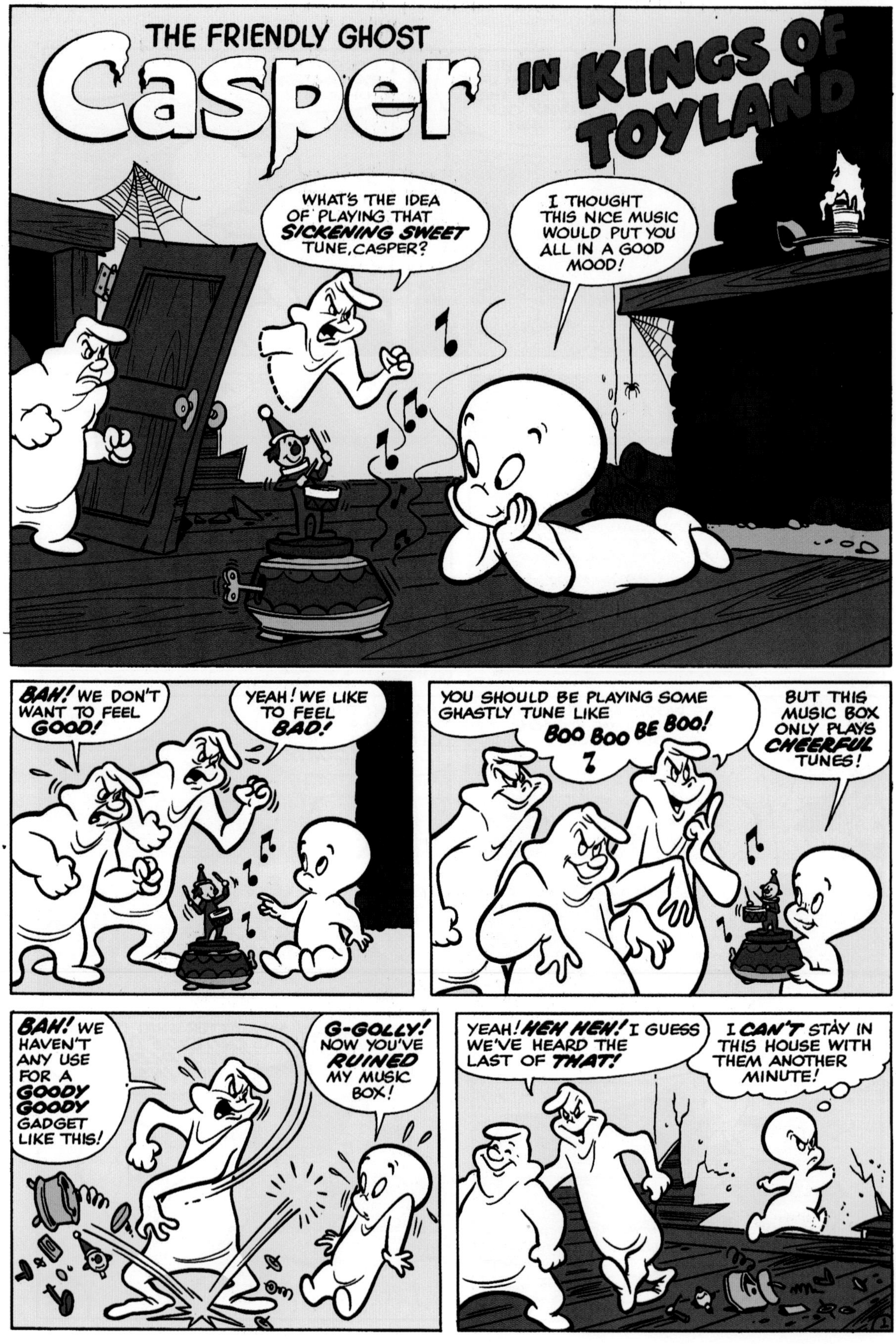
THE FRIENDLY GHOST
Casper
IN KINGS OF TOYLAND
WHAT'S THE IDEA OF PLAYING THAT SICKENING SWEET TUNE, CASPER?
I THOUGHT THIS NICE MUSIC WOULD PUT YOU ALL IN A GOOD MOOD!
BAH! WE DON'T WANT TO FEEL GOOD!
YEAH! WE LIKE TO FEEL BAD!
YOU SHOULD BE PLAYING SOME GHASTLY TUNE LIKE BOO BOO BE BOO!
BUT THIS MUSIC BOX ONLY PLAYS CHEERFUL TUNES!
BAH! WE HAVEN'T ANY USE FOR A GOODY GOODY GADGET LIKE THIS!
G-GOLLY! NOW YOU'VE RUINED MY MUSIC BOX!
YEAH! HEH HEH! I GUESS WE'VE HEARD THE LAST OF THAT!
I CAN'T STAY IN THIS HOUSE WITH THEM ANOTHER MINUTE!

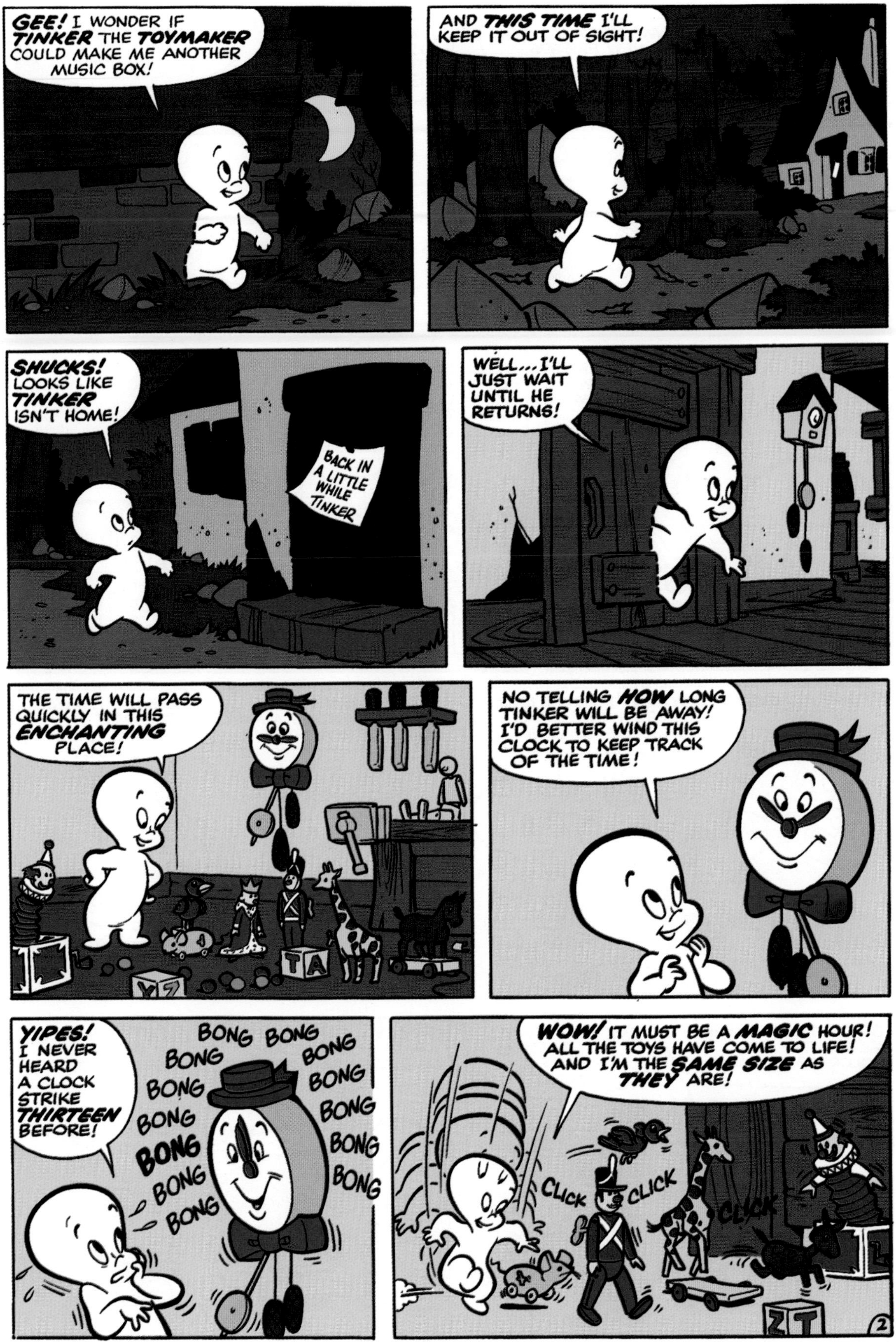
GEE! I WONDER IF TINKER THE TOYMAKER COULD MAKE ME ANOTHER MUSIC BOX!
AND THIS TIME I'LL KEEP IT OUT OF SIGHT!
SHUCKS! LOOKS LIKE TINKER ISN'T HOME!
BACK IN A LITTLE WHILE TINKER
WELL... I'LL JUST WAIT UNTIL HE RETURNS!
THE TIME WILL PASS QUICKLY IN THIS ENCHANTING PLACE!
NO TELLING HOW LONG TINKER WILL BE AWAY! I'D BETTER WIND THIS CLOCK TO KEEP TRACK OF THE TIME!
YIPES! I NEVER HEARD A CLOCK STRIKE THIRTEEN BEFORE!
BONG BONG BONG BONG BONG BONG BONG BONG BONG BONG BONG BONG BONG
WOW! IT MUST BE A MAGIC HOUR! ALL THE TOYS HAVE COME TO LIFE! AND I'M THE SAME SIZE AS THEY ARE!
CLICK CLICK CLICK
2

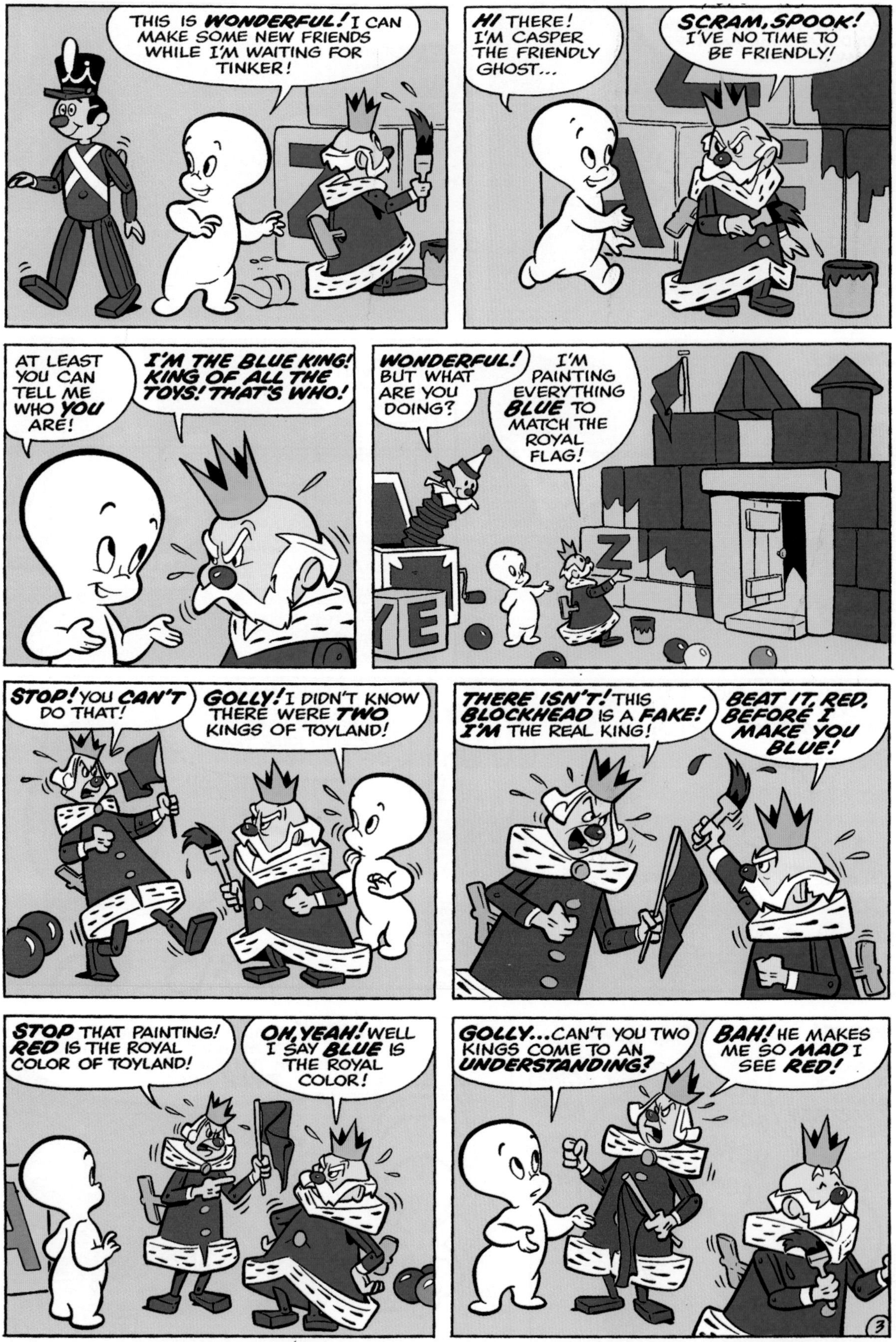
THIS IS WONDERFUL! I CAN MAKE SOME NEW FRIENDS WHILE I'M WAITING FOR TINKER!
HI THERE! I'M CASPER THE FRIENDLY GHOST...
SCRAM, SPOOK! I'VE NO TIME TO BE FRIENDLY!
AT LEAST YOU CAN TELL ME WHO YOU ARE!
I'M THE BLUE KING! KING OF ALL THE TOYS! THAT'S WHO!
WONDERFUL! BUT WHAT ARE YOU DOING?
I'M PAINTING EVERYTHING BLUE TO MATCH THE ROYAL FLAG!
STOP! YOU CAN'T DO THAT!
GOLLY! I DIDN'T KNOW THERE WERE TWO KINGS OF TOYLAND!
THERE ISN'T! THIS BLOCKHEAD IS A FAKE! I'M THE REAL KING!
BEAT IT, RED, BEFORE I MAKE YOU BLUE!
STOP THAT PAINTING! RED IS THE ROYAL COLOR OF TOYLAND!
OH, YEAH! WELL I SAY BLUE IS THE ROYAL COLOR!
GOLLY...CAN'T YOU TWO KINGS COME TO AN UNDERSTANDING?
BAH! HE MAKES ME SO MAD I SEE RED!
3

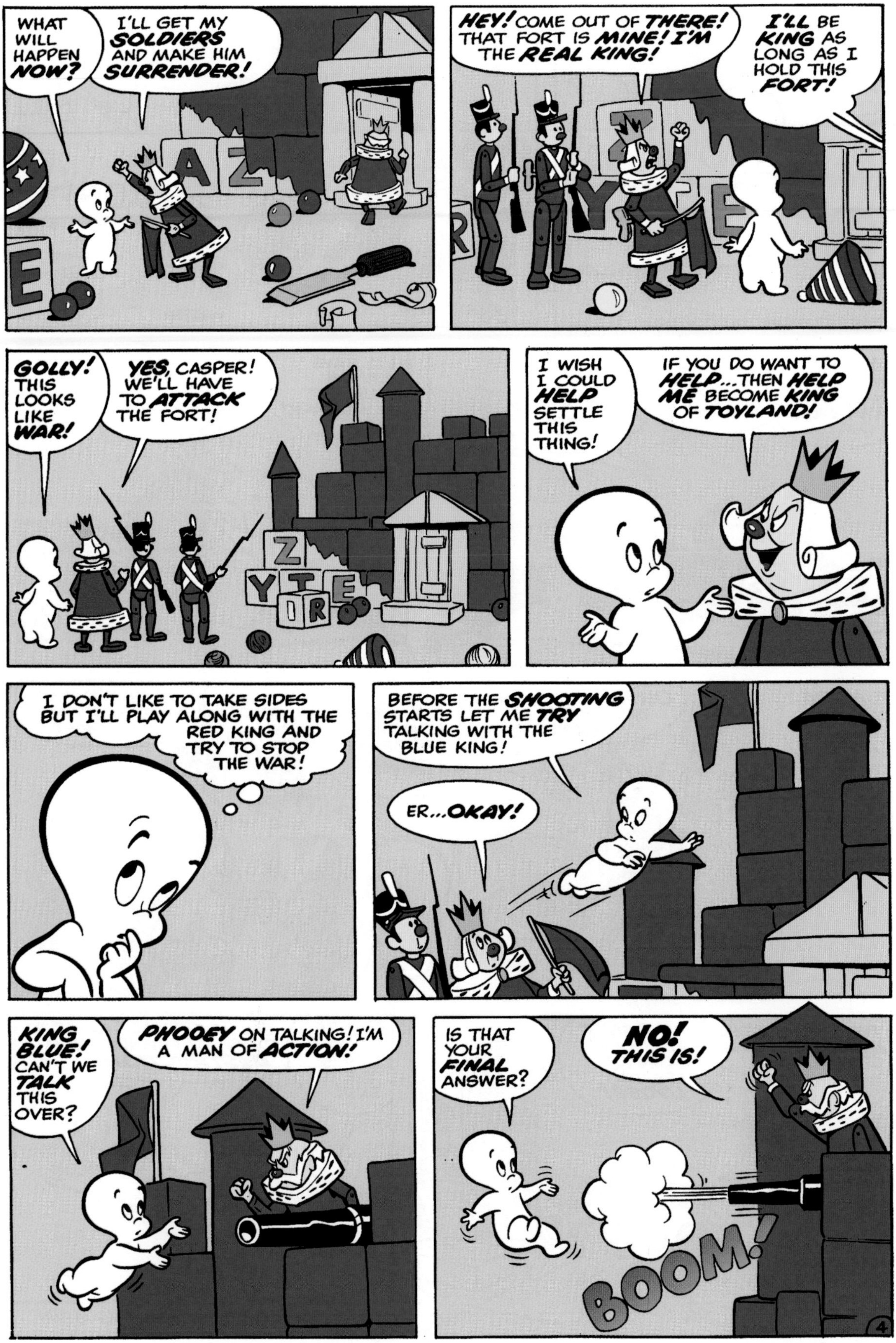
WHAT WILL HAPPEN NOW?
I'LL GET MY SOLDIERS AND MAKE HIM SURRENDER!
HEY! COME OUT OF THERE! THAT FORT IS MINE! I'M THE REAL KING!
I'LL BE KING AS LONG AS I HOLD THIS FORT!
GOLLY! THIS LOOKS LIKE WAR!
YES, CASPER! WE'LL HAVE TO ATTACK THE FORT!
I WISH I COULD HELP SETTLE THIS THING!
IF YOU DO WANT TO HELP...THEN HELP ME BECOME KING OF TOYLAND!
I DON'T LIKE TO TAKE SIDES BUT I'LL PLAY ALONG WITH THE RED KING AND TRY TO STOP THE WAR!
BEFORE THE SHOOTING STARTS LET ME TRY TALKING WITH THE BLUE KING!
ER...OKAY!
KING BLUE! CAN'T WE TALK THIS OVER?
PHOOEY ON TALKING! I'M A MAN OF ACTION!
IS THAT YOUR FINAL ANSWER?
NO! THIS IS!
BOOM!
4

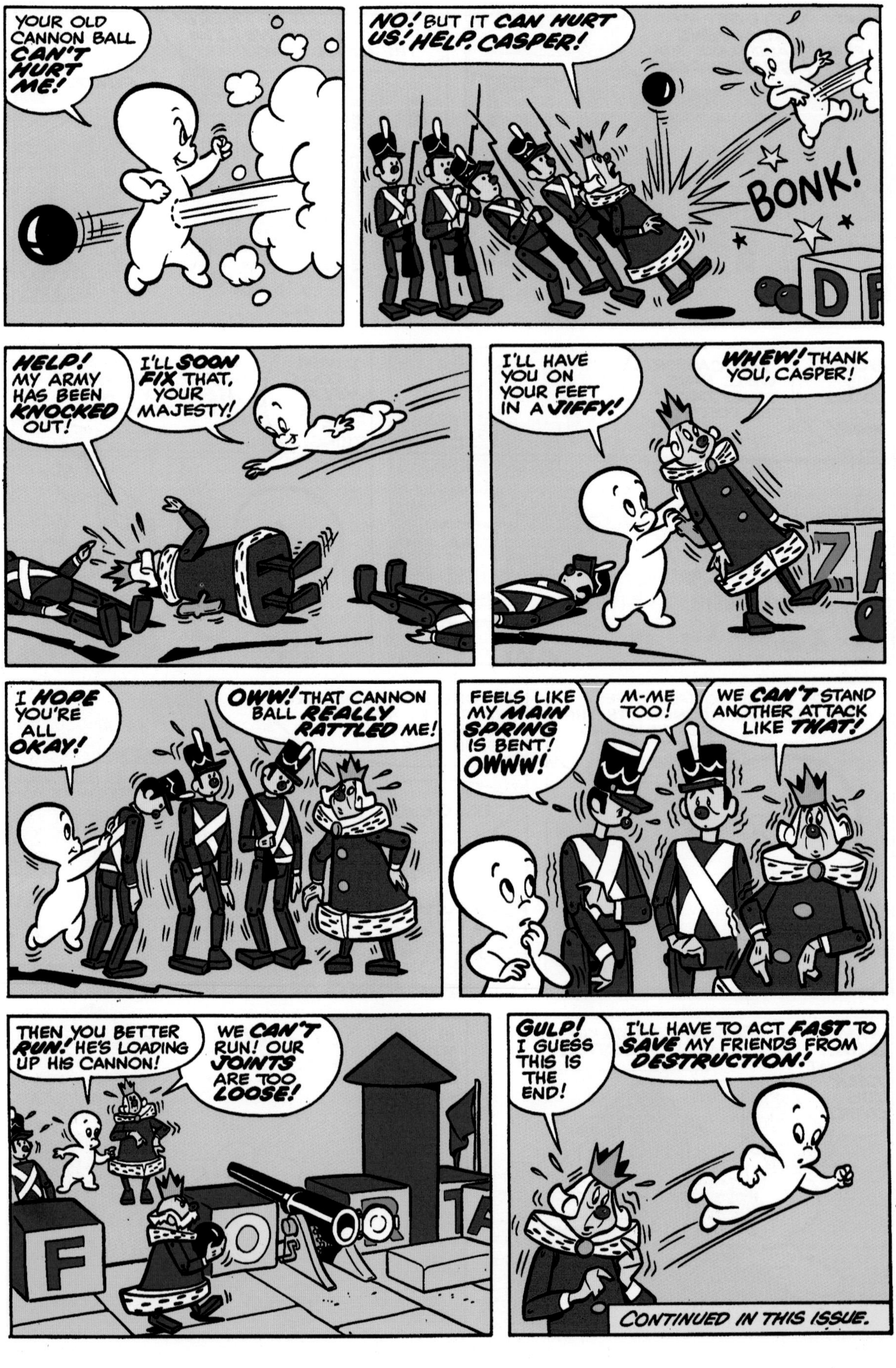
YOUR OLD CANNON BALL CAN'T HURT ME!
NO! BUT IT CAN HURT US! HELP, CASPER!
BONK!
HELP! MY ARMY HAS BEEN KNOCKED OUT!
I'LL SOON FIX THAT, YOUR MAJESTY!
I'LL HAVE YOU ON YOUR FEET IN A JIFFY!
WHEW! THANK YOU, CASPER!
I HOPE YOU'RE ALL OKAY!
OWW! THAT CANNON BALL REALLY RATTLED ME!
FEELS LIKE MY MAIN SPRING IS BENT! OWWW!
M-ME TOO!
WE CAN'T STAND ANOTHER ATTACK LIKE THAT!
THEN YOU BETTER RUN! HE'S LOADING UP HIS CANNON!
WE CAN'T RUN! OUR JOINTS ARE TOO LOOSE!
GULP! I GUESS THIS IS THE END!
I'LL HAVE TO ACT FAST TO SAVE MY FRIENDS FROM DESTRUCTION!
CONTINUED IN THIS ISSUE.

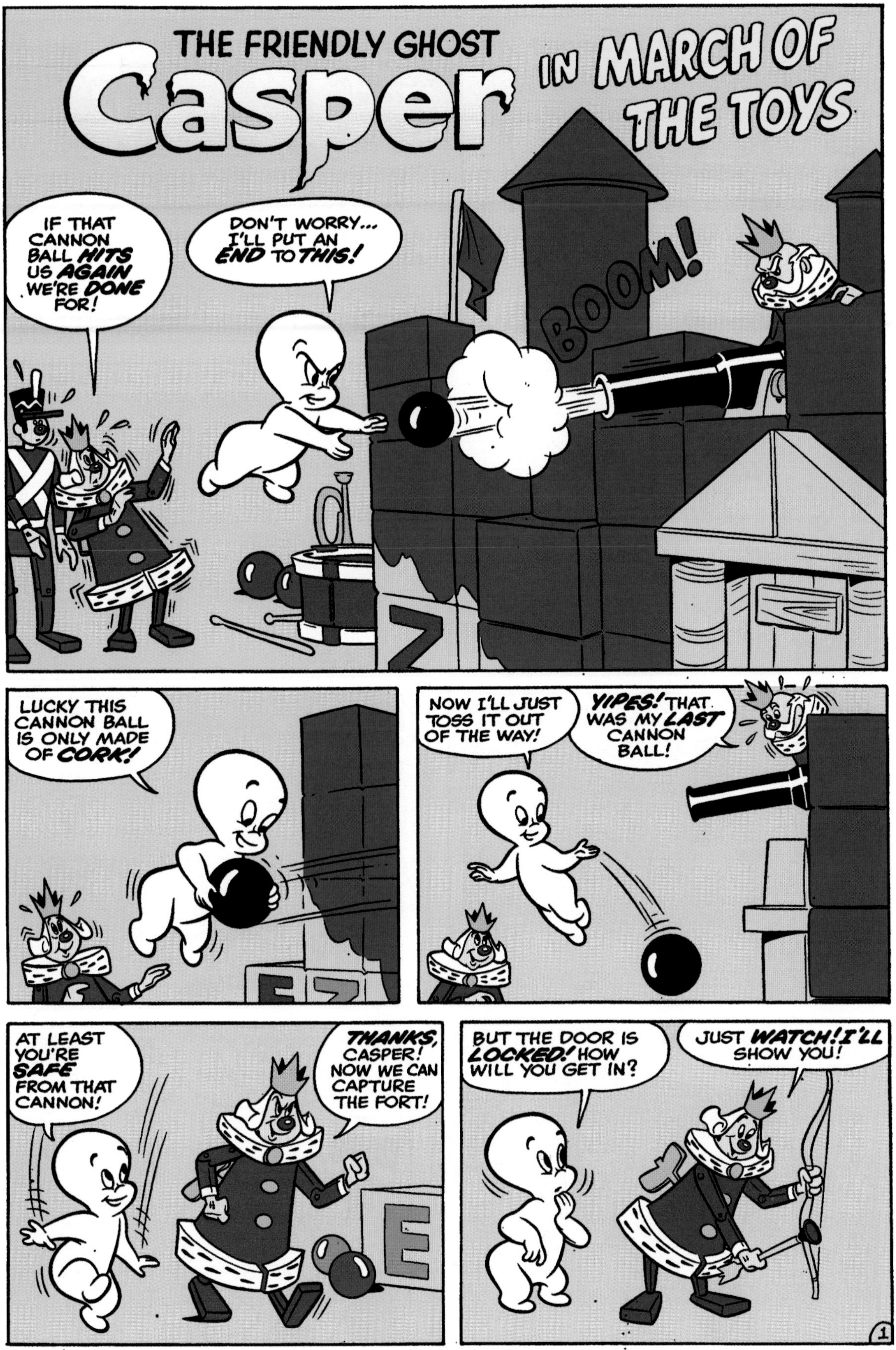
THE FRIENDLY GHOST
Casper
IN MARCH OF THE TOYS
IF THAT CANNON BALL HITS US AGAIN WE'RE DONE FOR!
DON'T WORRY... I'LL PUT AN END TO THIS!
BOOM!
LUCKY THIS CANNON BALL IS ONLY MADE OF CORK!
NOW I'LL JUST TOSS IT OUT OF THE WAY!
YIPES! THAT WAS MY LAST CANNON BALL!
AT LEAST YOU'RE SAFE FROM THAT CANNON!
THANKS, CASPER! NOW WE CAN CAPTURE THE FORT!
BUT THE DOOR IS LOCKED! HOW WILL YOU GET IN?
JUST WATCH! I'LL SHOW YOU!
1

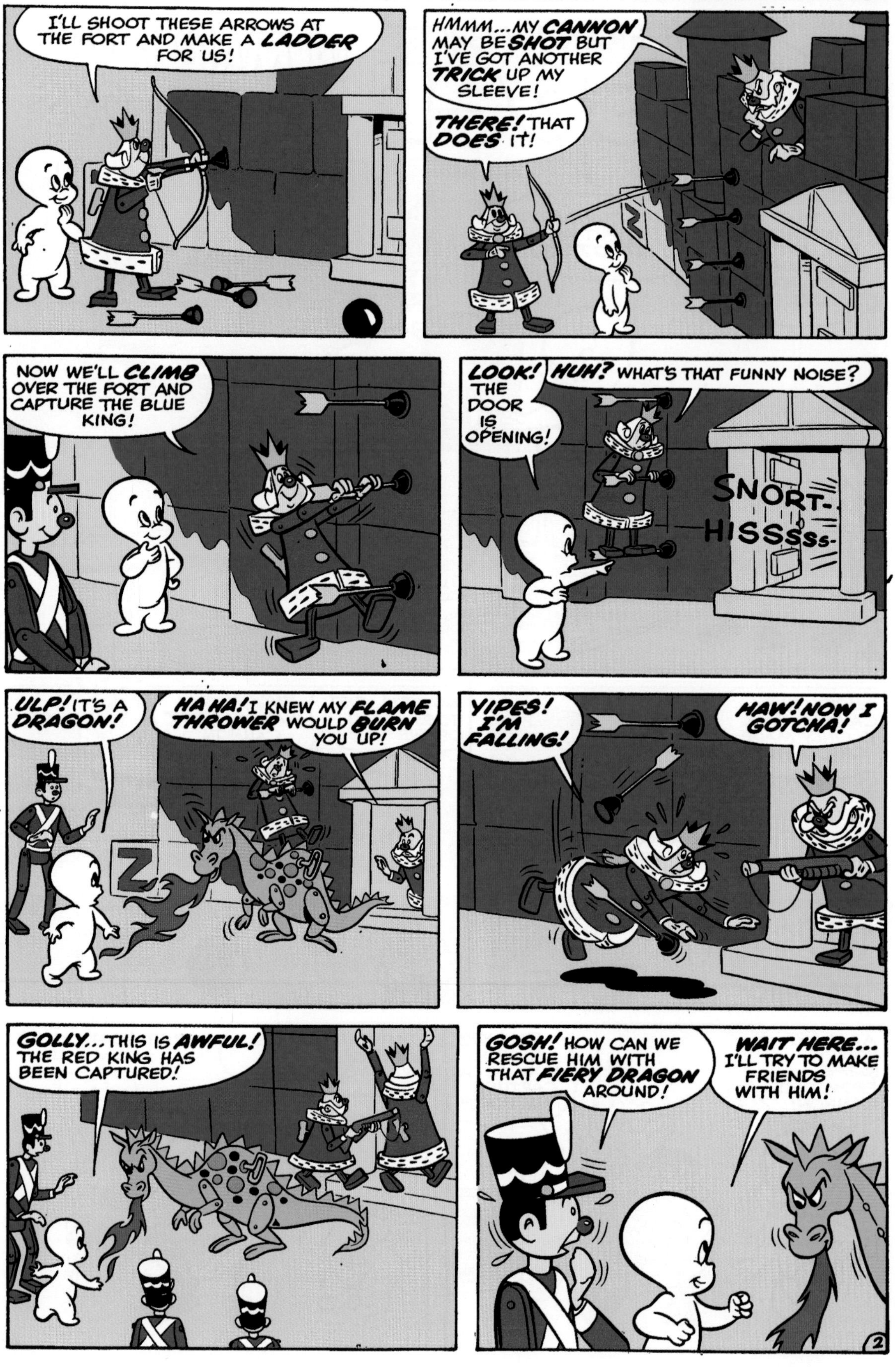
I'LL SHOOT THESE ARROWS AT THE FORT AND MAKE A LADDER FOR US!
HMMM... MY CANNON MAY BE SHOT BUT I'VE GOT ANOTHER TRICK UP MY SLEEVE!
THERE! THAT DOES IT!
NOW WE'LL CLIMB OVER THE FORT AND CAPTURE THE BLUE KING!
LOOK! THE DOOR IS OPENING!
HUH? WHAT'S THAT FUNNY NOISE?
SNORT-HISSSSS-
ULP! IT'S A DRAGON!
HA HA! I KNEW MY FLAME THROWER WOULD BURN YOU UP!
YIPES! I'M FALLING!
HAW! NOW I GOTCHA!
GOLLY... THIS IS AWFUL! THE RED KING HAS BEEN CAPTURED!
GOSH! HOW CAN WE RESCUE HIM WITH THAT FIERY DRAGON AROUND!
WAIT HERE... I'LL TRY TO MAKE FRIENDS WITH HIM!
2

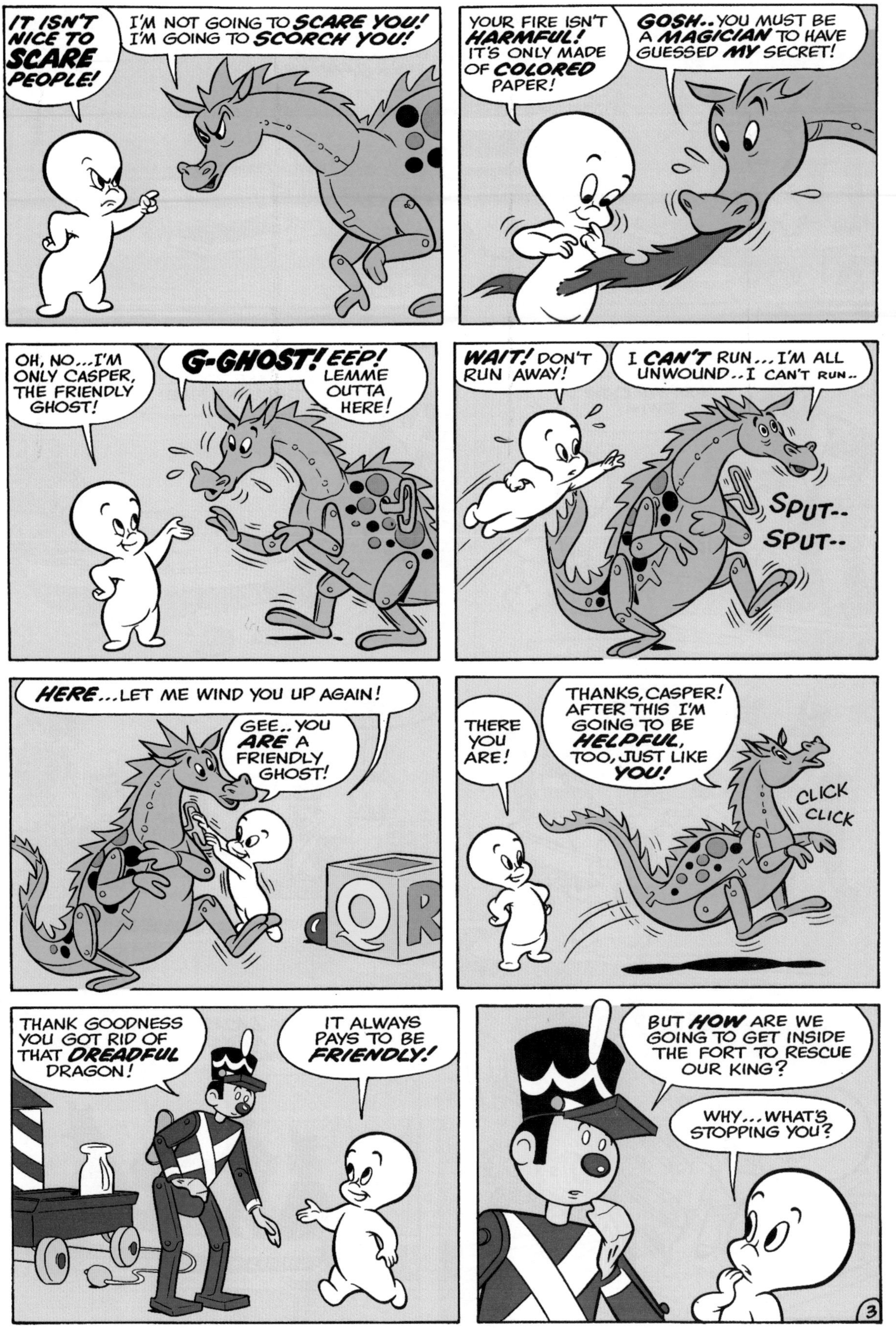
IT ISN'T NICE TO SCARE PEOPLE!
I'M NOT GOING TO SCARE YOU! I'M GOING TO SCORCH YOU!
YOUR FIRE ISN'T HARMFUL! IT'S ONLY MADE OF COLORED PAPER!
GOSH.. YOU MUST BE A MAGICIAN TO HAVE GUESSED MY SECRET!
OH, NO...I'M ONLY CASPER, THE FRIENDLY GHOST!
G-GHOST! EEP! LEMME OUTTA HERE!
WAIT! DON'T RUN AWAY!
I CAN'T RUN... I'M ALL UNWOUND.. I CAN'T RUN..
SPUT-- SPUT--
HERE...LET ME WIND YOU UP AGAIN!
GEE.. YOU ARE A FRIENDLY GHOST!
THERE YOU ARE!
THANKS, CASPER! AFTER THIS I'M GOING TO BE HELPFUL, TOO, JUST LIKE YOU!
CLICK CLICK
THANK GOODNESS YOU GOT RID OF THAT DREADFUL DRAGON!
IT ALWAYS PAYS TO BE FRIENDLY!
BUT HOW ARE WE GOING TO GET INSIDE THE FORT TO RESCUE OUR KING?
WHY...WHAT'S STOPPING YOU?
3

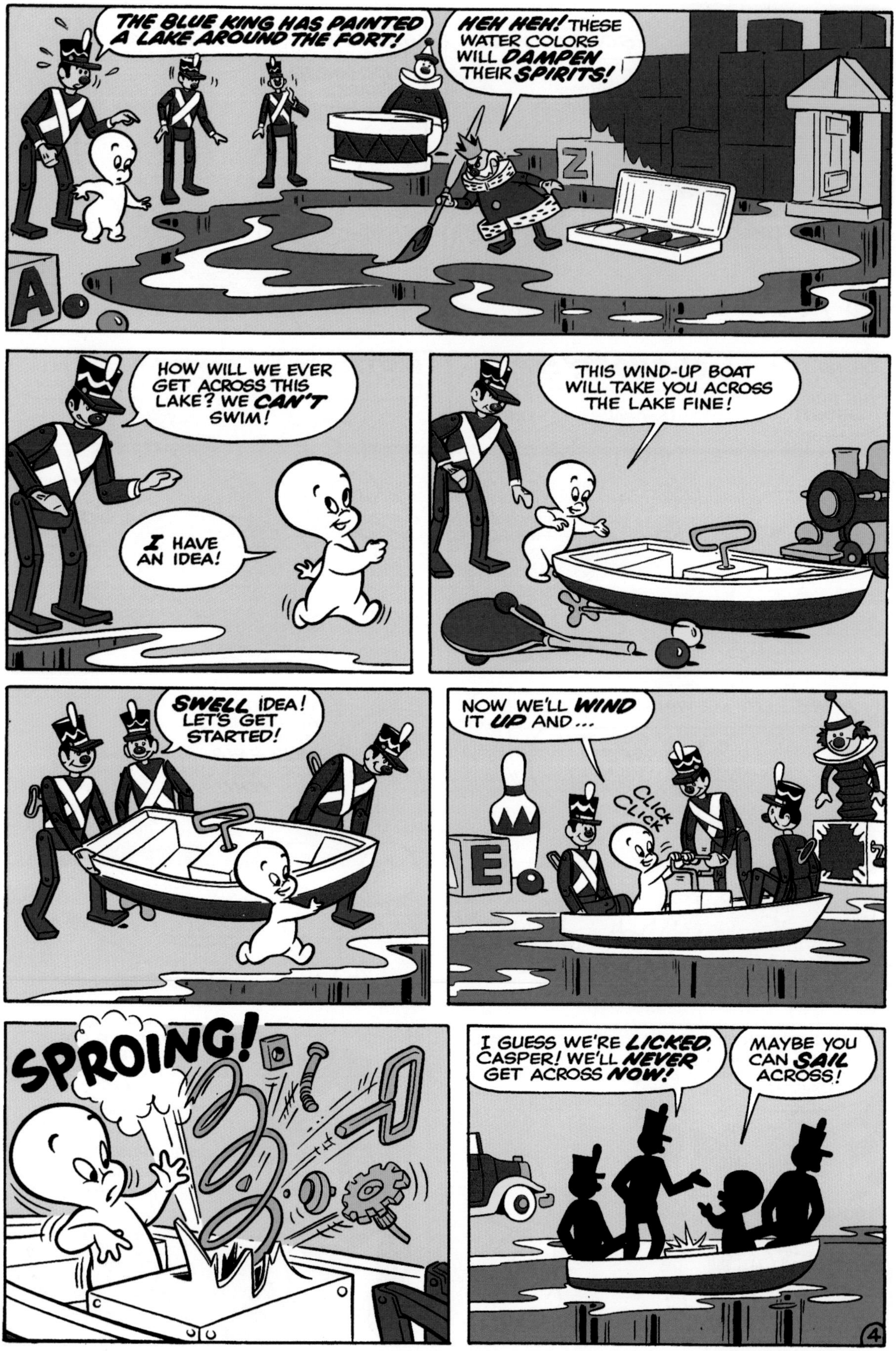
THE BLUE KING HAS PAINTED A LAKE AROUND THE FORT!
HEH HEH! THESE WATER COLORS WILL DAMPEN THEIR SPIRITS!
Z
A
HOW WILL WE EVER GET ACROSS THIS LAKE? WE CAN'T SWIM!
I HAVE AN IDEA!
THIS WIND-UP BOAT WILL TAKE YOU ACROSS THE LAKE FINE!
SWELL IDEA! LET'S GET STARTED!
NOW WE'LL WIND IT UP AND...
CLICK CLICK
E
SPROING!
I GUESS WE'RE LICKED, CASPER! WE'LL NEVER GET ACROSS NOW!
MAYBE YOU CAN SAIL ACROSS!
4

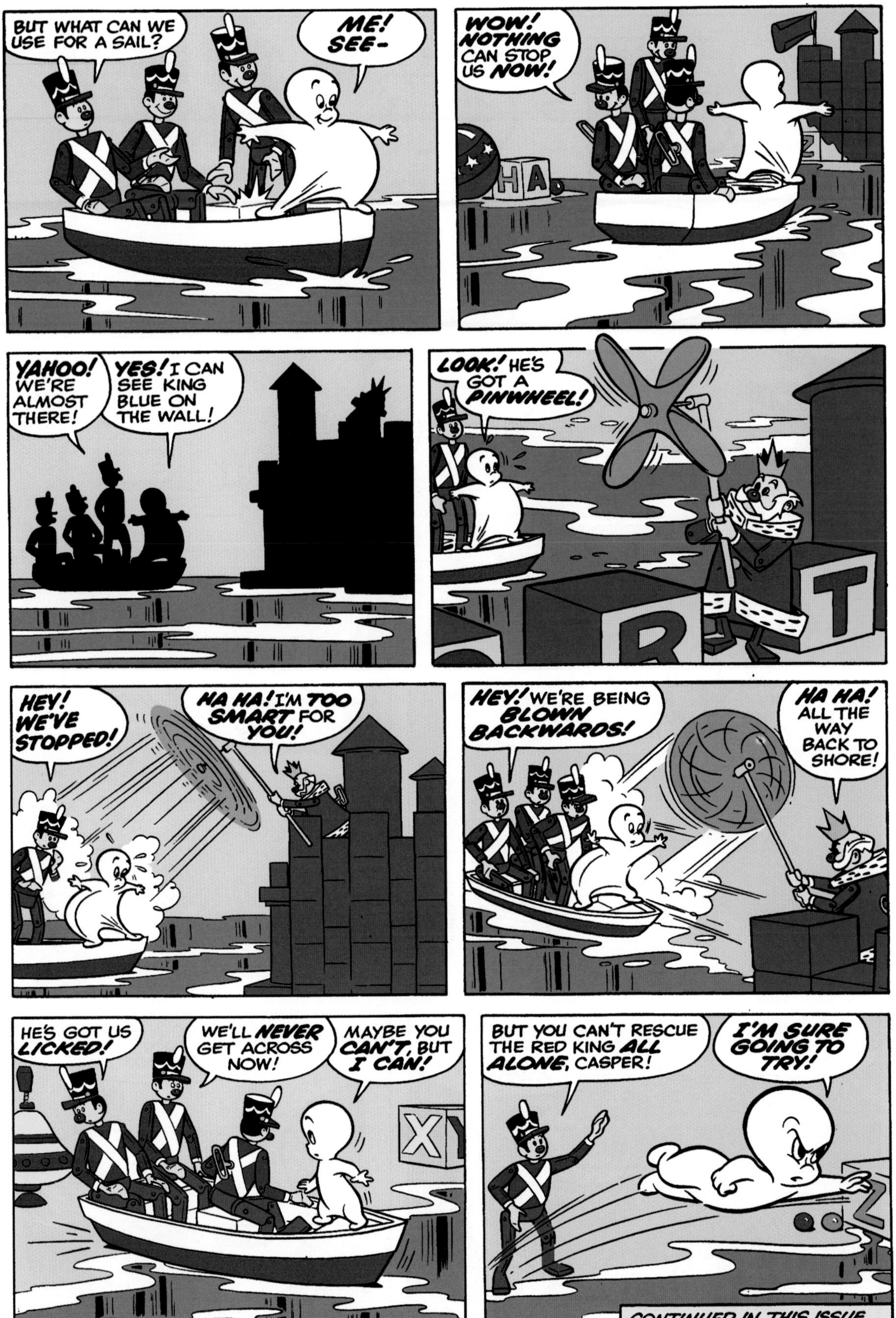
BUT WHAT CAN WE USE FOR A SAIL?
ME! SEE-
WOW! NOTHING CAN STOP US NOW!
YAHOO! WE'RE ALMOST THERE!
YES! I CAN SEE KING BLUE ON THE WALL!
LOOK! HE'S GOT A PINWHEEL!
HEY! WE'VE STOPPED!
HA HA! I'M TOO SMART FOR YOU!
HEY! WE'RE BEING BLOWN BACKWARDS!
HA HA! ALL THE WAY BACK TO SHORE!
HE'S GOT US LICKED!
WE'LL NEVER GET ACROSS NOW!
MAYBE YOU CAN'T, BUT I CAN!
BUT YOU CAN'T RESCUE THE RED KING ALL ALONE, CASPER!
I'M SURE GOING TO TRY!
CONTINUED IN THIS ISSUE.

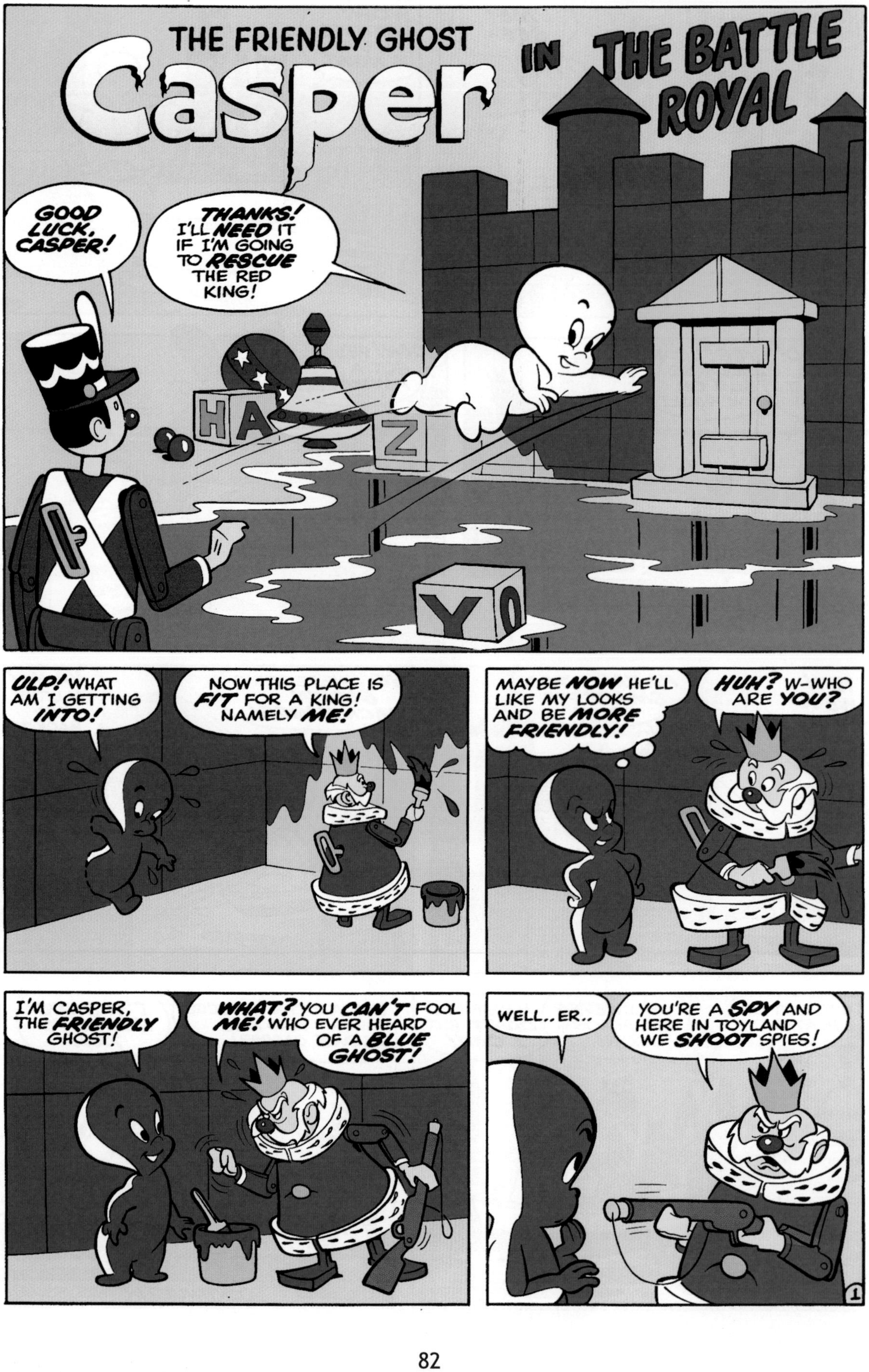
THE FRIENDLY GHOST
Casper
IN THE BATTLE ROYAL
GOOD LUCK, CASPER!
THANKS! I'LL NEED IT IF I'M GOING TO RESCUE THE RED KING!
HA
Z
YO
ULP! WHAT AM I GETTING INTO!
NOW THIS PLACE IS FIT FOR A KING! NAMELY ME!
MAYBE NOW HE'LL LIKE MY LOOKS AND BE MORE FRIENDLY!
HUH? W-WHO ARE YOU?
I'M CASPER, THE FRIENDLY GHOST!
WHAT? YOU CAN'T FOOL ME! WHO EVER HEARD OF A BLUE GHOST!
WELL.. ER..
YOU'RE A SPY AND HERE IN TOYLAND WE SHOOT SPIES!
1

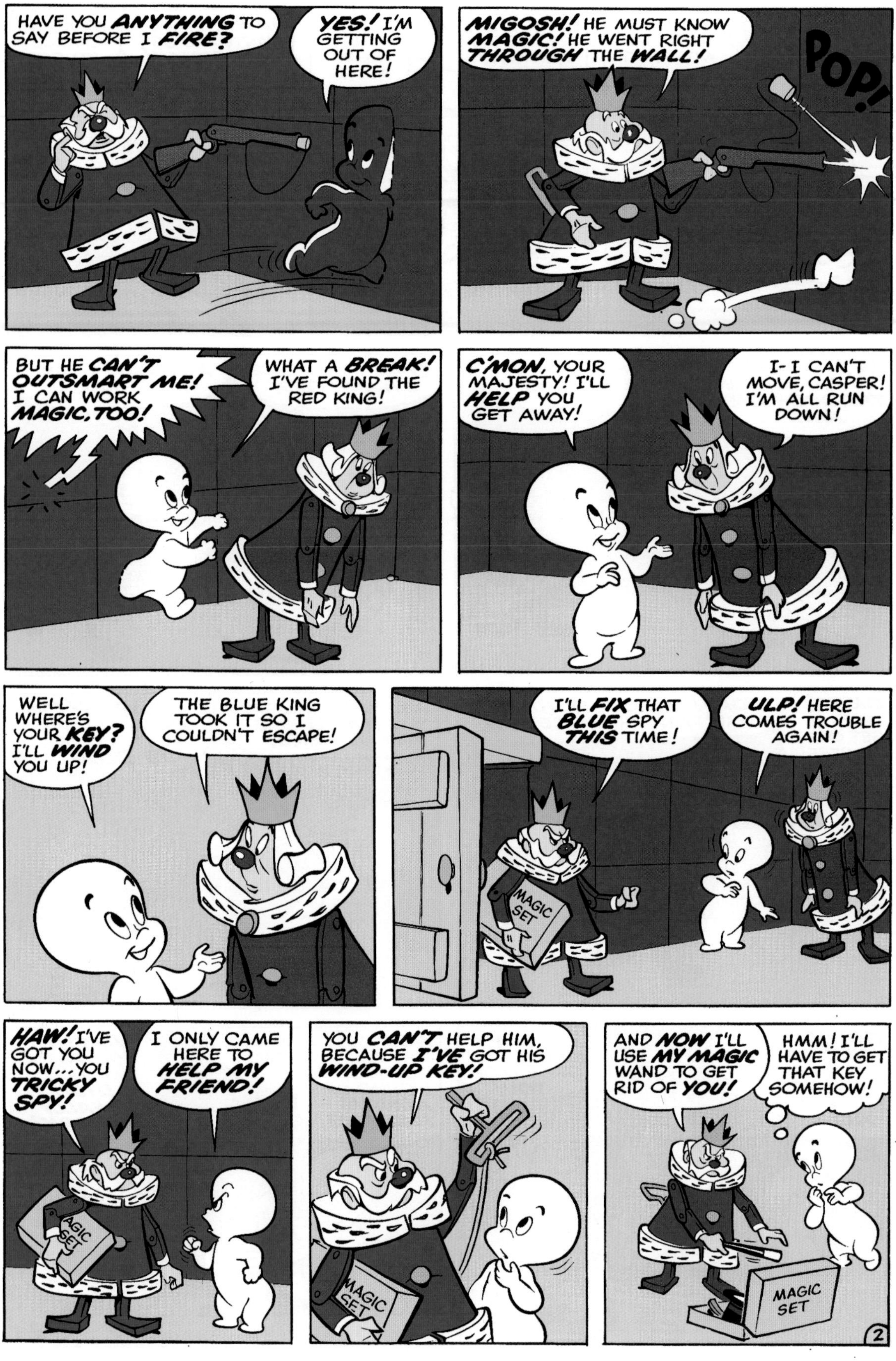
HAVE YOU ANYTHING TO SAY BEFORE I FIRE?
YES! I'M GETTING OUT OF HERE!
MIGOSH! HE MUST KNOW MAGIC! HE WENT RIGHT THROUGH THE WALL!
POP!
BUT HE CAN'T OUTSMART ME! I CAN WORK MAGIC, TOO!
WHAT A BREAK! I'VE FOUND THE RED KING!
C'MON, YOUR MAJESTY! I'LL HELP YOU GET AWAY!
I-I CAN'T MOVE, CASPER! I'M ALL RUN DOWN!
WELL WHERE'S YOUR KEY? I'LL WIND YOU UP!
THE BLUE KING TOOK IT SO I COULDN'T ESCAPE!
I'LL FIX THAT BLUE SPY THIS TIME!
ULP! HERE COMES TROUBLE AGAIN!
MAGIC SET
HAW! I'VE GOT YOU NOW... YOU TRICKY SPY!
I ONLY CAME HERE TO HELP MY FRIEND!
YOU CAN'T HELP HIM, BECAUSE I'VE GOT HIS WIND-UP KEY!
AND NOW I'LL USE MY MAGIC WAND TO GET RID OF YOU!
HMM! I'LL HAVE TO GET THAT KEY SOMEHOW!
MAGIC SET
2

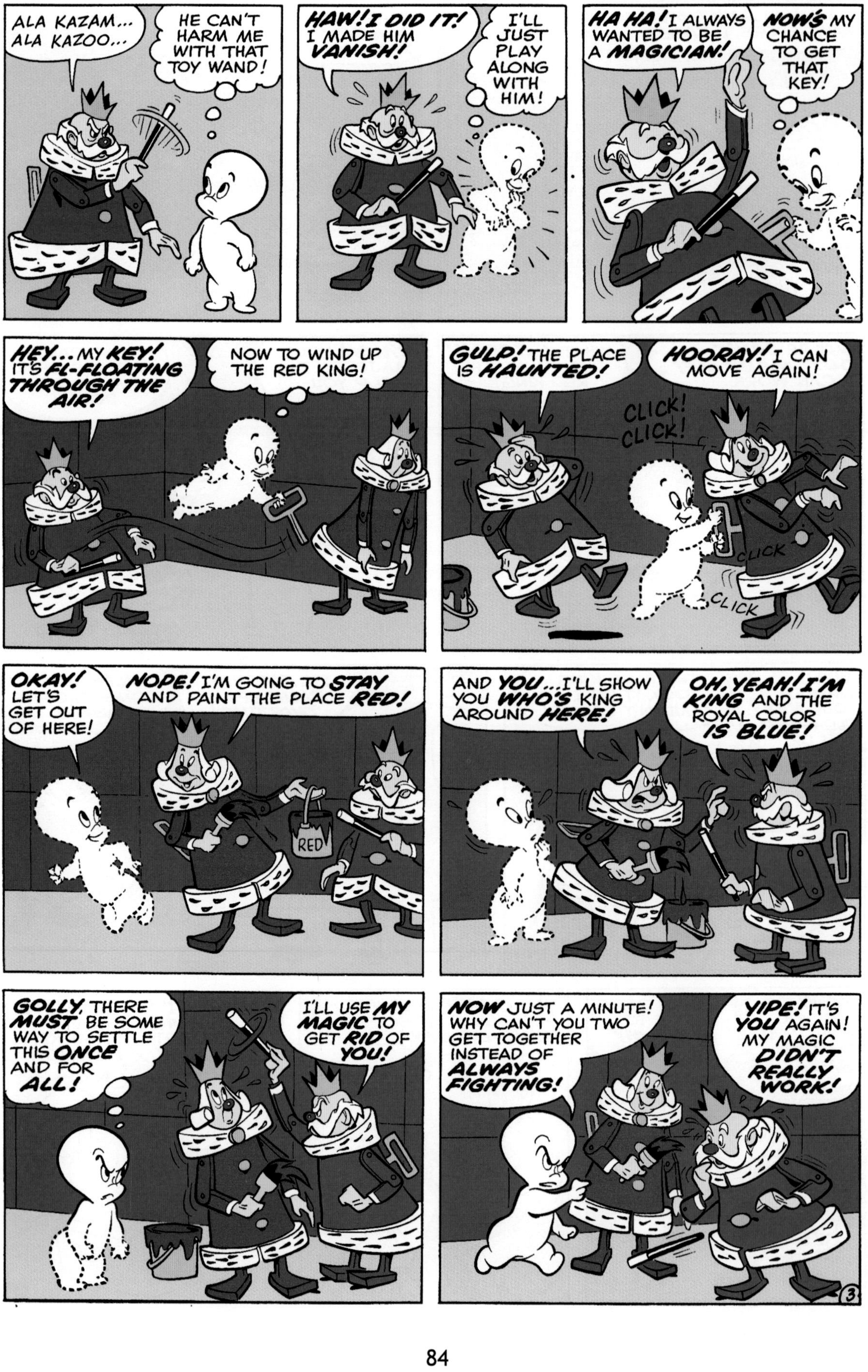
ALA KAZAM... ALA KAZOO...
HE CAN'T HARM ME WITH THAT TOY WAND!
HAW! I DID IT! I MADE HIM VANISH!
I'LL JUST PLAY ALONG WITH HIM!
HA HA! I ALWAYS WANTED TO BE A MAGICIAN!
NOW'S MY CHANCE TO GET THAT KEY!
HEY... MY KEY! IT'S FL-FLOATING THROUGH THE AIR!
NOW TO WIND UP THE RED KING!
GULP! THE PLACE IS HAUNTED!
HOORAY! I CAN MOVE AGAIN!
CLICK! CLICK!
CLICK
CLICK
OKAY! LET'S GET OUT OF HERE!
NOPE! I'M GOING TO STAY AND PAINT THE PLACE RED!
RED
AND YOU...I'LL SHOW YOU WHO'S KING AROUND HERE!
OH, YEAH! I'M KING AND THE ROYAL COLOR IS BLUE!
GOLLY, THERE MUST BE SOME WAY TO SETTLE THIS ONCE AND FOR ALL!
I'LL USE MY MAGIC TO GET RID OF YOU!
NOW JUST A MINUTE! WHY CAN'T YOU TWO GET TOGETHER INSTEAD OF ALWAYS FIGHTING!
YIPE! IT'S YOU AGAIN! MY MAGIC DIDN'T REALLY WORK!
3

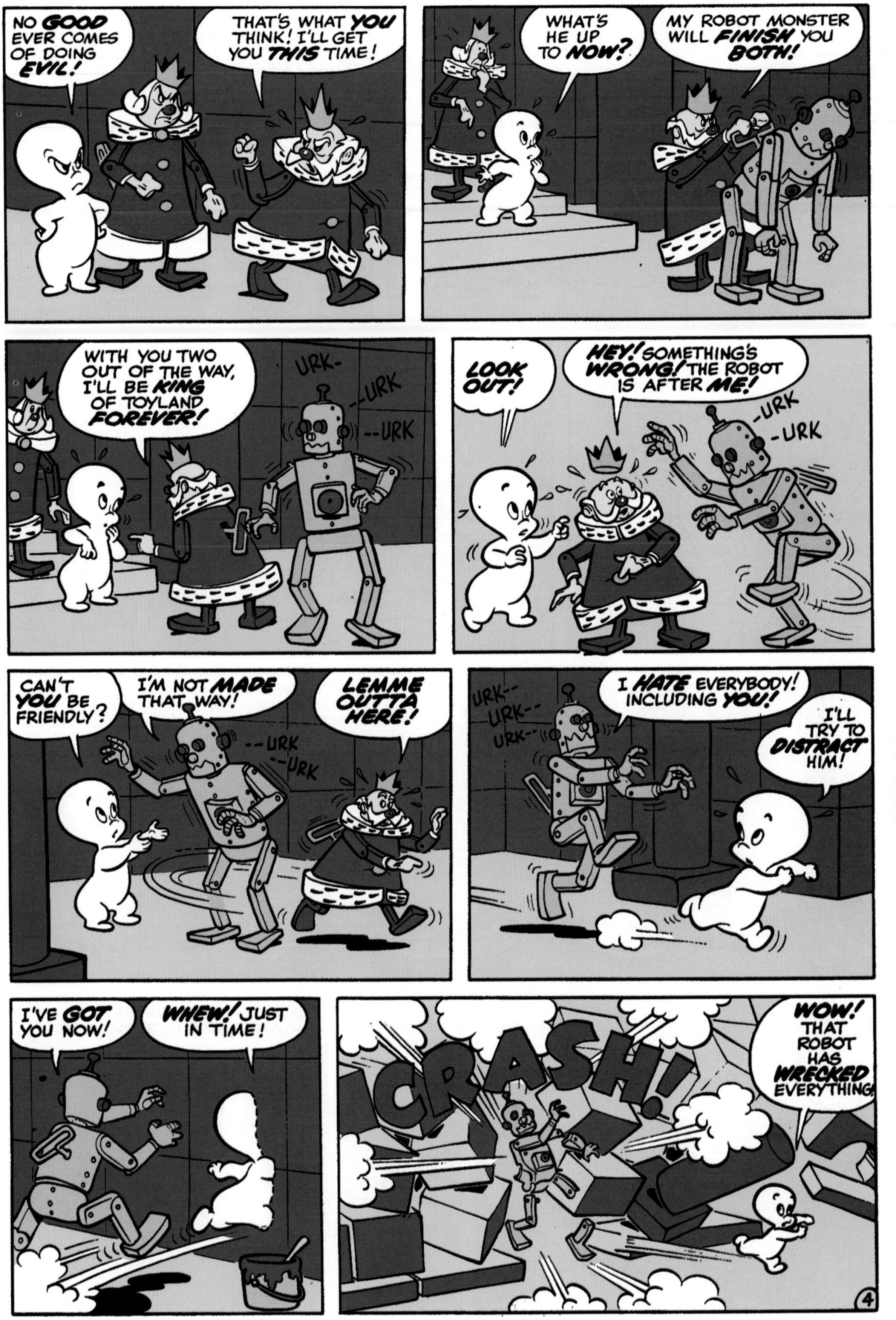
NO GOOD EVER COMES OF DOING EVIL!
THAT'S WHAT YOU THINK! I'LL GET YOU THIS TIME!
WHAT'S HE UP TO NOW?
MY ROBOT MONSTER WILL FINISH YOU BOTH!
WITH YOU TWO OUT OF THE WAY, I'LL BE KING OF TOYLAND FOREVER!
URK- --URK --URK
LOOK OUT!
HEY! SOMETHING'S WRONG! THE ROBOT IS AFTER ME!
-URK -URK
CAN'T YOU BE FRIENDLY?
I'M NOT MADE THAT WAY!
--URK --URK
LEMME OUTTA HERE!
URK-- URK-- URK--
I HATE EVERYBODY! INCLUDING YOU!
I'LL TRY TO DISTRACT HIM!
I'VE GOT YOU NOW!
WHEW! JUST IN TIME!
CRASH!
WOW! THAT ROBOT HAS WRECKED EVERYTHING!
4

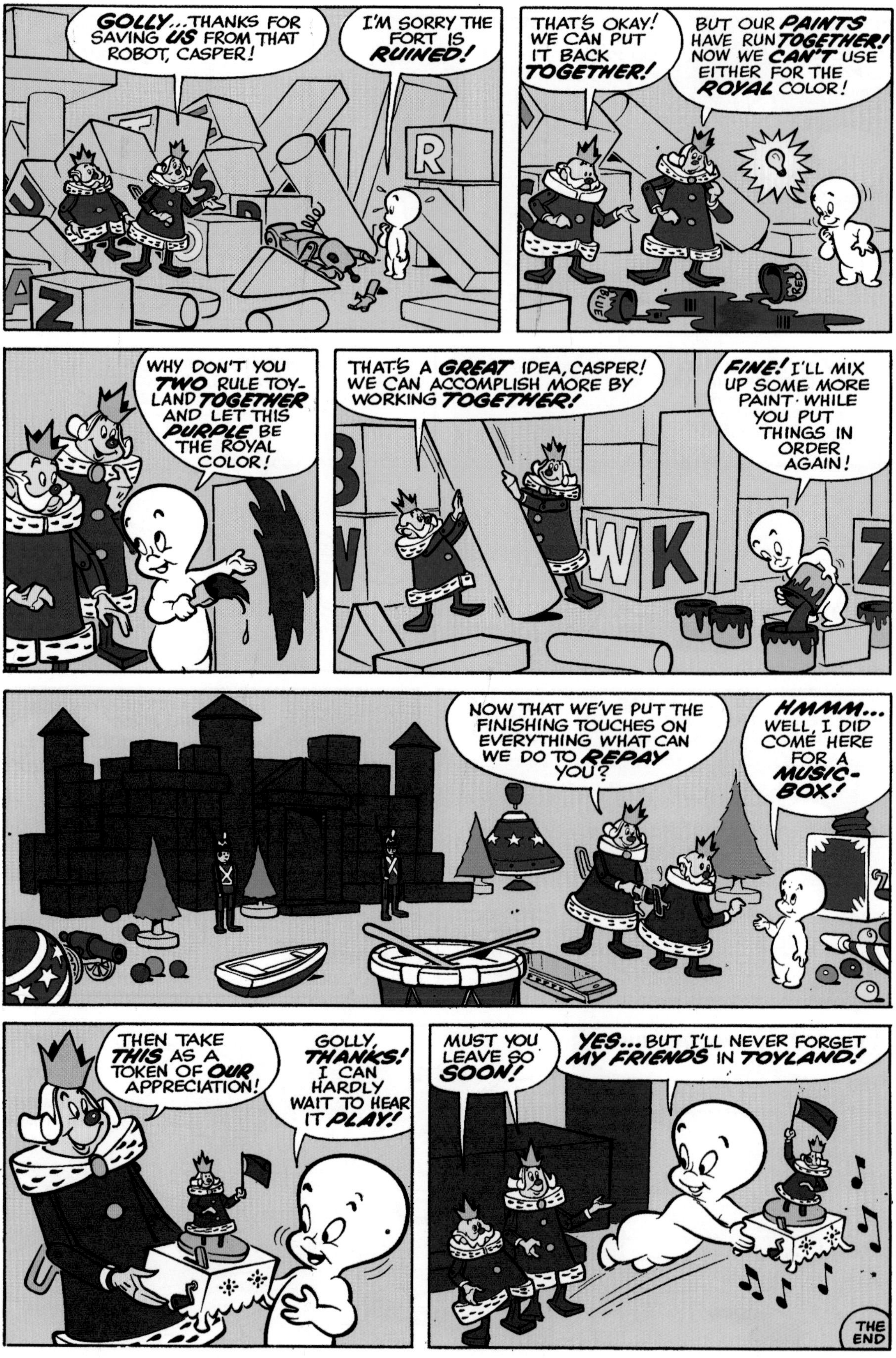
GOLLY...THANKS FOR SAVING US FROM THAT ROBOT, CASPER!
I'M SORRY THE FORT IS RUINED!
R
THAT'S OKAY! WE CAN PUT IT BACK TOGETHER!
BUT OUR PAINTS HAVE RUN TOGETHER! NOW WE CAN'T USE EITHER FOR THE ROYAL COLOR!
BLUE
RED
WHY DON'T YOU TWO RULE TOY-LAND TOGETHER AND LET THIS PURPLE BE THE ROYAL COLOR!
THAT'S A GREAT IDEA, CASPER! WE CAN ACCOMPLISH MORE BY WORKING TOGETHER!
FINE! I'LL MIX UP SOME MORE PAINT WHILE YOU PUT THINGS IN ORDER AGAIN!
W K
NOW THAT WE'VE PUT THE FINISHING TOUCHES ON EVERYTHING WHAT CAN WE DO TO REPAY YOU?
HMMM... WELL, I DID COME HERE FOR A MUSIC-BOX!
THEN TAKE THIS AS A TOKEN OF OUR APPRECIATION!
GOLLY, THANKS! I CAN HARDLY WAIT TO HEAR IT PLAY!
MUST YOU LEAVE SO SOON!
YES... BUT I'LL NEVER FORGET MY FRIENDS IN TOYLAND!
THE END

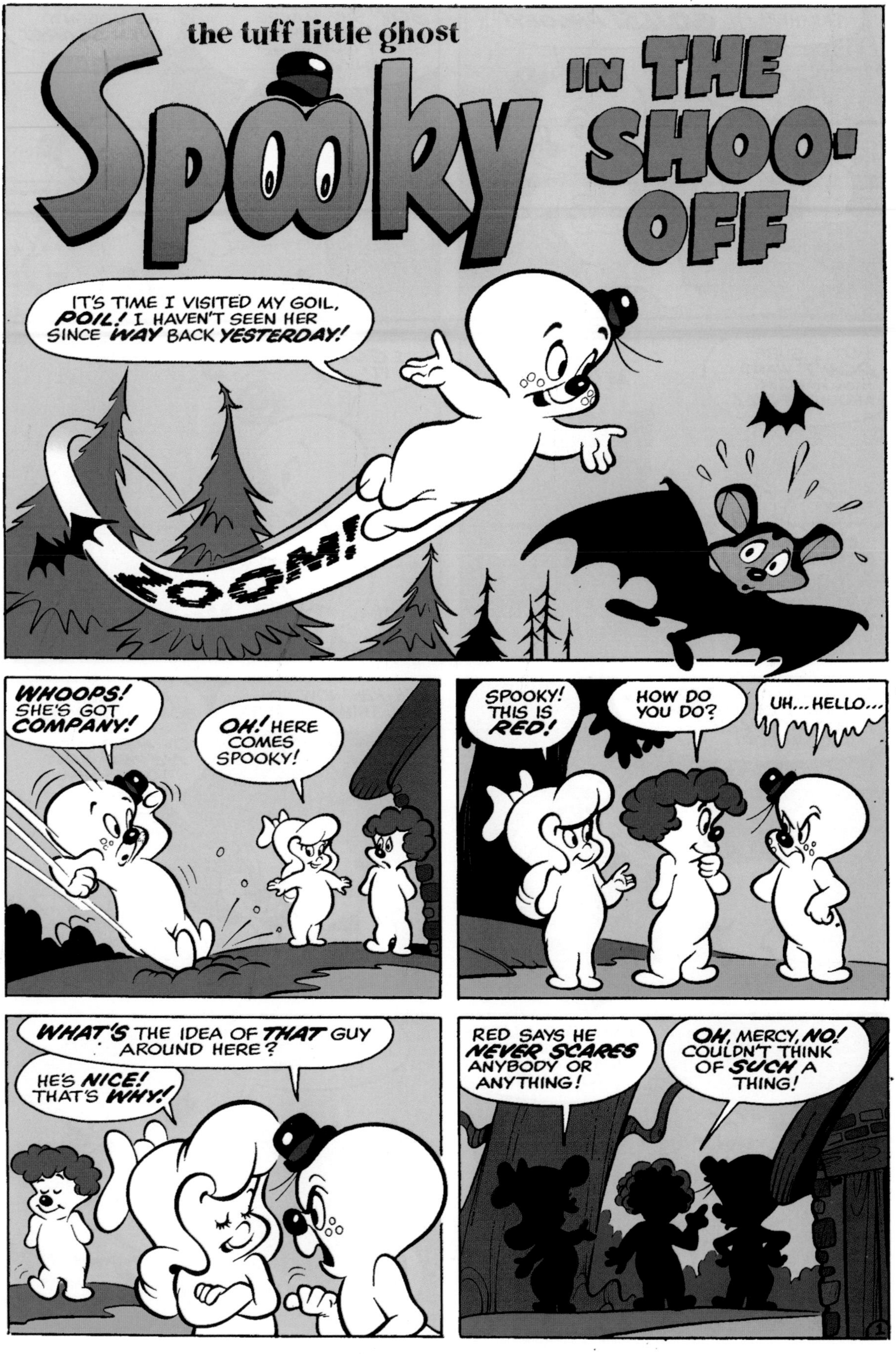
the tuff little ghost
Spooky
IN THE SHOO-OFF
IT'S TIME I VISITED MY GOIL, POIL! I HAVEN'T SEEN HER SINCE WAY BACK YESTERDAY!
ZOOM!
WHOOPS! SHE'S GOT COMPANY!
OH! HERE COMES SPOOKY!
SPOOKY! THIS IS RED!
HOW DO YOU DO?
UH... HELLO...
WHAT'S THE IDEA OF THAT GUY AROUND HERE?
HE'S NICE! THAT'S WHY!
RED SAYS HE NEVER SCARES ANYBODY OR ANYTHING!
OH, MERCY, NO! COULDN'T THINK OF SUCH A THING!

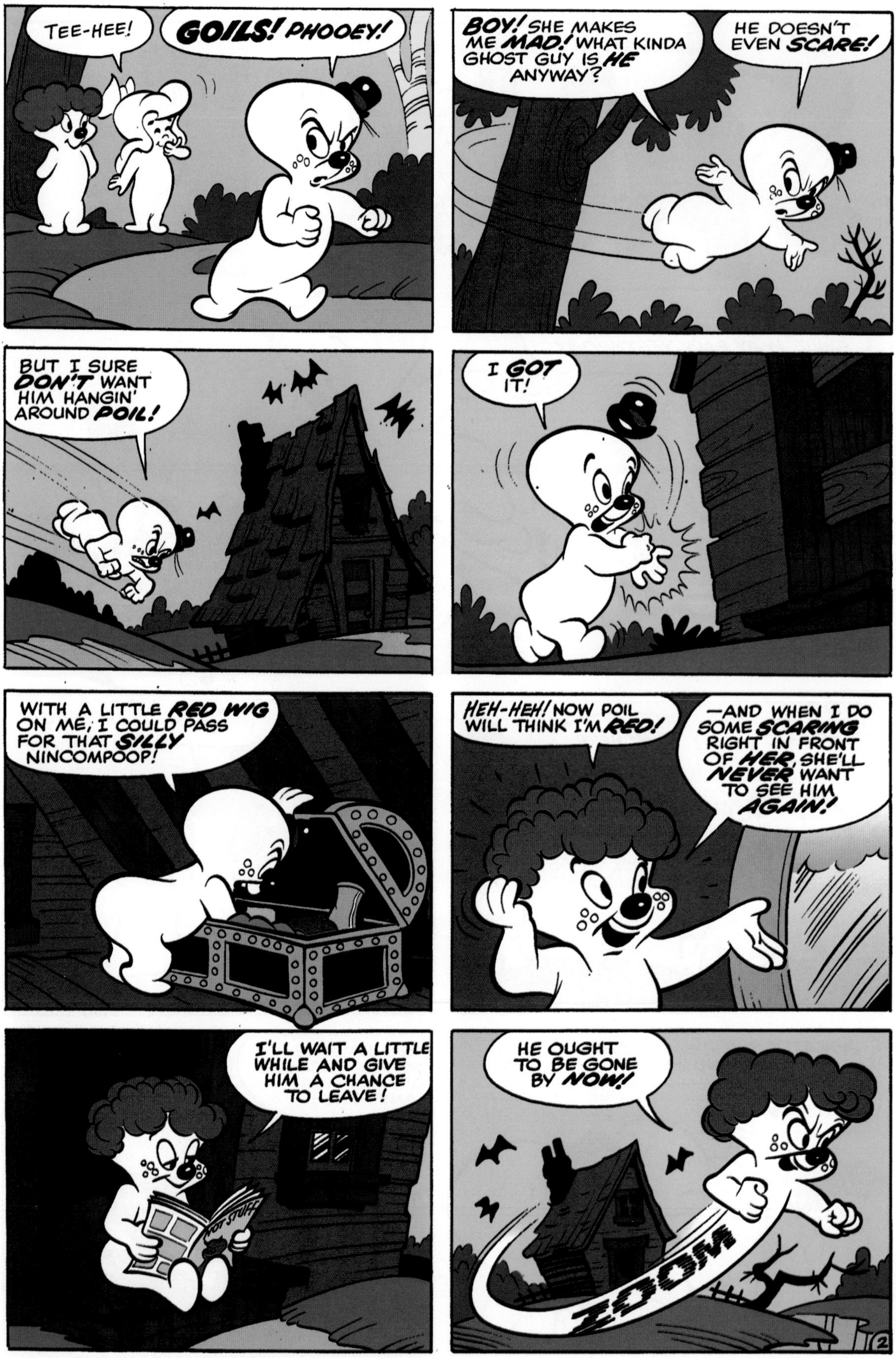

TEE-HEE!
GOILS! PHOOEY!
BOY! SHE MAKES ME MAD! WHAT KINDA GHOST GUY IS HE ANYWAY?
HE DOESN'T EVEN SCARE!
BUT I SURE DON'T WANT HIM HANGIN' AROUND POIL!
I GOT IT!
WITH A LITTLE RED WIG ON ME, I COULD PASS FOR THAT SILLY NINCOMPOOP!
HEH-HEH! NOW POIL WILL THINK I'M RED!
—AND WHEN I DO SOME SCARING RIGHT IN FRONT OF HER, SHE'LL NEVER WANT TO SEE HIM AGAIN!
I'LL WAIT A LITTLE WHILE AND GIVE HIM A CHANCE TO LEAVE!
HE OUGHT TO BE GONE BY NOW!
ZOOM

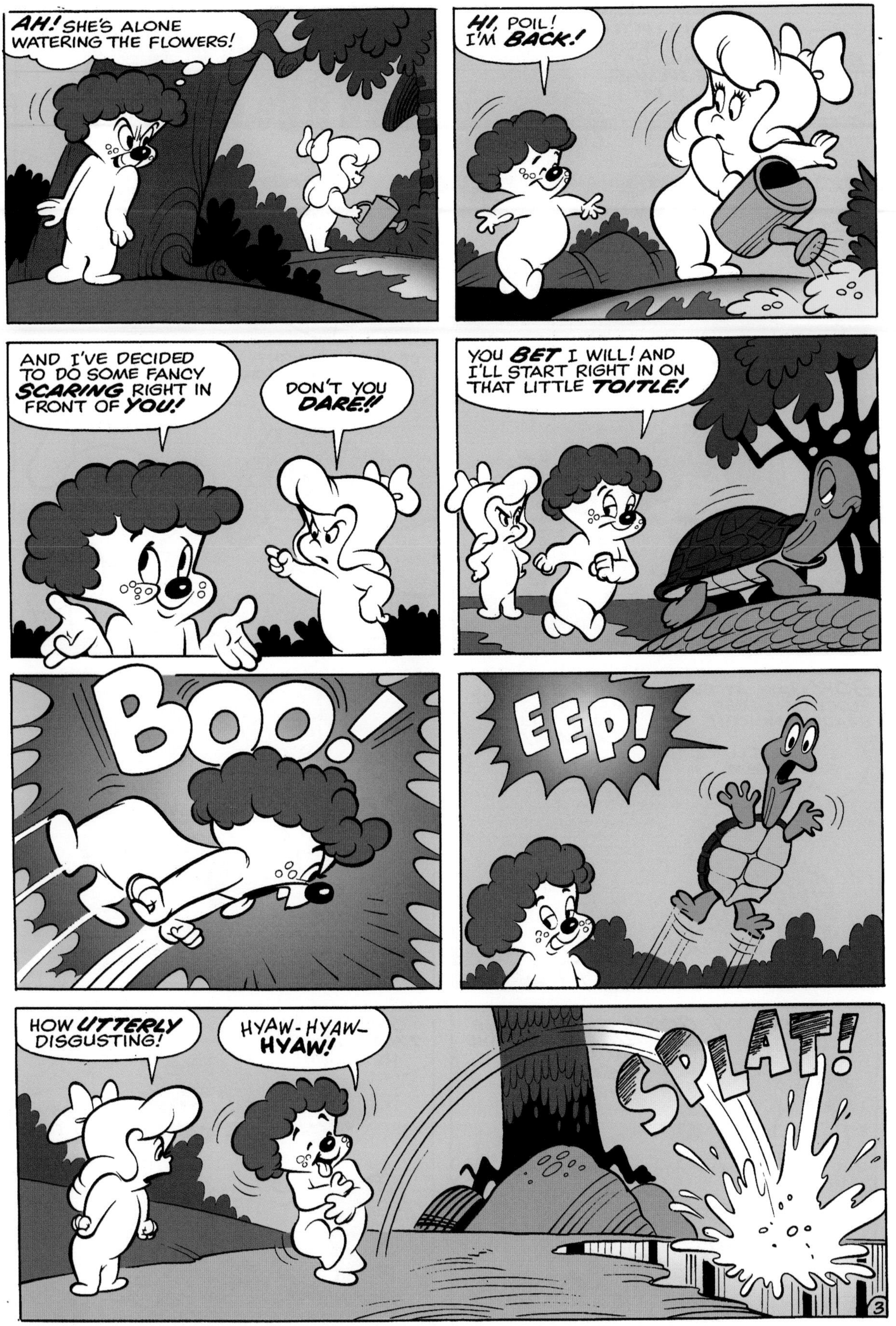
AH! SHE'S ALONE WATERING THE FLOWERS!
HI, POIL! I'M BACK!
AND I'VE DECIDED TO DO SOME FANCY SCARING RIGHT IN FRONT OF YOU!
DON'T YOU DARE!!
YOU BET I WILL! AND I'LL START RIGHT IN ON THAT LITTLE TOITLE!
BOO!
EEP!
HOW UTTERLY DISGUSTING!
HYAW-HYAW-HYAW!
SPLAT!
3

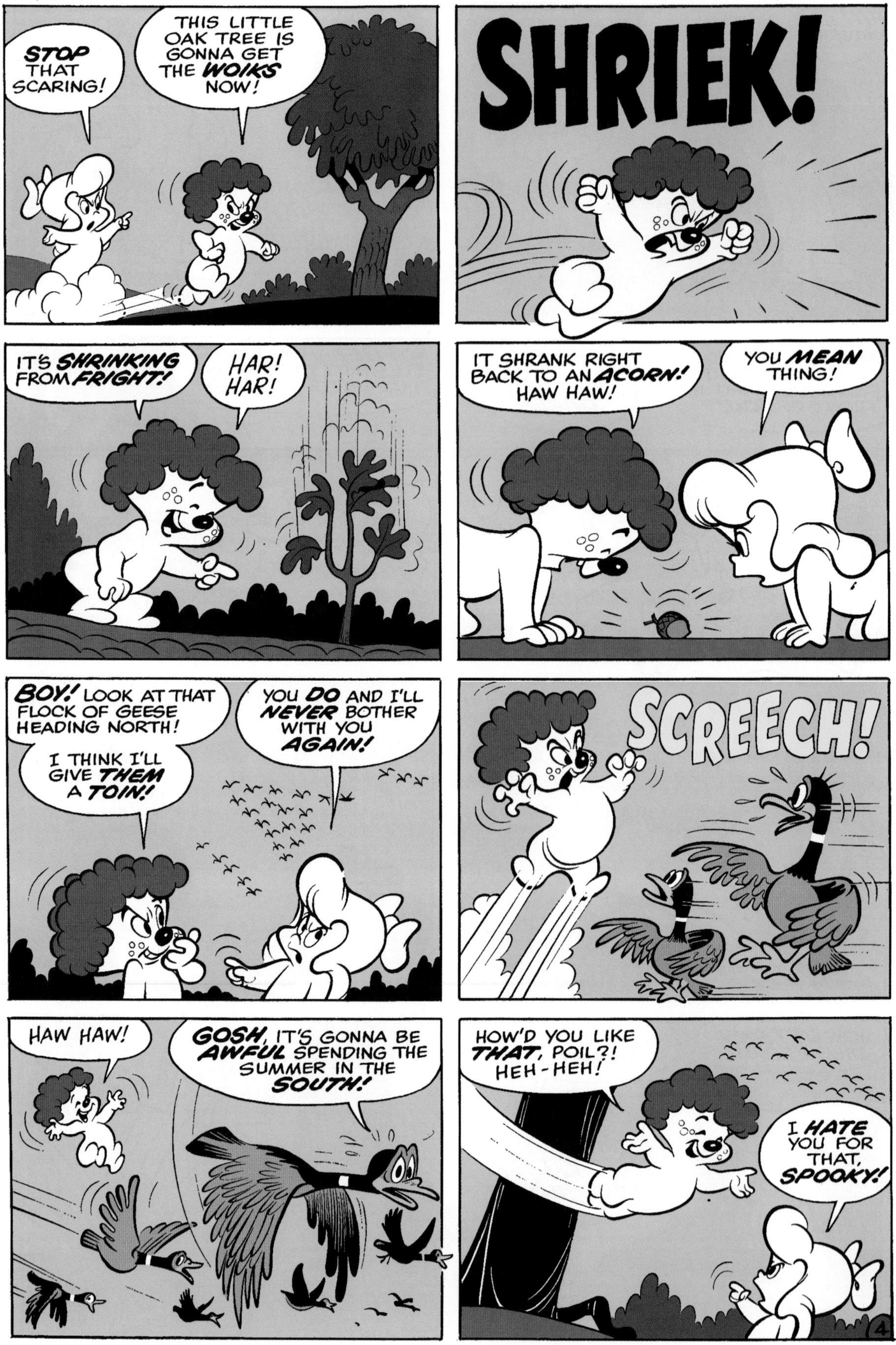
STOP THAT SCARING!
THIS LITTLE OAK TREE IS GONNA GET THE WOIKS NOW!
SHRIEK!
IT'S SHRINKING FROM FRIGHT!
HAR! HAR!
IT SHRANK RIGHT BACK TO AN ACORN! HAW HAW!
YOU MEAN THING!
BOY! LOOK AT THAT FLOCK OF GEESE HEADING NORTH!
I THINK I'LL GIVE THEM A TOIN!
YOU DO AND I'LL NEVER BOTHER WITH YOU AGAIN!
SCREECH!
HAW HAW!
GOSH, IT'S GONNA BE AWFUL SPENDING THE SUMMER IN THE SOUTH!
HOW'D YOU LIKE THAT, POIL?! HEH-HEH!
I HATE YOU FOR THAT, SPOOKY!
4

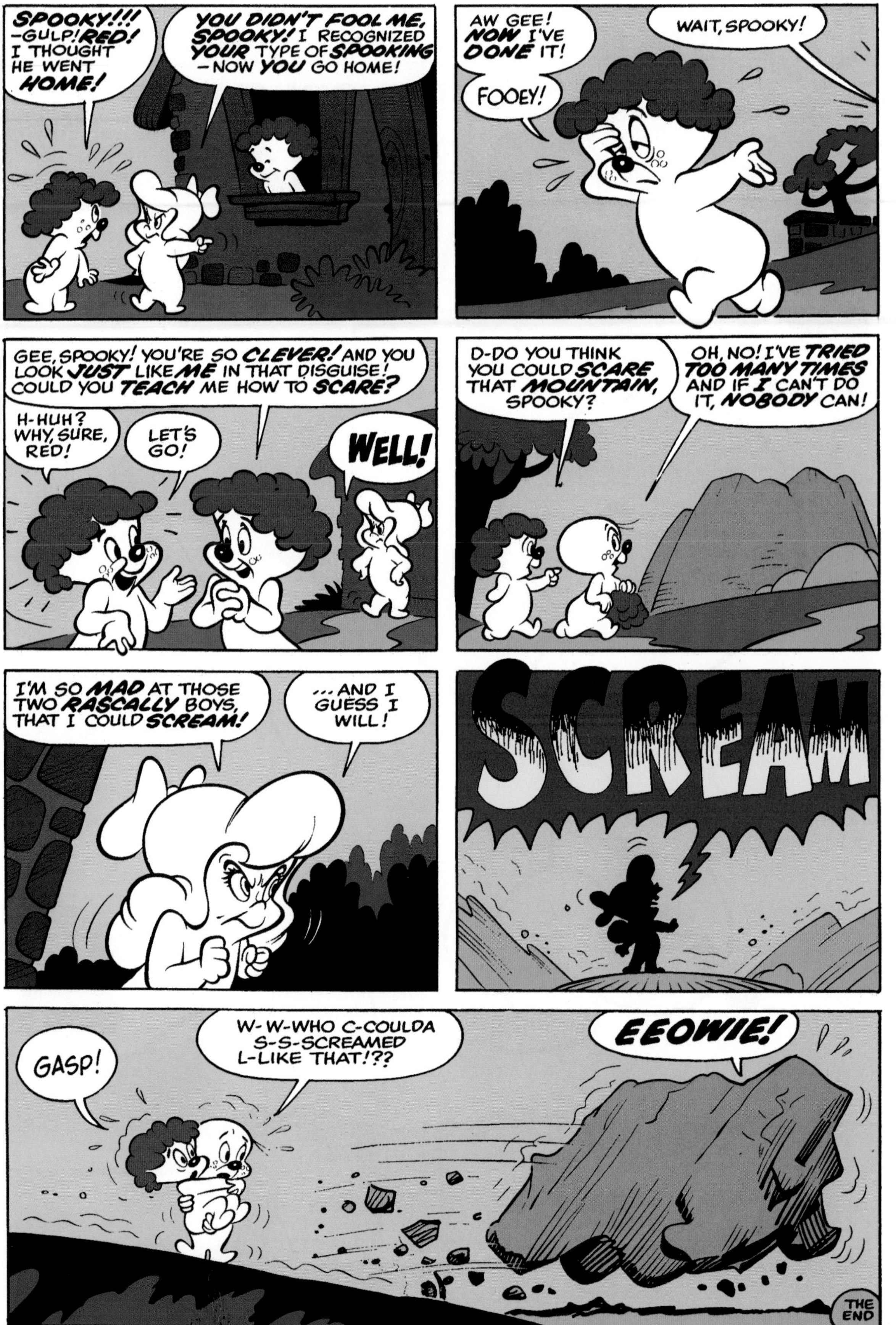
SPOOKY!!! —GULP! RED! I THOUGHT HE WENT HOME!
YOU DIDN'T FOOL ME, SPOOKY! I RECOGNIZED YOUR TYPE OF SPOOKING —NOW YOU GO HOME!
AW GEE! NOW I'VE DONE IT!
FOOEY!
WAIT, SPOOKY!
GEE, SPOOKY! YOU'RE SO CLEVER! AND YOU LOOK JUST LIKE ME IN THAT DISGUISE! COULD YOU TEACH ME HOW TO SCARE?
H-HUH? WHY, SURE, RED!
LET'S GO!
WELL!
D-DO YOU THINK YOU COULD SCARE THAT MOUNTAIN, SPOOKY?
OH, NO! I'VE TRIED TOO MANY TIMES AND IF I CAN'T DO IT, NOBODY CAN!
I'M SO MAD AT THOSE TWO RASCALLY BOYS, THAT I COULD SCREAM!
...AND I GUESS I WILL!
SCREAM
GASP!
W-W-WHO C-COULDA S-S-SCREAMED L-LIKE THAT!??
EEOWIE!
THE END

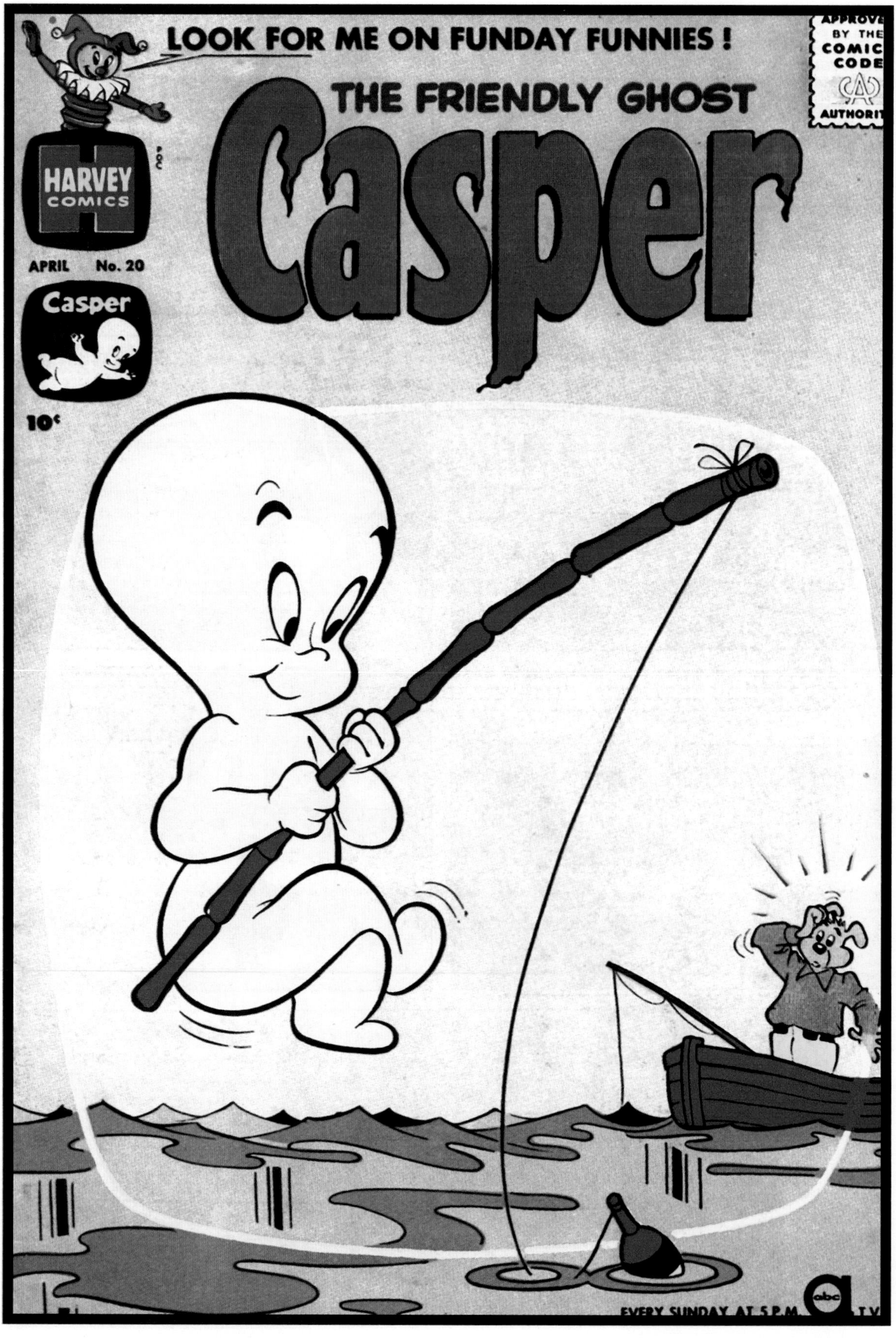

LOOK FOR ME ON FUNDAY FUNNIES !
APPROVED BY THE COMICS CODE AUTHORITY
THE FRIENDLY GHOST
Casper
HARVEY COMICS
APRIL No. 20
Casper
10¢
EVERY SUNDAY AT 5 P.M. abc TV

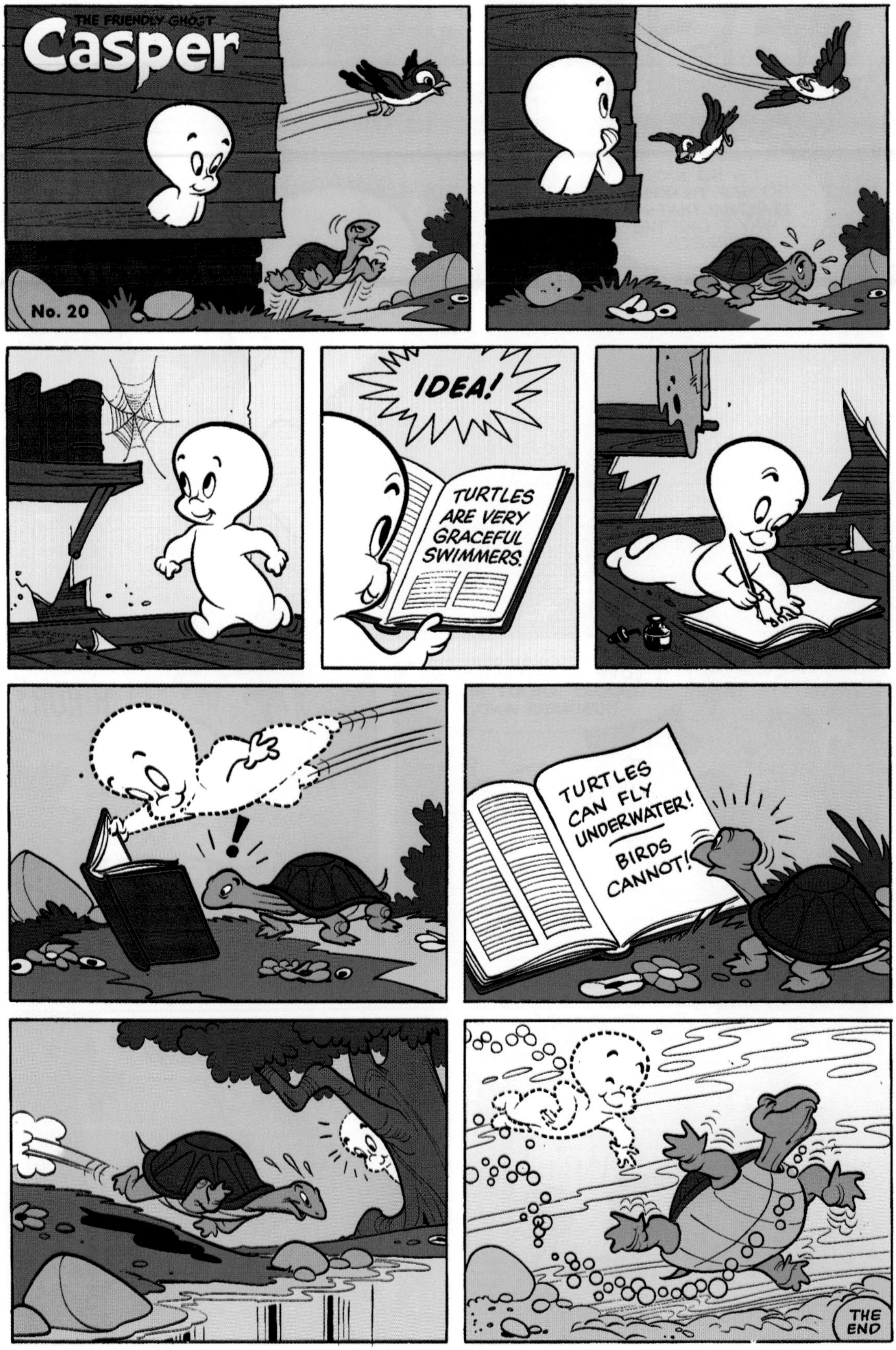
THE FRIENDLY GHOST
Casper
No. 20
IDEA!
TURTLES ARE VERY GRACEFUL SWIMMERS.
TURTLES CAN FLY UNDERWATER!
BIRDS CANNOT!
THE END

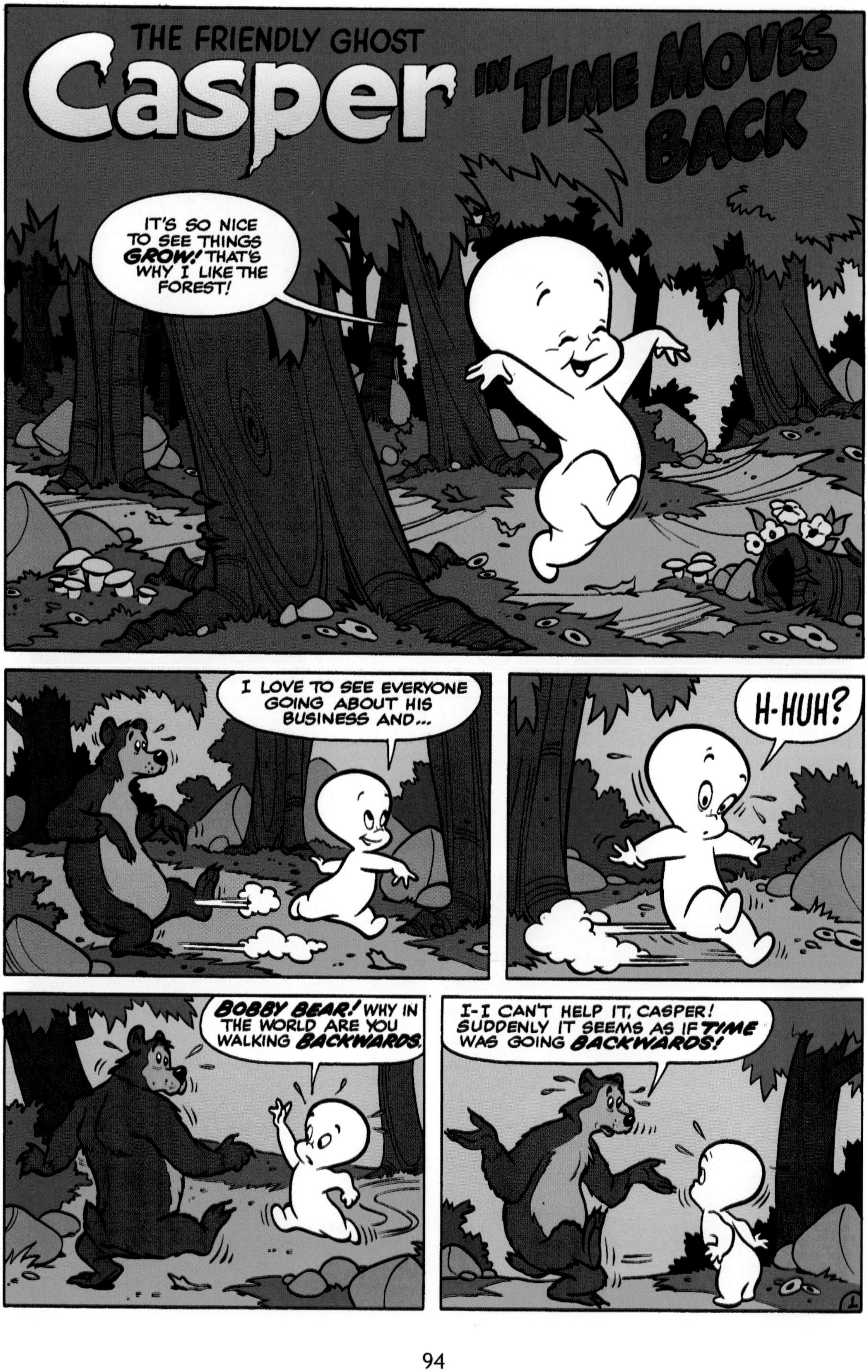
THE FRIENDLY GHOST
Casper IN TIME MOVES BACK
IT'S SO NICE TO SEE THINGS GROW! THAT'S WHY I LIKE THE FOREST!
I LOVE TO SEE EVERYONE GOING ABOUT HIS BUSINESS AND...
H-HUH?
BOBBY BEAR! WHY IN THE WORLD ARE YOU WALKING BACKWARDS?
I-I CAN'T HELP IT, CASPER! SUDDENLY IT SEEMS AS IF TIME WAS GOING BACKWARDS!
1

I'VE HAD LUNCH BUT THE WAY THINGS ARE GOING I WON'T BE HAVING MY SUPPER!
WHY NOT?
'CAUSE I'LL BE HAVING MY BREAKFAST AGAIN AND I DON'T FEEL LIKE IT! SOB!
WHAT COULD BE THE MATTER WITH HIM?
OH, WELL! MAYBE IT WAS JUST SOMETHING HE ATE!
BOO HOO!
SOMETHING TINY SOUNDS SAD!
BOO HOO!
A SPIDER SOBBING! I NEVER EXPECTED A SPIDER TO CRY!
SOB!
I'VE SPENT SO MUCH TIME BUILDING A BEAUTIFUL WEB, BUT NOW I'M UNBUILDING IT!
UNBUILDING IT? WHY?
I CAN'T HELP IT! I JUST STARTED DOING THINGS BACKWARDS! SOB!
2

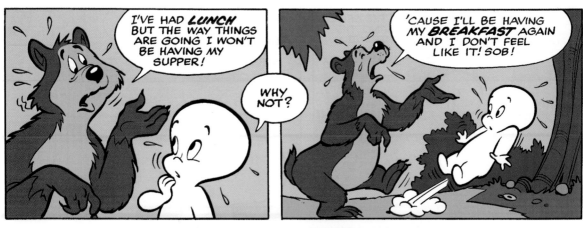

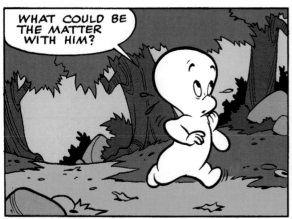

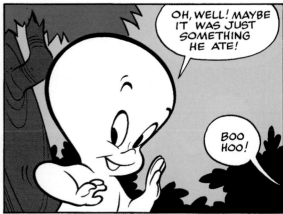

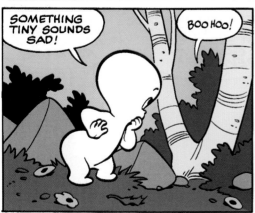

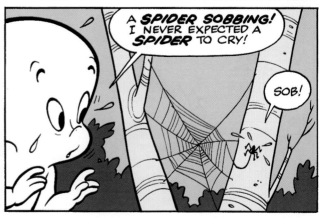

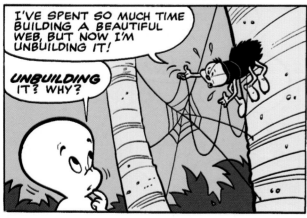

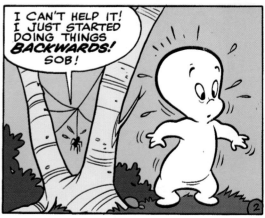

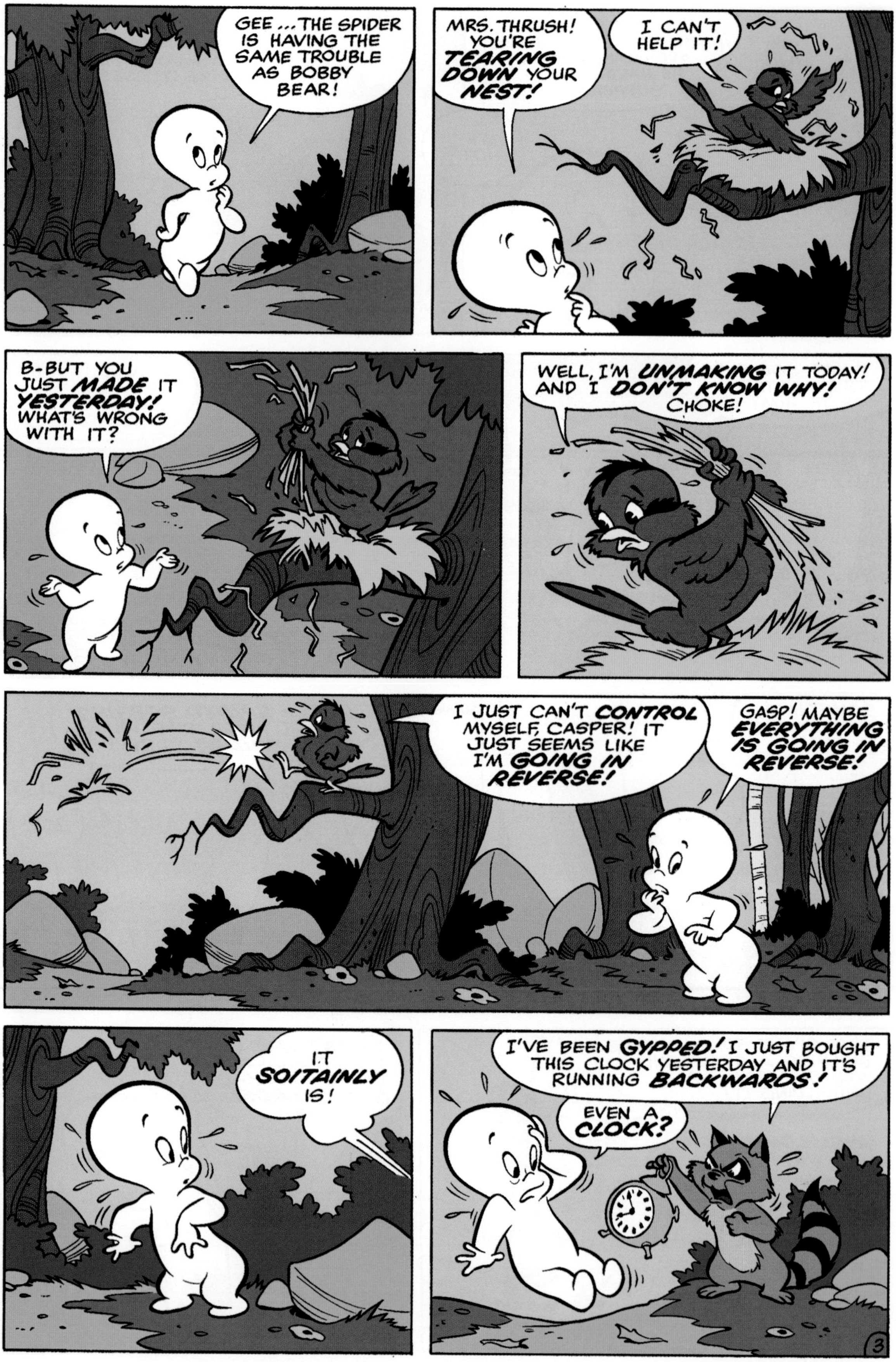
GEE ... THE SPIDER IS HAVING THE SAME TROUBLE AS BOBBY BEAR!
MRS. THRUSH! YOU'RE TEARING DOWN YOUR NEST!
I CAN'T HELP IT!
B-BUT YOU JUST MADE IT YESTERDAY! WHAT'S WRONG WITH IT?
WELL, I'M UNMAKING IT TODAY! AND I DON'T KNOW WHY! CHOKE!
I JUST CAN'T CONTROL MYSELF, CASPER! IT JUST SEEMS LIKE I'M GOING IN REVERSE!
GASP! MAYBE EVERYTHING IS GOING IN REVERSE!
IT SOITAINLY IS!
I'VE BEEN GYPPED! I JUST BOUGHT THIS CLOCK YESTERDAY AND IT'S RUNNING BACKWARDS!
EVEN A CLOCK?
3

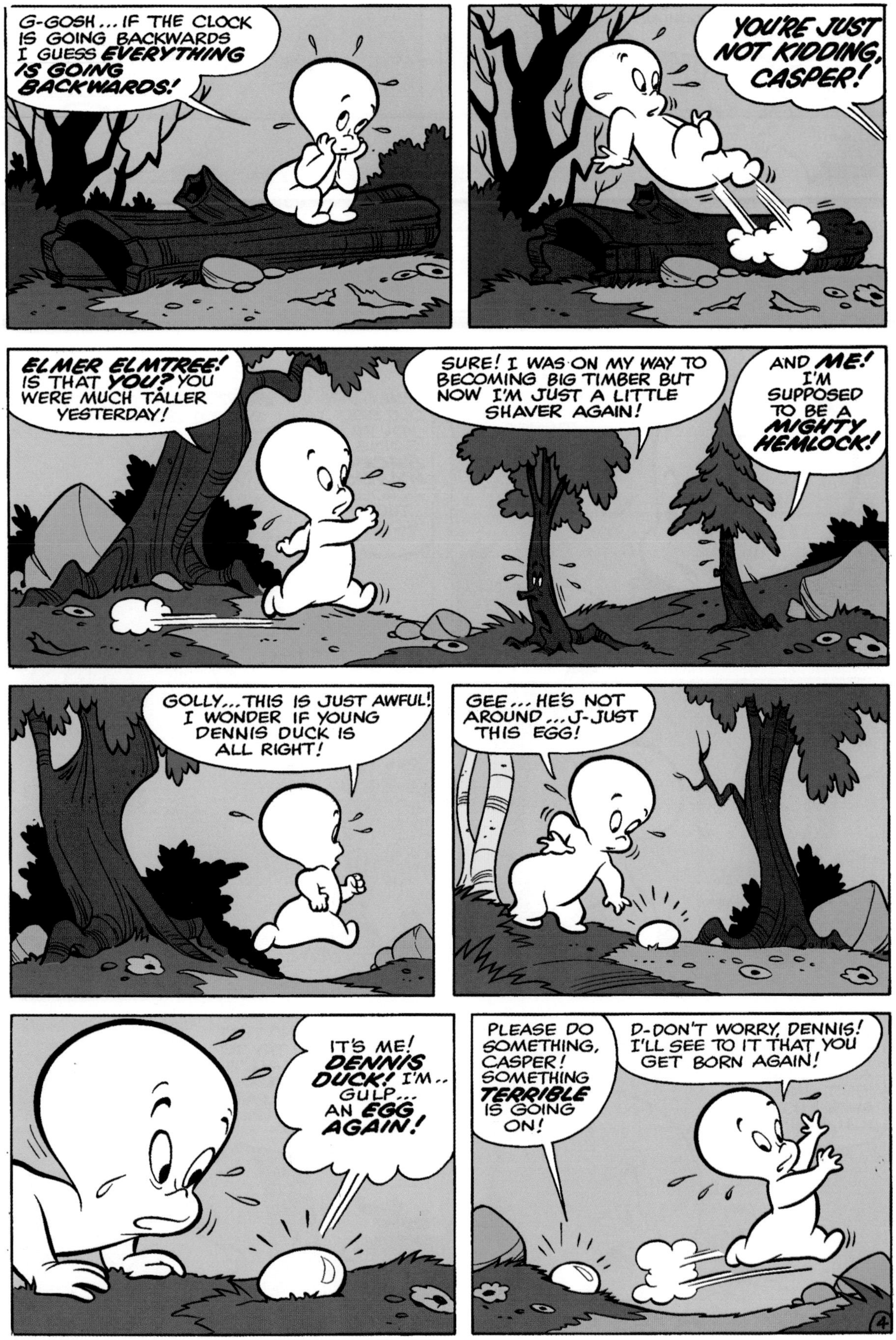
G-GOSH... IF THE CLOCK IS GOING BACKWARDS I GUESS EVERYTHING IS GOING BACKWARDS!
YOU'RE JUST NOT KIDDING, CASPER!
ELMER ELMTREE! IS THAT YOU? YOU WERE MUCH TALLER YESTERDAY!
SURE! I WAS ON MY WAY TO BECOMING BIG TIMBER BUT NOW I'M JUST A LITTLE SHAVER AGAIN!
AND ME! I'M SUPPOSED TO BE A MIGHTY HEMLOCK!
GOLLY... THIS IS JUST AWFUL! I WONDER IF YOUNG DENNIS DUCK IS ALL RIGHT!
GEE... HE'S NOT AROUND... J-JUST THIS EGG!
IT'S ME! DENNIS DUCK! I'M.. GULP... AN EGG AGAIN!
PLEASE DO SOMETHING, CASPER! SOMETHING TERRIBLE IS GOING ON!
D-DON'T WORRY, DENNIS! I'LL SEE TO IT THAT YOU GET BORN AGAIN!
4

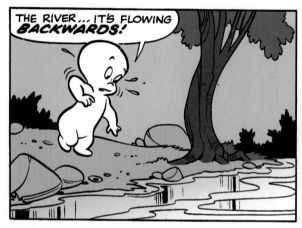

THE RIVER... IT'S FLOWING *BACKWARDS!*

...SOB...RIGHT BACK WHERE I STARTED FROM! A LITTLE *TRICKLE!*

WHAT'S *HAPPENING?* WHAT CAN I DO TO MAKE THINGS RIGHT?

WHY... OLD SOL... YOU'RE GOING *BACK-WARDS* ACROSS THE SKY?

YES, CASPER...I'M AFRAID I'M GOING TO SET IN THE *EAST*... BUT I *KNOW* WHAT'S GOING ON!

WHY THINGS MIGHT GET WORSE AND WORSE AND... *ULP...*

THERE'S A PESKY *SORCERER* WHO'S DOING ALL THIS! HE ISN'T FAR AWAY FROM YOU, CASPER!

I'VE GOT TO FIND THAT SORCERER AND TRY TO MAKE HIM STOP ALL THIS BACKWARD BUSINESS OR WE'LL MOVE CLEAR BACK TO THE...GULP... *STONE AGE!*

CONTINUED IN THIS ISSUE.

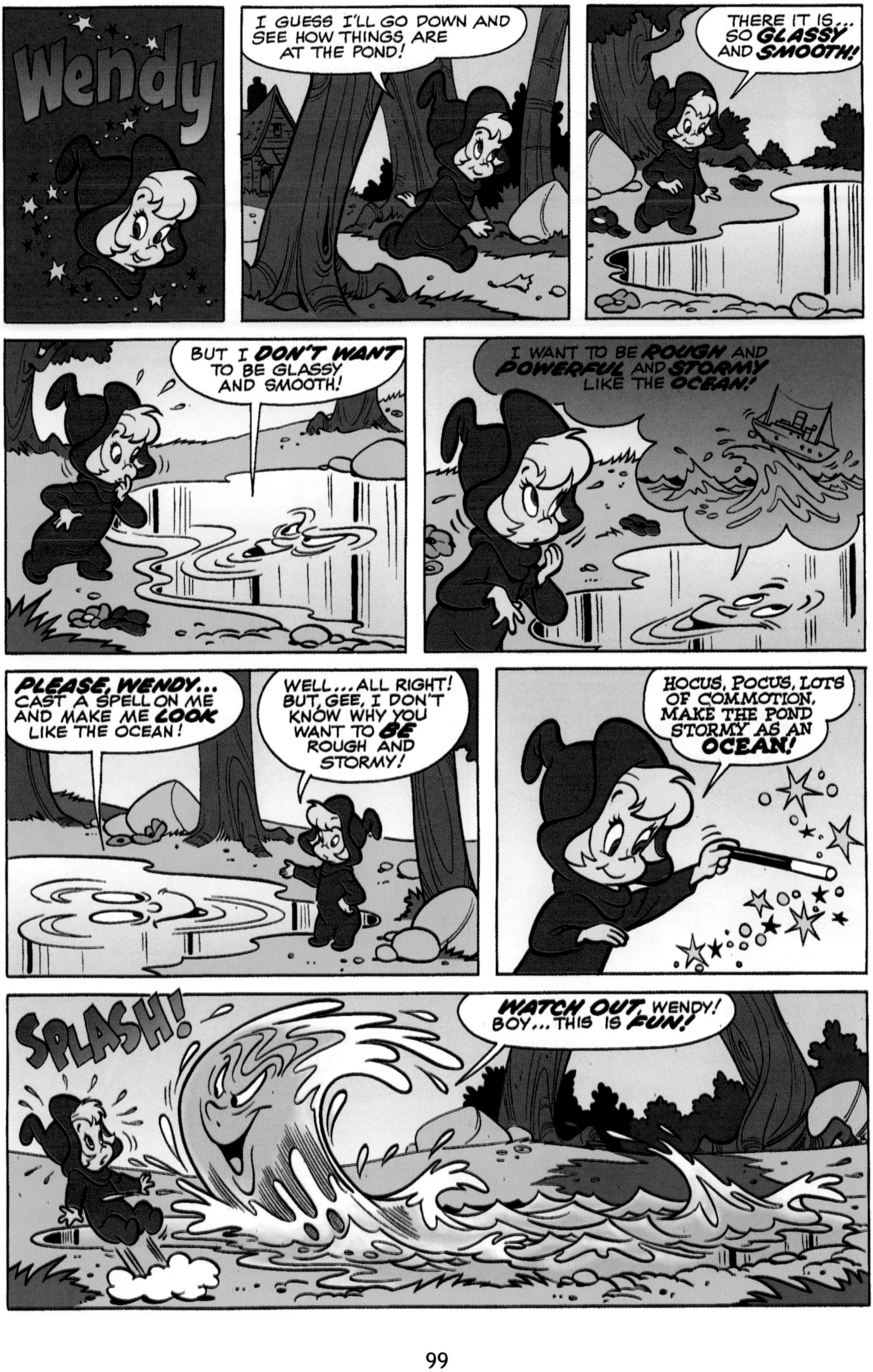
Wendy
I GUESS I'LL GO DOWN AND SEE HOW THINGS ARE AT THE POND!
THERE IT IS... SO GLASSY AND SMOOTH!
BUT I DON'T WANT TO BE GLASSY AND SMOOTH!
I WANT TO BE ROUGH AND POWERFUL AND STORMY LIKE THE OCEAN!
PLEASE, WENDY... CAST A SPELL ON ME AND MAKE ME LOOK LIKE THE OCEAN!
WELL... ALL RIGHT! BUT, GEE, I DON'T KNOW WHY YOU WANT TO BE ROUGH AND STORMY!
HOCUS, POCUS, LOTS OF COMMOTION, MAKE THE POND STORMY AS AN OCEAN!
SPLASH!
WATCH OUT, WENDY! BOY... THIS IS FUN!

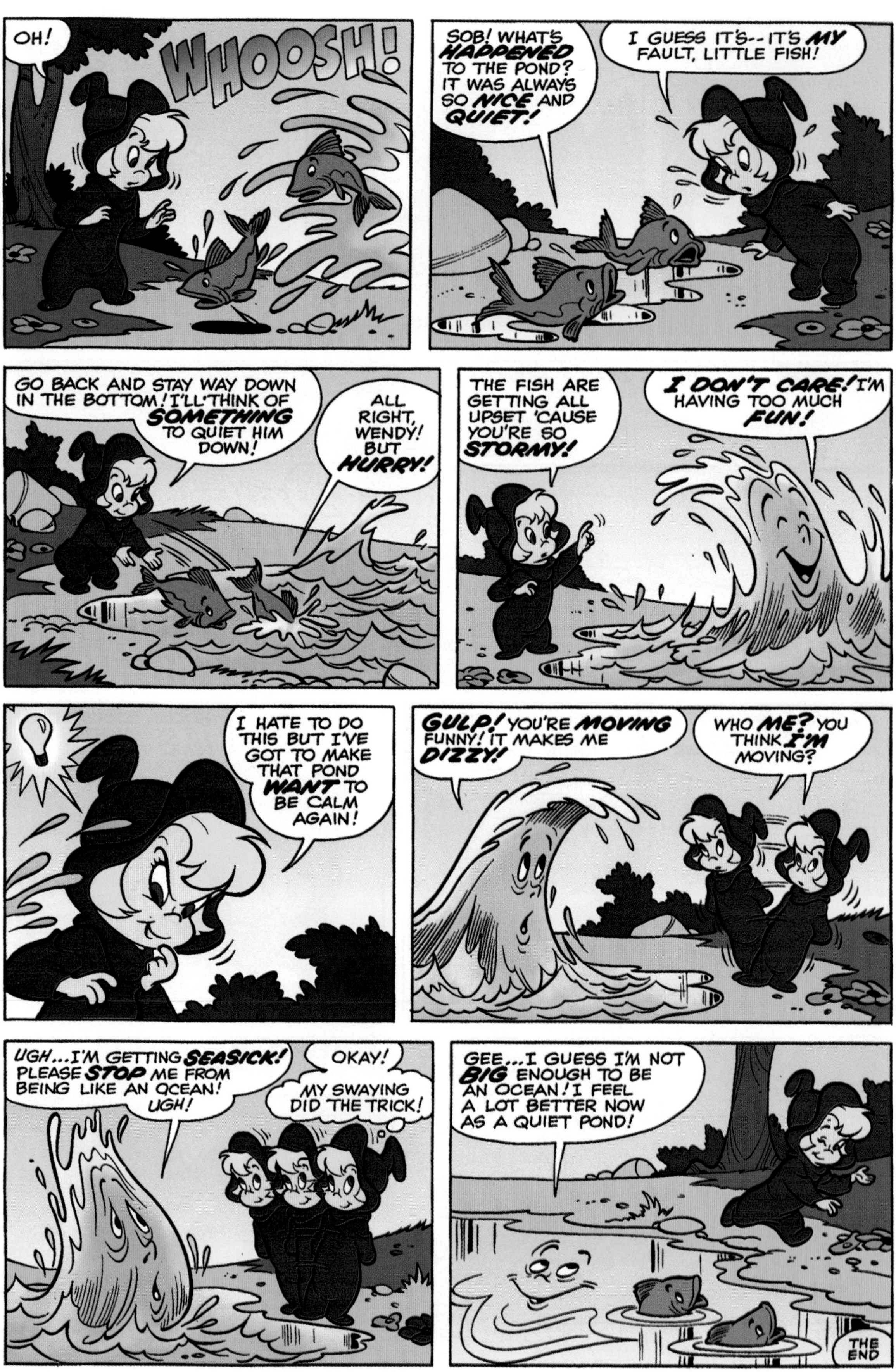
OH!
WHOOSH!
SOB! WHAT'S HAPPENED TO THE POND? IT WAS ALWAYS SO NICE AND QUIET!
I GUESS IT'S-- IT'S MY FAULT, LITTLE FISH!
GO BACK AND STAY WAY DOWN IN THE BOTTOM! I'LL THINK OF SOMETHING TO QUIET HIM DOWN!
ALL RIGHT, WENDY! BUT HURRY!
THE FISH ARE GETTING ALL UPSET 'CAUSE YOU'RE SO STORMY!
I DON'T CARE! I'M HAVING TOO MUCH FUN!
I HATE TO DO THIS BUT I'VE GOT TO MAKE THAT POND WANT TO BE CALM AGAIN!
GULP! YOU'RE MOVING FUNNY! IT MAKES ME DIZZY!
WHO ME? YOU THINK I'M MOVING?
UGH...I'M GETTING SEASICK! PLEASE STOP ME FROM BEING LIKE AN OCEAN! UGH!
OKAY!
MY SWAYING DID THE TRICK!
GEE...I GUESS I'M NOT BIG ENOUGH TO BE AN OCEAN! I FEEL A LOT BETTER NOW AS A QUIET POND!
THE END

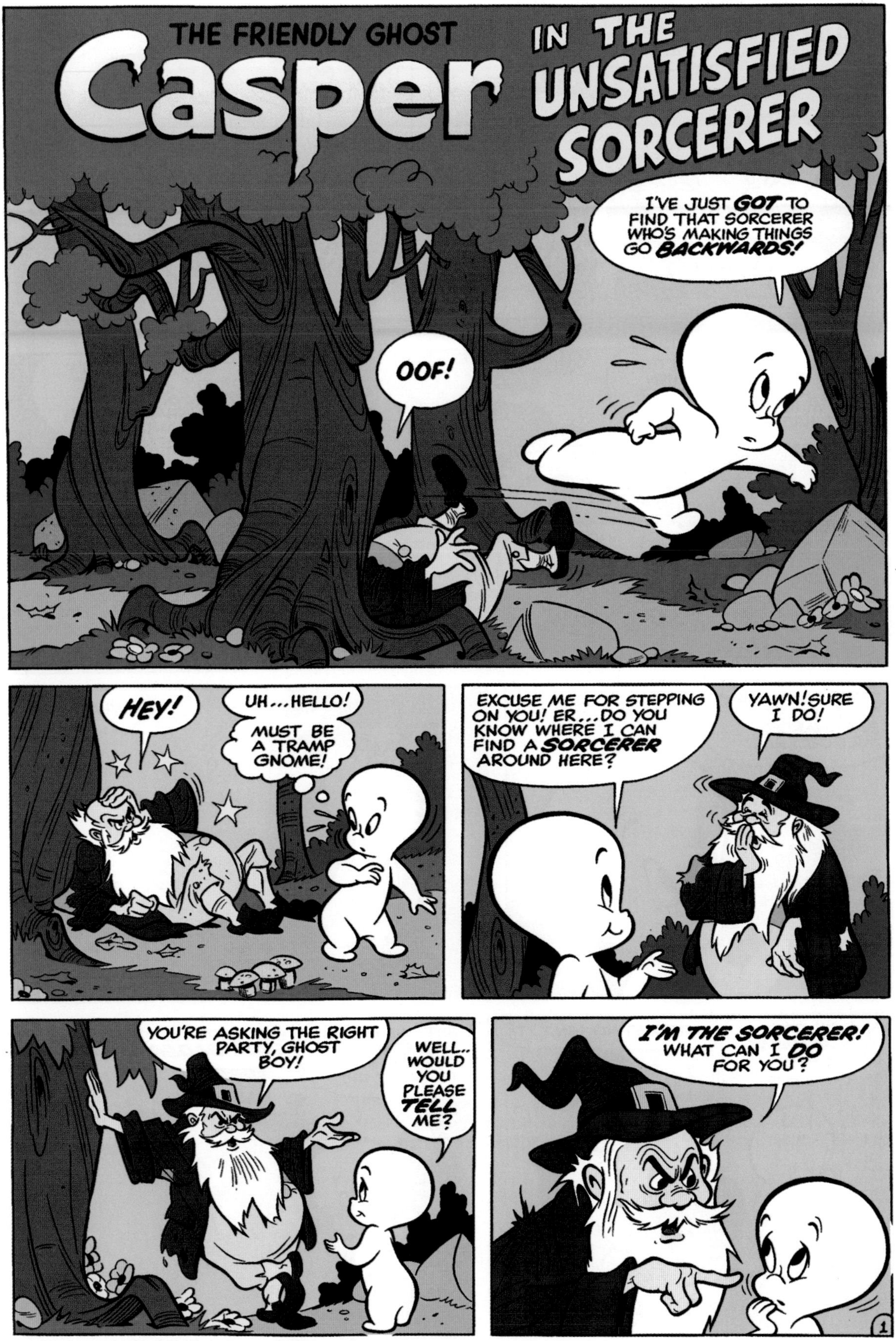
THE FRIENDLY GHOST
Casper
IN THE UNSATISFIED SORCERER
I'VE JUST GOT TO FIND THAT SORCERER WHO'S MAKING THINGS GO BACKWARDS!
OOF!
HEY!
UH...HELLO!
MUST BE A TRAMP GNOME!
EXCUSE ME FOR STEPPING ON YOU! ER...DO YOU KNOW WHERE I CAN FIND A SORCERER AROUND HERE?
YAWN! SURE I DO!
YOU'RE ASKING THE RIGHT PARTY, GHOST BOY!
WELL.. WOULD YOU PLEASE TELL ME?
I'M THE SORCERER! WHAT CAN I DO FOR YOU?
1

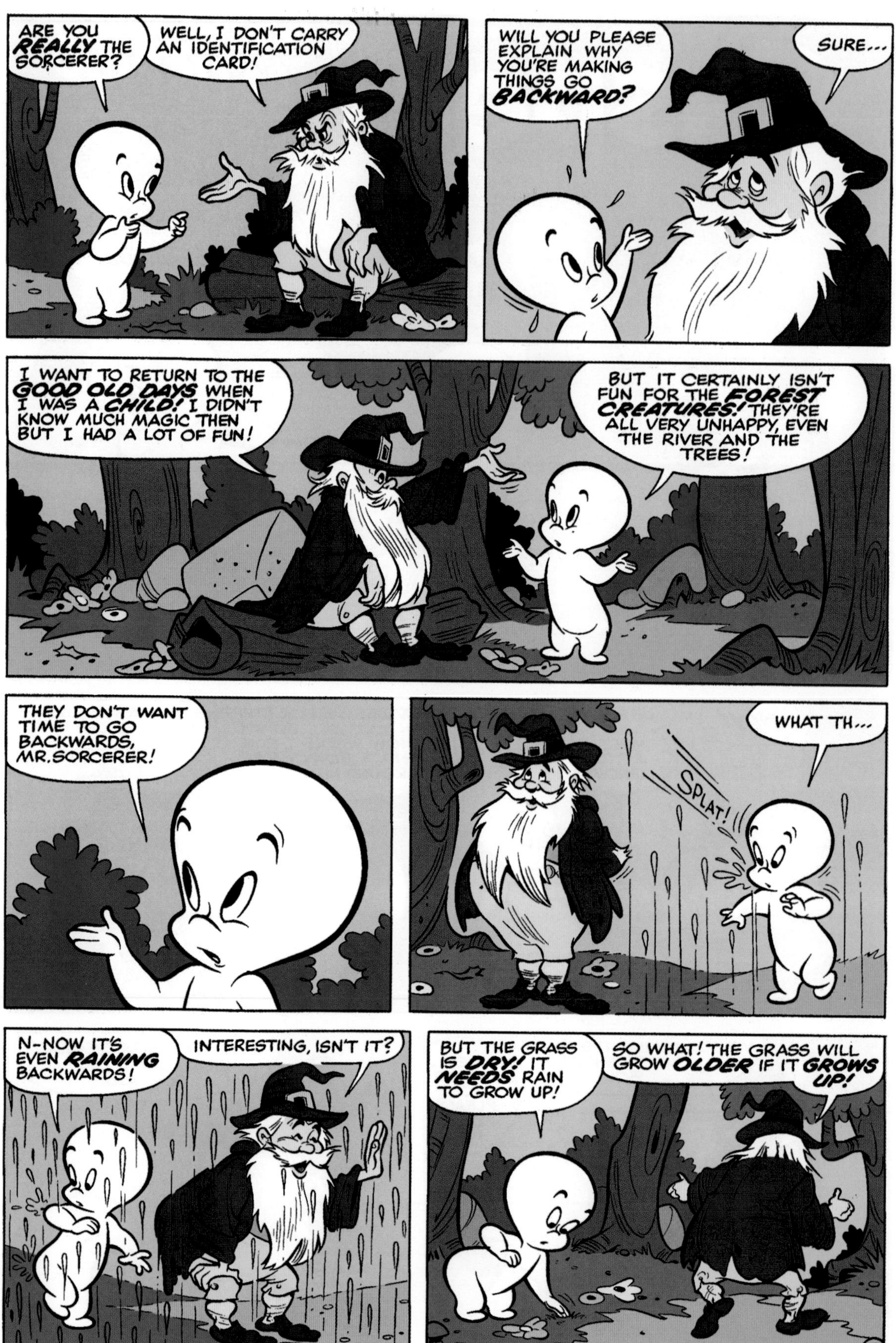
ARE YOU REALLY THE SORCERER?
WELL, I DON'T CARRY AN IDENTIFICATION CARD!
WILL YOU PLEASE EXPLAIN WHY YOU'RE MAKING THINGS GO BACKWARD?
SURE...
I WANT TO RETURN TO THE GOOD OLD DAYS WHEN I WAS A CHILD! I DIDN'T KNOW MUCH MAGIC THEN BUT I HAD A LOT OF FUN!
BUT IT CERTAINLY ISN'T FUN FOR THE FOREST CREATURES! THEY'RE ALL VERY UNHAPPY, EVEN THE RIVER AND THE TREES!
THEY DON'T WANT TIME TO GO BACKWARDS, MR. SORCERER!
WHAT TH...
SPLAT!
N-NOW IT'S EVEN RAINING BACKWARDS!
INTERESTING, ISN'T IT?
BUT THE GRASS IS DRY! IT NEEDS RAIN TO GROW UP!
SO WHAT! THE GRASS WILL GROW OLDER IF IT GROWS UP!
2

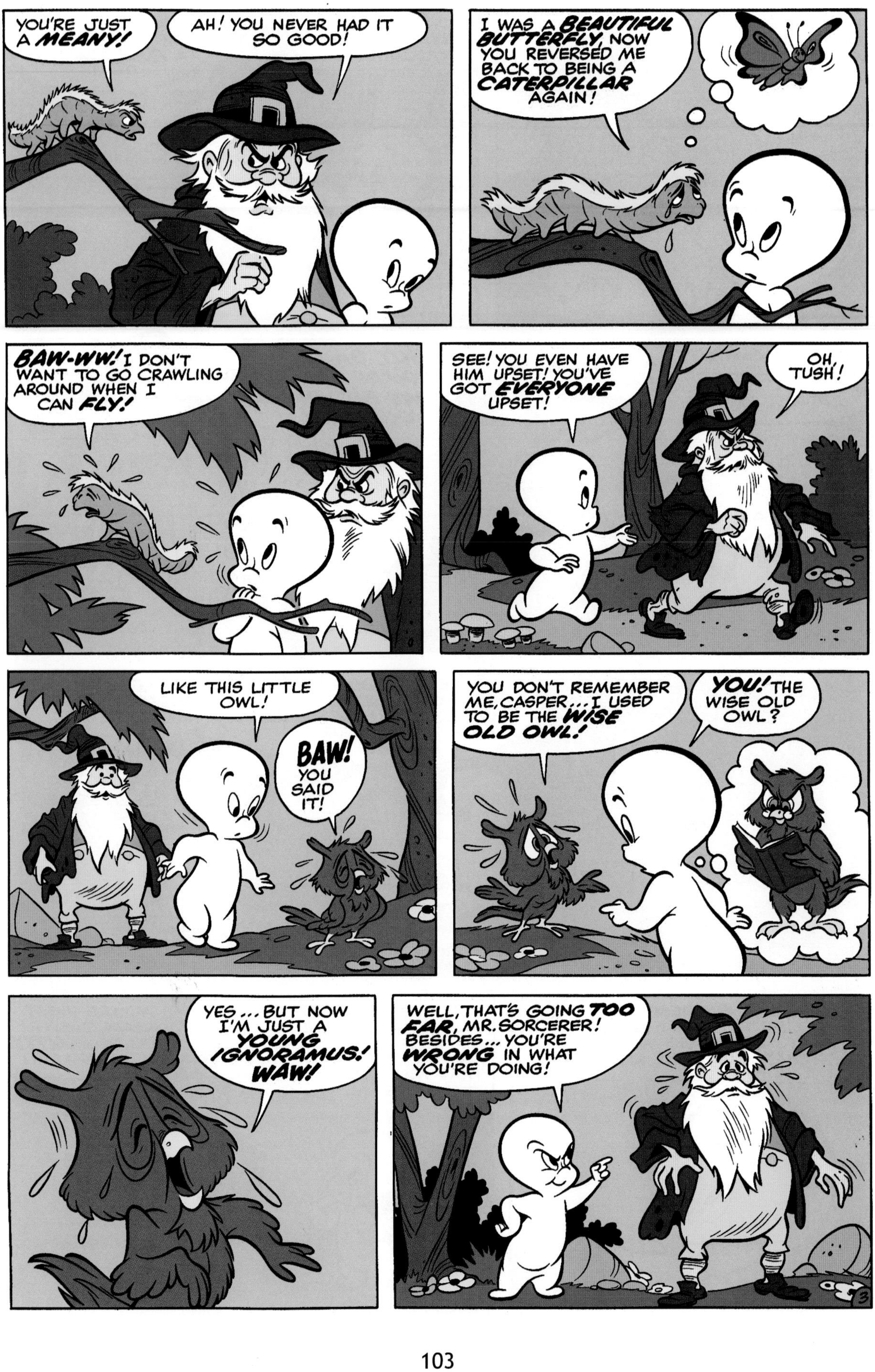

YOU'RE JUST A MEANY!
AH! YOU NEVER HAD IT SO GOOD!
I WAS A BEAUTIFUL BUTTERFLY, NOW YOU REVERSED ME BACK TO BEING A CATERPILLAR AGAIN!
BAW-WW! I DON'T WANT TO GO CRAWLING AROUND WHEN I CAN FLY!
SEE! YOU EVEN HAVE HIM UPSET! YOU'VE GOT EVERYONE UPSET!
OH, TUSH!
LIKE THIS LITTLE OWL!
BAW! YOU SAID IT!
YOU DON'T REMEMBER ME, CASPER... I USED TO BE THE WISE OLD OWL!
YOU! THE WISE OLD OWL?
YES... BUT NOW I'M JUST A YOUNG IGNORAMUS! WAW!
WELL, THAT'S GOING TOO FAR, MR. SORCERER! BESIDES... YOU'RE WRONG IN WHAT YOU'RE DOING!
3

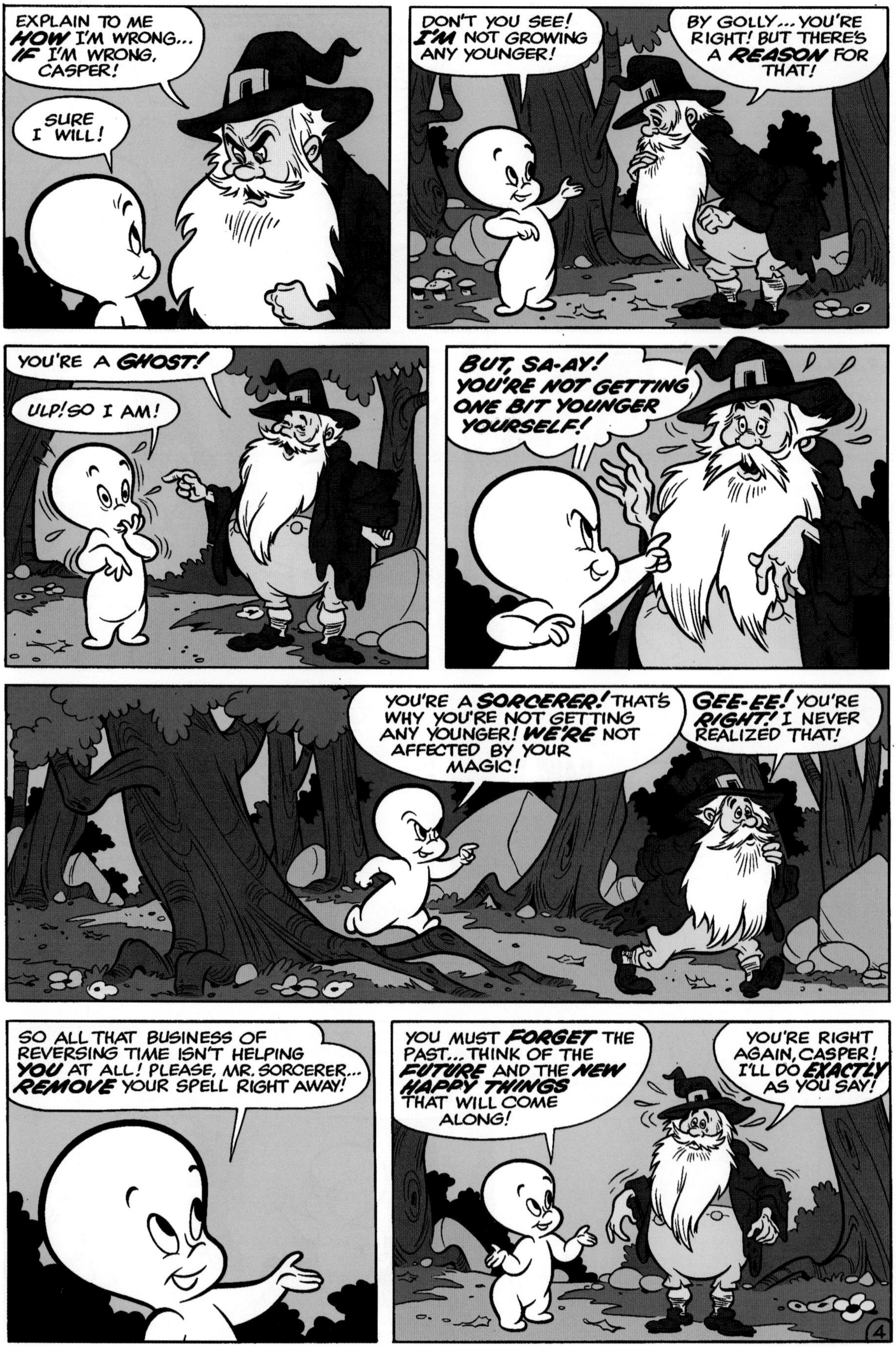
EXPLAIN TO ME HOW I'M WRONG... IF I'M WRONG, CASPER!
SURE I WILL!
DON'T YOU SEE! I'M NOT GROWING ANY YOUNGER!
BY GOLLY... YOU'RE RIGHT! BUT THERE'S A REASON FOR THAT!
YOU'RE A GHOST!
ULP! SO I AM!
BUT, SA-AY! YOU'RE NOT GETTING ONE BIT YOUNGER YOURSELF!
YOU'RE A SORCERER! THAT'S WHY YOU'RE NOT GETTING ANY YOUNGER! WE'RE NOT AFFECTED BY YOUR MAGIC!
GEE-EE! YOU'RE RIGHT! I NEVER REALIZED THAT!
SO ALL THAT BUSINESS OF REVERSING TIME ISN'T HELPING YOU AT ALL! PLEASE, MR. SORCERER... REMOVE YOUR SPELL RIGHT AWAY!
YOU MUST FORGET THE PAST... THINK OF THE FUTURE AND THE NEW HAPPY THINGS THAT WILL COME ALONG!
YOU'RE RIGHT AGAIN, CASPER! I'LL DO EXACTLY AS YOU SAY!
4

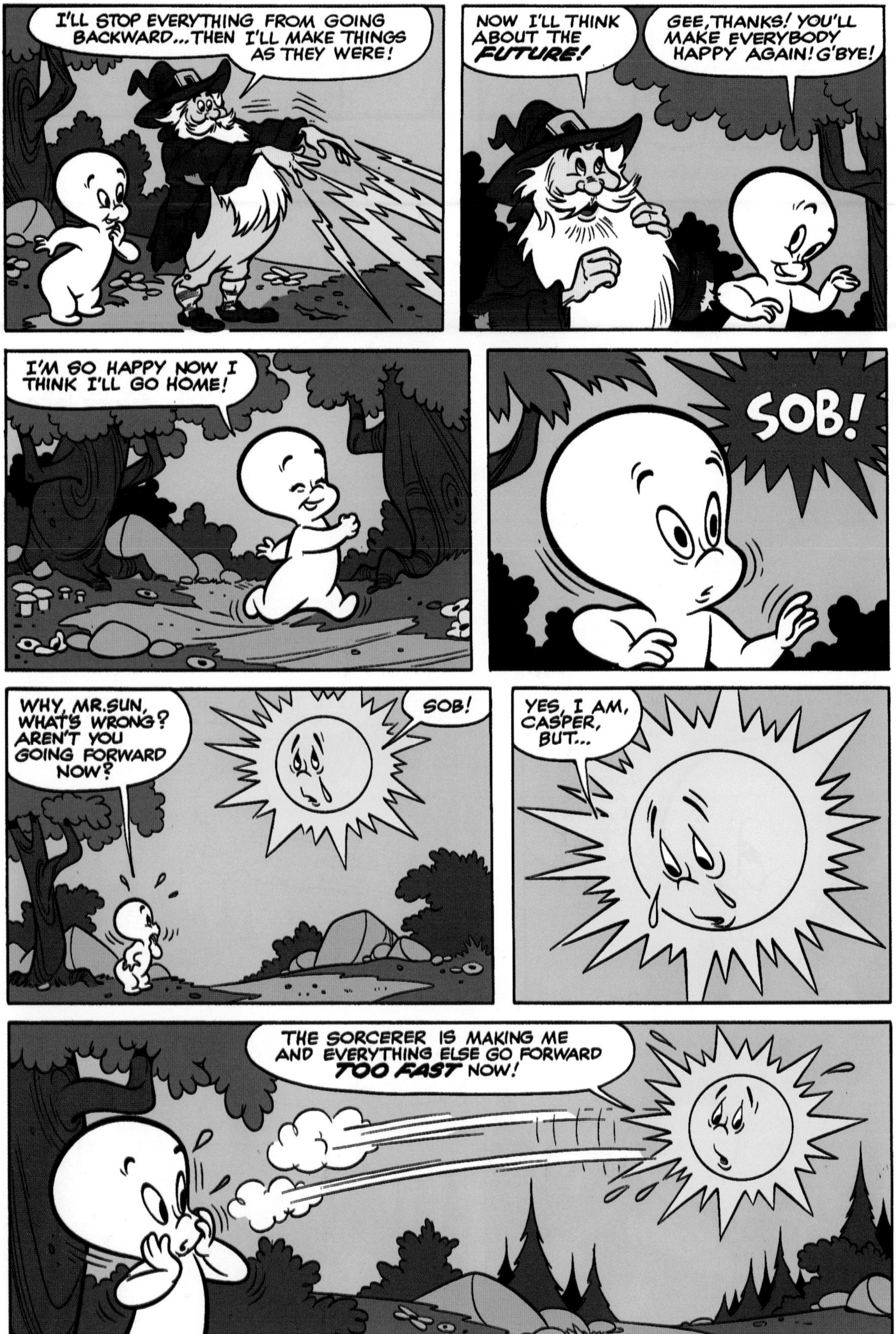
I'LL STOP EVERYTHING FROM GOING BACKWARD...THEN I'LL MAKE THINGS AS THEY WERE!
NOW I'LL THINK ABOUT THE FUTURE!
GEE, THANKS! YOU'LL MAKE EVERYBODY HAPPY AGAIN! G'BYE!
I'M SO HAPPY NOW I THINK I'LL GO HOME!
SOB!
WHY, MR.SUN, WHAT'S WRONG? AREN'T YOU GOING FORWARD NOW?
SOB!
YES, I AM, CASPER, BUT...
THE SORCERER IS MAKING ME AND EVERYTHING ELSE GO FORWARD TOO FAST NOW!

CONTINUED IN THIS ISSUE—

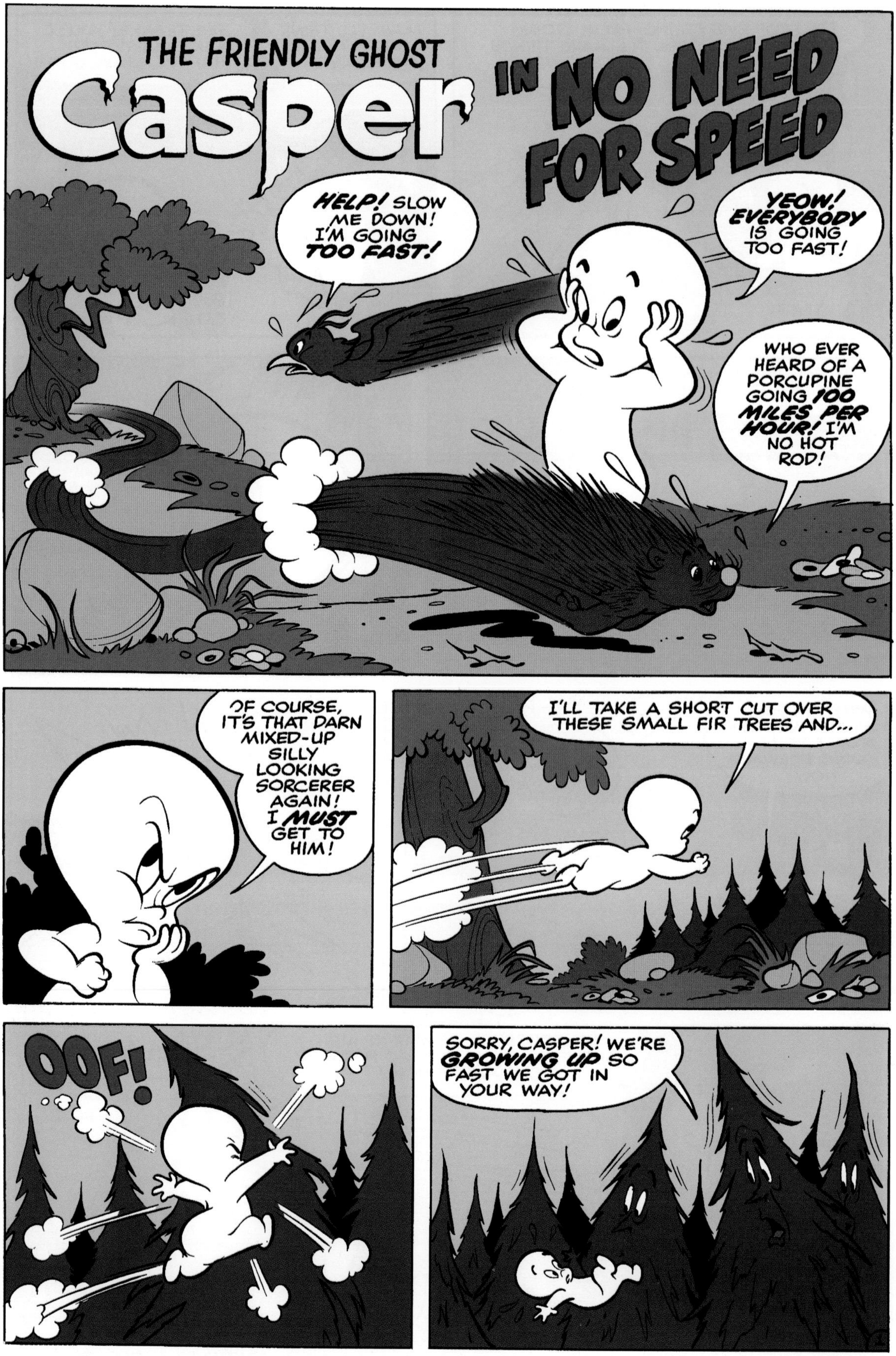

THE FRIENDLY GHOST
Casper
IN NO NEED FOR SPEED
HELP! SLOW ME DOWN! I'M GOING TOO FAST!
YEOW! EVERYBODY IS GOING TOO FAST!
WHO EVER HEARD OF A PORCUPINE GOING 100 MILES PER HOUR! I'M NO HOT ROD!
OF COURSE, IT'S THAT DARN MIXED-UP SILLY LOOKING SORCERER AGAIN! I MUST GET TO HIM!
I'LL TAKE A SHORT CUT OVER THESE SMALL FIR TREES AND...
OOF!
SORRY, CASPER! WE'RE GROWING UP SO FAST WE GOT IN YOUR WAY!

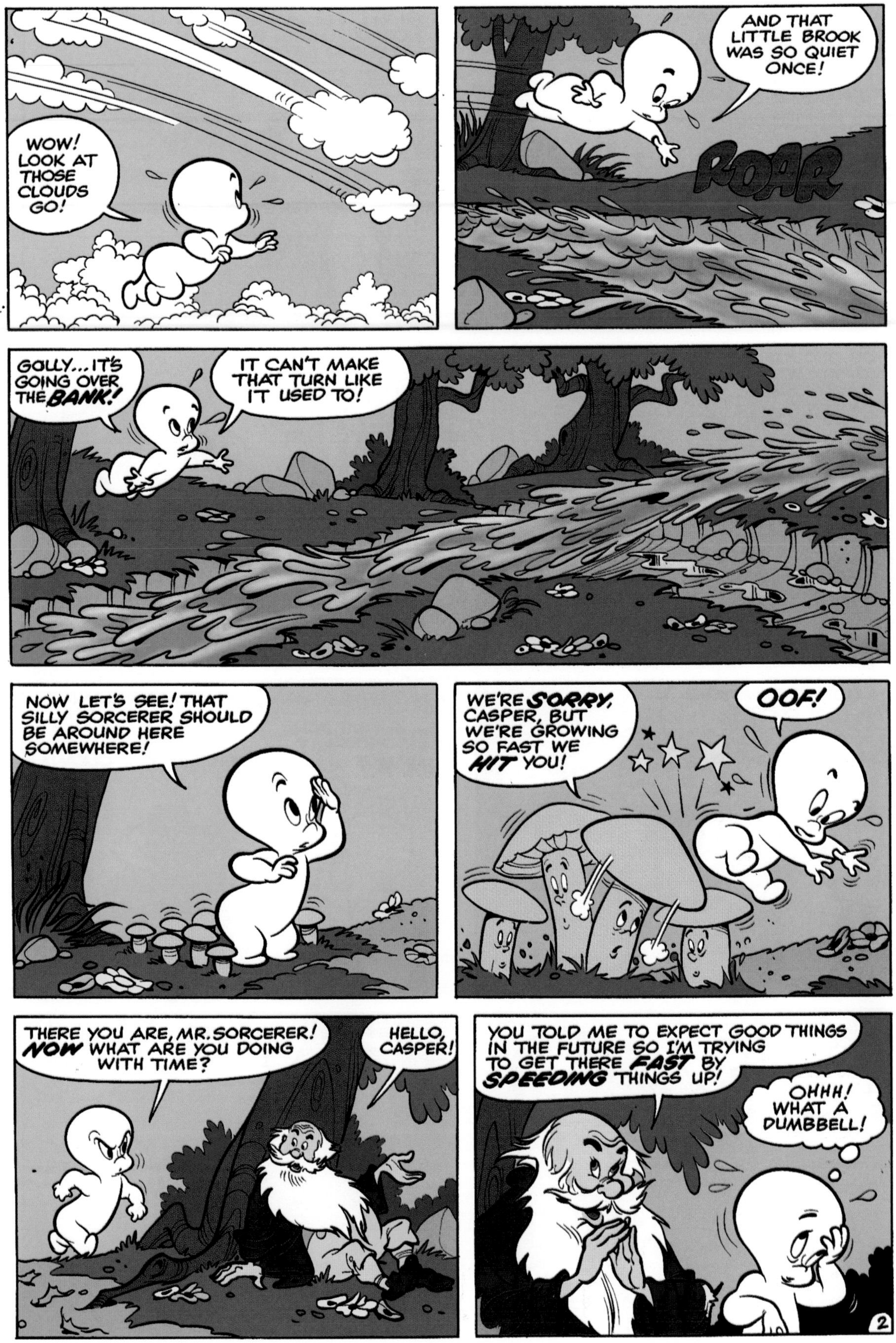
WOW! LOOK AT THOSE CLOUDS GO!
AND THAT LITTLE BROOK WAS SO QUIET ONCE!
ROAR
GOLLY... IT'S GOING OVER THE BANK!
IT CAN'T MAKE THAT TURN LIKE IT USED TO!
NOW LET'S SEE! THAT SILLY SORCERER SHOULD BE AROUND HERE SOMEWHERE!
WE'RE SORRY, CASPER, BUT WE'RE GROWING SO FAST WE HIT YOU!
OOF!
THERE YOU ARE, MR. SORCERER! NOW WHAT ARE YOU DOING WITH TIME?
HELLO, CASPER!
YOU TOLD ME TO EXPECT GOOD THINGS IN THE FUTURE SO I'M TRYING TO GET THERE FAST BY SPEEDING THINGS UP!
OHHH! WHAT A DUMBBELL!
2

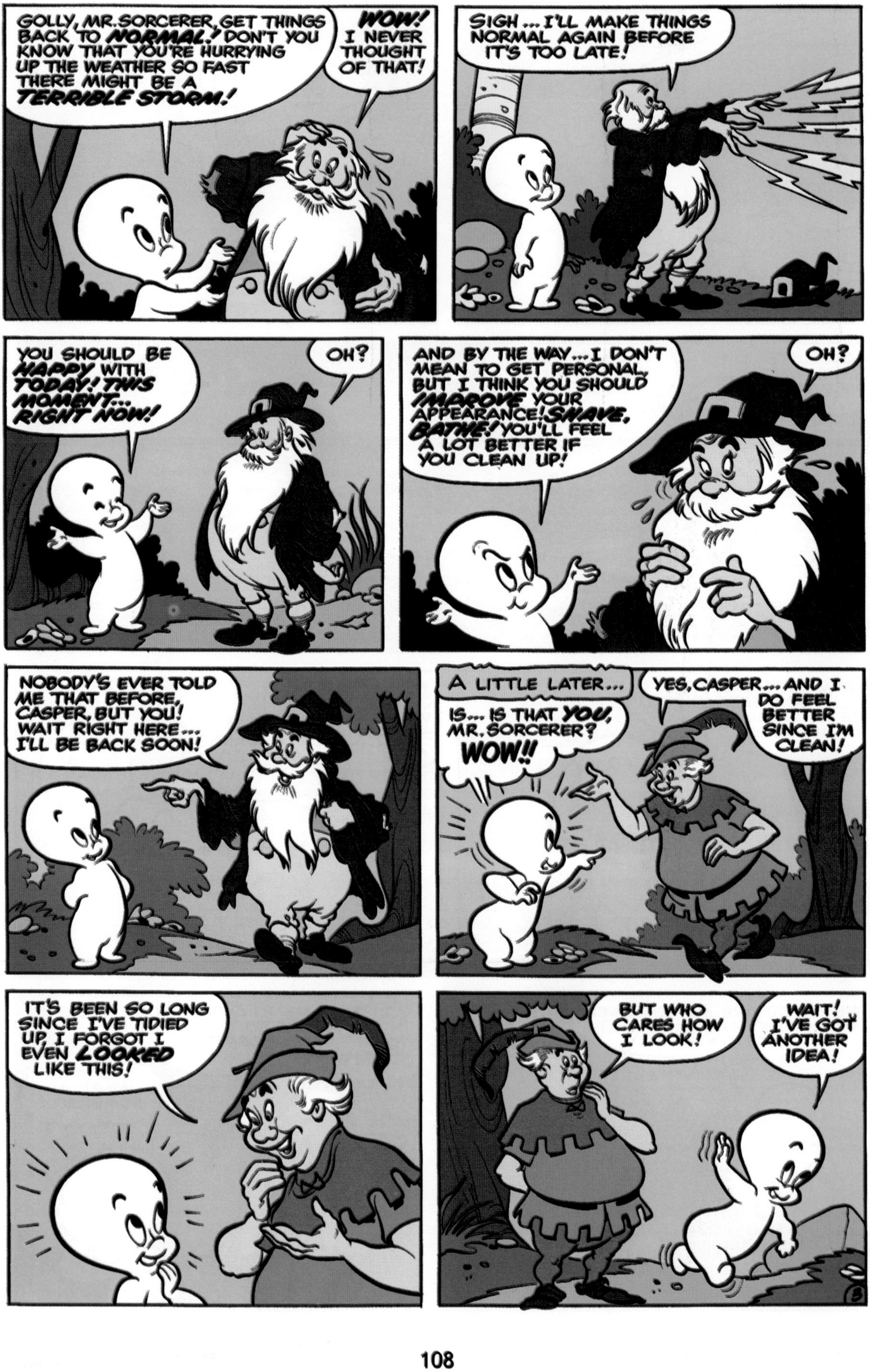
GOLLY, MR. SORCERER, GET THINGS BACK TO NORMAL! DON'T YOU KNOW THAT YOU'RE HURRYING UP THE WEATHER SO FAST THERE MIGHT BE A TERRIBLE STORM!
WOW! I NEVER THOUGHT OF THAT!
SIGH ... I'LL MAKE THINGS NORMAL AGAIN BEFORE IT'S TOO LATE!
YOU SHOULD BE HAPPY WITH TODAY! THIS MOMENT... RIGHT NOW!
OH?
AND BY THE WAY... I DON'T MEAN TO GET PERSONAL, BUT I THINK YOU SHOULD IMPROVE YOUR APPEARANCE! SHAVE, BATHE! YOU'LL FEEL A LOT BETTER IF YOU CLEAN UP!
OH?
NOBODY'S EVER TOLD ME THAT BEFORE, CASPER, BUT YOU! WAIT RIGHT HERE... I'LL BE BACK SOON!
A LITTLE LATER...
IS... IS THAT YOU, MR. SORCERER? WOW!!
YES, CASPER... AND I DO FEEL BETTER SINCE I'M CLEAN!
IT'S BEEN SO LONG SINCE I'VE TIDIED UP, I FORGOT I EVEN LOOKED LIKE THIS!
BUT WHO CARES HOW I LOOK!
WAIT! I'VE GOT ANOTHER IDEA!
8

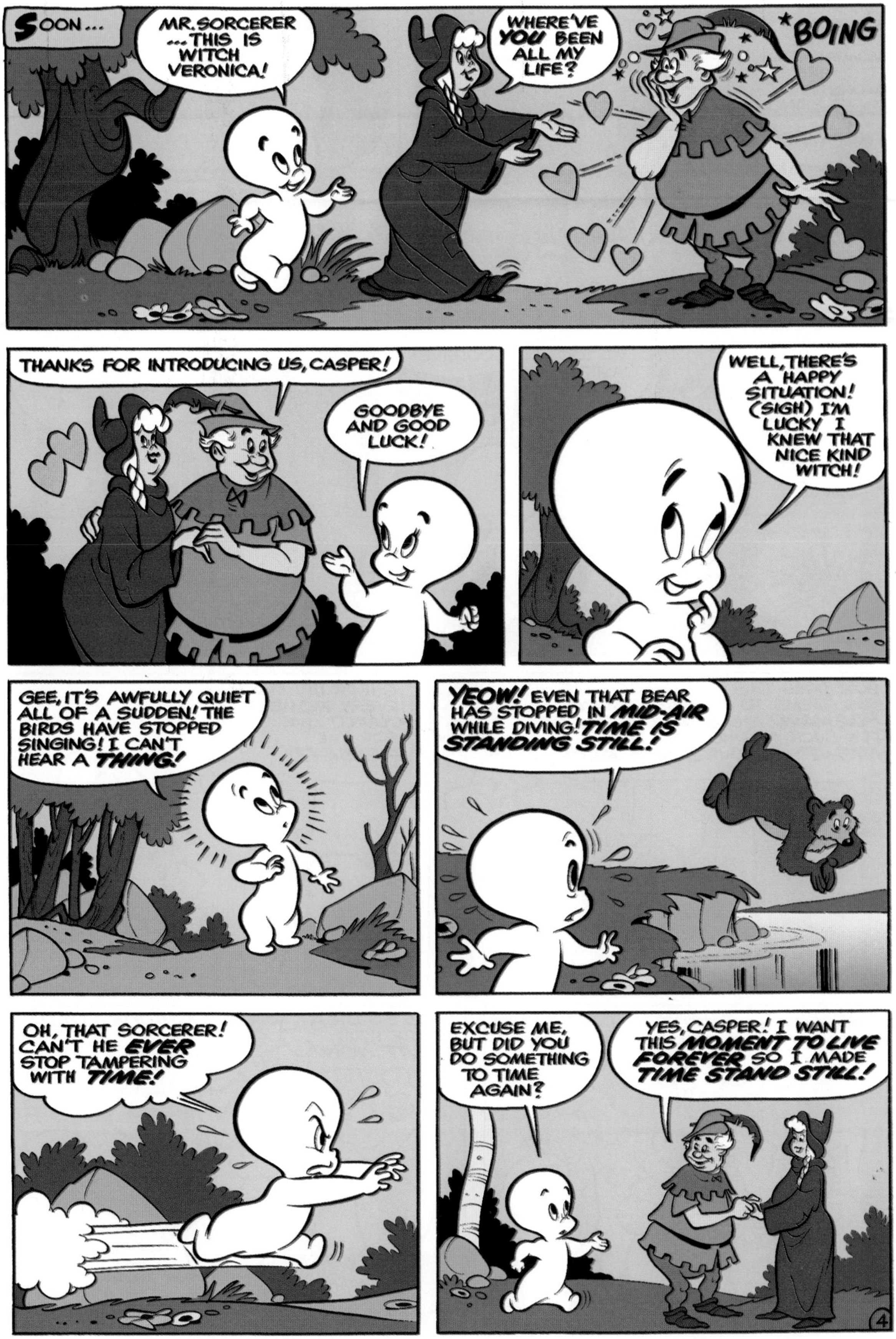
SOON...
MR. SORCERER ...THIS IS WITCH VERONICA!
WHERE'VE YOU BEEN ALL MY LIFE?
BOING
THANKS FOR INTRODUCING US, CASPER!
GOODBYE AND GOOD LUCK!
WELL, THERE'S A HAPPY SITUATION! (SIGH) I'M LUCKY I KNEW THAT NICE KIND WITCH!
GEE, IT'S AWFULLY QUIET ALL OF A SUDDEN! THE BIRDS HAVE STOPPED SINGING! I CAN'T HEAR A THING!
YEOW! EVEN THAT BEAR HAS STOPPED IN MID-AIR WHILE DIVING! TIME IS STANDING STILL!
OH, THAT SORCERER! CAN'T HE EVER STOP TAMPERING WITH TIME!
EXCUSE ME, BUT DID YOU DO SOMETHING TO TIME AGAIN?
YES, CASPER! I WANT THIS MOMENT TO LIVE FOREVER SO I MADE TIME STAND STILL!
4

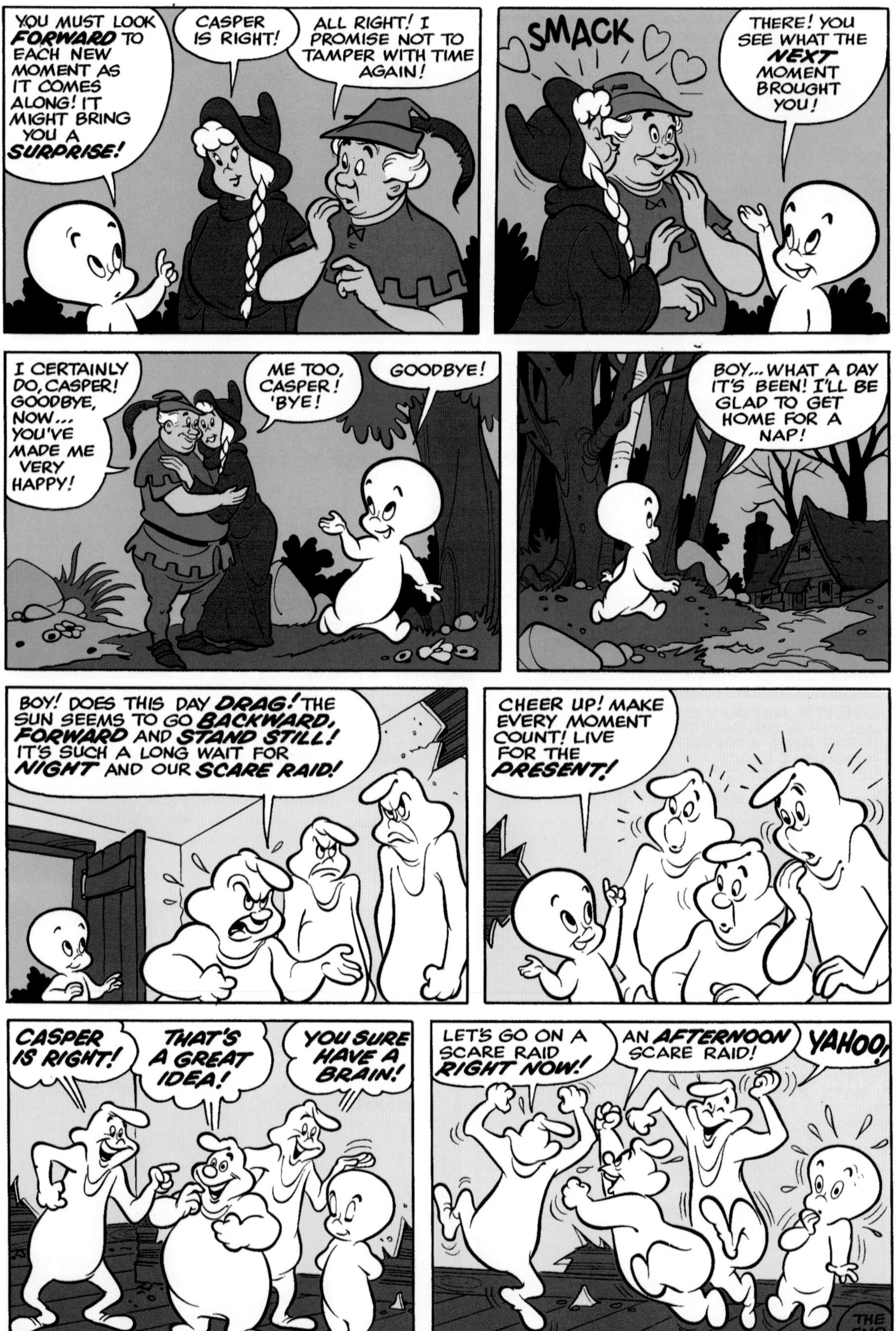
YOU MUST LOOK FORWARD TO EACH NEW MOMENT AS IT COMES ALONG! IT MIGHT BRING YOU A SURPRISE!
CASPER IS RIGHT!
ALL RIGHT! I PROMISE NOT TO TAMPER WITH TIME AGAIN!
SMACK
THERE! YOU SEE WHAT THE NEXT MOMENT BROUGHT YOU!
I CERTAINLY DO, CASPER! GOODBYE, NOW... YOU'VE MADE ME VERY HAPPY!
ME TOO, CASPER! 'BYE!
GOODBYE!
BOY... WHAT A DAY IT'S BEEN! I'LL BE GLAD TO GET HOME FOR A NAP!
BOY! DOES THIS DAY DRAG! THE SUN SEEMS TO GO BACKWARD, FORWARD AND STAND STILL! IT'S SUCH A LONG WAIT FOR NIGHT AND OUR SCARE RAID!
CHEER UP! MAKE EVERY MOMENT COUNT! LIVE FOR THE PRESENT!
CASPER IS RIGHT!
THAT'S A GREAT IDEA!
YOU SURE HAVE A BRAIN!
LET'S GO ON A SCARE RAID RIGHT NOW!
AN AFTERNOON SCARE RAID!
YAHOO!
THE END

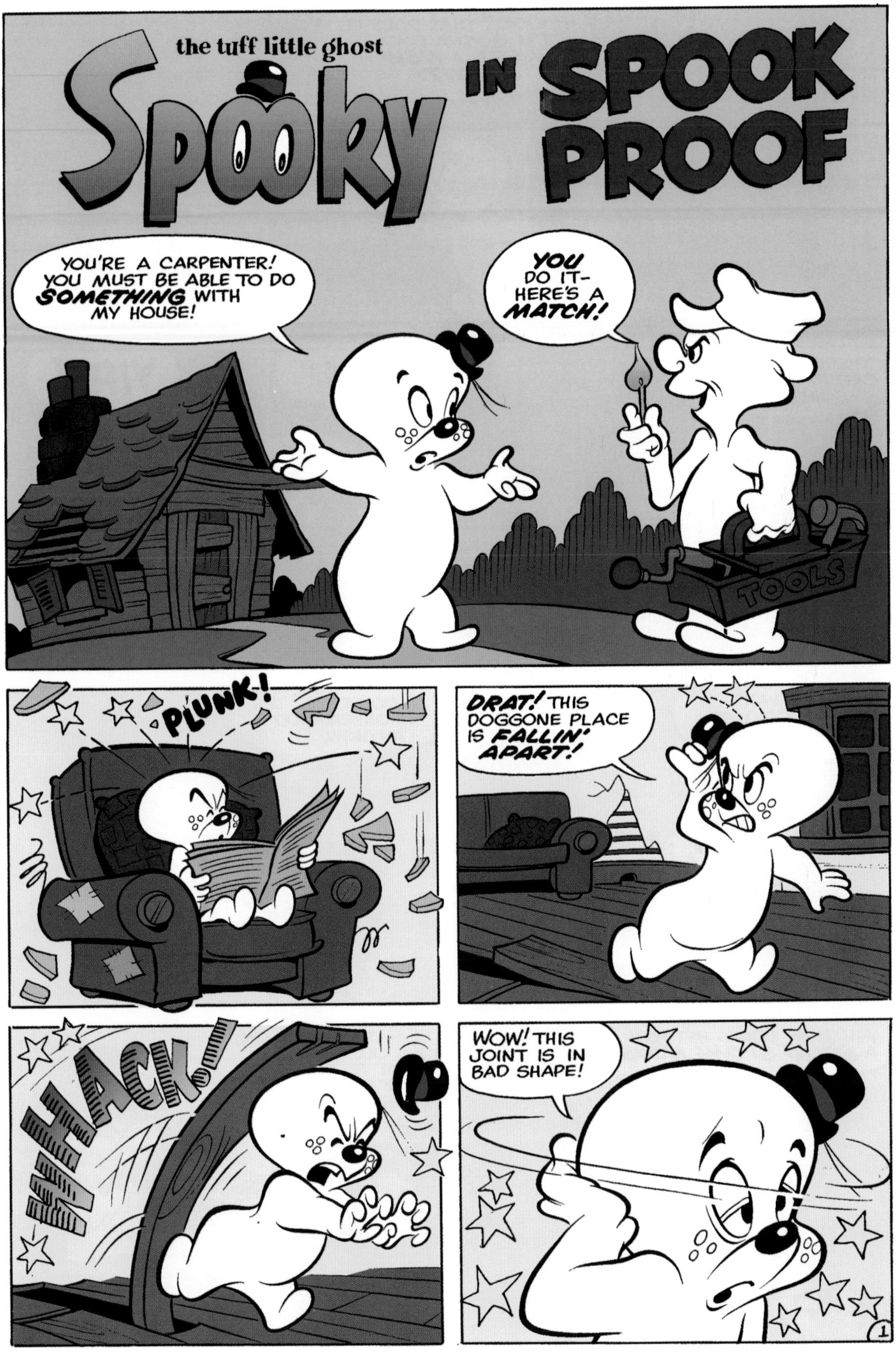
the tuff little ghost
Spooky IN SPOOK PROOF
YOU'RE A CARPENTER! YOU MUST BE ABLE TO DO SOMETHING WITH MY HOUSE!
YOU DO IT- HERE'S A MATCH!
TOOLS
PLUNK!
DRAT! THIS DOGGONE PLACE IS FALLIN' APART!
WHACK!!
WOW! THIS JOINT IS IN BAD SHAPE!
1

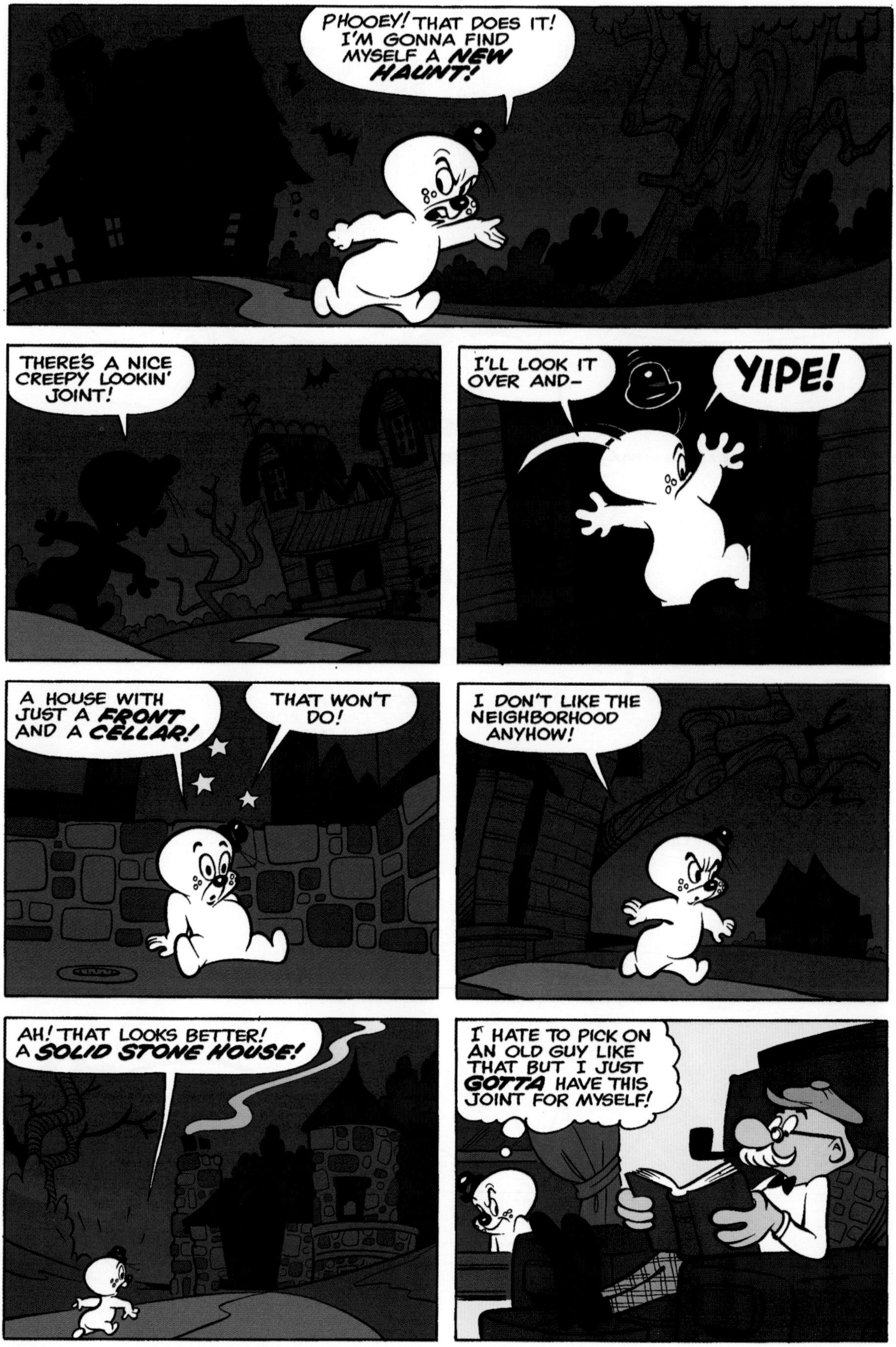
PHOOEY! THAT DOES IT! I'M GONNA FIND MYSELF A NEW HAUNT!
THERE'S A NICE CREEPY LOOKIN' JOINT!
I'LL LOOK IT OVER AND–
YIPE!
A HOUSE WITH JUST A FRONT AND A CELLAR!
THAT WON'T DO!
I DON'T LIKE THE NEIGHBORHOOD ANYHOW!
AH! THAT LOOKS BETTER! A SOLID STONE HOUSE!
I HATE TO PICK ON AN OLD GUY LIKE THAT BUT I JUST GOTTA HAVE THIS JOINT FOR MYSELF!

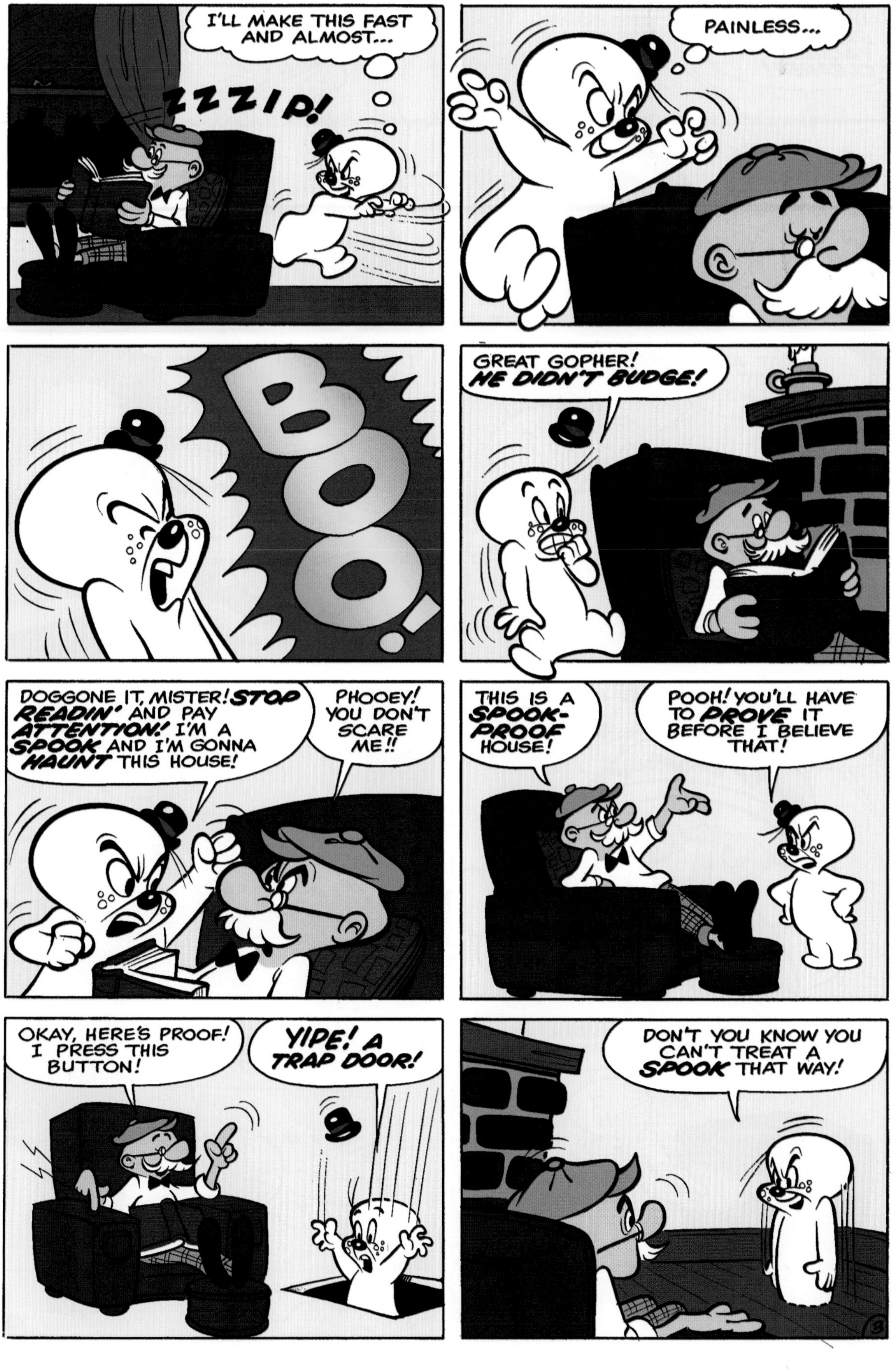
I'LL MAKE THIS FAST AND ALMOST...
ZZZIP!
PAINLESS...
BOO!
GREAT GOPHER! HE DIDN'T BUDGE!
DOGGONE IT, MISTER! STOP READIN' AND PAY ATTENTION! I'M A SPOOK AND I'M GONNA HAUNT THIS HOUSE!
PHOOEY! YOU DON'T SCARE ME!!
THIS IS A SPOOK-PROOF HOUSE!
POOH! YOU'LL HAVE TO PROVE IT BEFORE I BELIEVE THAT!
OKAY, HERE'S PROOF! I PRESS THIS BUTTON!
YIPE! A TRAP DOOR!
DON'T YOU KNOW YOU CAN'T TREAT A SPOOK THAT WAY!
3

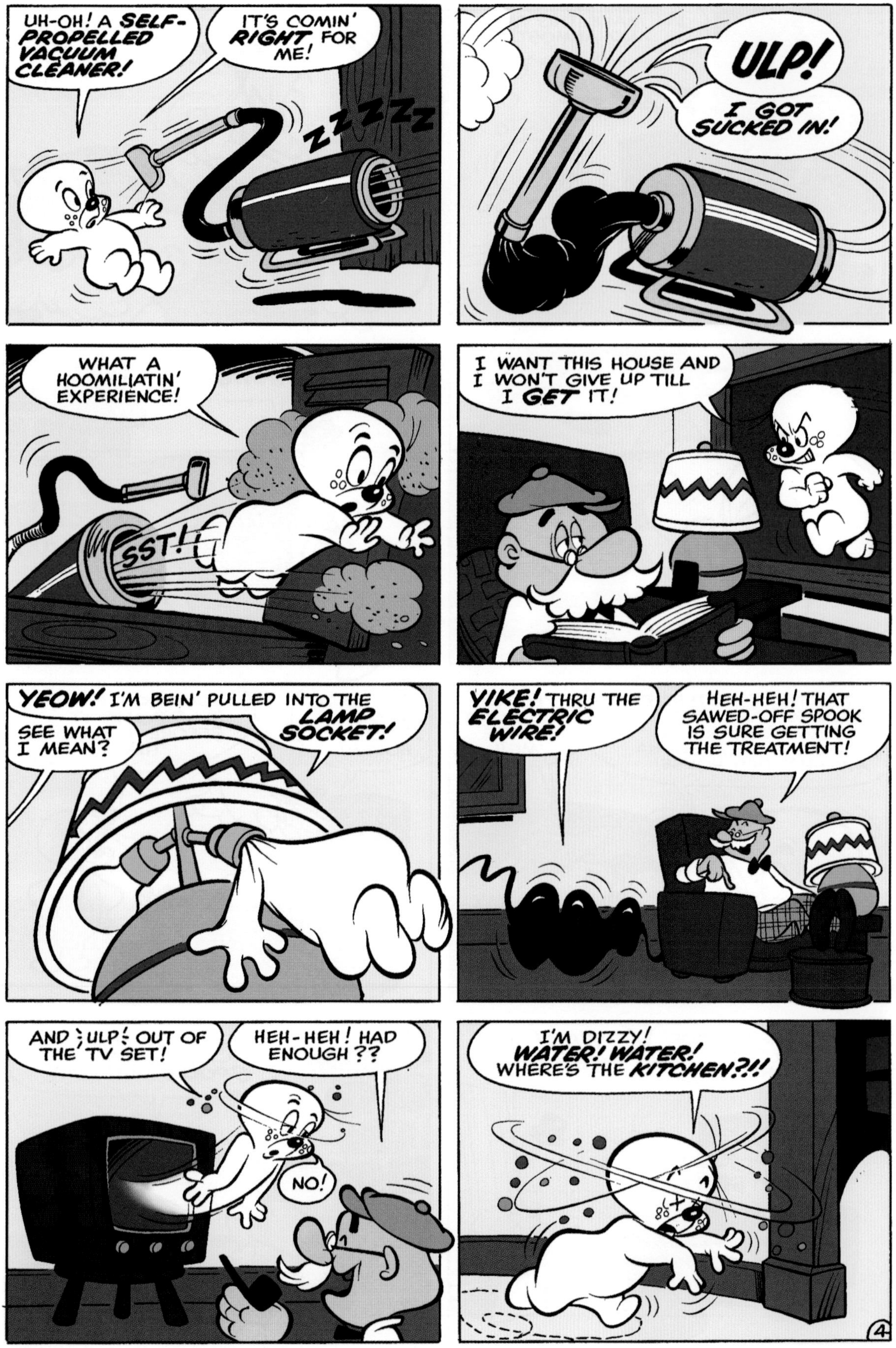
UH-OH! A SELF-PROPELLED VACUUM CLEANER!
IT'S COMIN' RIGHT FOR ME!
ZZZZZZ
ULP!
I GOT SUCKED IN!
WHAT A HOOMILIATIN' EXPERIENCE!
SST!
I WANT THIS HOUSE AND I WON'T GIVE UP TILL I GET IT!
YEOW! I'M BEIN' PULLED INTO THE LAMP SOCKET!
SEE WHAT I MEAN?
YIKE! THRU THE ELECTRIC WIRE!
HEH-HEH! THAT SAWED-OFF SPOOK IS SURE GETTING THE TREATMENT!
AND -ULP!- OUT OF THE TV SET!
HEH-HEH! HAD ENOUGH??
NO!
I'M DIZZY! WATER! WATER! WHERE'S THE KITCHEN?!!
4

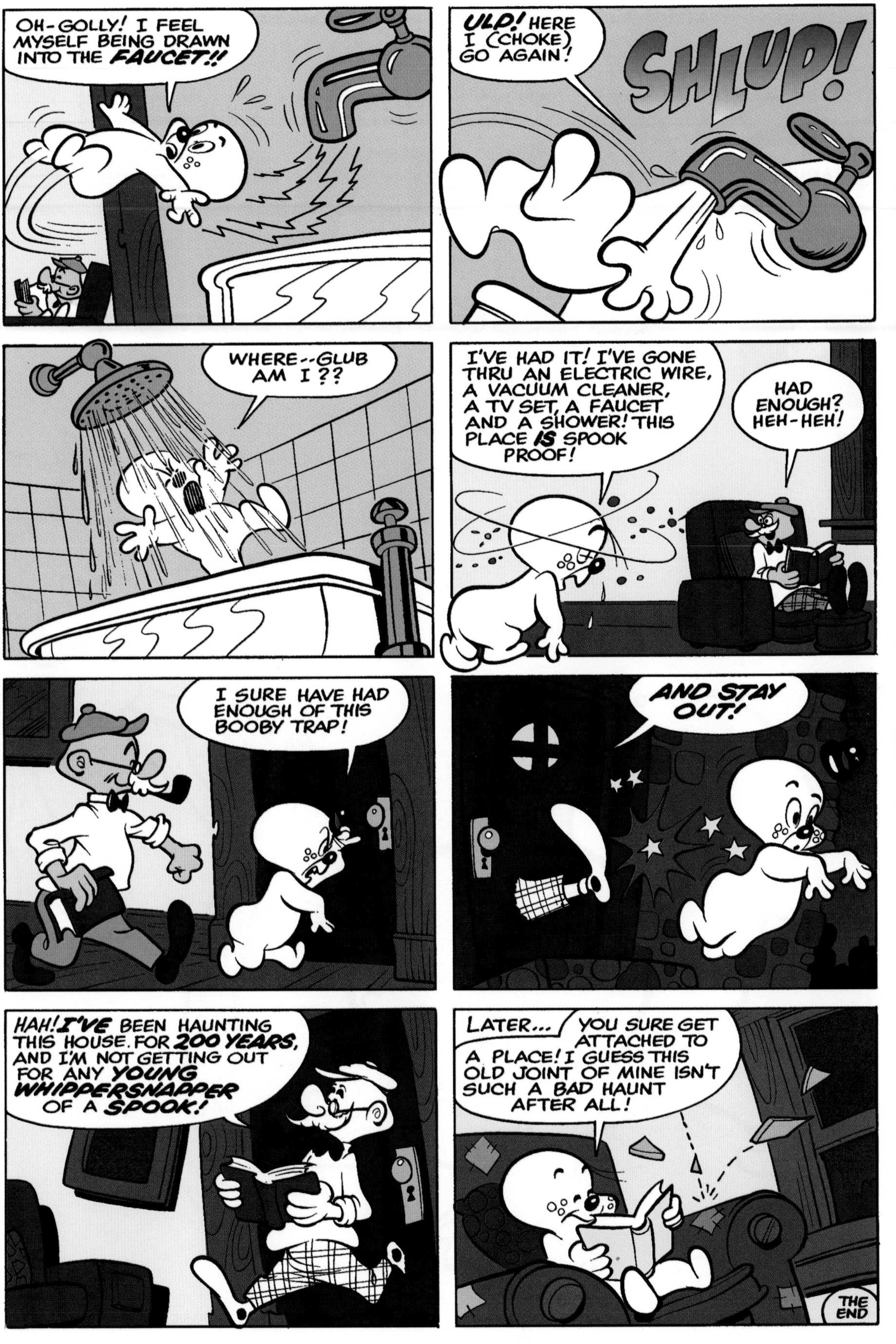
OH-GOLLY! I FEEL MYSELF BEING DRAWN INTO THE FAUCET!!
ULP! HERE I (CHOKE) GO AGAIN!
SHLUP!
WHERE--GLUB AM I??
I'VE HAD IT! I'VE GONE THRU AN ELECTRIC WIRE, A VACUUM CLEANER, A TV SET, A FAUCET AND A SHOWER! THIS PLACE IS SPOOK PROOF!
HAD ENOUGH? HEH-HEH!
I SURE HAVE HAD ENOUGH OF THIS BOOBY TRAP!
AND STAY OUT!
HAH! I'VE BEEN HAUNTING THIS HOUSE FOR 200 YEARS, AND I'M NOT GETTING OUT FOR ANY YOUNG WHIPPERSNAPPER OF A SPOOK!
LATER...
YOU SURE GET ATTACHED TO A PLACE! I GUESS THIS OLD JOINT OF MINE ISN'T SUCH A BAD HAUNT AFTER ALL!
THE END

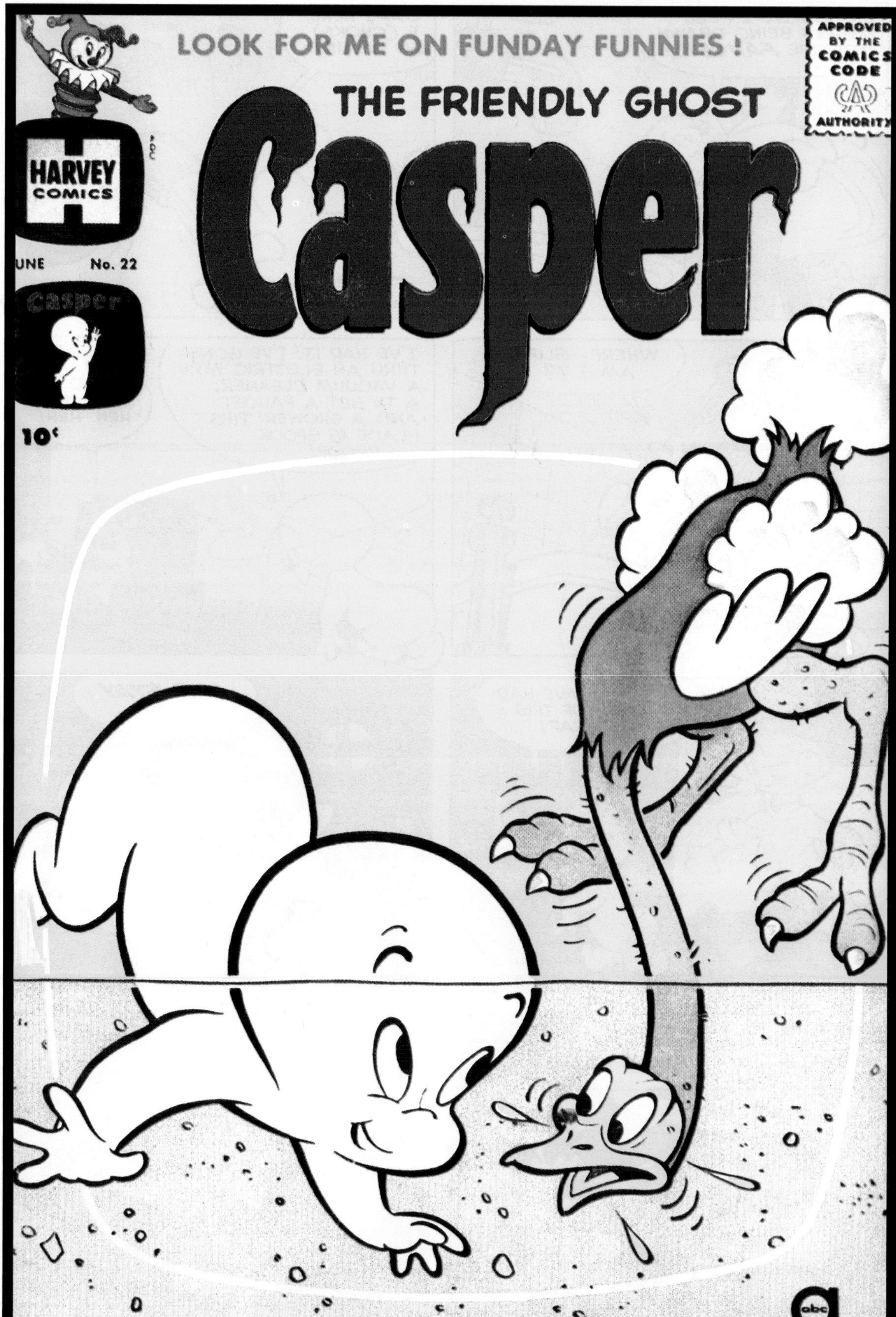
LOOK FOR ME ON FUNDAY FUNNIES !
THE FRIENDLY GHOST
Casper
HARVEY COMICS
UNE No. 22
Casper
10¢
APPROVED BY THE COMICS CODE AUTHORITY
EVERY SUNDAY AT 5 P.M. abc T.V.

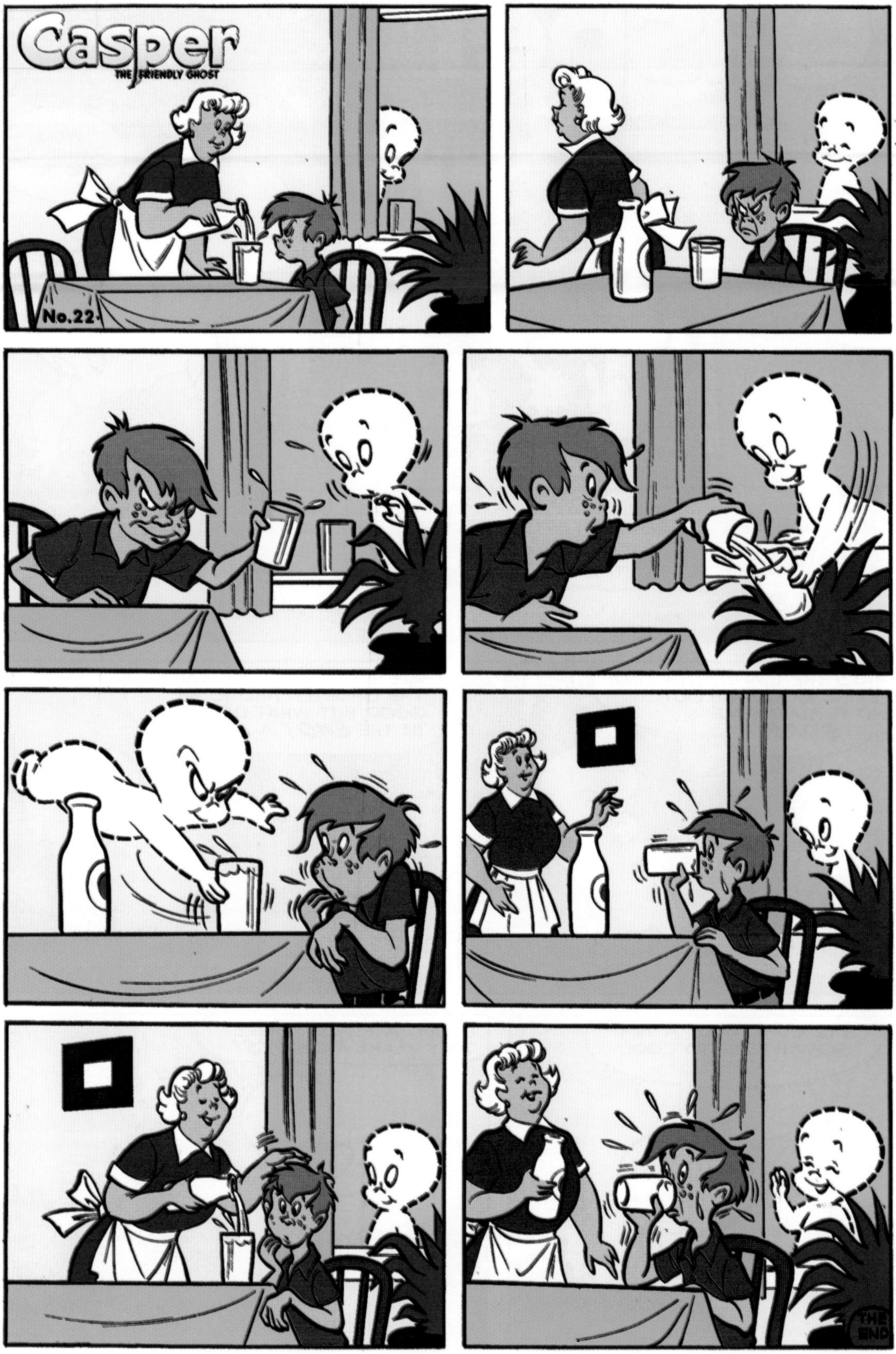
Casper
THE FRIENDLY GHOST
No.22
WOW!
THE END

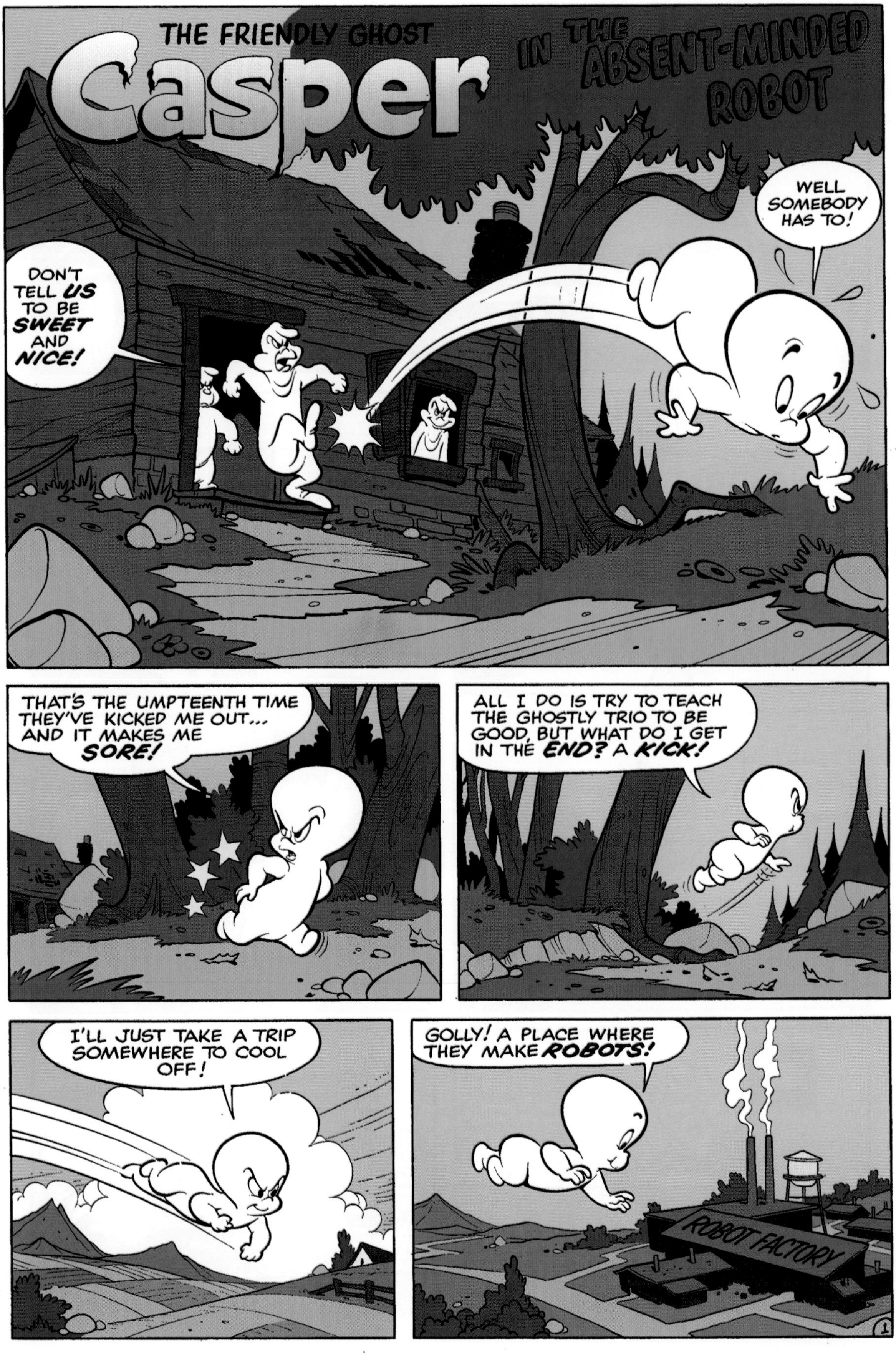
THE FRIENDLY GHOST
Casper
IN THE ABSENT-MINDED ROBOT
DON'T TELL US TO BE SWEET AND NICE!
WELL SOMEBODY HAS TO!
THAT'S THE UMPTEENTH TIME THEY'VE KICKED ME OUT... AND IT MAKES ME SORE!
ALL I DO IS TRY TO TEACH THE GHOSTLY TRIO TO BE GOOD, BUT WHAT DO I GET IN THE END? A KICK!
I'LL JUST TAKE A TRIP SOMEWHERE TO COOL OFF!
GOLLY! A PLACE WHERE THEY MAKE ROBOTS!
ROBOT FACTORY

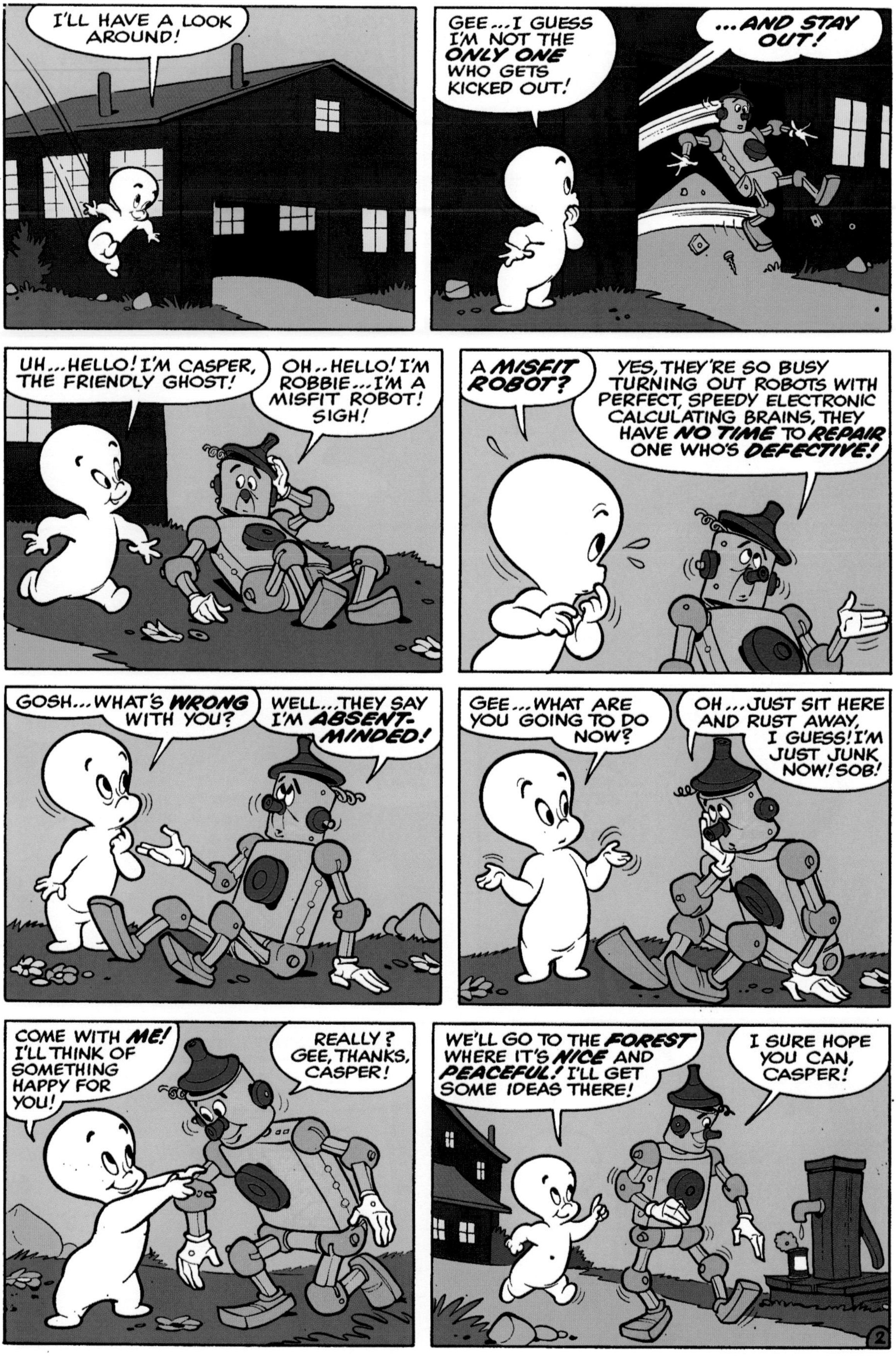
I'LL HAVE A LOOK AROUND!
GEE...I GUESS I'M NOT THE ONLY ONE WHO GETS KICKED OUT!
...AND STAY OUT!
UH...HELLO! I'M CASPER, THE FRIENDLY GHOST!
OH..HELLO! I'M ROBBIE...I'M A MISFIT ROBOT! SIGH!
A MISFIT ROBOT?
YES, THEY'RE SO BUSY TURNING OUT ROBOTS WITH PERFECT, SPEEDY ELECTRONIC CALCULATING BRAINS, THEY HAVE NO TIME TO REPAIR ONE WHO'S DEFECTIVE!
GOSH...WHAT'S WRONG WITH YOU?
WELL...THEY SAY I'M ABSENT-MINDED!
GEE...WHAT ARE YOU GOING TO DO NOW?
OH...JUST SIT HERE AND RUST AWAY, I GUESS! I'M JUST JUNK NOW! SOB!
COME WITH ME! I'LL THINK OF SOMETHING HAPPY FOR YOU!
REALLY? GEE, THANKS, CASPER!
WE'LL GO TO THE FOREST WHERE IT'S NICE AND PEACEFUL! I'LL GET SOME IDEAS THERE!
I SURE HOPE YOU CAN, CASPER!
2

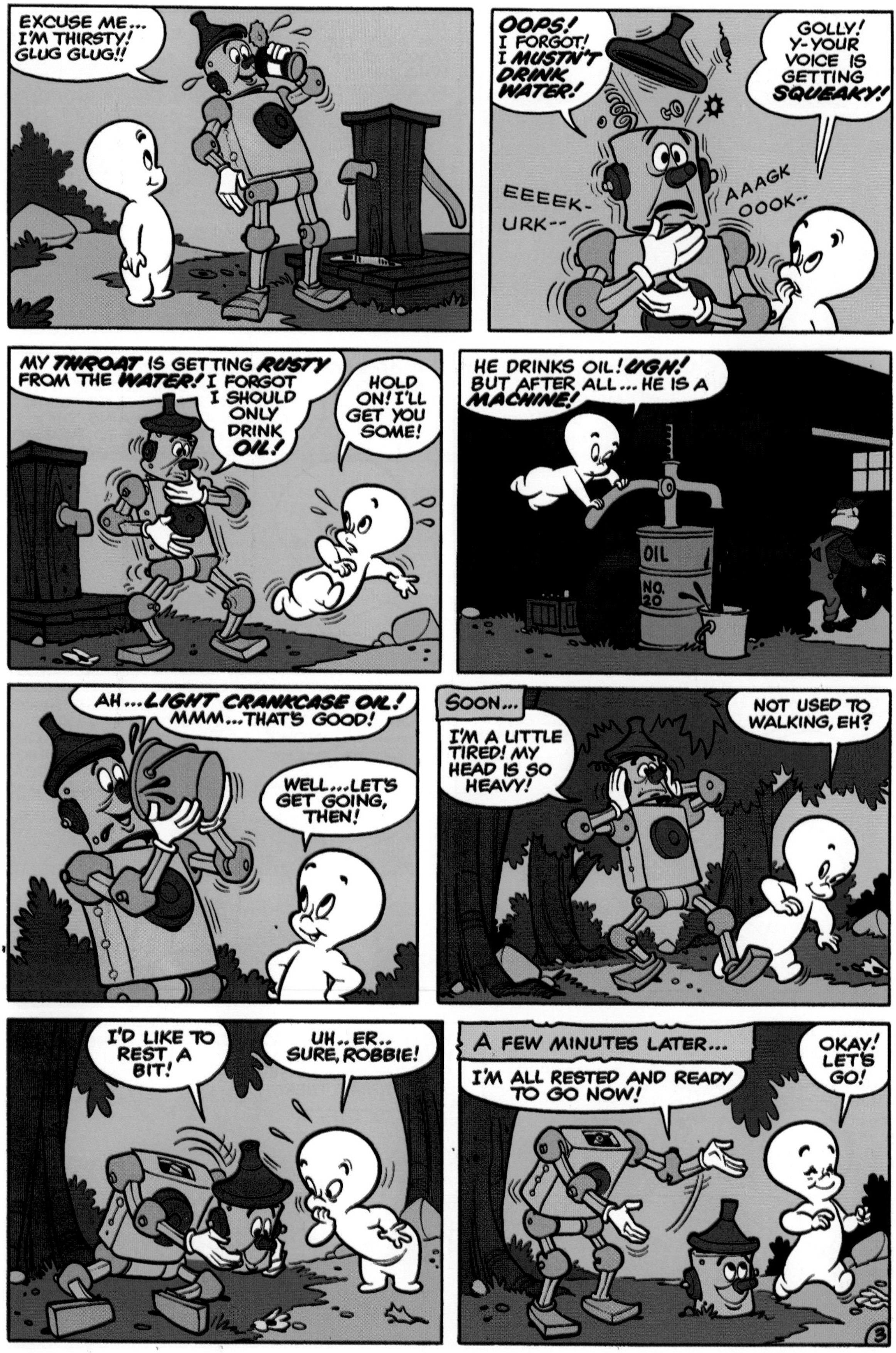
EXCUSE ME... I'M THIRSTY! GLUG GLUG!!
OOPS! I FORGOT! I MUSTN'T DRINK WATER!
GOLLY! Y-YOUR VOICE IS GETTING SQUEAKY!
EEEEK-URK--
AAAGK OOOK--
MY THROAT IS GETTING RUSTY FROM THE WATER! I FORGOT I SHOULD ONLY DRINK OIL!
HOLD ON! I'LL GET YOU SOME!
HE DRINKS OIL! UGH! BUT AFTER ALL... HE IS A MACHINE!
OIL NO. 20
AH... LIGHT CRANKCASE OIL! MMM... THAT'S GOOD!
WELL... LET'S GET GOING, THEN!
SOON...
I'M A LITTLE TIRED! MY HEAD IS SO HEAVY!
NOT USED TO WALKING, EH?
I'D LIKE TO REST A BIT!
UH.. ER.. SURE, ROBBIE!
A FEW MINUTES LATER...
I'M ALL RESTED AND READY TO GO NOW!
OKAY! LET'S GO!
3

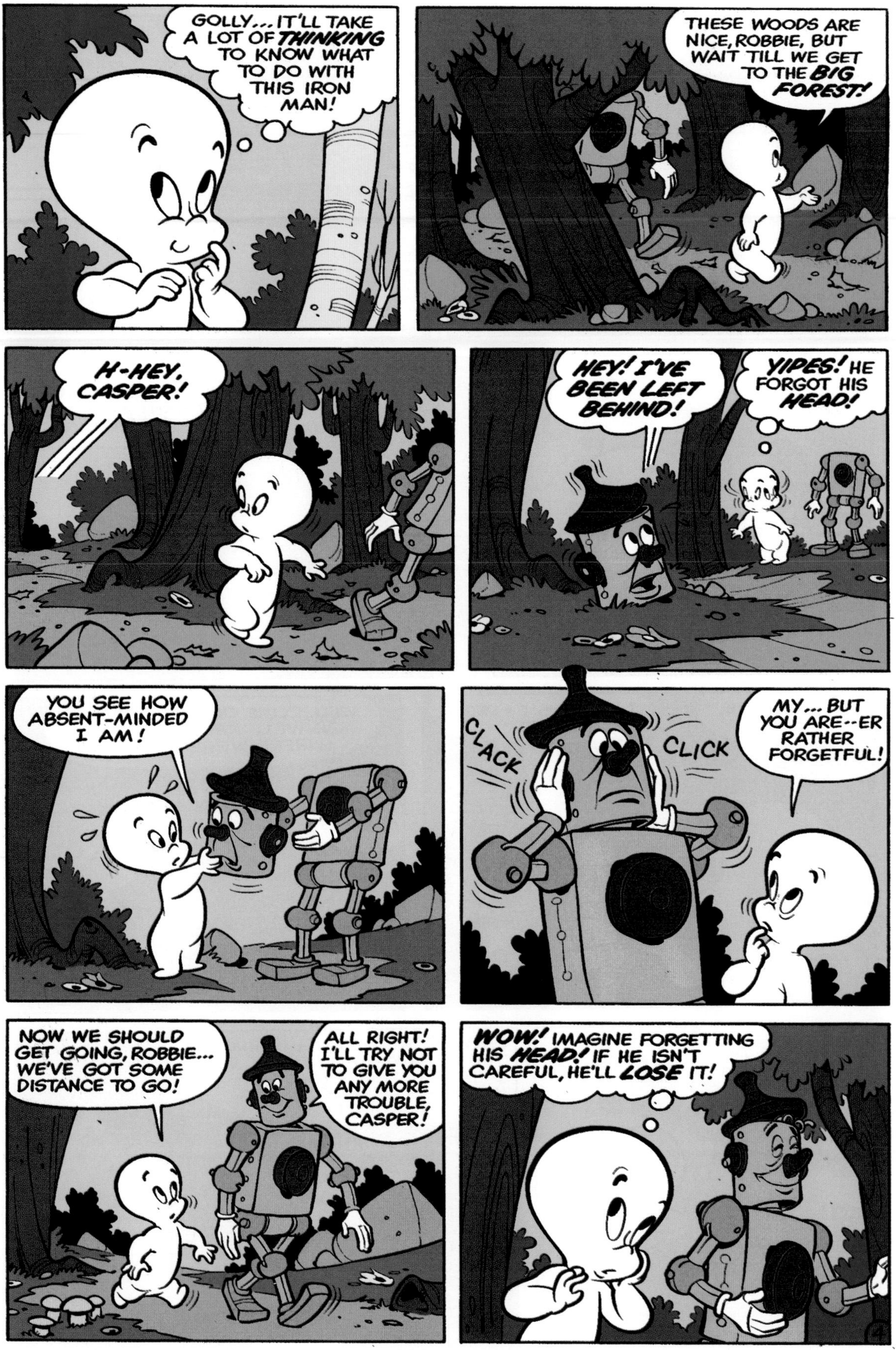
GOLLY... IT'LL TAKE A LOT OF THINKING TO KNOW WHAT TO DO WITH THIS IRON MAN!
THESE WOODS ARE NICE, ROBBIE, BUT WAIT TILL WE GET TO THE BIG FOREST!
H-HEY, CASPER!
HEY! I'VE BEEN LEFT BEHIND!
YIPES! HE FORGOT HIS HEAD!
YOU SEE HOW ABSENT-MINDED I AM!
CLACK
CLICK
MY... BUT YOU ARE--ER RATHER FORGETFUL!
NOW WE SHOULD GET GOING, ROBBIE... WE'VE GOT SOME DISTANCE TO GO!
ALL RIGHT! I'LL TRY NOT TO GIVE YOU ANY MORE TROUBLE, CASPER!
WOW! IMAGINE FORGETTING HIS HEAD! IF HE ISN'T CAREFUL, HE'LL LOSE IT!
4

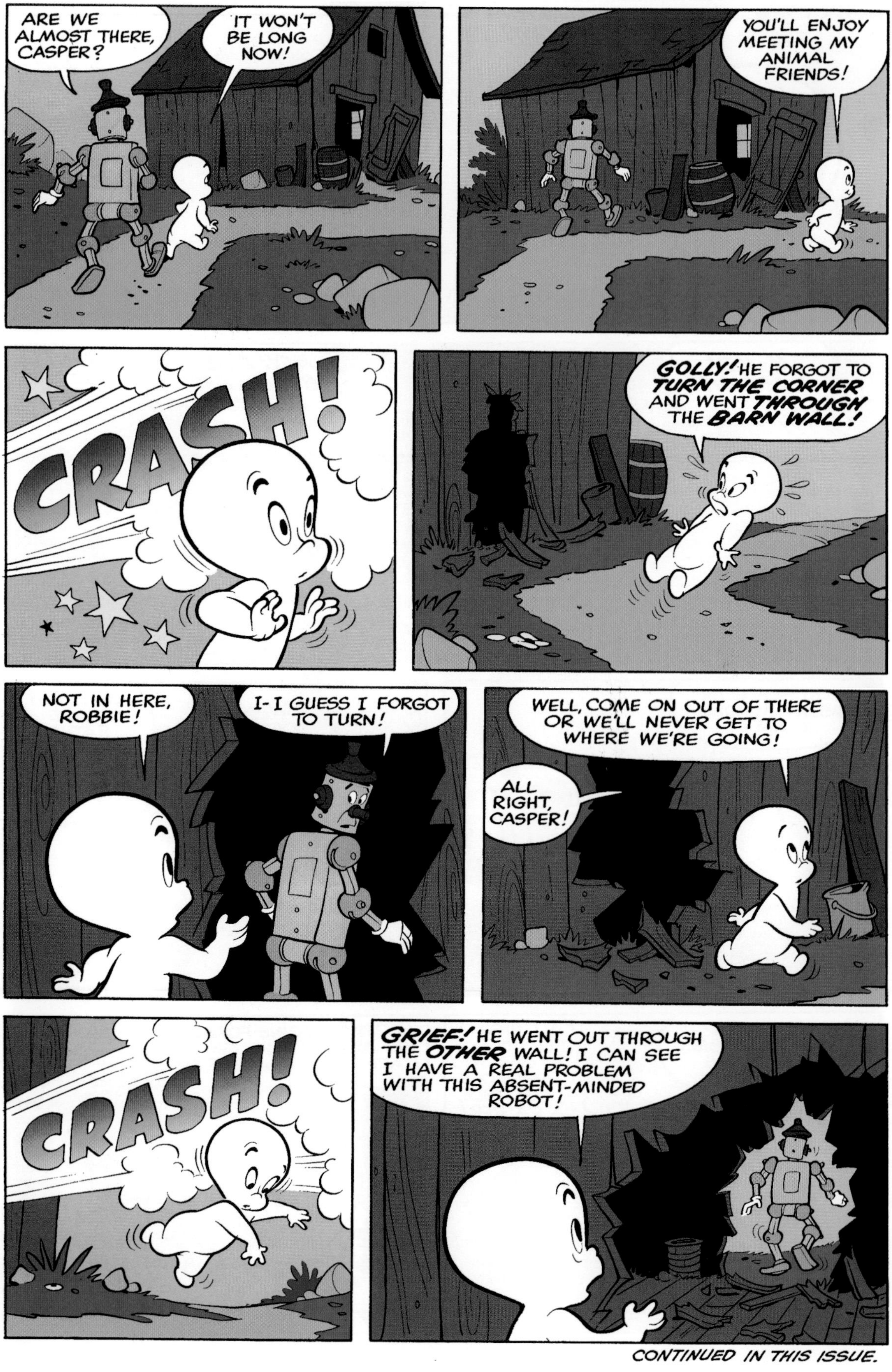
ARE WE ALMOST THERE, CASPER?
IT WON'T BE LONG NOW!
YOU'LL ENJOY MEETING MY ANIMAL FRIENDS!
CRASH!
GOLLY! HE FORGOT TO TURN THE CORNER AND WENT THROUGH THE BARN WALL!
NOT IN HERE, ROBBIE!
I-I GUESS I FORGOT TO TURN!
WELL, COME ON OUT OF THERE OR WE'LL NEVER GET TO WHERE WE'RE GOING!
ALL RIGHT, CASPER!
CRASH!
GRIEF! HE WENT OUT THROUGH THE OTHER WALL! I CAN SEE I HAVE A REAL PROBLEM WITH THIS ABSENT-MINDED ROBOT!

CONTINUED IN THIS ISSUE.

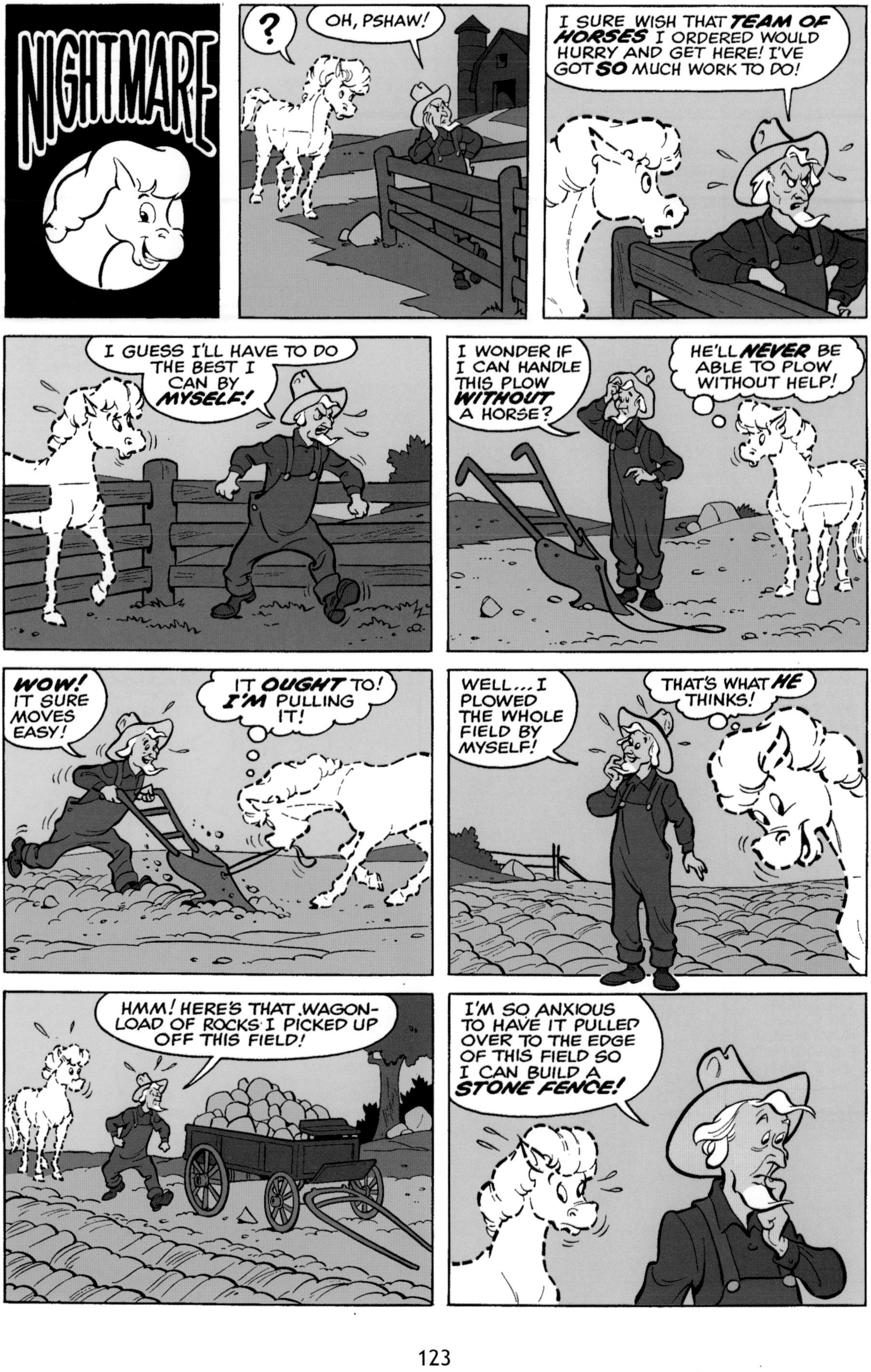
NIGHTMARE
?
OH, PSHAW!
I SURE WISH THAT TEAM OF HORSES I ORDERED WOULD HURRY AND GET HERE! I'VE GOT SO MUCH WORK TO DO!
I GUESS I'LL HAVE TO DO THE BEST I CAN BY MYSELF!
I WONDER IF I CAN HANDLE THIS PLOW WITHOUT A HORSE?
HE'LL NEVER BE ABLE TO PLOW WITHOUT HELP!
WOW! IT SURE MOVES EASY!
IT OUGHT TO! I'M PULLING IT!
WELL... I PLOWED THE WHOLE FIELD BY MYSELF!
THAT'S WHAT HE THINKS!
HMM! HERE'S THAT WAGON-LOAD OF ROCKS I PICKED UP OFF THIS FIELD!
I'M SO ANXIOUS TO HAVE IT PULLED OVER TO THE EDGE OF THIS FIELD SO I CAN BUILD A STONE FENCE!

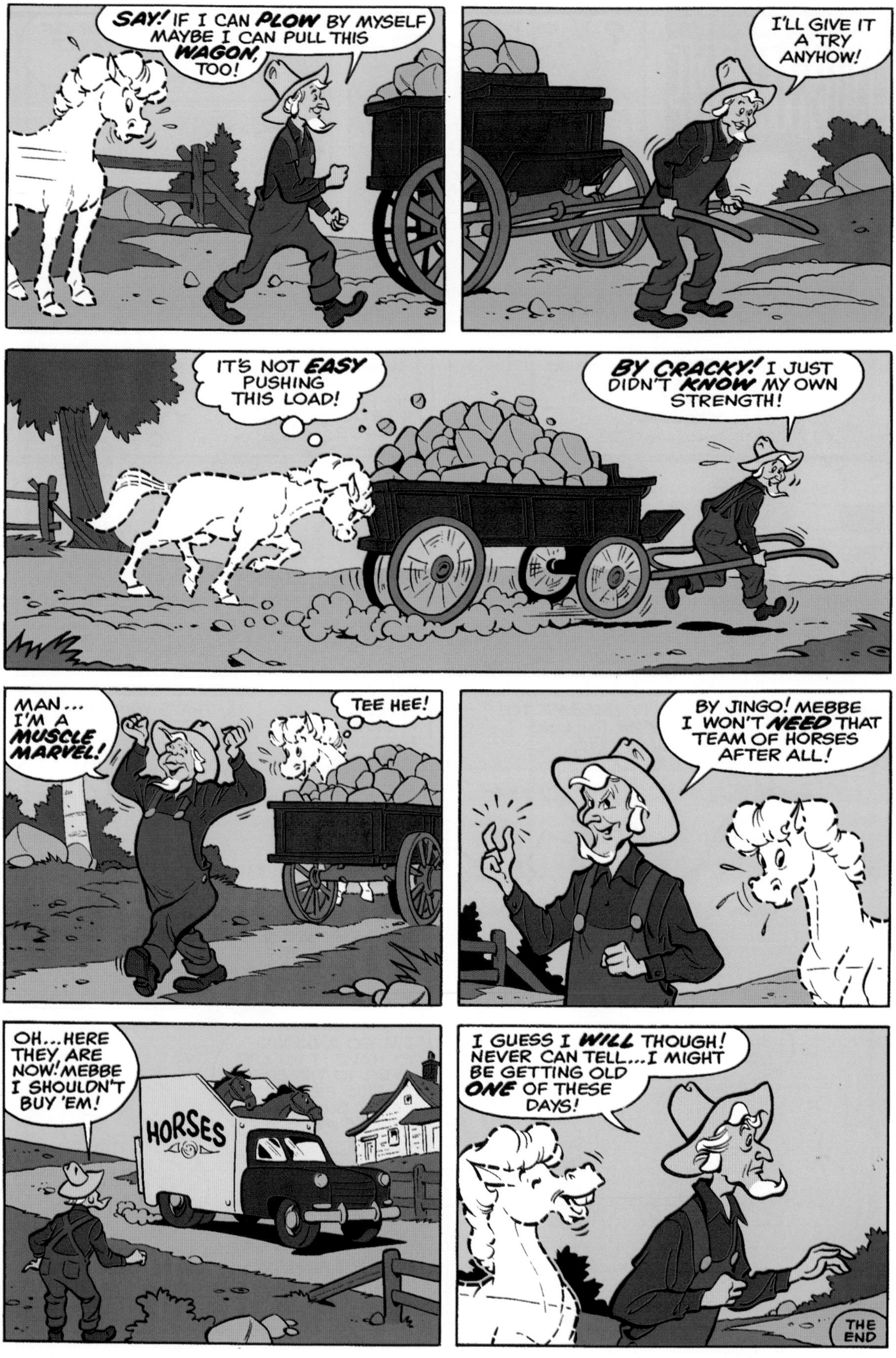
SAY! IF I CAN PLOW BY MYSELF MAYBE I CAN PULL THIS WAGON, TOO!
I'LL GIVE IT A TRY ANYHOW!
IT'S NOT EASY PUSHING THIS LOAD!
BY CRACKY! I JUST DIDN'T KNOW MY OWN STRENGTH!
MAN... I'M A MUSCLE MARVEL!
TEE HEE!
BY JINGO! MEBBE I WON'T NEED THAT TEAM OF HORSES AFTER ALL!
OH...HERE THEY ARE NOW! MEBBE I SHOULDN'T BUY 'EM!
HORSES
I GUESS I WILL THOUGH! NEVER CAN TELL...I MIGHT BE GETTING OLD ONE OF THESE DAYS!
THE END

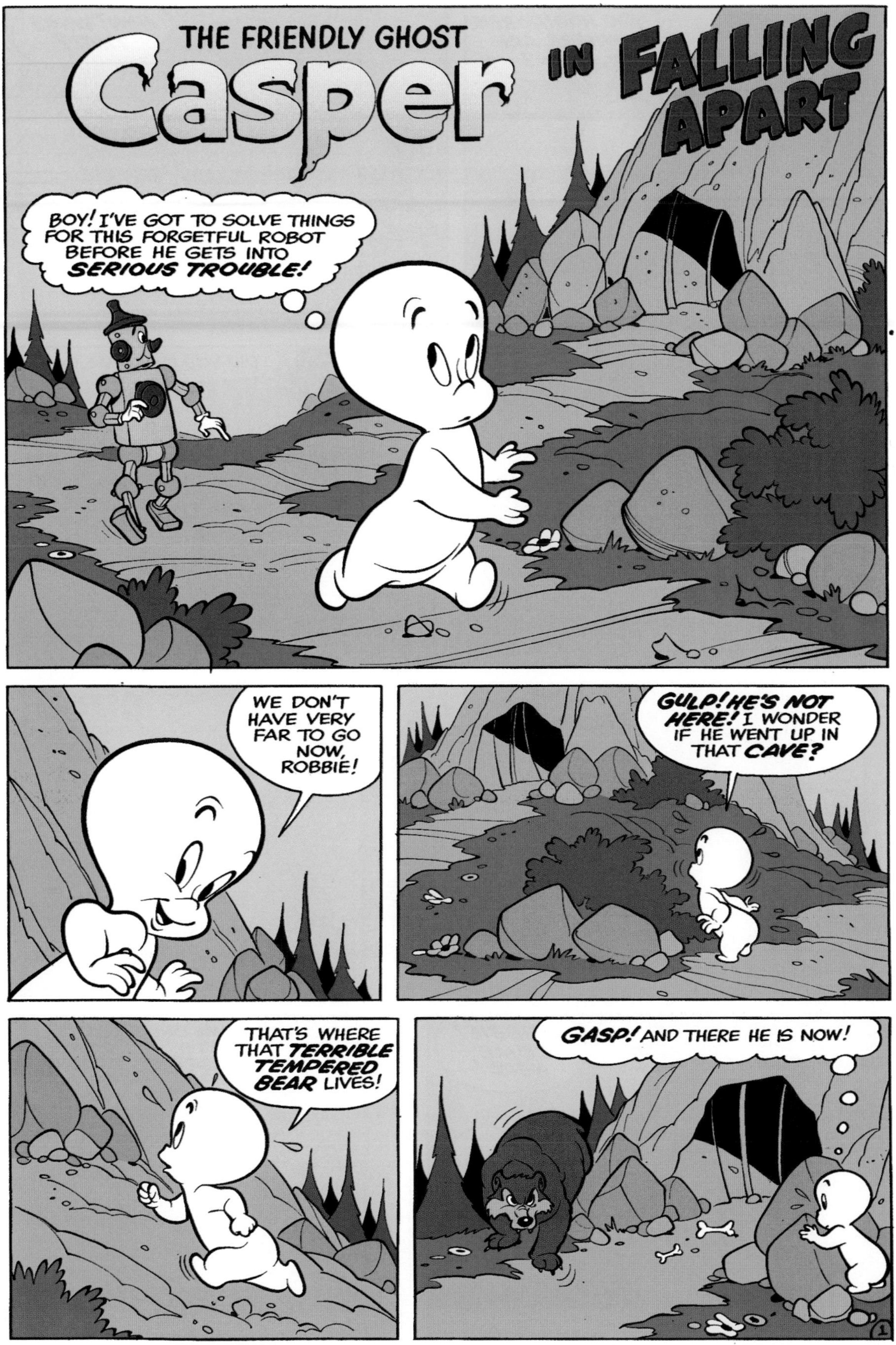
THE FRIENDLY GHOST
Casper
IN
FALLING APART
BOY! I'VE GOT TO SOLVE THINGS FOR THIS FORGETFUL ROBOT BEFORE HE GETS INTO SERIOUS TROUBLE!
WE DON'T HAVE VERY FAR TO GO NOW, ROBBIE!
GULP! HE'S NOT HERE! I WONDER IF HE WENT UP IN THAT CAVE?
THAT'S WHERE THAT TERRIBLE TEMPERED BEAR LIVES!
GASP! AND THERE HE IS NOW!
1

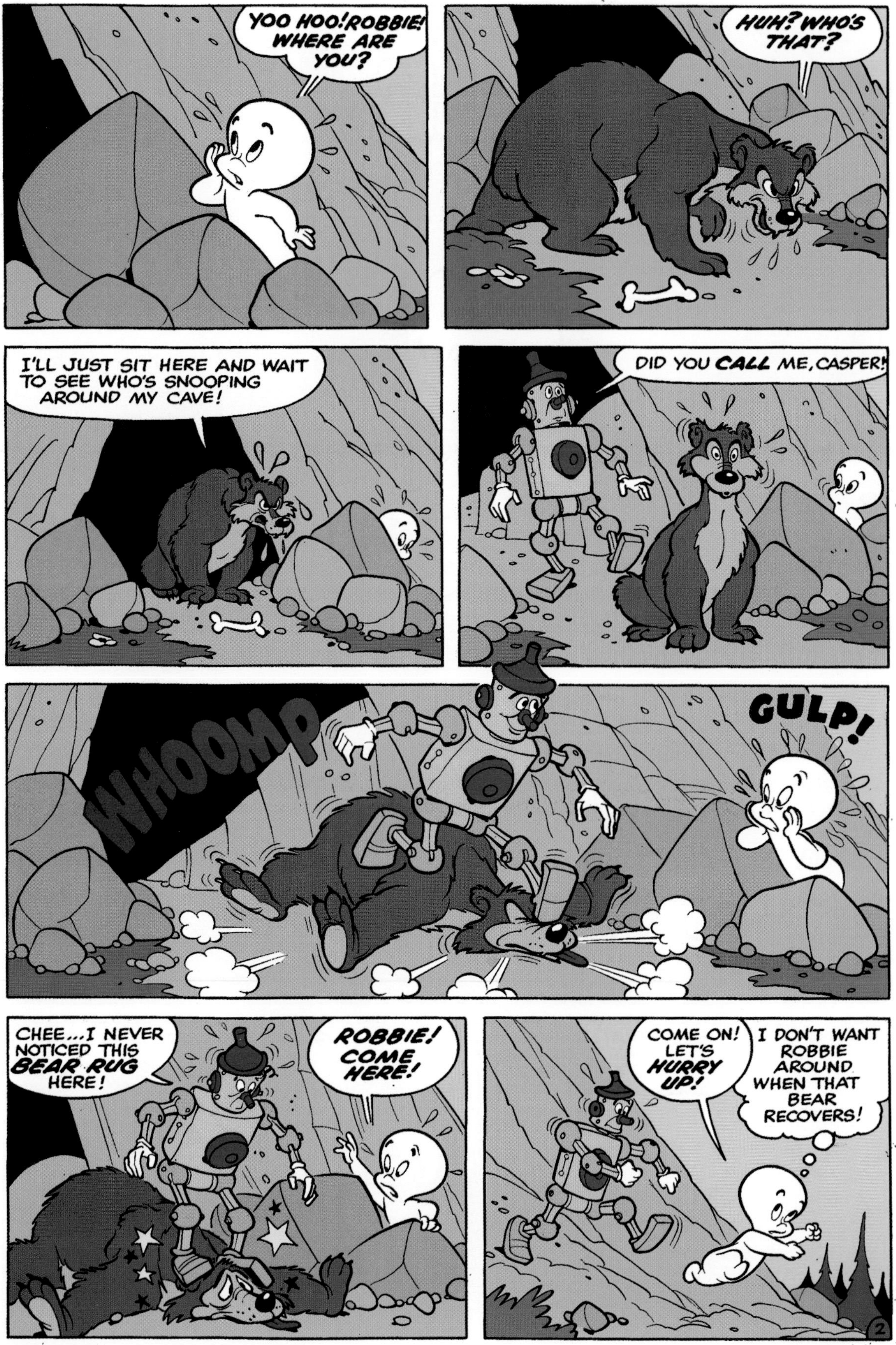
YOO HOO! ROBBIE! WHERE ARE YOU?
HUH? WHO'S THAT?
I'LL JUST SIT HERE AND WAIT TO SEE WHO'S SNOOPING AROUND MY CAVE!
DID YOU CALL ME, CASPER!
WHOOMP
GULP!
CHEE...I NEVER NOTICED THIS BEAR RUG HERE!
ROBBIE! COME HERE!
COME ON! LET'S HURRY UP!
I DON'T WANT ROBBIE AROUND WHEN THAT BEAR RECOVERS!
2

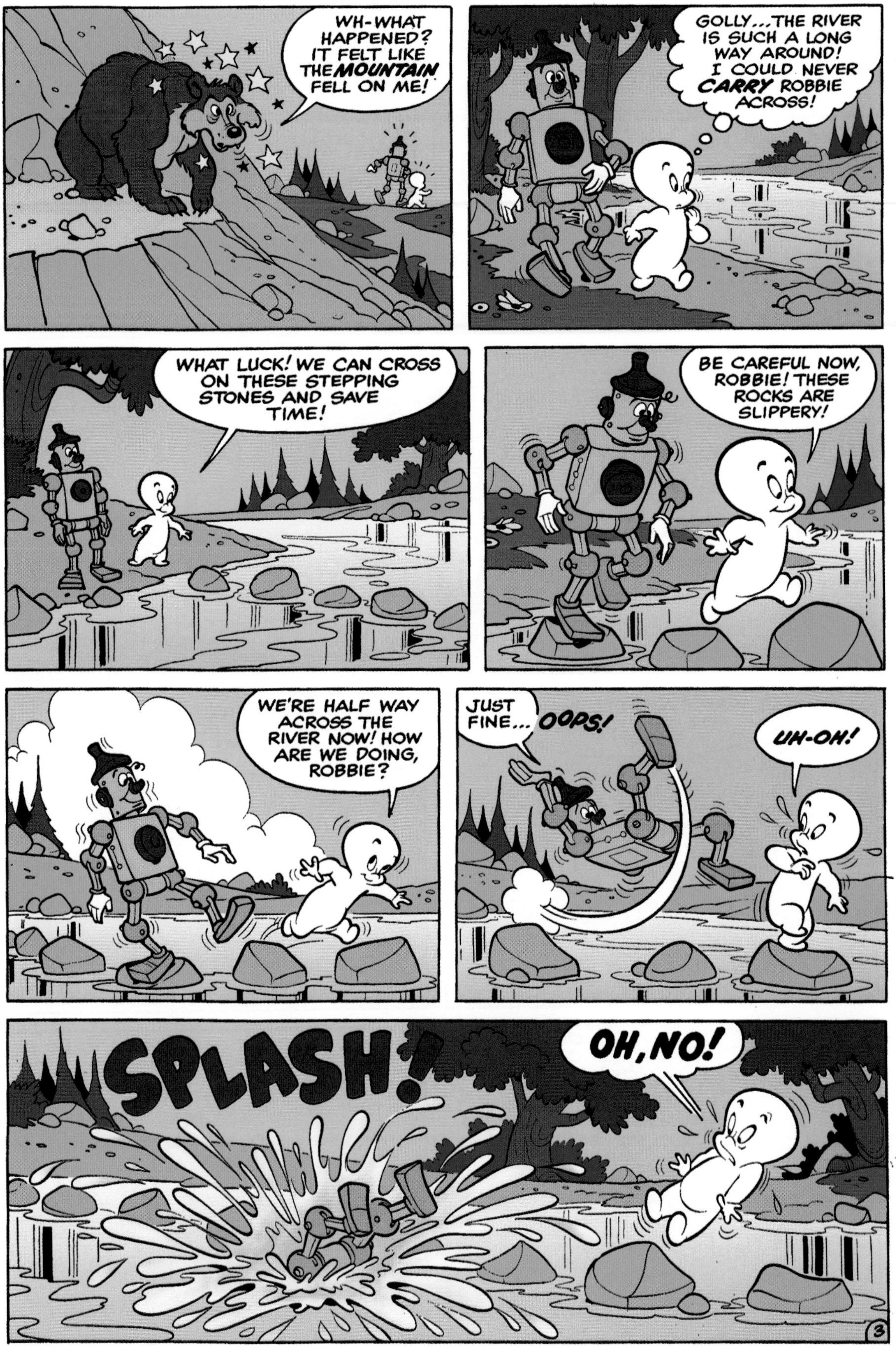
WH-WHAT HAPPENED? IT FELT LIKE THE MOUNTAIN FELL ON ME!
GOLLY... THE RIVER IS SUCH A LONG WAY AROUND! I COULD NEVER CARRY ROBBIE ACROSS!
WHAT LUCK! WE CAN CROSS ON THESE STEPPING STONES AND SAVE TIME!
BE CAREFUL NOW, ROBBIE! THESE ROCKS ARE SLIPPERY!
WE'RE HALF WAY ACROSS THE RIVER NOW! HOW ARE WE DOING, ROBBIE?
JUST FINE... OOPS!
UH-OH!
SPLASH!
OH, NO!
3

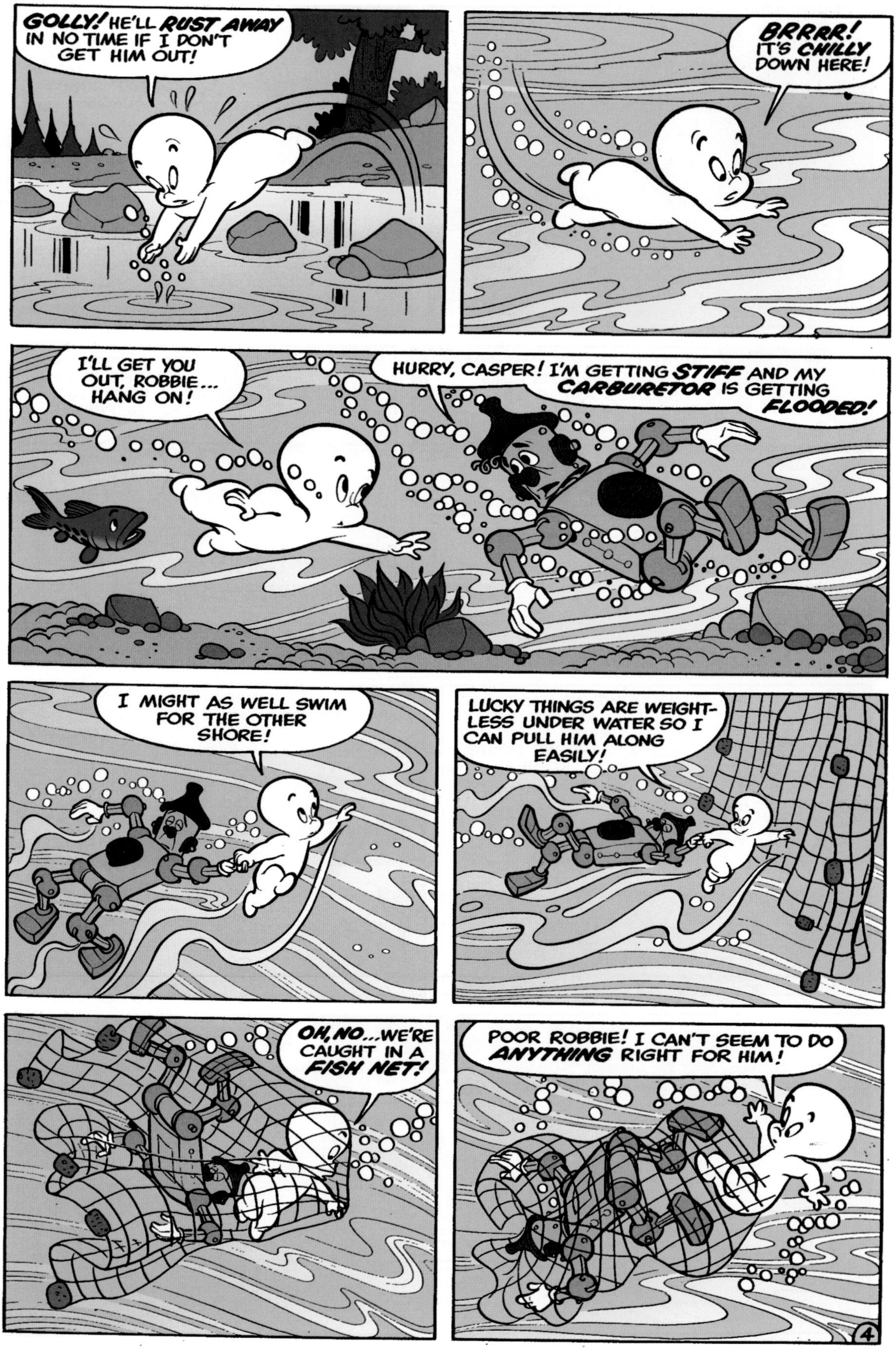
GOLLY! HE'LL RUST AWAY IN NO TIME IF I DON'T GET HIM OUT!
BRRRR! IT'S CHILLY DOWN HERE!
I'LL GET YOU OUT, ROBBIE... HANG ON!
HURRY, CASPER! I'M GETTING STIFF AND MY CARBURETOR IS GETTING FLOODED!
I MIGHT AS WELL SWIM FOR THE OTHER SHORE!
LUCKY THINGS ARE WEIGHT-LESS UNDER WATER SO I CAN PULL HIM ALONG EASILY!
OH, NO...WE'RE CAUGHT IN A FISH NET!
POOR ROBBIE! I CAN'T SEEM TO DO ANYTHING RIGHT FOR HIM!
4

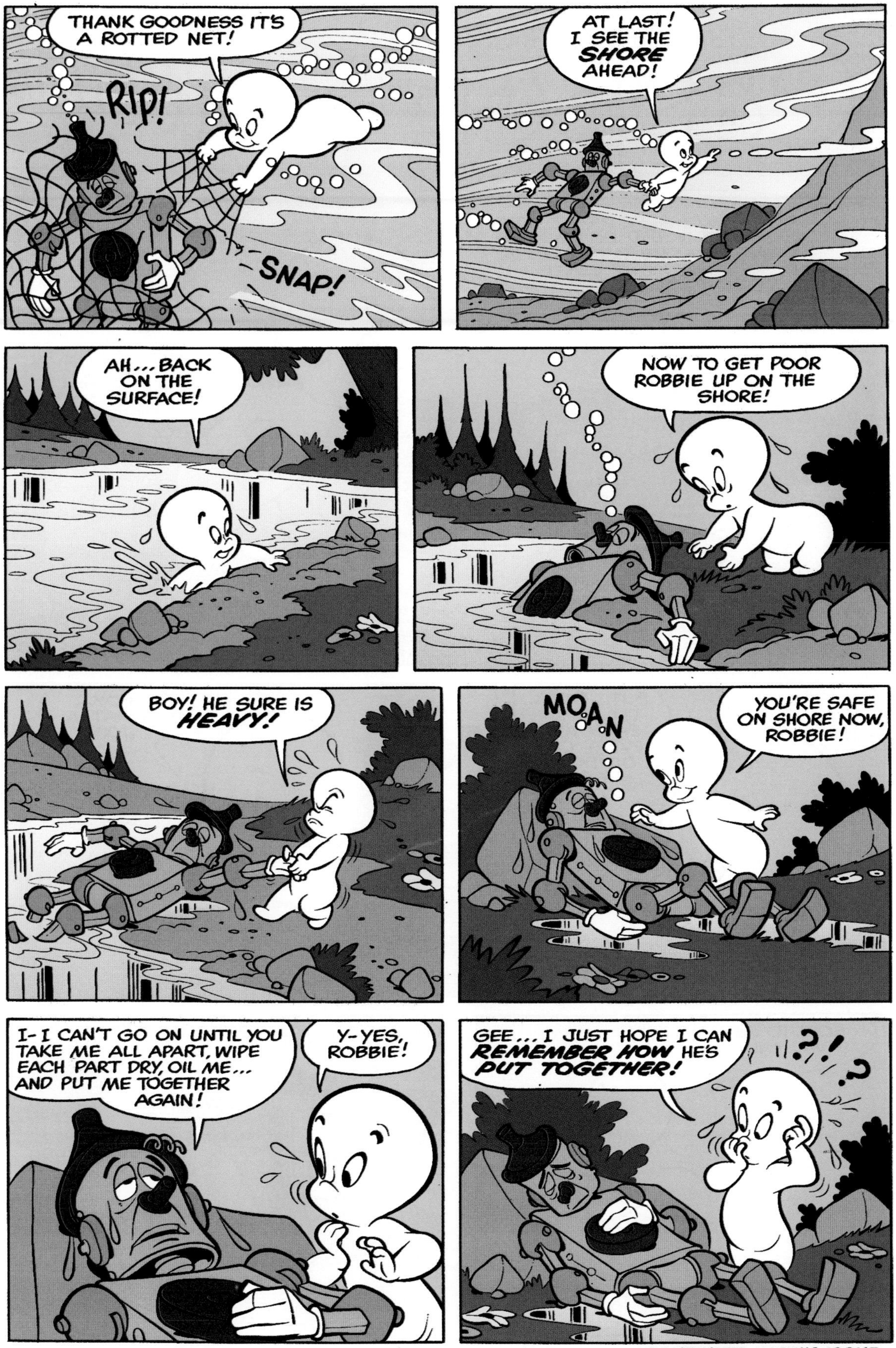
THANK GOODNESS IT'S A ROTTED NET!
RIP!
SNAP!
AT LAST! I SEE THE SHORE AHEAD!
AH... BACK ON THE SURFACE!
NOW TO GET POOR ROBBIE UP ON THE SHORE!
BOY! HE SURE IS HEAVY!
MOAN
YOU'RE SAFE ON SHORE NOW, ROBBIE!
I- I CAN'T GO ON UNTIL YOU TAKE ME ALL APART, WIPE EACH PART DRY, OIL ME... AND PUT ME TOGETHER AGAIN!
Y-YES, ROBBIE!
GEE... I JUST HOPE I CAN REMEMBER HOW HE'S PUT TOGETHER!

CONTINUED IN THIS ISSUE.

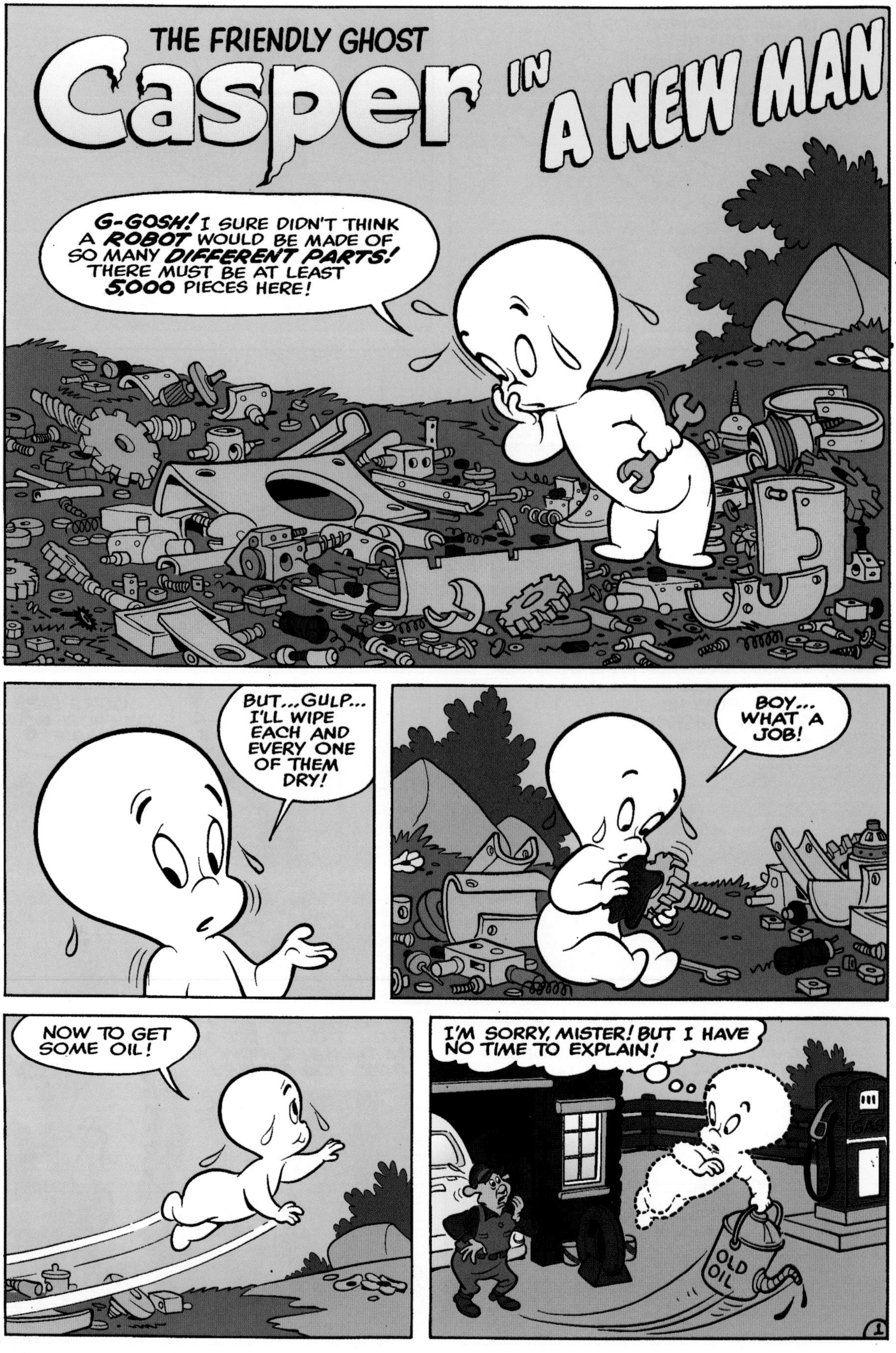
THE FRIENDLY GHOST
Casper
IN
A NEW MAN
G-GOSH! I SURE DIDN'T THINK A ROBOT WOULD BE MADE OF SO MANY DIFFERENT PARTS! THERE MUST BE AT LEAST 5,000 PIECES HERE!
BUT...GULP... I'LL WIPE EACH AND EVERY ONE OF THEM DRY!
BOY... WHAT A JOB!
NOW TO GET SOME OIL!
I'M SORRY, MISTER! BUT I HAVE NO TIME TO EXPLAIN!
GAS
OLD OIL
1

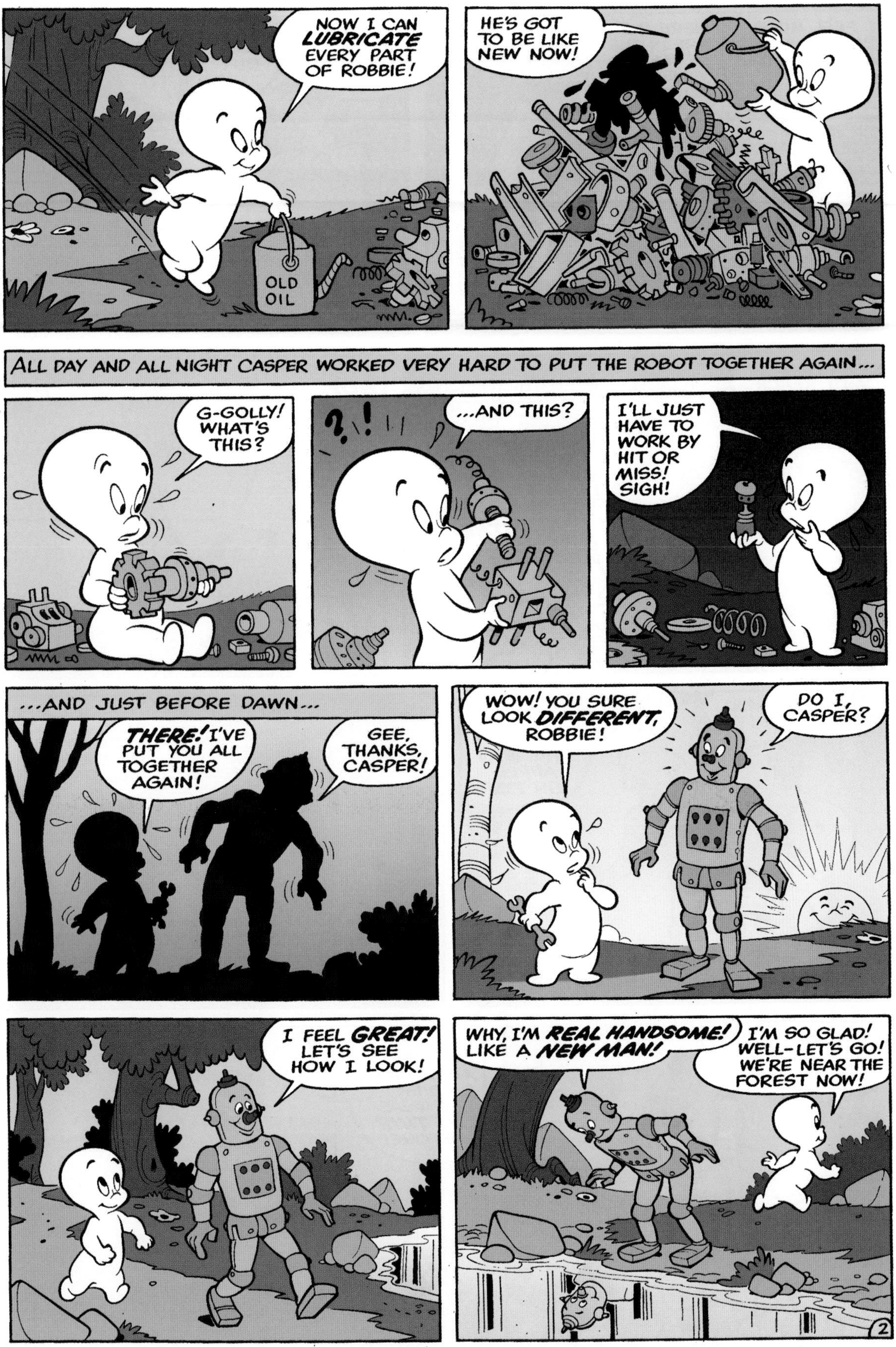
NOW I CAN LUBRICATE EVERY PART OF ROBBIE!
OLD OIL
HE'S GOT TO BE LIKE NEW NOW!
ALL DAY AND ALL NIGHT CASPER WORKED VERY HARD TO PUT THE ROBOT TOGETHER AGAIN...
G-GOLLY! WHAT'S THIS?
?!
...AND THIS?
I'LL JUST HAVE TO WORK BY HIT OR MISS! SIGH!
...AND JUST BEFORE DAWN...
THERE! I'VE PUT YOU ALL TOGETHER AGAIN!
GEE, THANKS, CASPER!
WOW! YOU SURE LOOK DIFFERENT, ROBBIE!
DO I, CASPER?
I FEEL GREAT! LET'S SEE HOW I LOOK!
WHY, I'M REAL HANDSOME! LIKE A NEW MAN!
I'M SO GLAD! WELL-LET'S GO! WE'RE NEAR THE FOREST NOW!
2

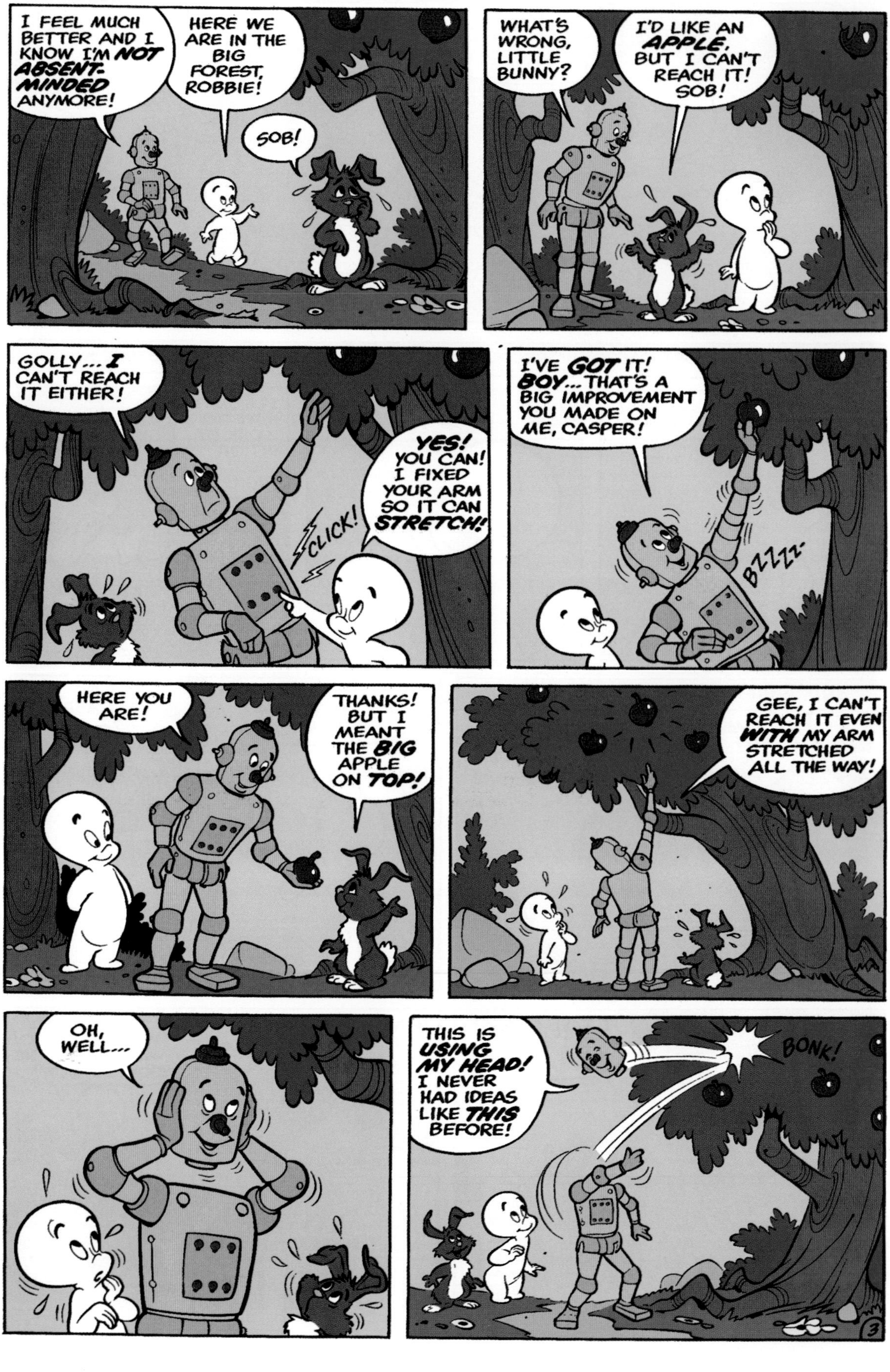
I FEEL MUCH BETTER AND I KNOW I'M NOT ABSENT-MINDED ANYMORE!
HERE WE ARE IN THE BIG FOREST, ROBBIE!
SOB!
WHAT'S WRONG, LITTLE BUNNY?
I'D LIKE AN APPLE, BUT I CAN'T REACH IT! SOB!
GOLLY... I CAN'T REACH IT EITHER!
YES! YOU CAN! I FIXED YOUR ARM SO IT CAN STRETCH!
CLICK!
I'VE GOT IT! BOY... THAT'S A BIG IMPROVEMENT YOU MADE ON ME, CASPER!
BZZZZ-
HERE YOU ARE!
THANKS! BUT I MEANT THE BIG APPLE ON TOP!
GEE, I CAN'T REACH IT EVEN WITH MY ARM STRETCHED ALL THE WAY!
OH, WELL...
THIS IS USING MY HEAD! I NEVER HAD IDEAS LIKE THIS BEFORE!
BONK!
3

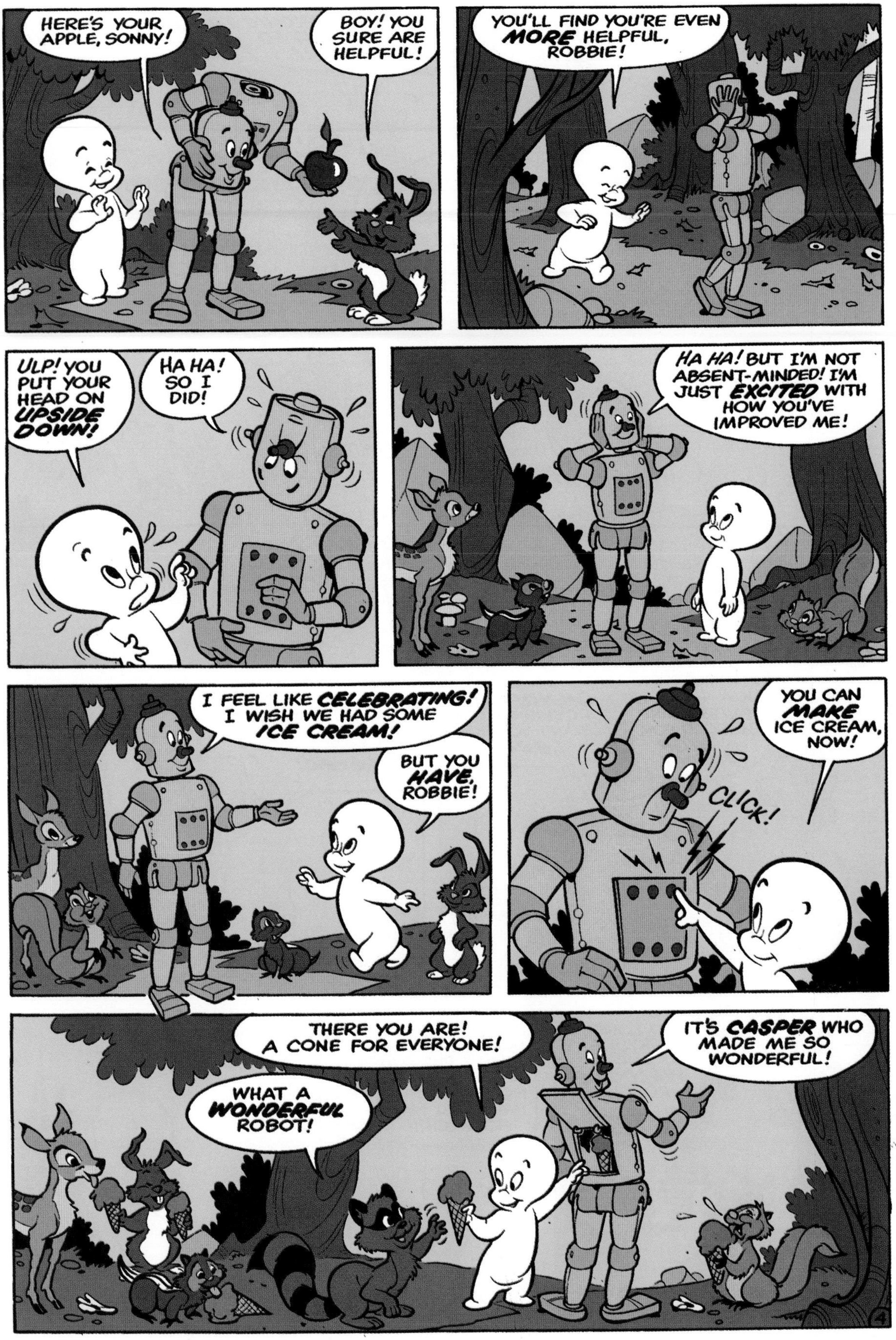
HERE'S YOUR APPLE, SONNY!
BOY! YOU SURE ARE HELPFUL!
YOU'LL FIND YOU'RE EVEN MORE HELPFUL, ROBBIE!
ULP! YOU PUT YOUR HEAD ON UPSIDE DOWN!
HA HA! SO I DID!
HA HA! BUT I'M NOT ABSENT-MINDED! I'M JUST EXCITED WITH HOW YOU'VE IMPROVED ME!
I FEEL LIKE CELEBRATING! I WISH WE HAD SOME ICE CREAM!
BUT YOU HAVE, ROBBIE!
YOU CAN MAKE ICE CREAM, NOW!
CLICK!
THERE YOU ARE! A CONE FOR EVERYONE!
IT'S CASPER WHO MADE ME SO WONDERFUL!
WHAT A WONDERFUL ROBOT!
4

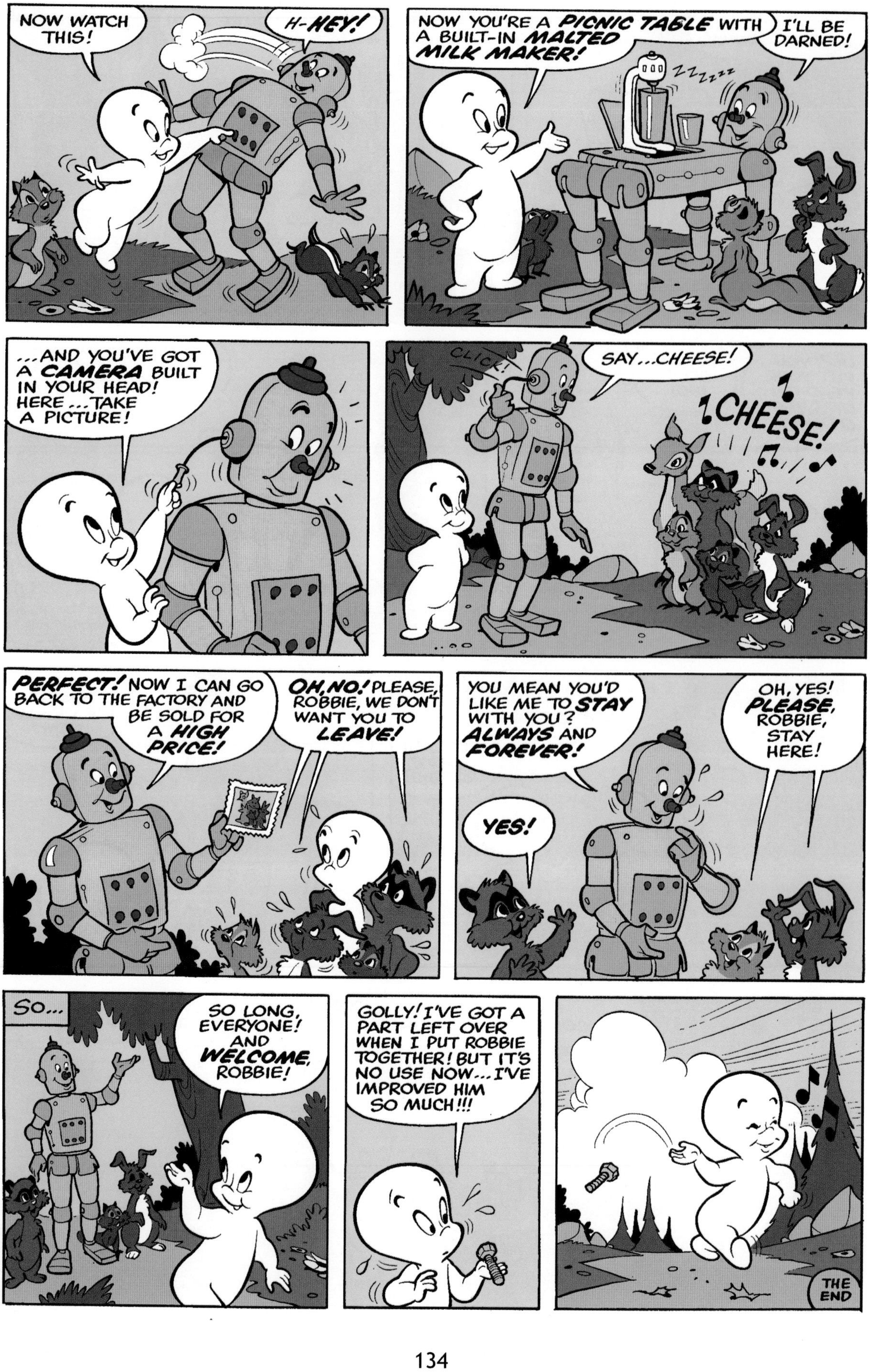
NOW WATCH THIS!
H-HEY!
NOW YOU'RE A PICNIC TABLE WITH A BUILT-IN MALTED MILK MAKER!
I'LL BE DARNED!
...AND YOU'VE GOT A CAMERA BUILT IN YOUR HEAD! HERE...TAKE A PICTURE!
CLICK!
SAY...CHEESE!
CHEESE!
PERFECT! NOW I CAN GO BACK TO THE FACTORY AND BE SOLD FOR A HIGH PRICE!
OH, NO! PLEASE, ROBBIE, WE DON'T WANT YOU TO LEAVE!
YOU MEAN YOU'D LIKE ME TO STAY WITH YOU? ALWAYS AND FOREVER!
OH, YES! PLEASE, ROBBIE, STAY HERE!
YES!
SO...
SO LONG, EVERYONE! AND WELCOME, ROBBIE!
GOLLY! I'VE GOT A PART LEFT OVER WHEN I PUT ROBBIE TOGETHER! BUT IT'S NO USE NOW...I'VE IMPROVED HIM SO MUCH!!!
THE END

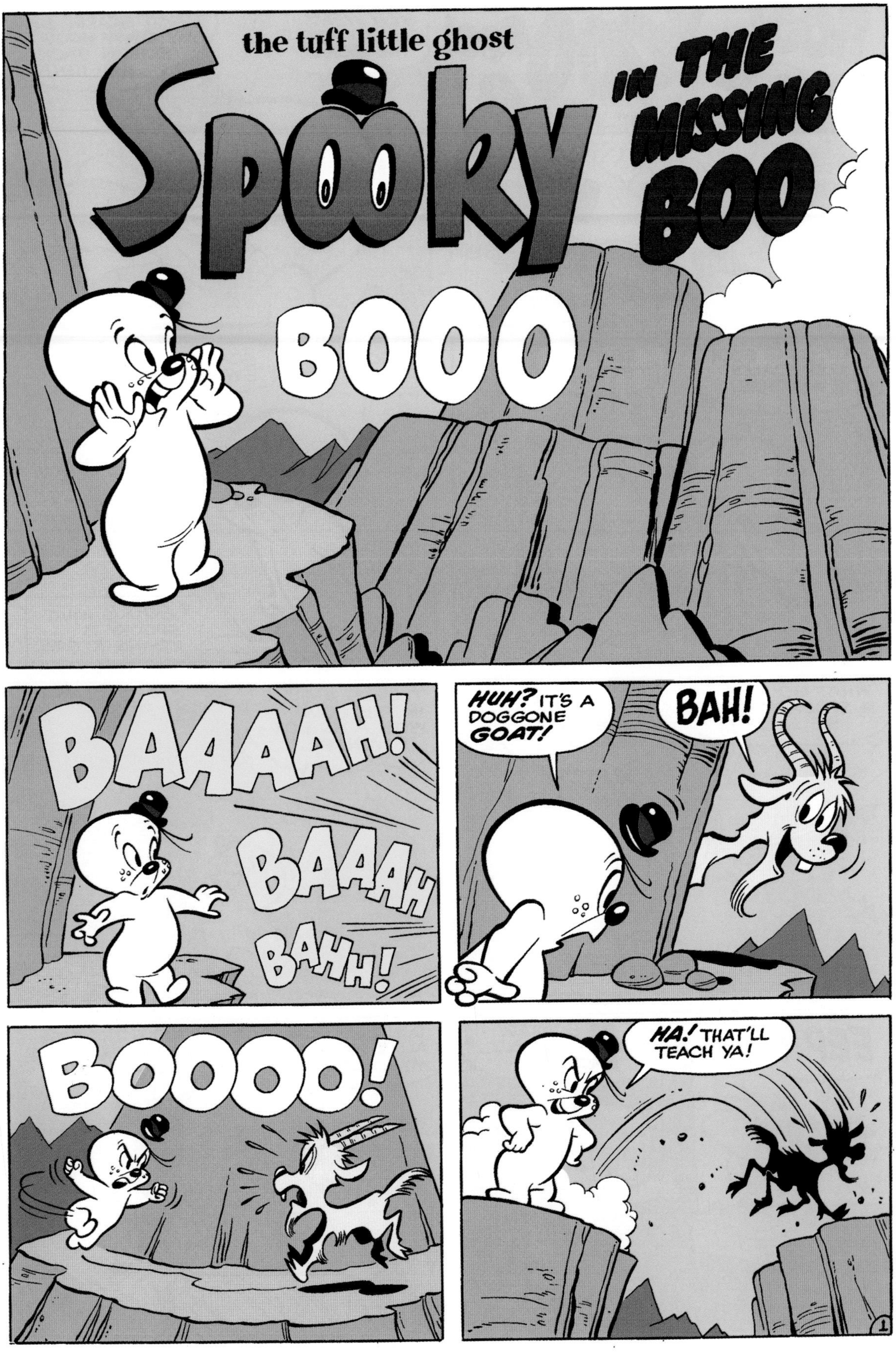
the tuff little ghost
Spooky
IN THE MISSING BOO
BOOO
BAAAAH!
BAAAAH
BAHH!
HUH? IT'S A DOGGONE GOAT!
BAH!
BOOOO!
HA! THAT'LL TEACH YA!
1

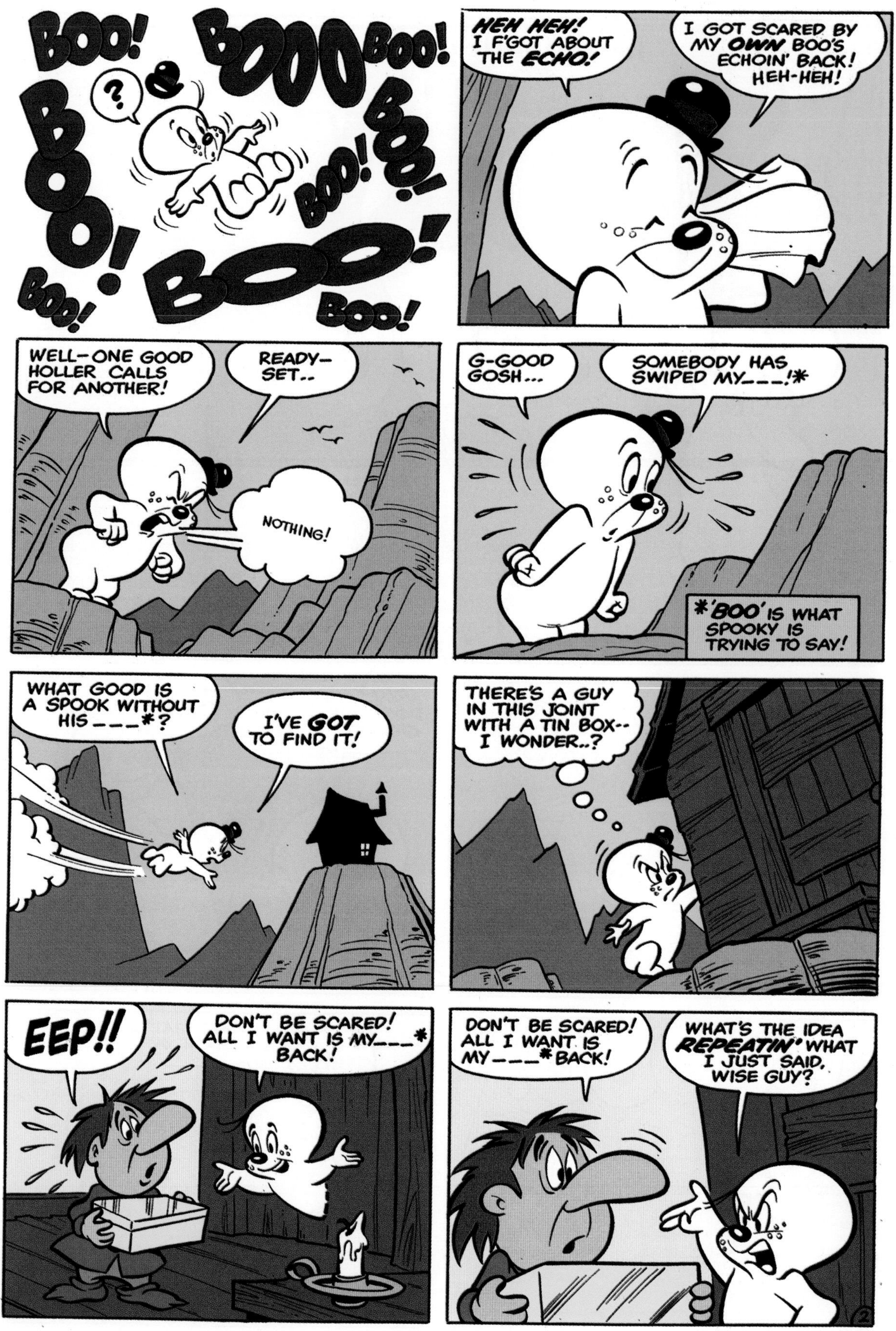
BOO! BOOOO BOO! BOO! BOO! BOO! BOO! BOO! BOO! BOO!
?
HEH HEH! I F'GOT ABOUT THE ECHO!
I GOT SCARED BY MY OWN BOO'S ECHOIN' BACK! HEH-HEH!
WELL-ONE GOOD HOLLER CALLS FOR ANOTHER!
READY- SET..
NOTHING!
G-GOOD GOSH...
SOMEBODY HAS SWIPED MY___!*
*'BOO' IS WHAT SPOOKY IS TRYING TO SAY!
WHAT GOOD IS A SPOOK WITHOUT HIS___*?
I'VE GOT TO FIND IT!
THERE'S A GUY IN THIS JOINT WITH A TIN BOX-- I WONDER..?
EEP!!
DON'T BE SCARED! ALL I WANT IS MY___* BACK!
DON'T BE SCARED! ALL I WANT IS MY___* BACK!
WHAT'S THE IDEA REPEATIN' WHAT I JUST SAID, WISE GUY?
2

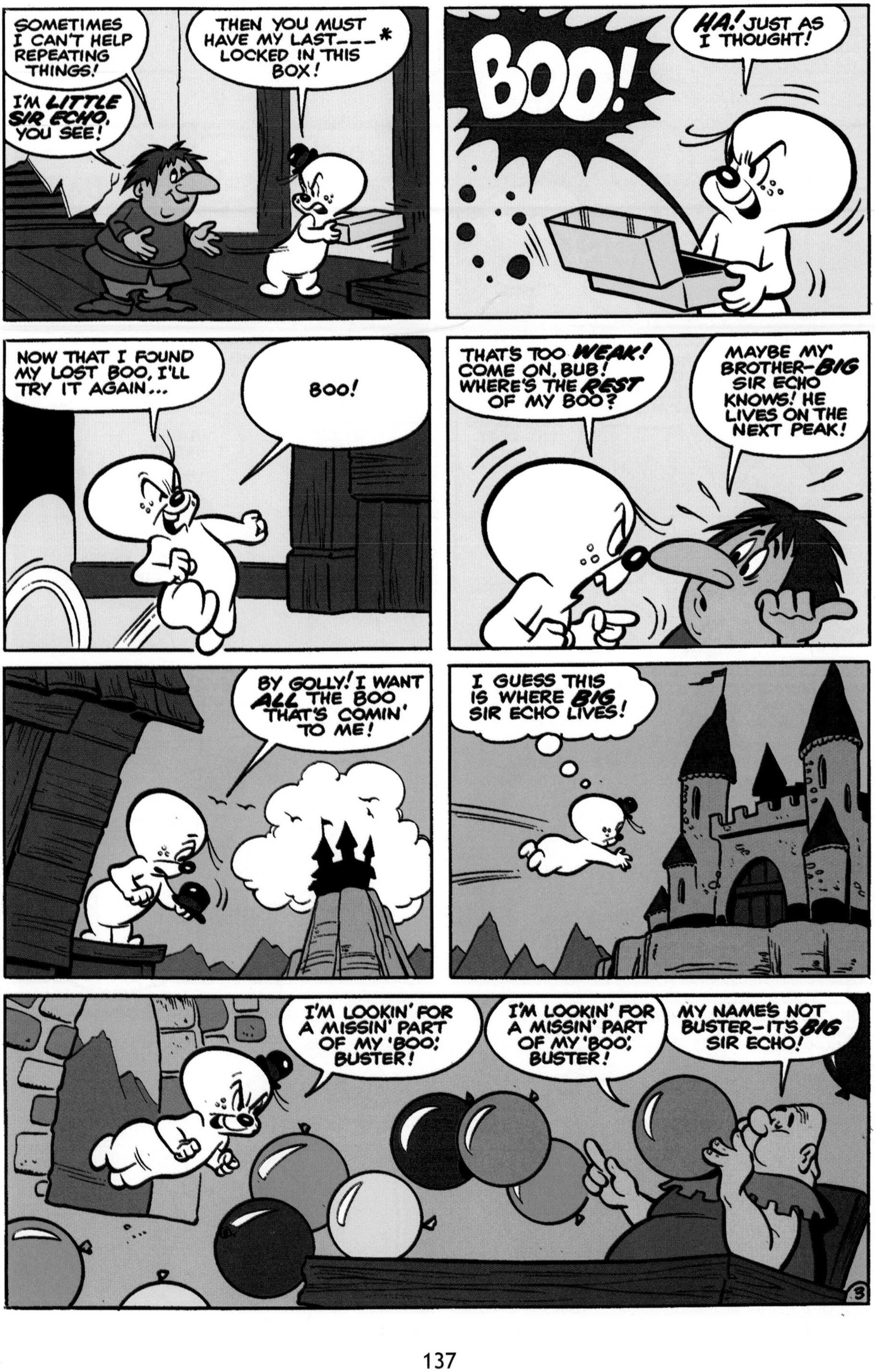
SOMETIMES I CAN'T HELP REPEATING THINGS!
I'M LITTLE SIR ECHO, YOU SEE!
THEN YOU MUST HAVE MY LAST---* LOCKED IN THIS BOX!
BOO!
HA! JUST AS I THOUGHT!
NOW THAT I FOUND MY LOST BOO, I'LL TRY IT AGAIN...
BOO!
THAT'S TOO WEAK! COME ON, BUB! WHERE'S THE REST OF MY BOO?
MAYBE MY BROTHER-BIG SIR ECHO KNOWS! HE LIVES ON THE NEXT PEAK!
BY GOLLY! I WANT ALL THE BOO THAT'S COMIN' TO ME!
I GUESS THIS IS WHERE BIG SIR ECHO LIVES!
I'M LOOKIN' FOR A MISSIN' PART OF MY 'BOO', BUSTER!
I'M LOOKIN' FOR A MISSIN' PART OF MY 'BOO', BUSTER!
MY NAME'S NOT BUSTER-IT'S BIG SIR ECHO!
3

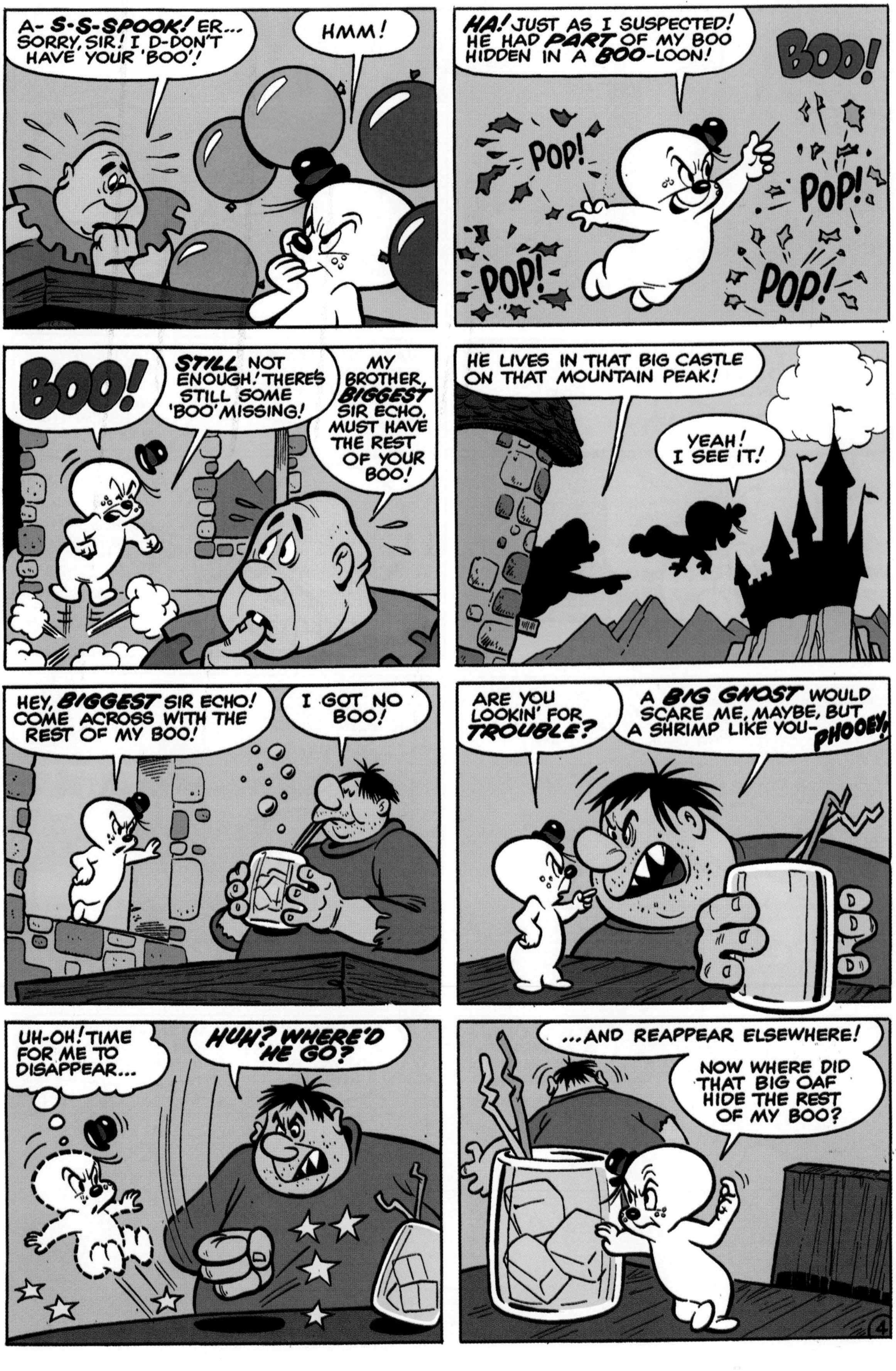
A- S-S-SPOOK! ER... SORRY, SIR! I D-DON'T HAVE YOUR 'BOO'!
HMM!
HA! JUST AS I SUSPECTED! HE HAD PART OF MY BOO HIDDEN IN A BOO-LOON!
BOO!
POP!
POP!
POP!
POP!
BOO!
STILL NOT ENOUGH! THERE'S STILL SOME 'BOO' MISSING!
MY BROTHER, BIGGEST SIR ECHO, MUST HAVE THE REST OF YOUR BOO!
HE LIVES IN THAT BIG CASTLE ON THAT MOUNTAIN PEAK!
YEAH! I SEE IT!
HEY, BIGGEST SIR ECHO! COME ACROSS WITH THE REST OF MY BOO!
I GOT NO BOO!
ARE YOU LOOKIN' FOR TROUBLE?
A BIG GHOST WOULD SCARE ME, MAYBE, BUT A SHRIMP LIKE YOU- PHOOEY!
UH-OH! TIME FOR ME TO DISAPPEAR...
HUH? WHERE'D HE GO?
...AND REAPPEAR ELSEWHERE!
NOW WHERE DID THAT BIG OAF HIDE THE REST OF MY BOO?
4

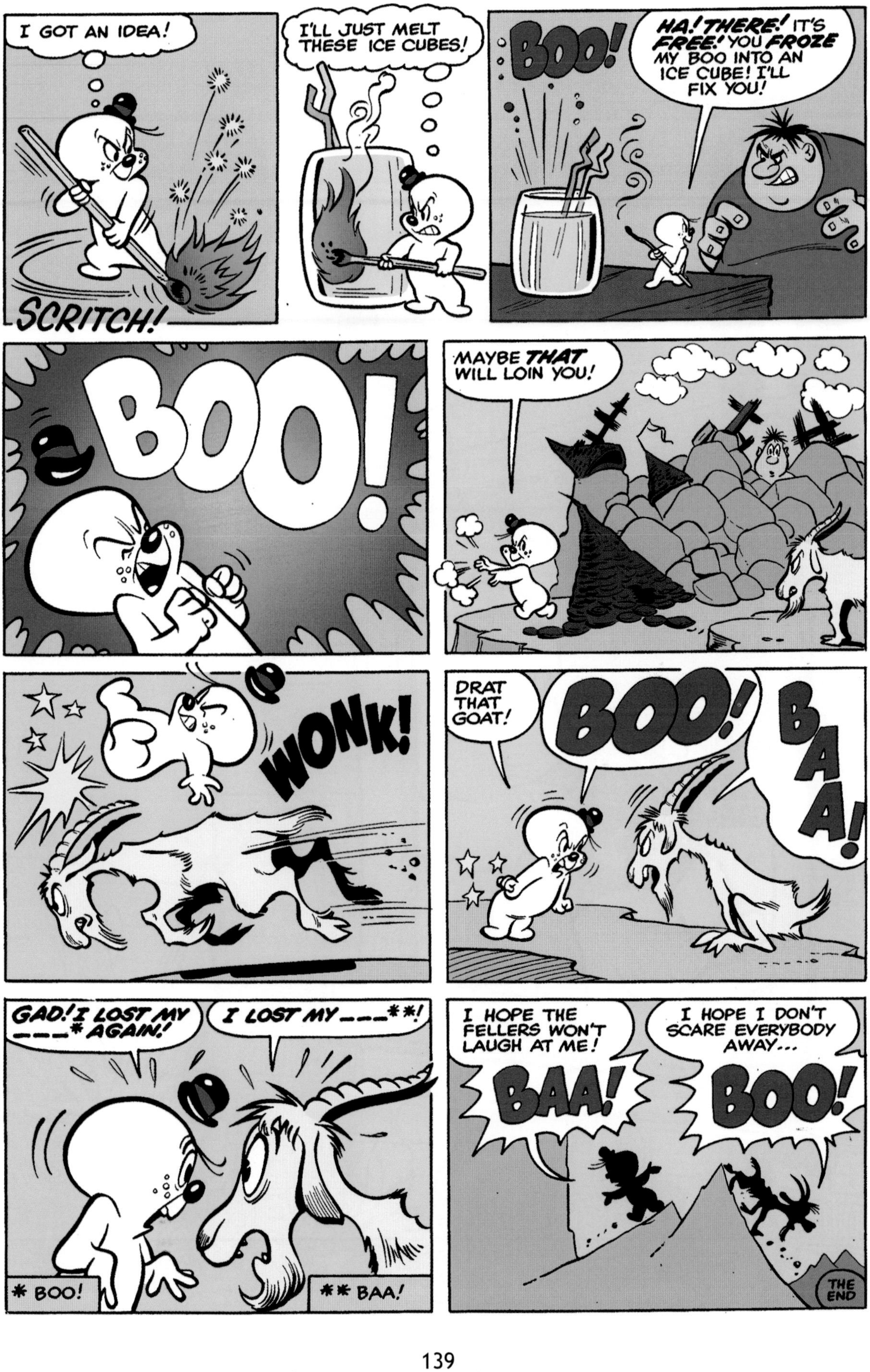

I GOT AN IDEA!
SCRITCH!
I'LL JUST MELT THESE ICE CUBES!
BOO!
HA! THERE! IT'S FREE! YOU FROZE MY BOO INTO AN ICE CUBE! I'LL FIX YOU!
BOO!
MAYBE THAT WILL LOIN YOU!
WONK!
DRAT THAT GOAT!
BOO!
BAA!
GAD! I LOST MY ---* AGAIN!
I LOST MY ---**!
* BOO!
** BAA!
I HOPE THE FELLERS WON'T LAUGH AT ME!
I HOPE I DON'T SCARE EVERYBODY AWAY...
BAA!
BOO!
THE END

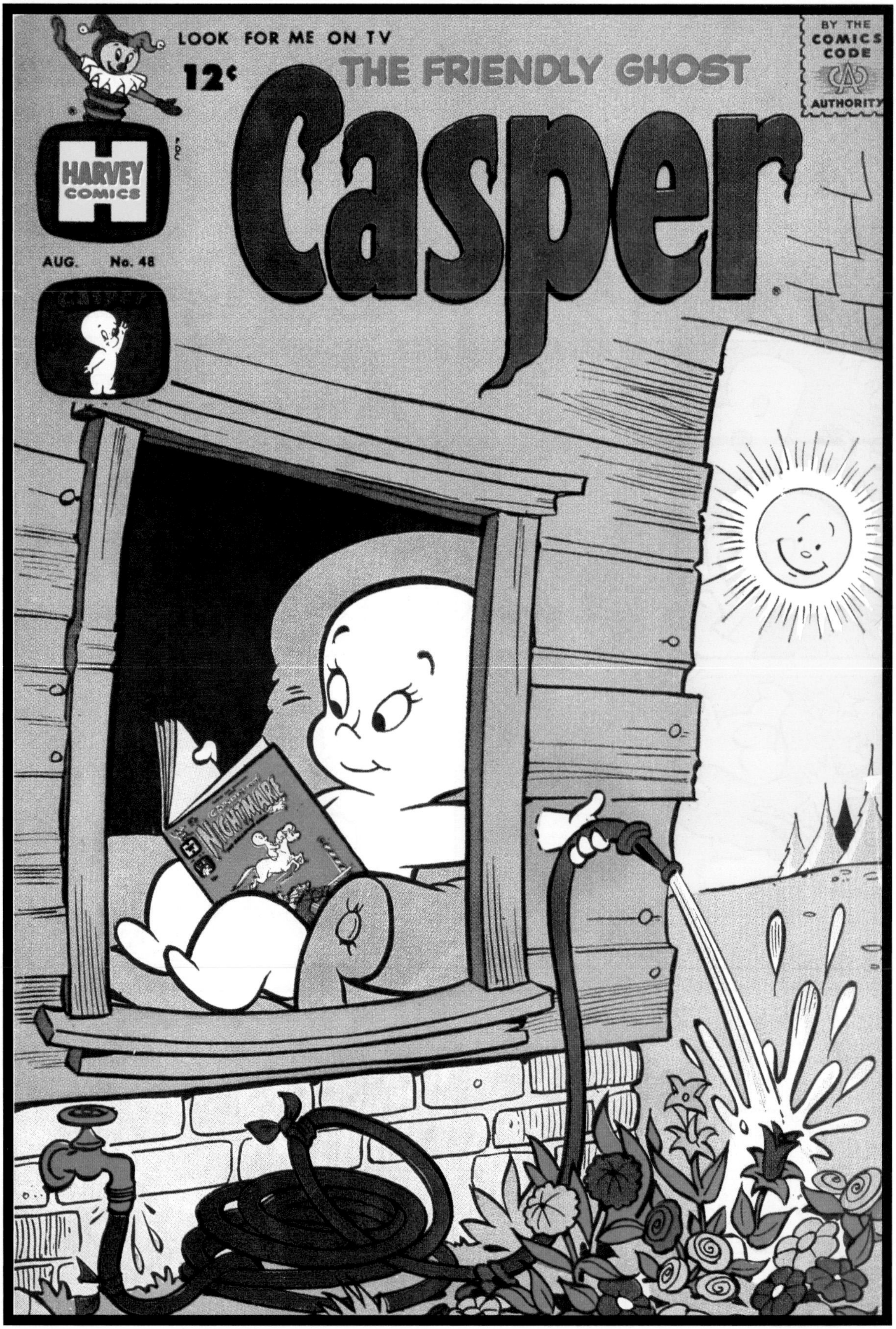
LOOK FOR ME ON TV
12¢
THE FRIENDLY GHOST
Casper
HARVEY COMICS
AUG. No. 48
BY THE COMICS CODE AUTHORITY
NIGHTMARE

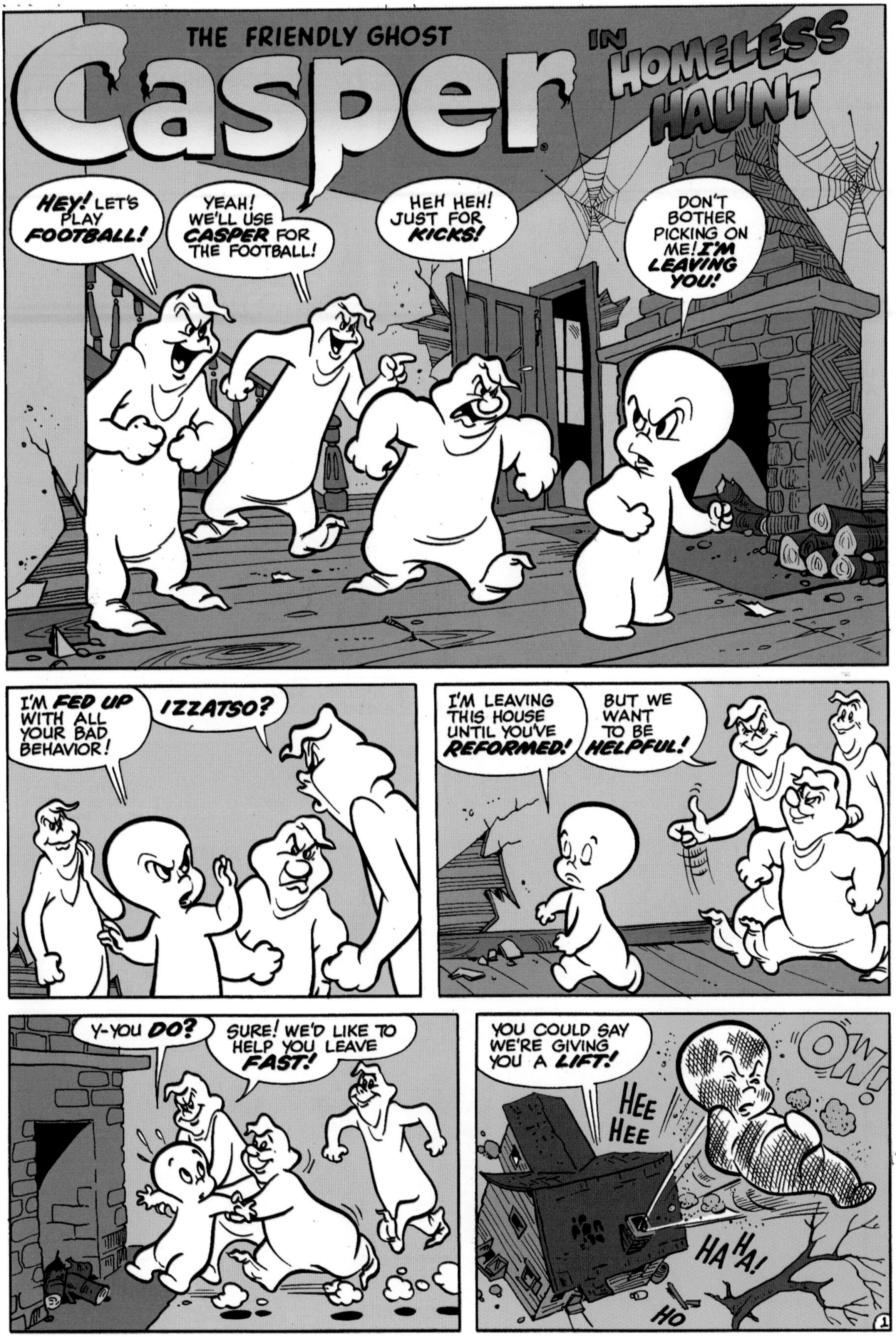
THE FRIENDLY GHOST
Casper
IN HOMELESS HAUNT
HEY! LET'S PLAY FOOTBALL!
YEAH! WE'LL USE CASPER FOR THE FOOTBALL!
HEH HEH! JUST FOR KICKS!
DON'T BOTHER PICKING ON ME! I'M LEAVING YOU!
I'M FED UP WITH ALL YOUR BAD BEHAVIOR!
IZZATSO?
I'M LEAVING THIS HOUSE UNTIL YOU'VE REFORMED!
BUT WE WANT TO BE HELPFUL!
Y-YOU DO?
SURE! WE'D LIKE TO HELP YOU LEAVE FAST!
YOU COULD SAY WE'RE GIVING YOU A LIFT!
HEE HEE
OW!
HA HA!
HO
1

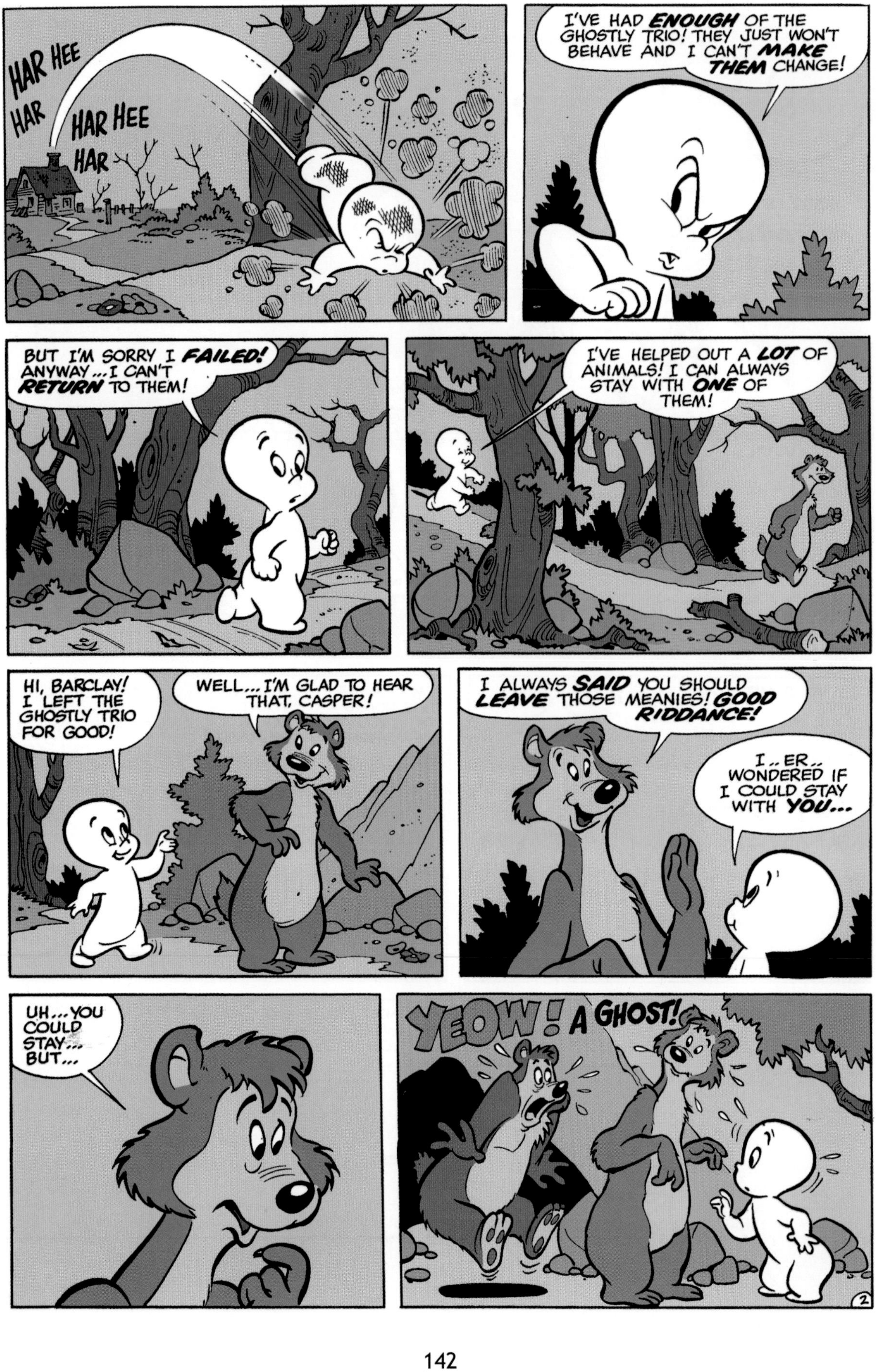
HAR HEE
HAR
HAR HEE
HAR
I'VE HAD ENOUGH OF THE GHOSTLY TRIO! THEY JUST WON'T BEHAVE AND I CAN'T MAKE THEM CHANGE!
BUT I'M SORRY I FAILED! ANYWAY... I CAN'T RETURN TO THEM!
I'VE HELPED OUT A LOT OF ANIMALS! I CAN ALWAYS STAY WITH ONE OF THEM!
HI, BARCLAY! I LEFT THE GHOSTLY TRIO FOR GOOD!
WELL... I'M GLAD TO HEAR THAT, CASPER!
I ALWAYS SAID YOU SHOULD LEAVE THOSE MEANIES! GOOD RIDDANCE!
I.. ER.. WONDERED IF I COULD STAY WITH YOU...
UH... YOU COULD STAY... BUT...
YEOW! A GHOST!
2

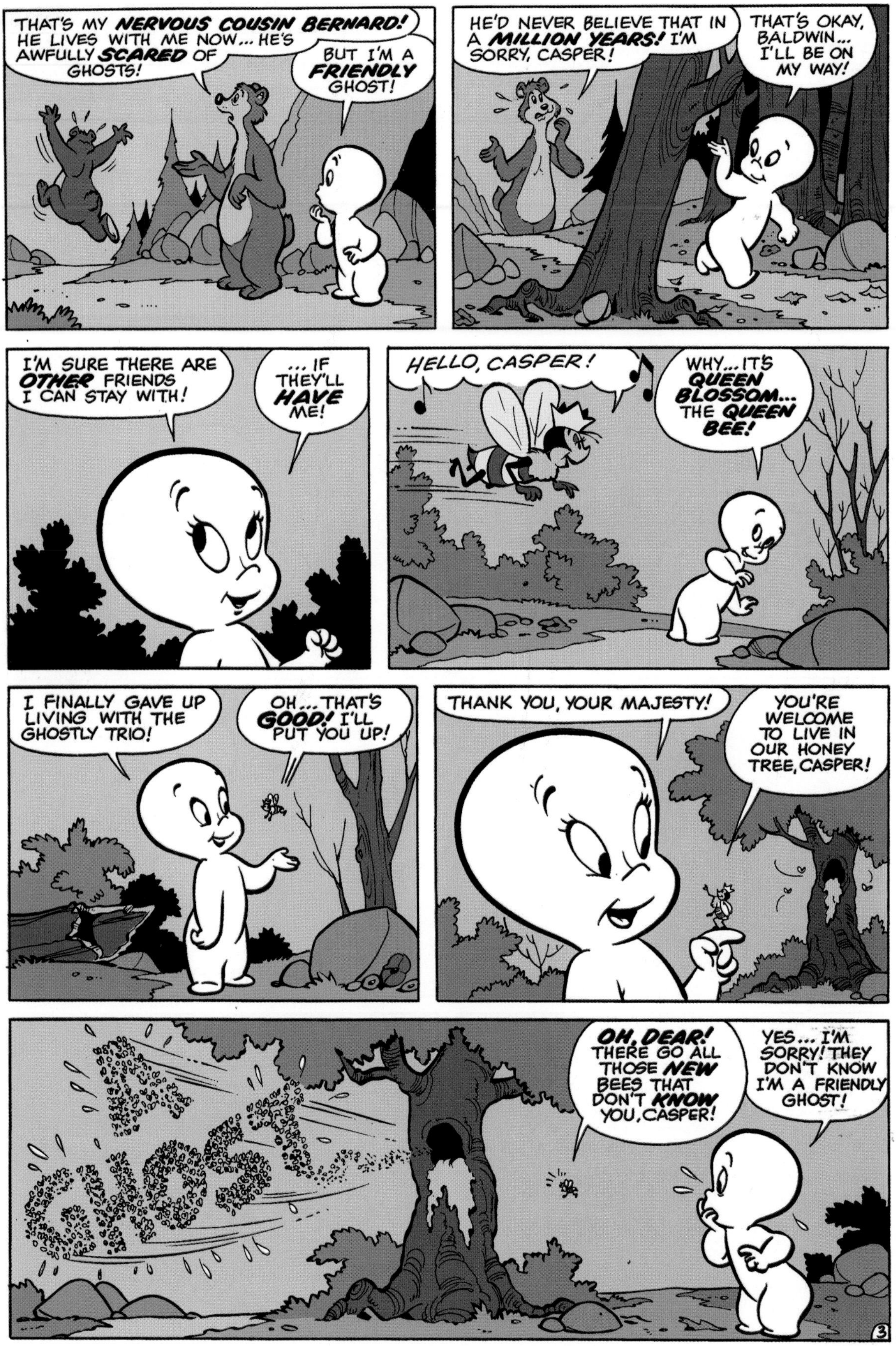
THAT'S MY NERVOUS COUSIN BERNARD! HE LIVES WITH ME NOW... HE'S AWFULLY SCARED OF GHOSTS!
BUT I'M A FRIENDLY GHOST!
HE'D NEVER BELIEVE THAT IN A MILLION YEARS! I'M SORRY, CASPER!
THAT'S OKAY, BALDWIN... I'LL BE ON MY WAY!
I'M SURE THERE ARE OTHER FRIENDS I CAN STAY WITH!
...IF THEY'LL HAVE ME!
HELLO, CASPER!
WHY... IT'S QUEEN BLOSSOM... THE QUEEN BEE!
I FINALLY GAVE UP LIVING WITH THE GHOSTLY TRIO!
OH... THAT'S GOOD! I'LL PUT YOU UP!
THANK YOU, YOUR MAJESTY!
YOU'RE WELCOME TO LIVE IN OUR HONEY TREE, CASPER!
OH, DEAR! THERE GO ALL THOSE NEW BEES THAT DON'T KNOW YOU, CASPER!
YES... I'M SORRY! THEY DON'T KNOW I'M A FRIENDLY GHOST!
3

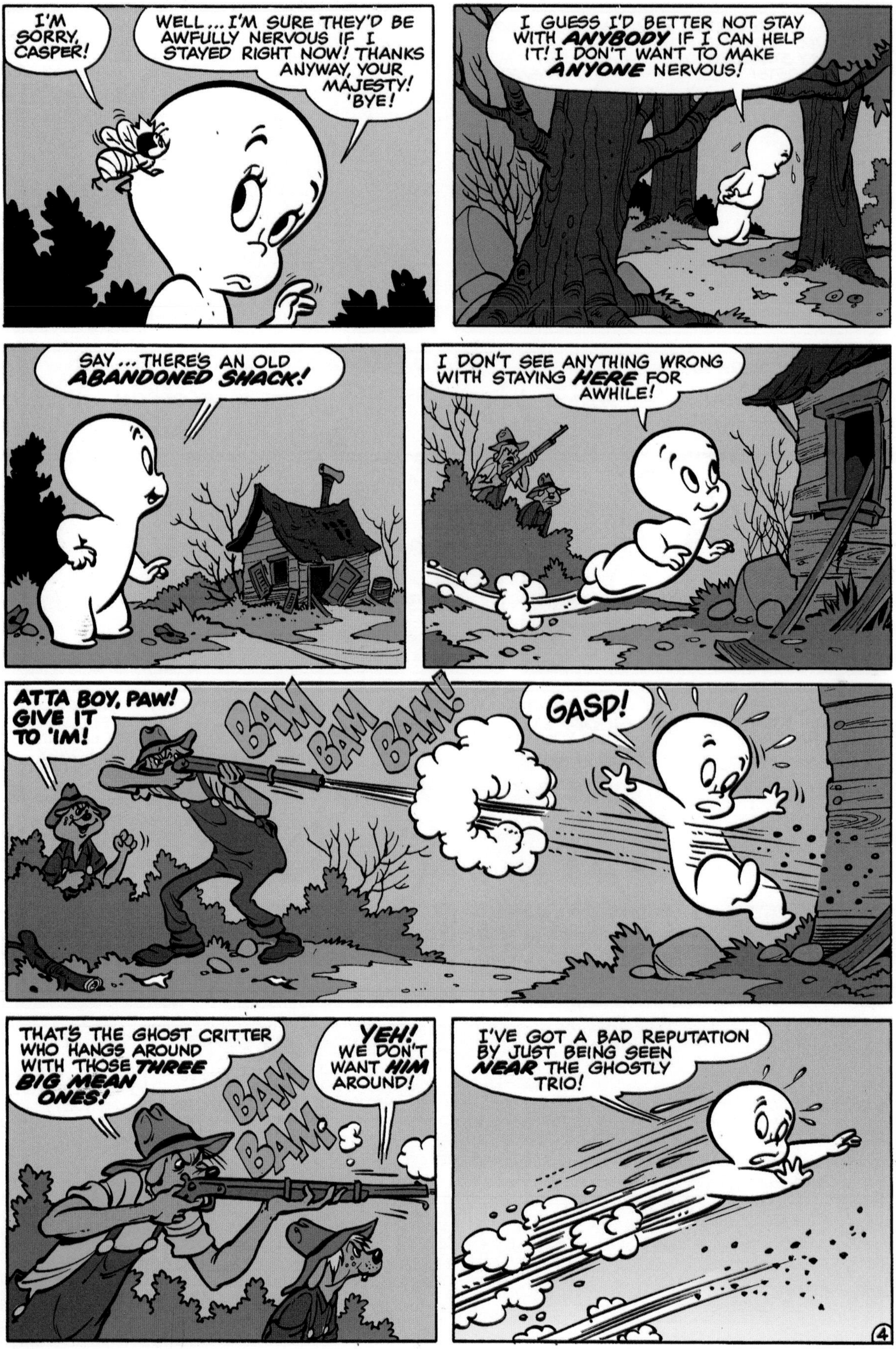
I'M SORRY, CASPER!
WELL ... I'M SURE THEY'D BE AWFULLY NERVOUS IF I STAYED RIGHT NOW! THANKS ANYWAY, YOUR MAJESTY! 'BYE!
I GUESS I'D BETTER NOT STAY WITH ANYBODY IF I CAN HELP IT! I DON'T WANT TO MAKE ANYONE NERVOUS!
SAY ... THERE'S AN OLD ABANDONED SHACK!
I DON'T SEE ANYTHING WRONG WITH STAYING HERE FOR AWHILE!
ATTA BOY, PAW! GIVE IT TO 'IM!
BAM BAM BAM!
GASP!
THAT'S THE GHOST CRITTER WHO HANGS AROUND WITH THOSE THREE BIG MEAN ONES!
BAM BAM!
YEH! WE DON'T WANT HIM AROUND!
I'VE GOT A BAD REPUTATION BY JUST BEING SEEN NEAR THE GHOSTLY TRIO!
4

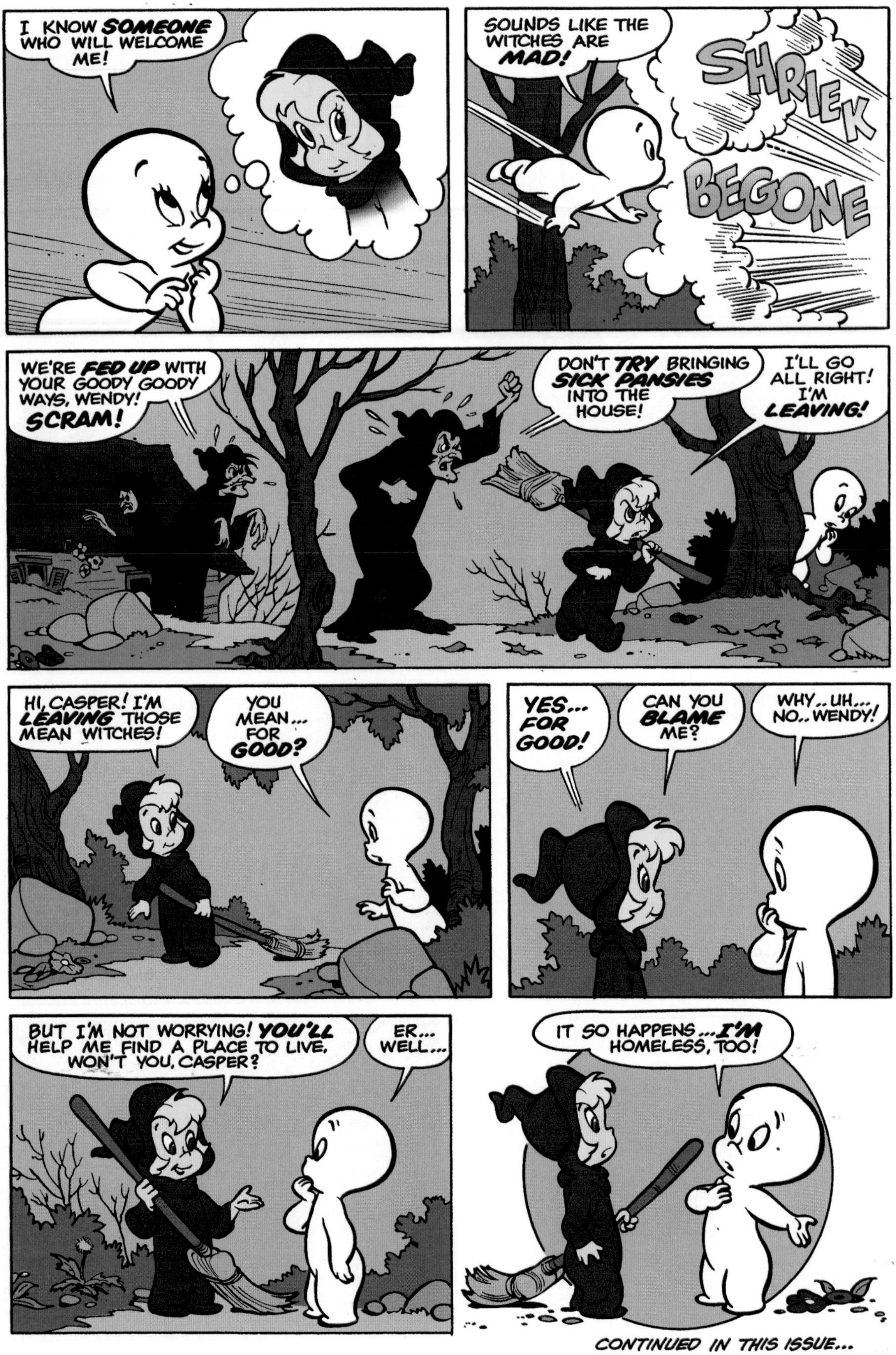
I KNOW SOMEONE WHO WILL WELCOME ME!
SOUNDS LIKE THE WITCHES ARE MAD!
SHRIEK
BEGONE
WE'RE FED UP WITH YOUR GOODY GOODY WAYS, WENDY! SCRAM!
DON'T TRY BRINGING SICK PANSIES INTO THE HOUSE!
I'LL GO ALL RIGHT! I'M LEAVING!
HI, CASPER! I'M LEAVING THOSE MEAN WITCHES!
YOU MEAN... FOR GOOD?
YES... FOR GOOD!
CAN YOU BLAME ME?
WHY..UH... NO..WENDY!
BUT I'M NOT WORRYING! YOU'LL HELP ME FIND A PLACE TO LIVE, WON'T YOU, CASPER?
ER... WELL...
IT SO HAPPENS...I'M HOMELESS, TOO!

CONTINUED IN THIS ISSUE...

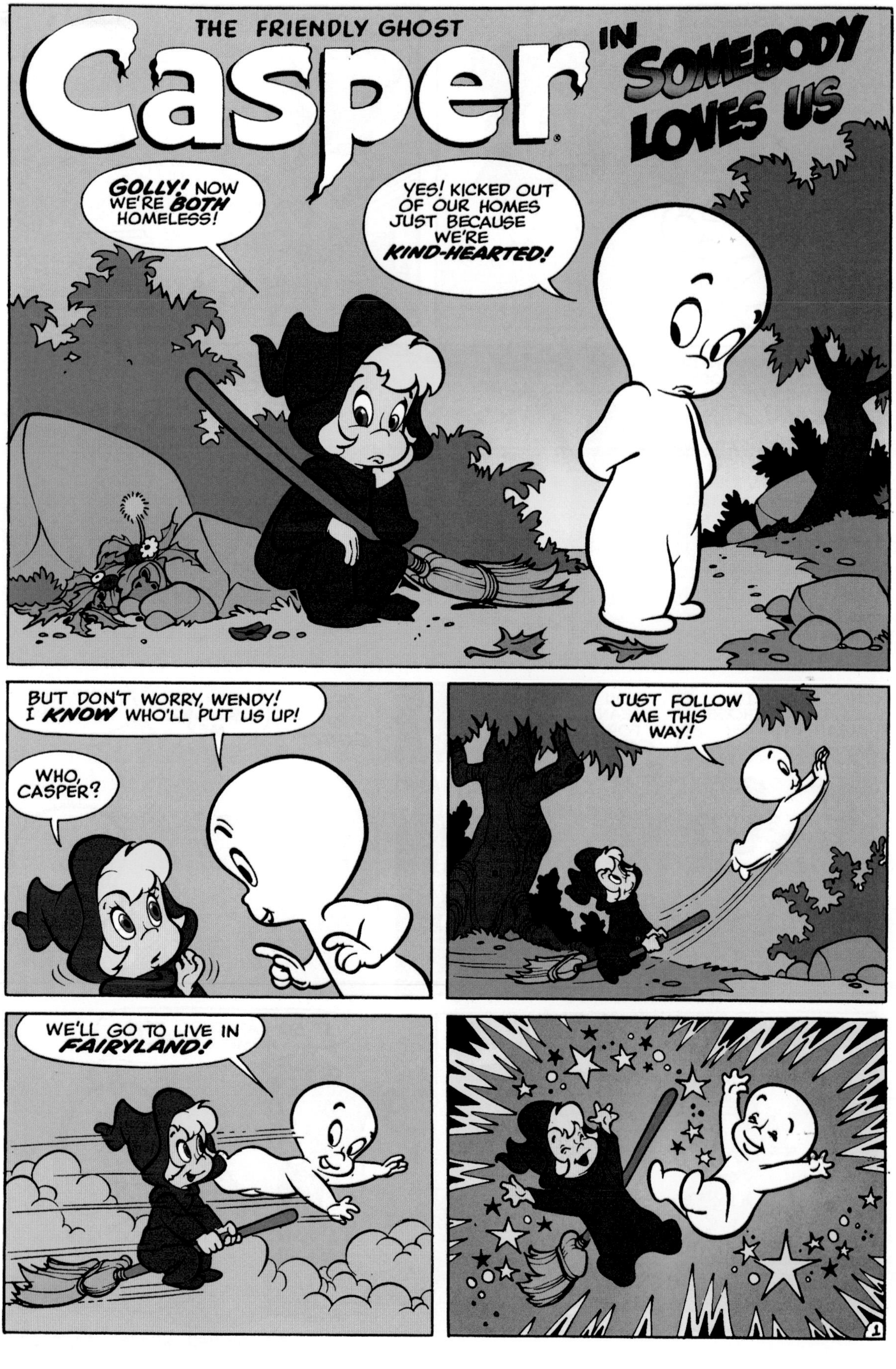

THE FRIENDLY GHOST
Casper
IN SOMEBODY LOVES US
GOLLY! NOW WE'RE BOTH HOMELESS!
YES! KICKED OUT OF OUR HOMES JUST BECAUSE WE'RE KIND-HEARTED!
BUT DON'T WORRY, WENDY! I KNOW WHO'LL PUT US UP!
WHO, CASPER?
JUST FOLLOW ME THIS WAY!
WE'LL GO TO LIVE IN FAIRYLAND!
1

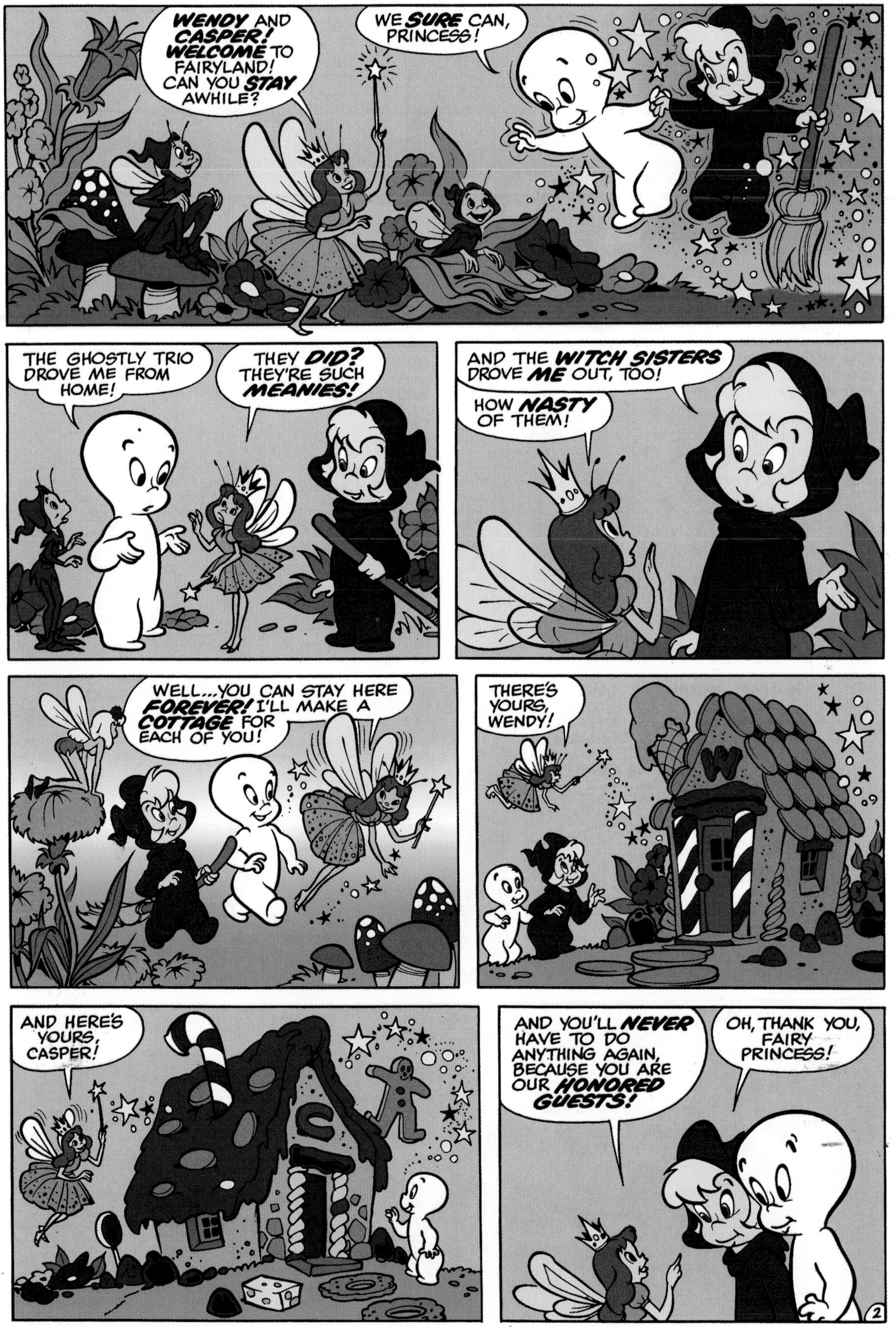
WENDY AND CASPER! WELCOME TO FAIRYLAND! CAN YOU STAY AWHILE?
WE SURE CAN, PRINCESS!
THE GHOSTLY TRIO DROVE ME FROM HOME!
THEY DID? THEY'RE SUCH MEANIES!
AND THE WITCH SISTERS DROVE ME OUT, TOO!
HOW NASTY OF THEM!
WELL...YOU CAN STAY HERE FOREVER! I'LL MAKE A COTTAGE FOR EACH OF YOU!
THERE'S YOURS, WENDY!
AND HERE'S YOURS, CASPER!
AND YOU'LL NEVER HAVE TO DO ANYTHING AGAIN, BECAUSE YOU ARE OUR HONORED GUESTS!
OH, THANK YOU, FAIRY PRINCESS!
2

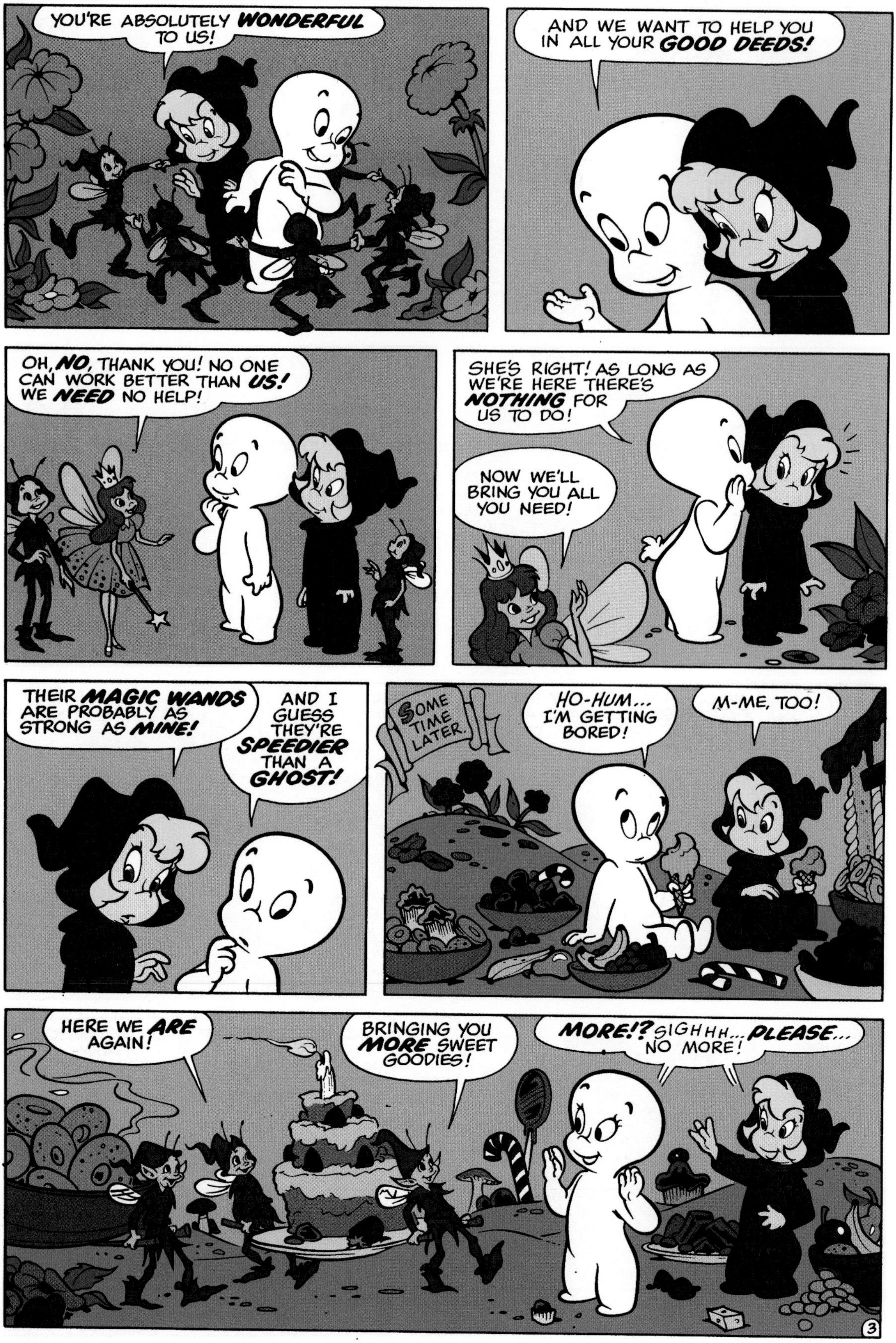
YOU'RE ABSOLUTELY WONDERFUL TO US!
AND WE WANT TO HELP YOU IN ALL YOUR GOOD DEEDS!
OH, NO, THANK YOU! NO ONE CAN WORK BETTER THAN US! WE NEED NO HELP!
SHE'S RIGHT! AS LONG AS WE'RE HERE THERE'S NOTHING FOR US TO DO!
NOW WE'LL BRING YOU ALL YOU NEED!
THEIR MAGIC WANDS ARE PROBABLY AS STRONG AS MINE!
AND I GUESS THEY'RE SPEEDIER THAN A GHOST!
SOME TIME LATER.
HO-HUM... I'M GETTING BORED!
M-ME, TOO!
HERE WE ARE AGAIN!
BRINGING YOU MORE SWEET GOODIES!
MORE!? SIGHHH... PLEASE... NO MORE!
3

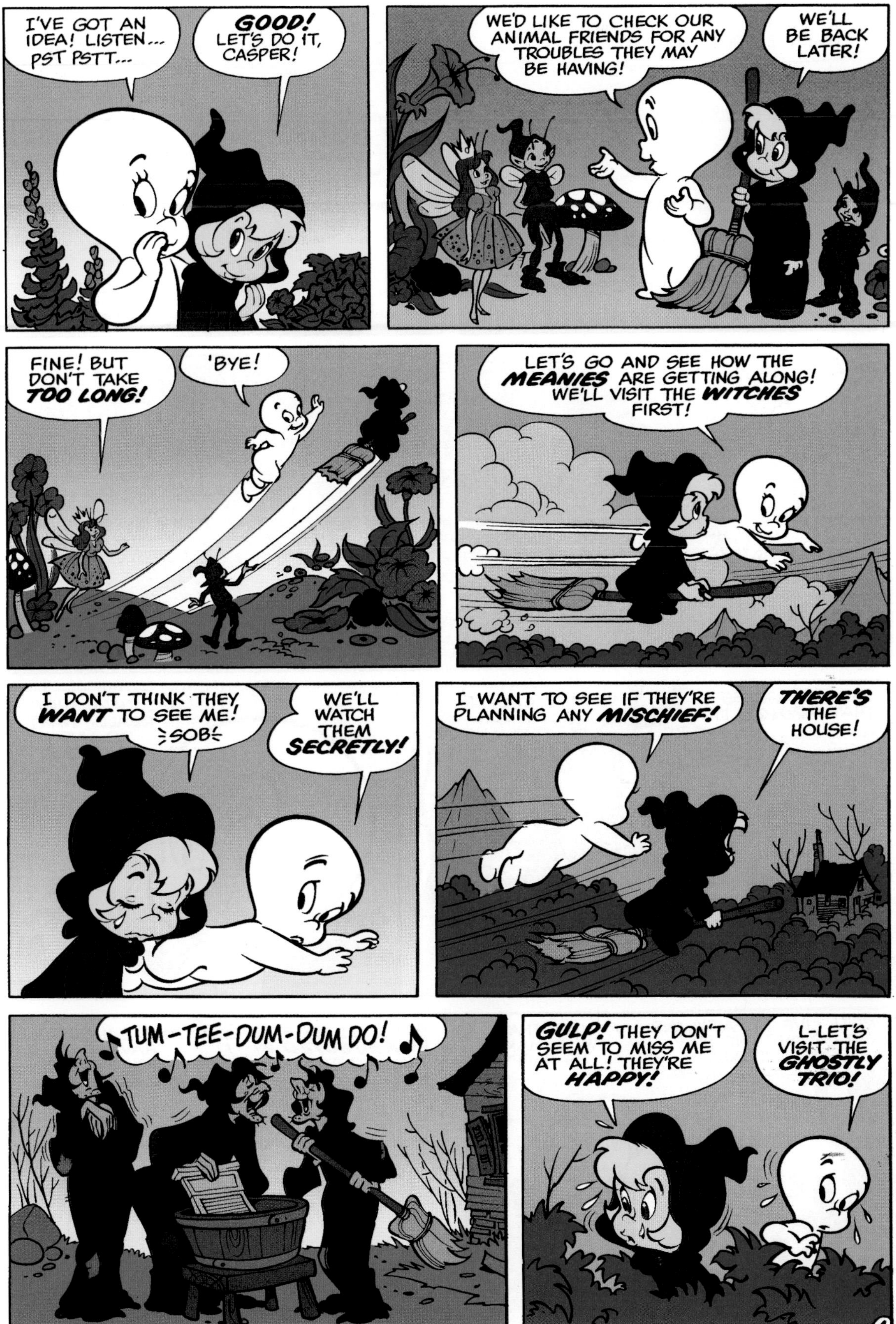
I'VE GOT AN IDEA! LISTEN... PST PSTT...
GOOD! LET'S DO IT, CASPER!
WE'D LIKE TO CHECK OUR ANIMAL FRIENDS FOR ANY TROUBLES THEY MAY BE HAVING!
WE'LL BE BACK LATER!
FINE! BUT DON'T TAKE TOO LONG!
'BYE!
LET'S GO AND SEE HOW THE MEANIES ARE GETTING ALONG! WE'LL VISIT THE WITCHES FIRST!
I DON'T THINK THEY WANT TO SEE ME! SOB
WE'LL WATCH THEM SECRETLY!
I WANT TO SEE IF THEY'RE PLANNING ANY MISCHIEF!
THERE'S THE HOUSE!
TUM-TEE-DUM-DUM DO!
GULP! THEY DON'T SEEM TO MISS ME AT ALL! THEY'RE HAPPY!
L-LET'S VISIT THE GHOSTLY TRIO!
4

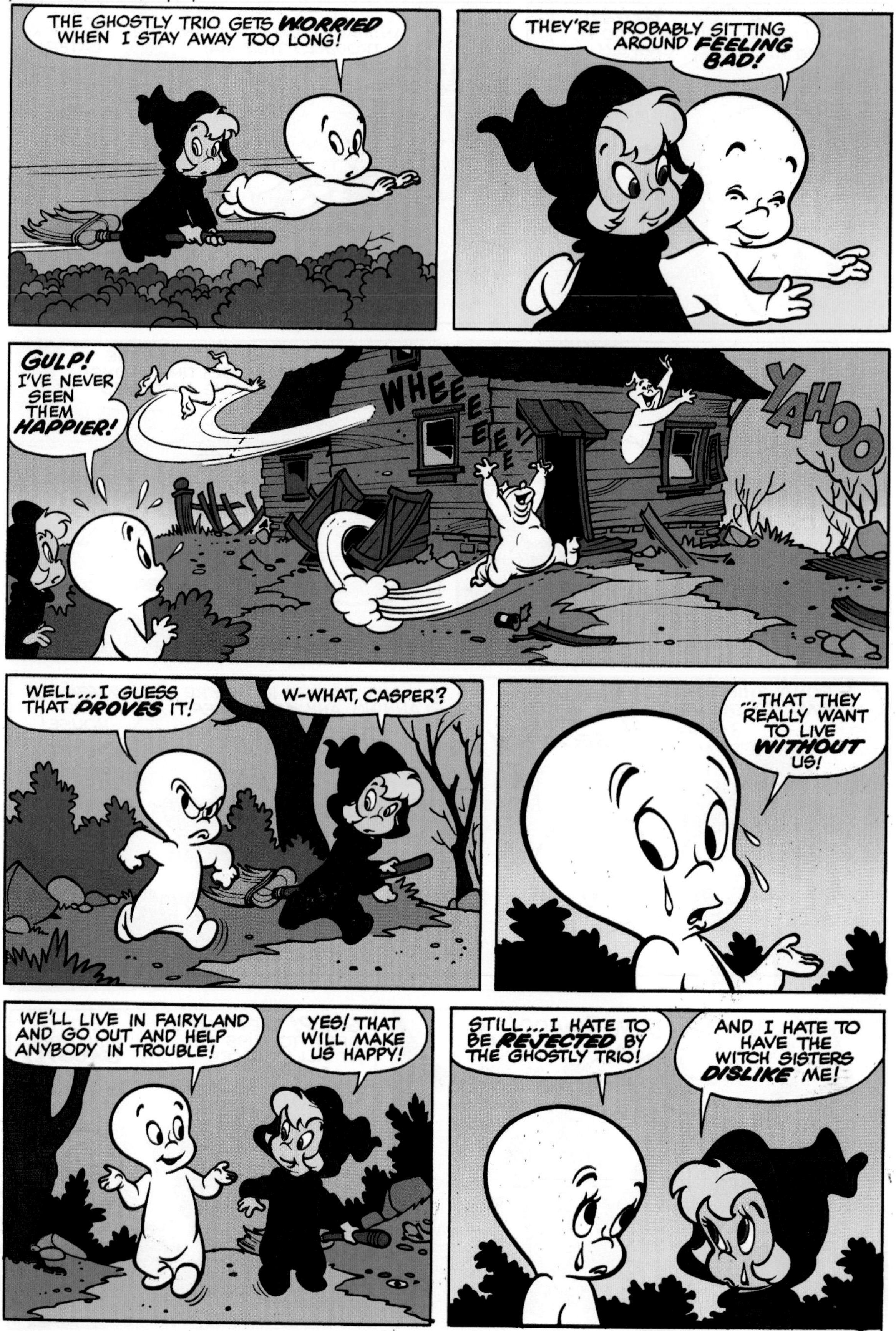
THE GHOSTLY TRIO GETS WORRIED WHEN I STAY AWAY TOO LONG!
THEY'RE PROBABLY SITTING AROUND FEELING BAD!
GULP! I'VE NEVER SEEN THEM HAPPIER!
WHEEEEEEE
YAHOO
WELL... I GUESS THAT PROVES IT!
W-WHAT, CASPER?
...THAT THEY REALLY WANT TO LIVE WITHOUT US!
WE'LL LIVE IN FAIRYLAND AND GO OUT AND HELP ANYBODY IN TROUBLE!
YES! THAT WILL MAKE US HAPPY!
STILL... I HATE TO BE REJECTED BY THE GHOSTLY TRIO!
AND I HATE TO HAVE THE WITCH SISTERS DISLIKE ME!
CONTINUED IN THIS ISSUE..

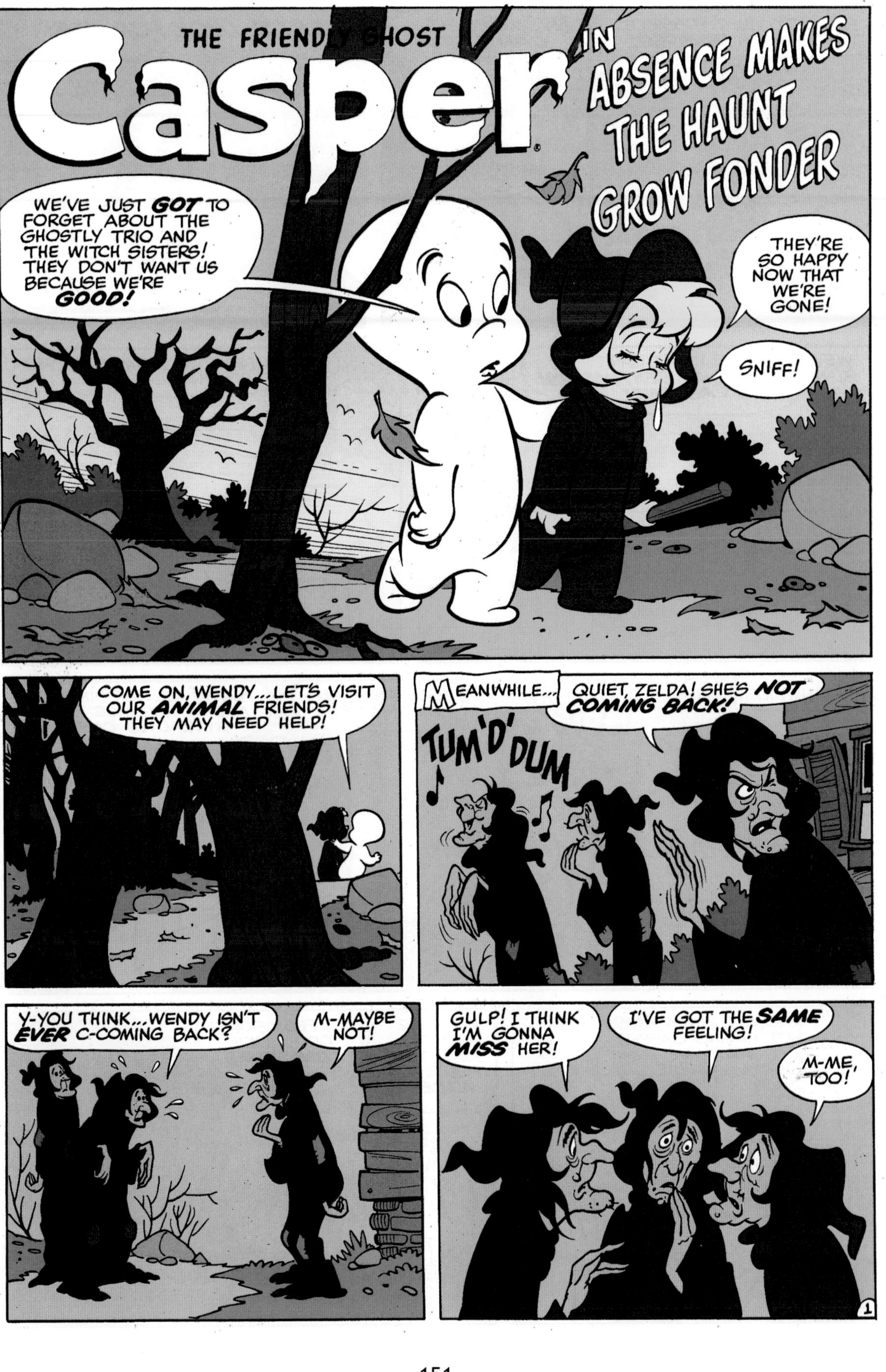

THE FRIENDLY GHOST
Casper
IN
ABSENCE MAKES THE HAUNT GROW FONDER
WE'VE JUST GOT TO FORGET ABOUT THE GHOSTLY TRIO AND THE WITCH SISTERS! THEY DON'T WANT US BECAUSE WE'RE GOOD!
THEY'RE SO HAPPY NOW THAT WE'RE GONE!
SNIFF!
COME ON, WENDY... LET'S VISIT OUR ANIMAL FRIENDS! THEY MAY NEED HELP!
MEANWHILE...
QUIET, ZELDA! SHE'S NOT COMING BACK!
TUM'D' DUM
Y-YOU THINK... WENDY ISN'T EVER C-COMING BACK?
M-MAYBE NOT!
GULP! I THINK I'M GONNA MISS HER!
I'VE GOT THE SAME FEELING!
M-ME, TOO!
1

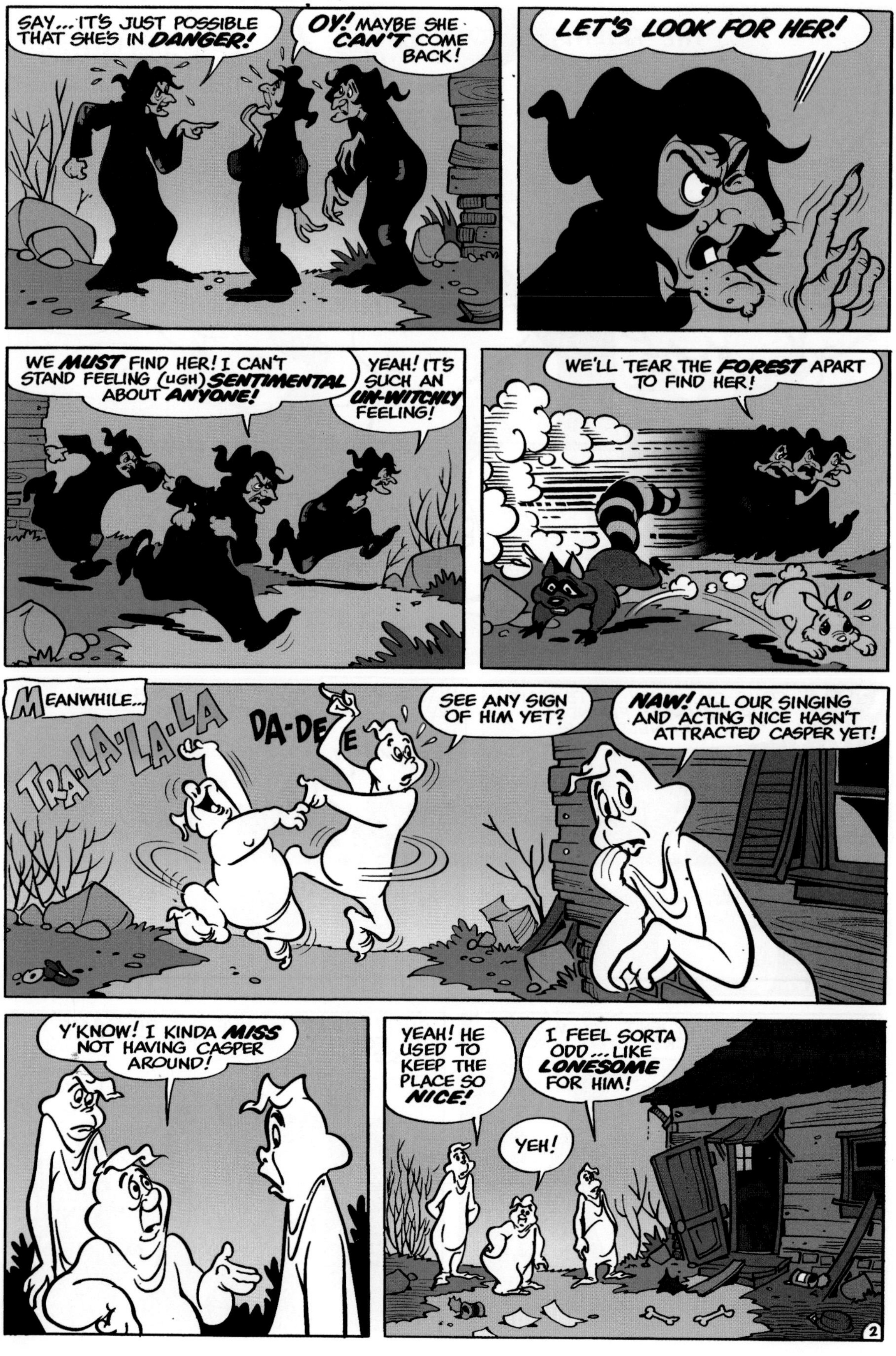
SAY... IT'S JUST POSSIBLE THAT SHE'S IN DANGER!
OY! MAYBE SHE CAN'T COME BACK!
LET'S LOOK FOR HER!
WE MUST FIND HER! I CAN'T STAND FEELING (UGH) SENTIMENTAL ABOUT ANYONE!
YEAH! IT'S SUCH AN UN-WITCHLY FEELING!
WE'LL TEAR THE FOREST APART TO FIND HER!
MEANWHILE...
TRA-LA-LA-LA
DA-DE-E
SEE ANY SIGN OF HIM YET?
NAW! ALL OUR SINGING AND ACTING NICE HASN'T ATTRACTED CASPER YET!
Y'KNOW! I KINDA MISS NOT HAVING CASPER AROUND!
YEAH! HE USED TO KEEP THE PLACE SO NICE!
I FEEL SORTA ODD... LIKE LONESOME FOR HIM!
YEH!
2

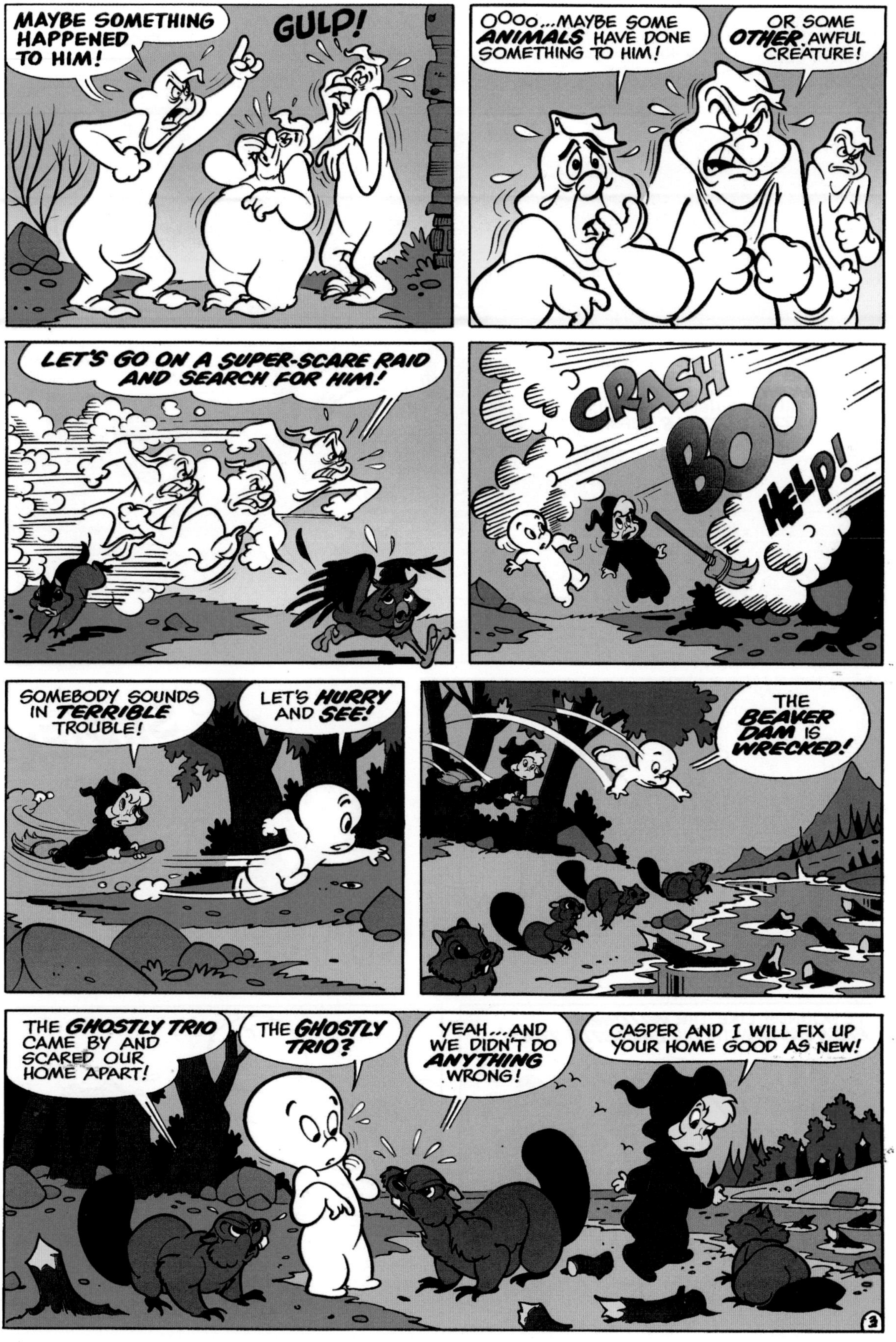
MAYBE SOMETHING HAPPENED TO HIM!
GULP!
OOOO...MAYBE SOME ANIMALS HAVE DONE SOMETHING TO HIM!
OR SOME OTHER AWFUL CREATURE!
LET'S GO ON A SUPER-SCARE RAID AND SEARCH FOR HIM!
CRASH
BOO
HELP!
SOMEBODY SOUNDS IN TERRIBLE TROUBLE!
LET'S HURRY AND SEE!
THE BEAVER DAM IS WRECKED!
THE GHOSTLY TRIO CAME BY AND SCARED OUR HOME APART!
THE GHOSTLY TRIO?
YEAH...AND WE DIDN'T DO ANYTHING WRONG!
CASPER AND I WILL FIX UP YOUR HOME GOOD AS NEW!
3

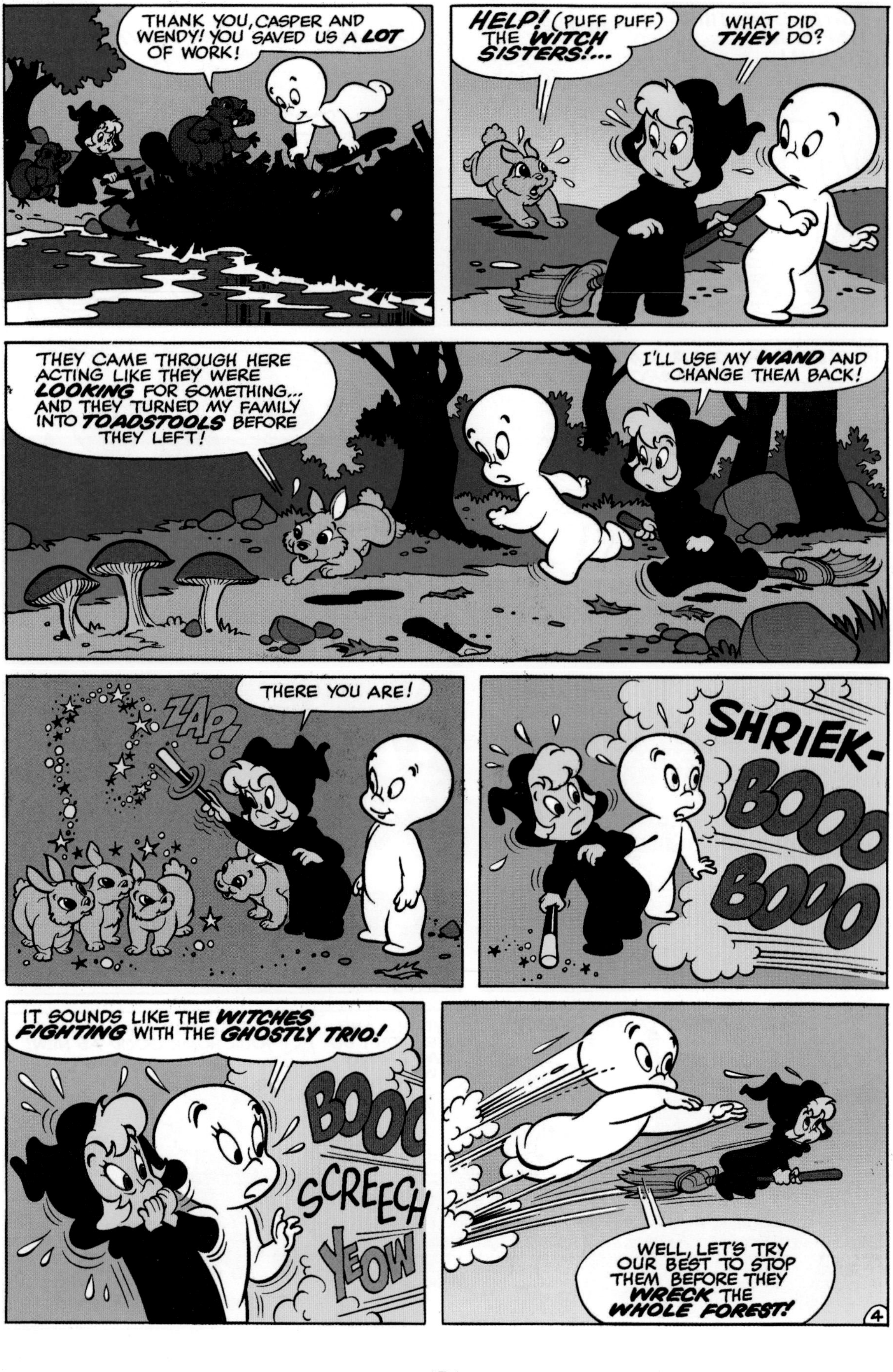
THANK YOU, CASPER AND WENDY! YOU SAVED US A LOT OF WORK!
HELP! (PUFF PUFF) THE WITCH SISTERS!...
WHAT DID THEY DO?
THEY CAME THROUGH HERE ACTING LIKE THEY WERE LOOKING FOR SOMETHING... AND THEY TURNED MY FAMILY INTO TOADSTOOLS BEFORE THEY LEFT!
I'LL USE MY WAND AND CHANGE THEM BACK!
THERE YOU ARE!
ZAP!
SHRIEK-BOOO BOOO
IT SOUNDS LIKE THE WITCHES FIGHTING WITH THE GHOSTLY TRIO!
BOOO
SCREECH
YEOW
WELL, LET'S TRY OUR BEST TO STOP THEM BEFORE THEY WRECK THE WHOLE FOREST!
4

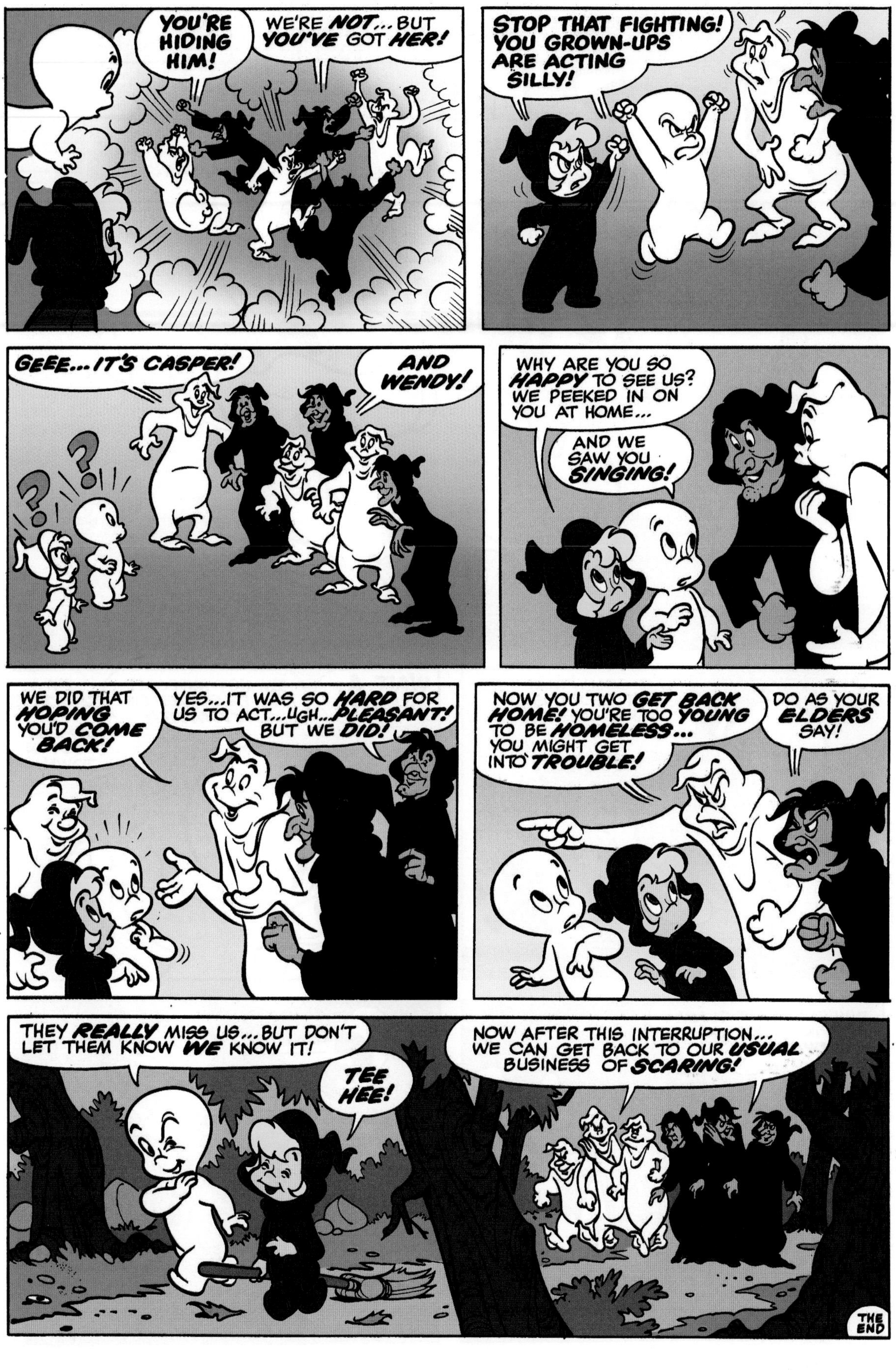
YOU'RE HIDING HIM!
WE'RE NOT... BUT YOU'VE GOT HER!
STOP THAT FIGHTING! YOU GROWN-UPS ARE ACTING SILLY!
GEEE... IT'S CASPER!
AND WENDY!
WHY ARE YOU SO HAPPY TO SEE US? WE PEEKED IN ON YOU AT HOME...
AND WE SAW YOU SINGING!
WE DID THAT HOPING YOU'D COME BACK!
YES...IT WAS SO HARD FOR US TO ACT...UGH...PLEASANT! BUT WE DID!
NOW YOU TWO GET BACK HOME! YOU'RE TOO YOUNG TO BE HOMELESS... YOU MIGHT GET INTO TROUBLE!
DO AS YOUR ELDERS SAY!
THEY REALLY MISS US... BUT DON'T LET THEM KNOW WE KNOW IT!
TEE HEE!
NOW AFTER THIS INTERRUPTION... WE CAN GET BACK TO OUR USUAL BUSINESS OF SCARING!
THE END

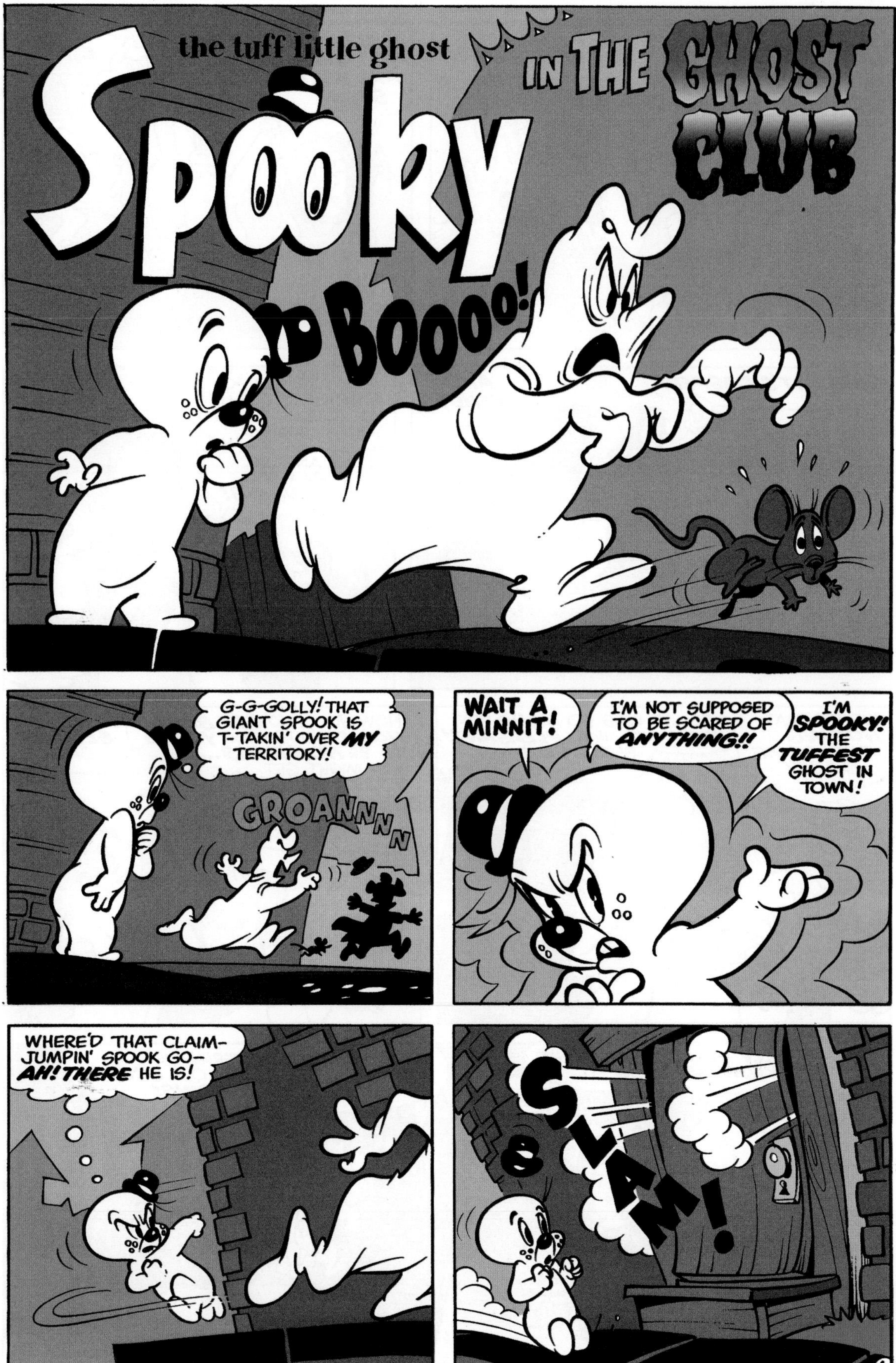

the tuff little ghost
Spooky
IN THE GHOST CLUB
BOOOO!
G-G-GOLLY! THAT GIANT SPOOK IS T-TAKIN' OVER MY TERRITORY!
GROANNNNN
WAIT A MINNIT!
I'M NOT SUPPOSED TO BE SCARED OF ANYTHING!!
I'M SPOOKY! THE TUFFEST GHOST IN TOWN!
WHERE'D THAT CLAIM-JUMPIN' SPOOK GO— AH! THERE HE IS!
SLAM!
1

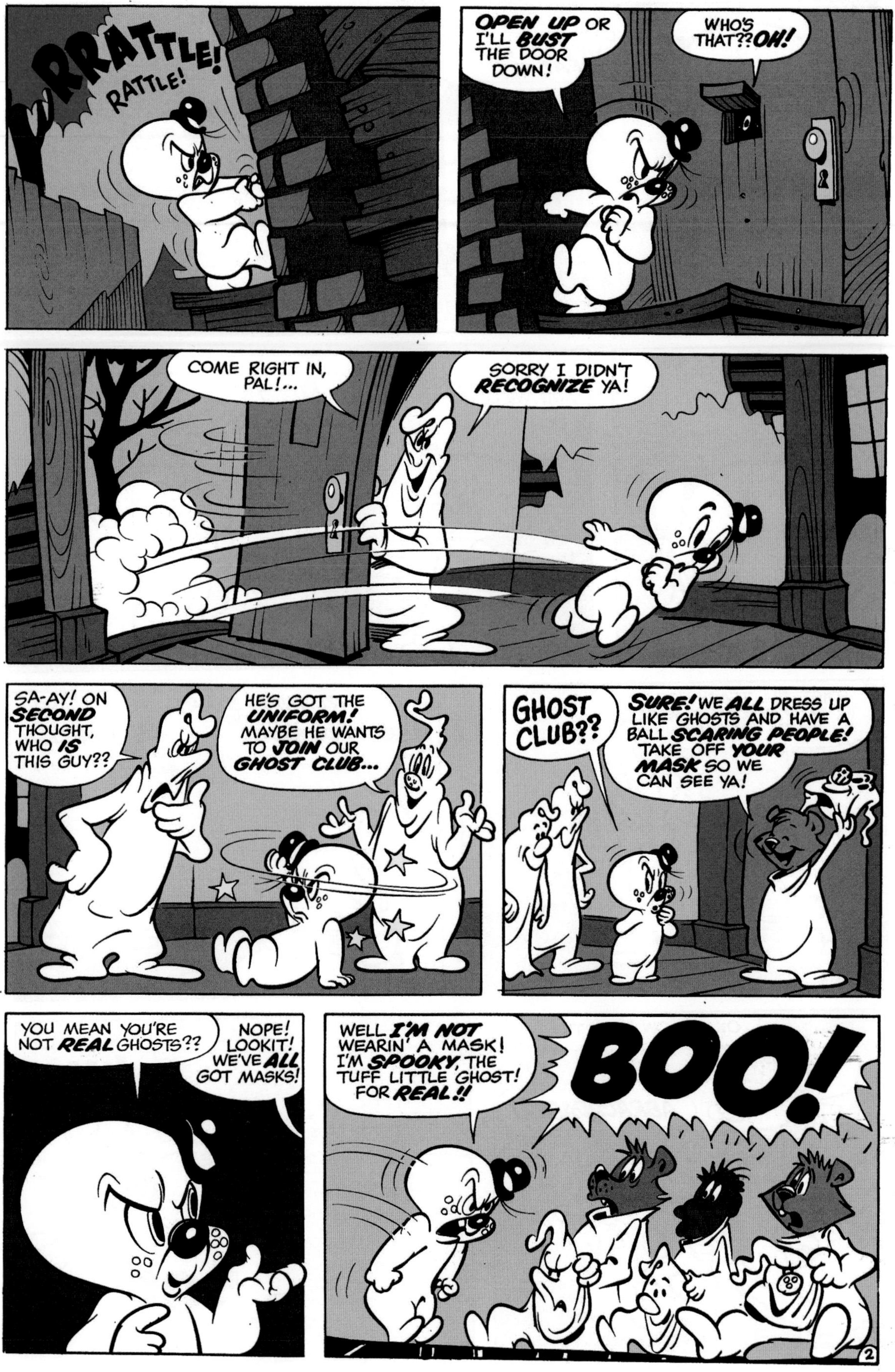
RRATTLE!
RATTLE!
OPEN UP OR I'LL BUST THE DOOR DOWN!
WHO'S THAT?? OH!
COME RIGHT IN, PAL!...
SORRY I DIDN'T RECOGNIZE YA!
SA-AY! ON SECOND THOUGHT, WHO IS THIS GUY??
HE'S GOT THE UNIFORM! MAYBE HE WANTS TO JOIN OUR GHOST CLUB...
GHOST CLUB??
SURE! WE ALL DRESS UP LIKE GHOSTS AND HAVE A BALL SCARING PEOPLE! TAKE OFF YOUR MASK SO WE CAN SEE YA!
YOU MEAN YOU'RE NOT REAL GHOSTS??
NOPE! LOOKIT! WE'VE ALL GOT MASKS!
WELL I'M NOT WEARIN' A MASK! I'M SPOOKY, THE TUFF LITTLE GHOST! FOR REAL!!
BOO!
2

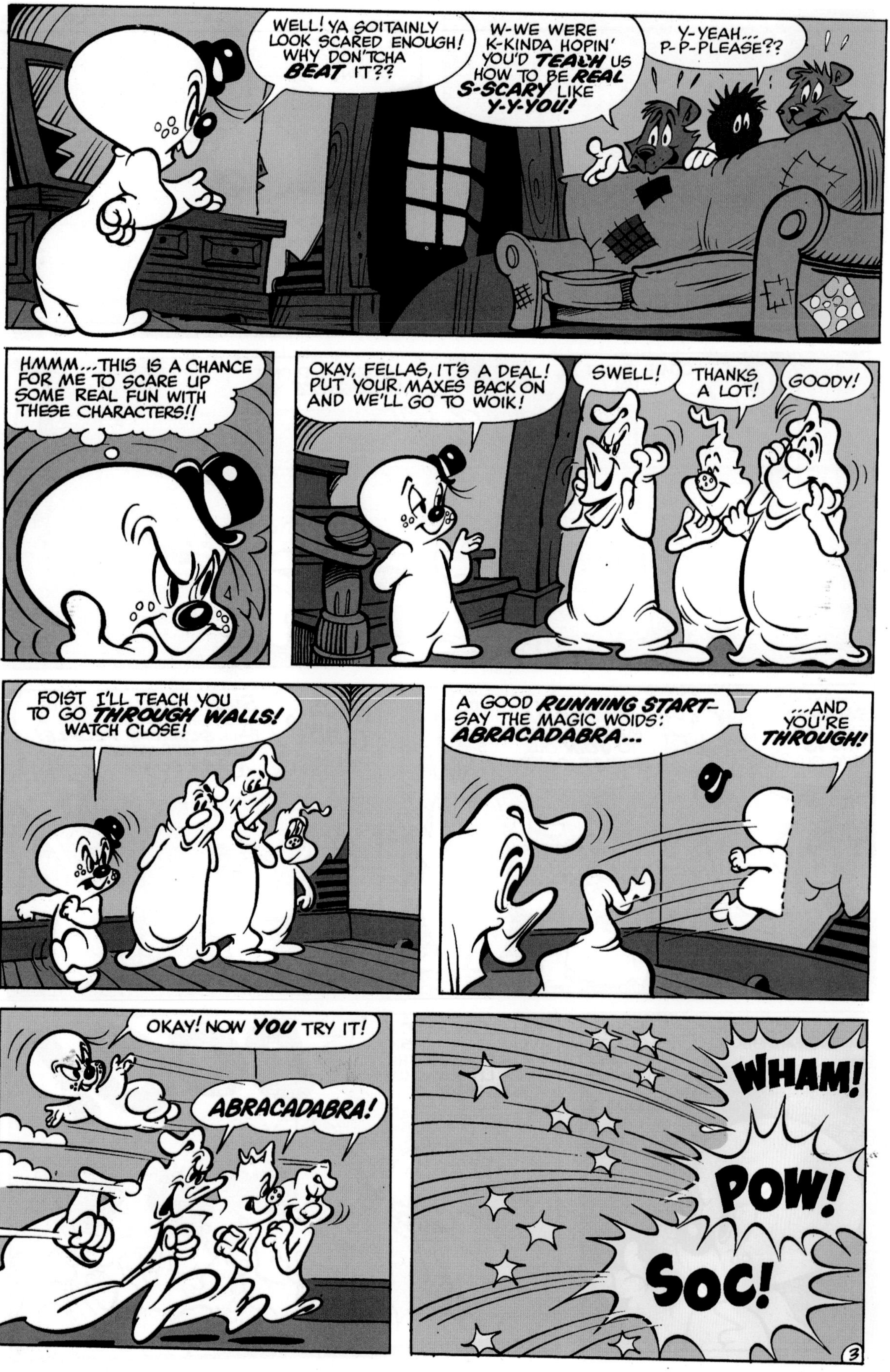
WELL! YA SOITAINLY LOOK SCARED ENOUGH! WHY DON'TCHA BEAT IT??
W-WE WERE K-KINDA HOPIN' YOU'D TEACH US HOW TO BE REAL S-SCARY LIKE Y-Y-YOU!
Y-YEAH... P-P-PLEASE??
HMMM... THIS IS A CHANCE FOR ME TO SCARE UP SOME REAL FUN WITH THESE CHARACTERS!!
OKAY, FELLAS, IT'S A DEAL! PUT YOUR MAXES BACK ON AND WE'LL GO TO WOIK!
SWELL!
THANKS A LOT!
GOODY!
FOIST I'LL TEACH YOU TO GO THROUGH WALLS! WATCH CLOSE!
A GOOD RUNNING START-SAY THE MAGIC WOIDS: ABRACADABRA...
...AND YOU'RE THROUGH!
OKAY! NOW YOU TRY IT!
ABRACADABRA!
WHAM!
POW!
SOC!
3

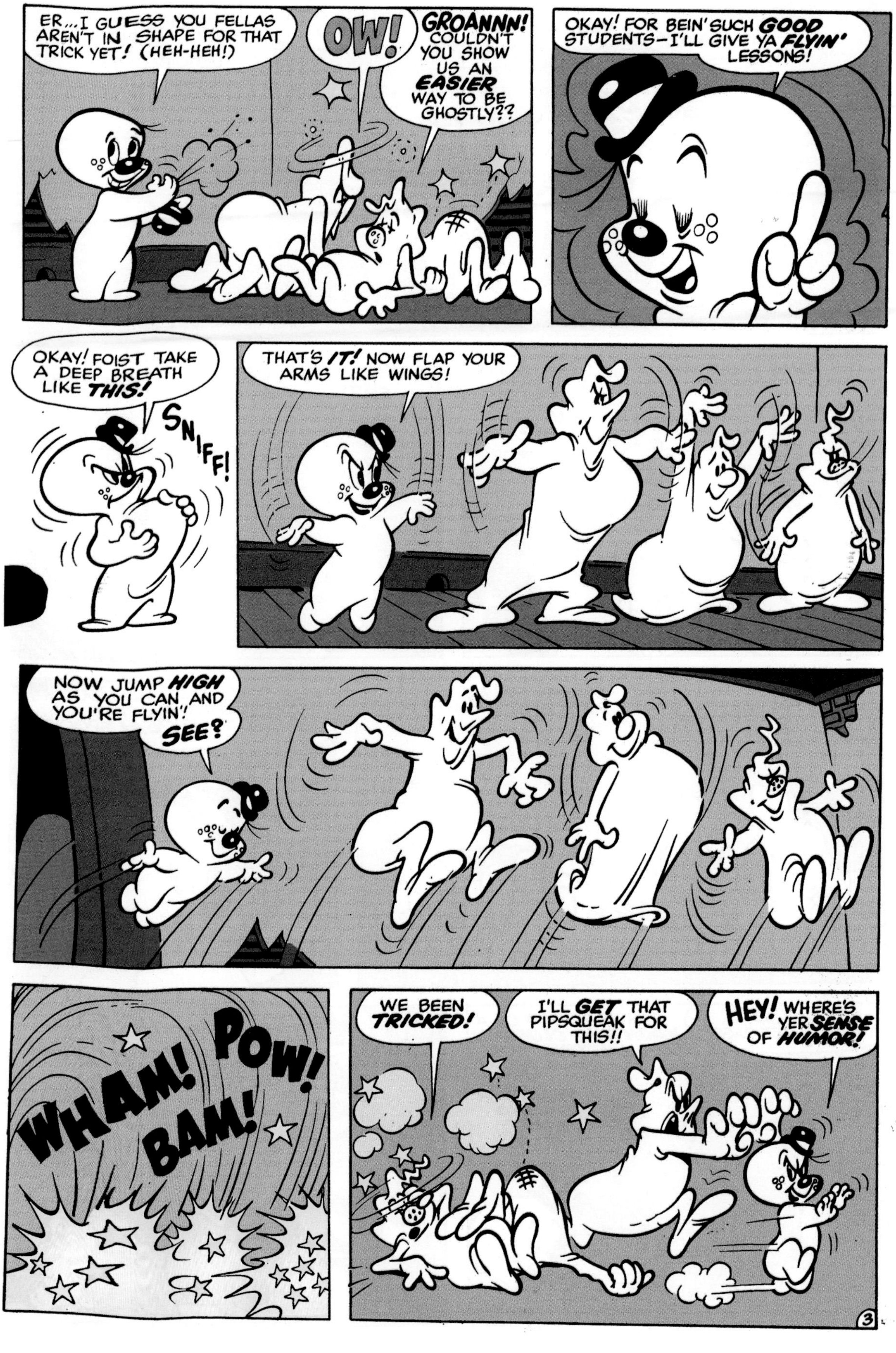
ER... I GUESS YOU FELLAS AREN'T IN SHAPE FOR THAT TRICK YET! (HEH-HEH!)
OW!
GROANNN! COULDN'T YOU SHOW US AN EASIER WAY TO BE GHOSTLY??
OKAY! FOR BEIN' SUCH GOOD STUDENTS—I'LL GIVE YA FLYIN' LESSONS!
OKAY! FOIST TAKE A DEEP BREATH LIKE THIS!
SNIFF!
THAT'S IT! NOW FLAP YOUR ARMS LIKE WINGS!
NOW JUMP HIGH AS YOU CAN AND YOU'RE FLYIN'! SEE?
WHAM! POW! BAM!
WE BEEN TRICKED!
I'LL GET THAT PIPSQUEAK FOR THIS!!
HEY! WHERE'S YER SENSE OF HUMOR!
3

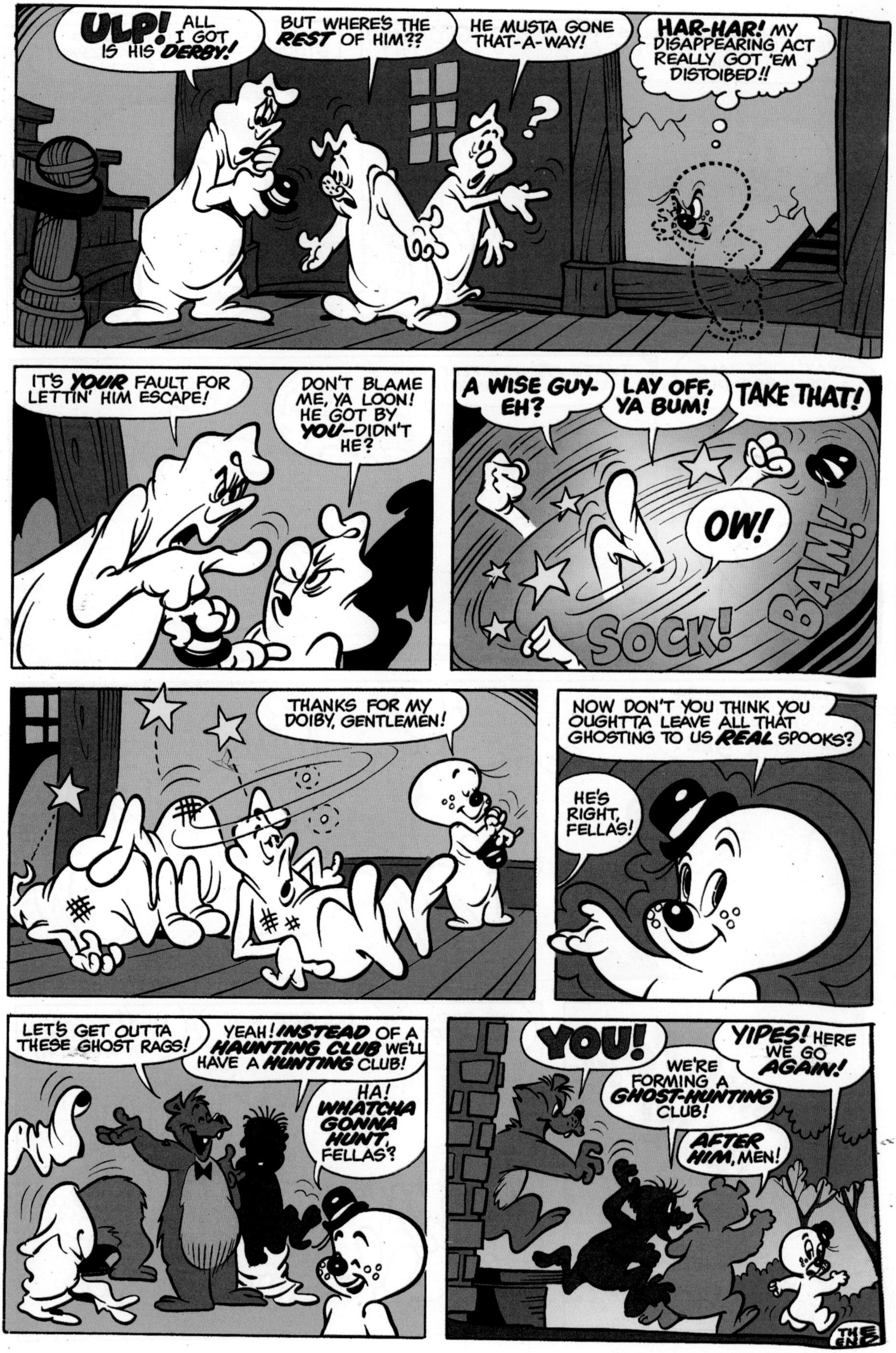
ULP! ALL I GOT IS HIS DERBY!
BUT WHERE'S THE REST OF HIM??
HE MUSTA GONE THAT-A-WAY!
HAR-HAR! MY DISAPPEARING ACT REALLY GOT 'EM DISTOIBED!!
IT'S YOUR FAULT FOR LETTIN' HIM ESCAPE!
DON'T BLAME ME, YA LOON! HE GOT BY YOU-DIDN'T HE?
A WISE GUY-EH?
LAY OFF, YA BUM!
TAKE THAT!
OW!
SOCK!
BAM!
THANKS FOR MY DOIBY, GENTLEMEN!
NOW DON'T YOU THINK YOU OUGHTTA LEAVE ALL THAT GHOSTING TO US REAL SPOOKS?
HE'S RIGHT, FELLAS!
LET'S GET OUTTA THESE GHOST RAGS!
YEAH! INSTEAD OF A HAUNTING CLUB WE'LL HAVE A HUNTING CLUB!
HA! WHATCHA GONNA HUNT, FELLAS?
YOU!
WE'RE FORMING A GHOST-HUNTING CLUB!
YIPES! HERE WE GO AGAIN!
AFTER HIM, MEN!
THE END